The American academy of arts and sciences

The Complete Works of Count Rumford

Vol. III.

The American academy of arts and sciences

The Complete Works of Count Rumford
Vol. III.

ISBN/EAN: 9783742801647

Manufactured in Europe, USA, Canada, Australia, Japa

Cover: Foto ©Andreas Hilbeck / pixelio.de

Manufactured and distributed by brebook publishing software (www.brebook.com)

The American academy of arts and sciences

The Complete Works of Count Rumford

THE
COMPLETE WORKS
OF
COUNT RUMFORD.

PUBLISHED BY THE AMERICAN ACADEMY OF
ARTS AND SCIENCES.

VOL. III.

BOSTON.
1874.

Cambridge:
Press of John Wilson and Son.

CONTENTS.

	Page
OF THE MANAGEMENT OF FIRE AND THE ECONOMY OF FUEL . . . . [Essay VI.]	1
ON THE CONSTRUCTION OF KITCHEN FIRE-PLACES AND KITCHEN UTENSILS; TOGETHER WITH REMARKS AND OBSERVATIONS RELATING TO THE VARIOUS PROCESSES OF COOKERY, AND PROPOSALS FOR IMPROVING THAT MOST USEFUL ART . . [Essay X.]	167
SUPPLEMENTARY OBSERVATIONS RELATING TO THE MANAGEMENT OF FIRES IN CLOSED FIRE-PLACES . . . . . . [Essay XIV.]	489

OF THE MANAGEMENT OF FIRE

AND

THE ECONOMY OF FUEL.

OF THE MANAGEMENT OF FIRE AND THE ECONOMY OF FUEL.

CHAPTER I.

The Subject of this Essay curious and interesting in a very high Degree. — All the Comforts, Conveniences, and Luxuries of Life are procured by the Assistance of FIRE *and of* HEAT. — *The Waste of Fuel very great. — Importance of the Economy of Fuel to Individuals, and to the Public. — Means used for estimating the Amount of the Waste of Fuel. — An Account of the first Kitchen of the House of Industry at Munich, and of the Expense of Fuel in that Kitchen compared with the Quantity consumed in the Kitchens of private Families. — An Account of several other Kitchens constructed on various Principles at Munich, under the Direction of the Author. — Introduction to a more scientific Investigation of the Subject under Consideration.*

NO subject of philosophical inquiry within the limits of human investigation is more calculated to excite admiration and to awaken curiosity than fire; and there is certainly none more extensively useful to mankind. It is owing, no doubt, to our being acquainted with it from our infancy, that we are not more struck with its appearance, and more sensible of the benefits we derive from it. Almost every comfort and convenience which man by his ingenuity procures for himself is obtained by its assistance; and he is not more distinguished from the brute creation by the use of speech, than by his power over that wonderful agent.

Having long been accustomed to consider the management of heat as a matter of the highest importance to mankind, a habit of attending carefully to every circumstance relative to this interesting subject that occasionally came under my observation soon led me to discover how much this science has been neglected, and how much room there is for very essential improvements in almost all those various operations in which heat is employed for the purposes of human life.

The great waste of fuel in all countries must be apparent to the most cursory observer; and the uses to which fire is employed are so very extensive, and the expense for fuel makes so considerable an article in the list of necessaries, that the importance of the subject cannot be denied.

And with regard to the economy of fuel, it has this in particular to recommend it, that whatever is saved by an individual is at the same time a positive saving to the whole community; for the less demand there is for any article in the market, the lower will be its price; and as all the subjects of useful industry — all the arts and manufactures, without exception — depend directly or indirectly on operations in which fire is necessary, it is of much importance to a manufacturing and commercial country to keep the price of fuel as low as possible; and even in countries where there are no manufactures, and where the inhabitants subsist entirely by agriculture, if wood be used as fuel, — as the proportion of woodland to arable must depend in a great measure on the consumption of fire-wood, — any saving of fuel will be attended with a proportional diminution of the forests reserved for fire-wood, consequently with an increase of the lands under cultivation, with an increase of inhabitants and of national wealth, strength and prosperity.

But what renders this subject peculiarly interesting is the great relief to the poor in all countries, and particularly in all cold climates, and in all great cities in every climate, that would result from any considerable diminution of the price of fuel, or from any simple contrivance by which a smaller quantity of this necessary article than they now are obliged to employ to make themselves comfortable might be made to perform the same services. Those who have never been exposed to the inclemencies of the seasons — who have never been eye-witnesses to the sufferings of the poor in their miserable habitations, pinched with cold and starving with hunger — can form no idea of the importance *to them* of the subject which I propose to treat in this Essay.

To all those who take pleasure in doing good to mankind by promoting useful knowledge, and facilitating the means of procuring the comforts and conveniencies of life, these investigations cannot but be very interesting.

Though it is generally acknowledged that there is a great waste of fuel in all countries, arising from ignorance and carelessness in the management of fire, yet few — very few, I believe — are aware of the real amount of this waste.

From the result of all my inquiries upon this subject, I have been led to conclude that not less than *seven eighths* of the heat generated, or which *with proper management might be generated*, from the fuel actually consumed, is carried up into the atmosphere with the smoke, and totally lost. And this opinion has not been formed hastily; on the contrary, it is the result of much attentive observation, and of many experiments. But in a matter of so much importance I feel it to be my duty not merely to give the public my *opinions*, but to lay before them the grounds upon which those opinions have been founded, in order that every one may judge for himself of the certainty or probability of my deductions.

It would not be difficult, merely from a consideration of the nature of heat,—of the manner in which it is generated in the combustion of fuel, and the manner in which it exists when generated,—to show that, as the process of boiling is commonly performed, there must of necessity be a very great loss of heat; for when the vessel, in which the fluid to be boiled is contained, is placed over an open or naked fire, not only by far the greater part of the radiant heat is totally lost, but also of that which exists in the flame, smoke, and hot vapour, a very small proportion only enters the vessel; the rest going off with great rapidity, by the chimney, into the higher regions of the atmosphere. But, without insisting upon these reasonings (though they are certainly incontrovertible), I shall endeavour to establish the facts in question upon still more solid ground,—that of actual experiment.

In the prosecution of the experiments necessary in this investigation, I proceeded in the following manner: As the quantity of heat which any given quantity of any given kind of fuel is capable of generating is not known, there is no fixed standard with which the result of an experiment can be compared, in order to ascertain exactly the proportion of the heat saved, or usefully employed, to that lost. Instead therefore of being able to determine this point *directly*, I was obliged to have recourse to *approximations*. Instead of determining the quantity of heat lost in any given operation, I endeavoured to find out with how much less fuel the same operation might be performed, by a more advantageous arrangement of the fire and disposition of the machinery: and several extensive public establishments, which have been erected in Bavaria within these last six or seven years, under my direction, by order of His Most Serene Highness, the ELECTOR PALATINE,—particularly an establishment for the poor of Munich (of which an account has been given to the public in my First Essay), and the establishment of a Public Academy for the education of one hundred and eighty young men, destined for the service of the State in the different civil and military departments,— the economical arrangements of these establishments afforded me a most favorable opportunity of putting into practice all my ideas relative to the management of fire; and of ascertaining, by numerous experiments made upon a large scale, and often varied and repeated, the real importance of the improvements I have introduced.

That many experiments have been actually made in these two establishments, during the seven years they have existed, will not be doubted by those who are informed that the kitchen, or rather the fire-place of the kitchen of the House of Industry, has been pulled

Of the Management of Fire

down and built entirely anew no less than *three times*, and that of the Military Academy *twice*, during that period; and that the forms of the boilers, and the internal construction of the fire-places, have been changed still oftener.

The importance of the improvements in the management of heat employed in culinary operations, which have resulted from these investigations, will appear by comparing the quantity of fuel now actually used in those kitchens to that consumed in performing the same operations in kitchens on the common construction. And this will at the same time show, in a clear and satisfactory manner, what I proposed to prove,— namely, that in all the common operations in which fire is employed there is a very great waste of fuel.

The waste of fuel in boiling water or any other liquid over an open fire, in the manner in which that process is commonly performed, and the great saving of fuel which will result from a more advantageous disposition and management of the fire, will be evident from the results of the following experiments, all of which were made by myself, and with the utmost care.

Experiment No. 1.— A copper boiler belonging to the kitchen of the Military Academy in Munich, 22 Rhinland inches in diameter above, 19$\frac{1}{2}$ inches in diameter below, and 24 inches in depth, and which weighed 50 lbs. weight of Bavaria ($=$61.92 lbs. Avoirdupois), being fixed in its fire-place, was filled with 95 Bavarian measures ($=$ 28 English wine-gallons) of water, which weighed 187 Bavarian pounds ($=$ 232.58 lbs. Avoirdupois); and this water being at the temperature of 58° F., a fire was lighted under the boiler with dry beech-wood, and the water was made to boil.

and was continued boiling two hours. The time employed and wood consumed in this experiment were as follows:—

	Time employed.		Wood consumed.
	h.	m.	lbs.
To make the water boil	1	1	11
To keep the water boiling	2	0	2¼
Total	3	1	13¼

Experiment No. 2.—The same boiler, containing the same quantity of water at the same temperature, being now removed to the kitchen of a private gentleman in the neighbourhood (Baron de Schwachheim, a brother of the Commandant of the Academy), and placed upon a tripod, a quantity of the same kind of wood used in the former experiment being provided, a fire was lighted under it by the gentleman's cook (directions having been given to be as sparing as possible of fuel), and it was made to boil and continued boiling two hours.

The result of the experiment was as follows:—

	Time employed.		Wood consumed.
	h.	m.	lbs.
To make the water boil	1	31	45
To keep it boiling	2	0	17½
Total	3	31	62½

As in these two experiments the same boiler was employed; as the quantity of water was the same, as also its temperature at the beginning of the experiments; and as it was made to continue boiling during the same length of time, it is evident that the quantities of wood consumed show the relative advantages of the different methods employed in the management of the fire. The difference of these quantities of fuel is very great (the one being only 13¼ lbs. and the other amounting to no less than 62½ lbs.). And this shows how very considerable the waste of fuel really is, in the manner in which it is commonly employed for culinary purposes, and how important the savings are which may be made by introducing a more advantageous arrangement for the management of fire. But great as these savings may appear to be, as shown by the results of the foregoing experiments, yet they are in fact still more considerable, as will be abundantly proved in the sequel. In the Experiment No. 2, in which the boiler was put over an open fire, great care was taken to place the fuel in the most advantageous manner; but in general little attention is paid to that circumstance, and the waste of fuel is greatly increased by such negligence. But in closed fire-places, upon a good construction, as the *proper place* for the fuel cannot be mistaken, and as it is fixed and bounded on all sides by a wall, the ignorance or inattention of those who take care of the fire can never be productive of any great waste of fuel; and this is an advantage of no small importance attending these fire-places.

Experiment No. 3. — A large copper sauce-pan or *casserole*, 11¼ inches in diameter above, 10⅜ in diameter below, and 3⅞ inches deep, containing 4 measures of water weighing 7$\frac{15}{16}$ lbs., and at the temperature of 58° F., being placed in its closed fire-place, and a fire being made under it with small pieces of dry beech-wood cut in lengths of about 4 inches, the water was made to boil, and was continued boiling two hours.

The result of the experiment was as follows: —

	Time employed.		Wood consumed.
	h.	m.	lbs.
To make the water boil	0	12	1
To keep it boiling	2	0	0½
Total	2	12	1½

Experiment No. 4.— The same sauce-pan, containing the same quantity of water, and at the same temperature as in the last experiment, was now taken from its proper fire-place, and placed upon a tripod; and a fire being made under it with dry beech-wood, the result of the experiment was as follows:—

	Time employed.	Wood consumed.
	h. m.	lbs.
To make the water boil	0 28	6
To keep it boiling	2 0	5¼
Total	2 28	11¼

The difference in the results of these two experiments is nearly the same as that in the results of those before mentioned, and they all tend to show that, in cooking or boiling over an open fire, nearly *five times* as much fuel is required as when the heat is confined in a closed fire-place, and its operation properly directed.

But I must again repeat, what I have already observed with respect to the two former experiments, as the Experiments No. 2 and No. 4 were both made with the utmost care, the results of them, compared with those which were made with the same boilers placed in closed fire-places, can give no adequate idea of the real loss of heat and waste of fuel which take place in the common operations of cookery.

From several estimates which I have made with great care relative to this subject, founded upon the quantity of fuel actually consumed in the kitchens of several private families, compared with the quantities of different kinds of food prepared for the table, it appears that at least *nine tenths* of the wood actually consumed in common kitchens, where cooking is carried on over an open fire, might be saved, by introducing the various improvements I have brought into use in the kitchens which have been constructed under my directions.

But it is not alone in kitchens, in which cooking is carried on over open fires, that useful alterations may be made: kitchens with closed fire-places, and indeed all the kitchens which have yet been contrived (as far as my knowledge extends), are susceptible of great improvement.

The various improvements that may be made in mechanical arrangements for the economy of fuel will appear in a striking manner from a detail of the different alterations which have from time to time been made in the kitchen of the House of Industry at Munich, and in that of the Military Academy, and of the effects produced by those progressive improvements.

The House of Industry being an establishment of public charity, and the number of those fed from the kitchen amounting from 1000 to 1500 persons daily, the economy of fuel, in a kitchen upon so large a scale, became an object of serious consideration; and I attended to this matter with peculiar pleasure, as it so completely coincided with my favorite philosophical pursuits.

The investigation of heat, and of the laws of its operations, had long occupied my attention, and I had been so fortunate, in the course of my experiments upon that subject, as to make some discoveries which were thought worthy of being inserted in the Philosophical Transactions of the Royal Society of London; and for my last paper upon that subject, published in the Transactions for the year 1792, I had the honour to receive the annual medal of the Society. I hope my mentioning this circumstance will not be attributed to ostentation. My motive in doing it is merely to show that, when I undertook to make the arrangements of which I am about to give an account, the subject was by no means new to me; but, on the contrary, that I was prepared, and in some measure qualified, for such investigation.

I conceive it to be the duty of those who propose useful improvements for the benefit of mankind not only to *merit*, but also to do every thing in their power to *obtain* the confidence of those to whom their proposals are submitted; and there appears to me to be a much greater degree of pride and arrogance displayed by an author *in taking it for granted* that the world is already sufficiently acquainted with his merit and his qualifications to treat the subject he undertakes to investigate, than in modestly pointing out the grounds upon which the confidence of the public in his knowledge of his subject and in his integrity may be founded.

But to return from this digression. In the first arrangement of the kitchen in the House of Industry at Munich, which was finished in the beginning of the year 1790, eight large copper boilers, each capable of containing about 38 English wine-gallons, were placed in such a manner in two rows, in a solid mass of brick-work, 3 feet high, 9 feet wide, and 18 feet long, built in the middle of the kitchen, that, from a single fire-place, situated at one end of this brick-work, by means of canals (furnished with valves or dampers) going from it through the solid mass of the brick-work to all the different boilers, these boilers were all heated, and made to boil with one single fire; and though none of them were in actual contact with the fire-place, and some of them were distant from it near 15 feet, yet they were all heated with great facility, and in a short space of time, by the heat which, upon opening the valves (which were of iron), was made to pass through the canals.

Each boiler having its separate canal and its separate valves, any single boiler, or any number of them, might be heated at pleasure, without heating the rest; and by opening the valves of any boiler more or less, more or less heat, as the occasion required, might be made to pass under the boiler; and when no more heat was wanting for any of the boilers, or when the fire was too strong, by opening a particular valve a communication with a waste canal was formed, by which all the heat, or any part of it at pleasure, might be made to pass off directly into the chimney, without going near any of the boilers.

The fire was regulated by a register in the door of the ash-pit, by which the air was admitted into the fire-place; and, when no more heat was wanted, the fire was put out by closing this register entirely, and by closing at the same time all the valves or dampers in the canals leading from the fire-place.

The fire-place was of an oval form, 3 feet long, 2 feet 3 inches wide, and about 18 inches high, vaulted above with *a double vault*, 4 inches of air being left between the two vaults; and the fuel was introduced into the fire-place by a passage closed by a *double* iron door, which door was kept constantly shut; and the fuel was burned upon an iron grate, the air which supplied the fire coming up from below the grate through the ash-pit.

The loss of heat in its passage from the fire-place to the boilers was prevented by making the canals of communication *double*, one within the other; the internal canal by which the heat passed, and which was 5 inches wide internally, and 6 inches high, being itself placed, and, as it were *insulated*, in a canal still larger, in such a manner that the canal by which the heat passed (which was constructed of very thin bricks, or rather tiles) was *surrounded on every side* with a wall, 2 inches thick, of *confined air*. The surrounding canal being formed in the solid body of the mass of brick-work, this arrangement of the double canals was entirely concealed. The double canals and the double vault over the fire-place were intended to serve the same purpose; namely, *to confine more effectually the heat*, and prevent its escape into the mass of brick-work, and its consequent loss.

Having found, in the course of my experiments, that confined air is the best barrier[*] that can be opposed to heat, to confine it, I endeavoured to avail myself of that discovery in these economical arrangements, and my attempts were not unsuccessful.

Not only the fire-place itself, and the canals of communication between the fire-place and the boilers, were surrounded by confined air, but it was also made use of for confining the heat in the boilers, and preventing its escaping into the atmosphere. This was done by making the covers of the boilers *double*. These covers (see the Figures 1 and 2, Plate I.) which were made of tin, or rather of thin iron plates tinned, were in the form of a hollow cone. The height of the cone was equal to about one third of its diameter, and the air which it contained was entirely shut up, the bottom of

[*] See Philosophical Transactions, 1792, Part 1. See also Vol. I., pp. 401 and following.

the cone being closed by a circular plate or thin sheet of tinned iron. The bottom of the cone was accurately fitted to the top of the boiler, which it completely closed, by means of a rim about 2 inches wide, which entered the boiler; which rim was soldered to the flat sheet of tinned iron which formed the bottom of the cover. The steam generated by the boiling liquid was carried off by a tube about half an inch in diameter, which passed through the hollow conical cover, and which was attached to the cover, both above and below, with solder, in such a manner that the air with which the hollow cone was filled remained completely confined, and cut off from all communications with the external air of the atmosphere, as well as with the steam generated in the boiler.

In some of the covers I filled the hollow of the cone with fur, but I did not find that these were sensibly better for confining the heat than those in which the cone was filled simply with air.

To convince the numerous strangers, who from curiosity visited this kitchen, of the great advantage of making use of double covers to confine the heat in the boilers, instead of using single covers for that purpose, a single cover was provided, which, as it was externally of the same form as the others, when it was placed upon a boiler, could not be distinguished from them; but as its bottom was wanting, and consequently there was no confined air interposed between the hot steam in the boiler and the external surface of the cover, on being placed upon a kettle actually boiling, this cover instantaneously became so exceedingly hot as actually to burn those who ventured to touch it; while a *double cover*, formed of the same materials, and placed in the same situation, was so moderately warm that the naked hand might be held upon it for any length of time without the least inconvenience.

As it was easy to conceive that what was so exceedingly hot as to burn the hand in an instant, upon touching it, could not fail to communicate a great deal of heat to the cold atmosphere which continually lay upon it, this experiment showed in a striking and *convincing* manner the utility of my double covers; and I have since had the satisfaction to see them gradually finding their way into common use.

It is perhaps quite unnecessary that I should inform my readers that one principal motive which induced me to take so much pains in the arrangement of this kitchen was a desire to introduce useful improvements, relative to the management of heat and the economy of fuel, into common practice. An establishment so interesting in all respects, so important in its consequences, and so perfectly new in Bavaria, as a public House of Industry upon a liberal and extensive plan, — where almost every trade and manufacture is carried on under the same roof, where the poor and indigent of both sexes, and of all ages, find a comfortable asylum, and employment suited to their strength and to their talents, and where industry is excited *not by punishments*, but by *the most liberal rewards*, and by the kindest usage, — such an establishment, I thought, could not fail to excite the curiosity of the public, and to draw together a great concourse of visitors; and as this appeared to me a favourable opportunity to draw the public attention to useful improvements, all my measures were taken accordingly; and not only the kitchen, but also the bake-house, the stoves for heating the rooms, the lamps, the various utensils and machines made use of in the different manufactories, all the different economical arrangements and contrivances for facilitating the operations of useful industry, were so many models expressly made for imitation.

But in the arrangements relative to the economy of fuel, besides a view to immediate public utility, another motive, not much less powerful, contributed to induce me to pay all possible attention to the subject; namely, a desire to acquire a more thorough knowledge relative to the nature of heat and of the laws of its operations; and with this view several parts were added to the machinery, which I suspected at the time to be too complicated to be really useful in common practice.

The steam, for instance, which arose from the boiling liquids, instead of being suffered to escape into the atmosphere, was carried up by tubes into a room immediately over the kitchen, where it was made to pass through a spiral worm placed in a large cask full of cold water, and condensed, giving out its heat to the water in the cask; which water thus warmed, without any new expense of fuel, was made use of next day, instead of cold water, for filling the boilers. That this water, so warmed, might not be cooled during the night, the cask that contained it was put into another cask still larger; and the space between the two casks was filled with wool. The cooling of the steam, in its passage from the boiler to the cask where it was condensed, was prevented by warm coverings of sheepskins with the wool on them, by which the tubes of communication, which were of tin, were defended from the cold air of the atmosphere.

By this contrivance, the heat, which would otherwise

have been carried off by the steam into the atmosphere and totally lost, was arrested in its flight, and brought back into the boiler, and made to work the second day.

By other contrivances, the smoke also was laid under contribution. After it had passed under the boilers, and just as it was about to escape by the chimney, it was stopped, and, by being made to pass under a large copper filled with cold water, was deprived of the greater part of the heat it still retained; and thinking it probable that considerable advantages would be derived from drying the wood very thoroughly, and even heating it, before it was made use of for fuel, the smoke from two of the boilers was made to pass under a plate of iron which formed the bottom of an oven, in which the wood, necessary for the consumption of the kitchen for one day (having previously been cut into billets of a proper size), was dried during 24 hours, previous to its being used.

In a smaller kitchen (adjoining to that I have been describing), which was constructed merely as a model for imitation, and which was constantly open for the inspection of the public, five boilers of different sizes, all heated by the same fire, were placed in a semicircular mass of brick-work, and the smoke, after having passed under all these five boilers, was made to heat, at pleasure, either an oven, or water which was contained in a wooden cask set upright upon the brick-work. A tube of copper, tinned on the outside, which went through the cask, gave a passage to the smoke, and this tube was connected with the bottom of the cask by means of a circular plate of copper through which the tube passed, which plate closed a circular opening in the bottom of the cask somewhat larger in diameter than the tube.

This circular plate was nailed to the bottom of the cask, and the joining made water-tight by interposing between the metallic plate and the wood a sheet of pasteboard; and the tube was fastened to the plate with solder. This tube (which was about 6 inches in diameter), as soon as it had passed the circular plate and entered the barrel, branched out into three smaller tubes, each about 4 inches in diameter, which, running parallel to each other through the whole length of the cask, went out of it above, by three different holes in the upper head of the cask, and ended in a canal which led to the chimney.

This tube, by which the smoke passed through the cask, was branched out into a number of branches in order to increase the surface, by which the heat of the smoke was communicated to the water in the cask. The cask was supplied with water from a reservoir placed in the upper part of the building, by means of a leaden pipe of communication from the one to the other; and the machinery was so contrived that, when any water was drawn out of the cask for use, it was immediately replaced from the reservoir; but as soon as the water in the cask had regained its proper height, the cold water from the reservoir ceased to flow in it.

Nothing more generally excited the surprise and curiosity of those who visited this kitchen, than to see water actually boiled in a wooden cask, and drawn from it boiling hot, by a brass cock. I have been the more particular in describing the manner in which this was done, as I have reason to think that a contrivance of this kind, or something similar to it, might, in many cases, be applied to useful purposes. No contrivance can possibly be invented by which heat can be communicated to fluids with so little loss; and as wood is not only an excellent non-conductor of heat itself, but may easily be surrounded by confined air, by furs, and other like bodies which are known to be useful in confining heat, the loss of heat, by the sides of a containing vessel composed of wood, might be almost entirely prevented.

Why should not the boilers for large salt-works and breweries, and those destined for other similar processes, in which great quantities of water are heated or evaporated, be constructed of wood, with horizontal tubes of iron or of copper, communicating with the fire-place, and running through them, for the circulation of the smoke? But this is not the place to enlarge upon this subject: I shall therefore leave it for the present, and return to my kitchens.

To prepare the soup furnished to the poor from the kitchen of the House of Industry, it was found necessary to keep up the fire near *five hours;* the soup, in order to its being good, requiring to be kept actually boiling above three hours.

The fuel made use of in this kitchen was dry beech-wood; a cord of which (or *klafter*, as it is called), 5 English feet 8 1/5 inches long, 5 feet 8 1/5 inches high, and 3 feet 1½ inches wide, and which weighed at an average about 2200 Bavarian pounds (= 2724 lbs. avoirdupois), cost at an average about 5¼ florins (= 9s. 6½d. sterling) in the market.

Of this wood the daily consumption, when soup was provided for 1000 persons, was about 300 lbs. Bavarian

weight, or about ⅓, or more exactly 5/33 of a cord or klafter, which cost 43 kreutzers (60 kreutzers making a florin), or about 1s. 3½d. sterling; and this gives 1/33 of a kreutzer, or 2/55 of a farthing, for the daily expense for fuel in cooking for each person.

To make an estimate of the daily expense for fuel in cooking the same quantity of the same kind of soup in private kitchens, we will suppose these 1000 persons, who were fed from the public kitchen of the House of Industry, to be separated into families of 5 persons each.

This would make just 200 families; and the quantity of wood consumed in the public kitchen daily for feeding 1000 persons (= 300 lbs.), being divided among 200 families, gives 1½ lbs. of wood for the daily consumption of each family; and, according to this estimate, 1 cord of wood, weighing 2200 lbs., ought to suffice for cooking for such a family 1466 days, or 4 years and 6 days.

But upon the most careful inquiries relative to the real consumption of fuel in private families in operations of cookery, as they are now generally performed over an open fire, I find that 5 Bavarian pounds of good peas-soup can hardly be prepared at a less expense of fuel than 15 lbs. of dry beech-wood of the best quality; consequently, a cord of such wood, instead of sufficing for preparing a soup daily for a family of 5 persons for 4 years, would hardly suffice for so long a time as 5 months.

And hence it appears that the consumption of fuel in the kitchens of private families is to that consumed in the first kitchen of the House of Industry at Munich, *in preparing the same quantity of the same kind of food* (peas-soup), as 10 to 1.* But it must be remembered that this difference in the quantities of fuel expended is not occasioned *entirely* by the difference between the two methods of managing the fire; for, exclusive of the effect produced by a given arrangement of the machinery, with the same arrangement, the greater the quantity of food prepared at once, or the larger the boiler (within certain limits, however, as will be seen hereafter), the less in proportion will be the quantity of fuel required; and the saving of fuel which arises from cooking upon a large scale is very considerable. But I shall take occasion to treat this part of my subject more fully elsewhere.

The kitchen in the House of Industry was finished in the beginning of the year 1790. And much about the same time, two other public kitchens upon a large scale were erected at Munich, under my directions; namely, the kitchen belonging to the Military Academy, and that belonging to the Military Hall (as it is called) in the English garden, in which building near 200 military officers messed daily during the annual encampments, for which purpose this building was erected.

There is likewise in the garden (which is 6 English miles in circumference) an inn, a farm-house, and a large dairy; and these establishments gave me an opportunity of constructing no less than four other kitchens, — namely, two for the inn, one for the farm-house, and one for the use of the dairy. And the uses for which these different kitchens were designed, and to which they were applied, were so various as not only

---

* Afterwards, on altering the kitchen of the House of Industry, and fitting it up on better principles, the economy of fuel was carried still farther, as will be seen in the sequel of this Essay.

to include almost every process of cookery, but also to afford opportunities of performing the same operations upon very different scales, and consequently of making many interesting experiments relative to the management of heat and the economy of fuel.

That I did not neglect these opportunities of pursuing with effect a subject which had long engaged my attention, and to which I was much attached, will readily be believed by those who know what ardour a curious subject of philosophical investigation is capable of inspiring in an inquisitive mind.

As the experiments I have made, or caused to be made, in the different establishments before mentioned, during the six or seven years that they have existed, are extremely numerous, it would take up too much time to give an account of them in detail: I shall therefore content myself with merely noticing the general results of them, and mentioning more particularly only such of them as appear to me to be most important. And in regard to the peculiar construction of the different kitchens above mentioned, as most of them have undergone many alterations, and as no one of them remains exactly in the same state in which it was first constructed, I do not think it necessary to be very particular in my account of them: I shall occasionally mention the principles on which they were constructed, and the faults I discovered in them; but when I shall come to speak of those improvements which have stood the test of actual experience, and which I can recommend as being worthy of imitation, I shall take care to be very exact and particular in my descriptions.

It will not be found very difficult, I fancy, from what has been said, to form a pretty just idea of the construction of the kitchen in the House of Industry above described, even without the help of a plan or drawing of it. That in the Military Academy was constructed upon a different principle. Instead of heating all the boilers from one and the same fireplace, almost every boiler had its own separate fireplace; and though the boilers were all furnished with double covers, similar to those made use of in the kitchen of the House of Industry, yet there was no attempt made to recover the heat carried off by the steam, but it was suffered to escape without hindrance into the atmosphere; it having been found, by the experiments made in the kitchen of the House of Industry, that when the fire is properly managed, — that is to say, when the heat is but just sufficient to keep the liquid boiling hot, or *very gently boiling*, — the quantity of steam generated is inconsiderable, and the heat carried off by it not worth the trouble of saving. Each fireplace was furnished with an iron grate, upon which the wood was burnt; and the opening into the fire, as well as that which communicated with the ash-pit, had in each its separate iron door.

Finding afterwards that the iron door which closed the opening by which the wood was introduced into the fire-place was much heated, and consequently that it caused a considerable loss of heat by communicating it to the cold atmosphere with which it was in contact; in order to remedy this evil without incurring the expense of double doors, the iron door was removed, and in its stead was placed a hollow cylinder, or rather truncated cone, of burnt clay or common earthen ware, which cone was 4 inches long, 6 inches in diameter internally, and 8 inches in diameter externally, at its larger end or base; and 5¼ inches in diameter internally, and 7¼ inches in diameter externally, at its smaller end; and being firmly fixed, with its axis in a horizontal position, and its larger end or base outwards, in the middle of the opening leading to the fire-place, and being well united with the solid brick-work by means of mortar, the cavity of this cone formed the opening by which the wood was introduced into the fire-place. This cavity being closed with a fit stopper of earthen ware, as earthen ware is a non-conductor of heat, or as heat cannot pass through it but with great difficulty and very slowly, the external surface of this cone and its stopper were never much heated, consequently the quantity of heat they could communicate to the atmosphere was but very trifling. This contrivance was afterwards rendered much more simple by substituting, instead of the hollow cone, a tile, 10 inches square, and about 2¼ inches thick, with a conical hole in its centre, 6 inches in diameter externally, and 5¼ inches in diameter within, provided with a fit baked earthen stopper. (See the Figures No. 6, 7, and 8, Plate I.)

A perforated square tile is preferable to a hollow cylinder for forming a passage into the fire-place, not only because it is cheaper, stronger, and more durable, but also because it may, on account of its form, be more easily and more firmly fixed in its place, and united with the rest of the brick-work.

If proper moulds be provided for forming these perforated tiles and their stoppers, they may be afforded for a mere trifle. In Munich they are made of the very best earth, by the Elector's potter; and they cost no more than 24 kreutzers, or something less than 9d. sterling, for a tile with its stopper. I had several made of sandstone by a stone-cutter, but they cost me 1 florin and 30 kreutzers, or about 2s. 9d. sterling each.

Though those made of stone answered perfectly well, yet I found them not better than those made of earthen ware; and as these last are much cheaper, and I believe equally durable, they ought certainly to be preferred. That the stopper may be made to fit with accuracy the hole it is intended to close (which is necessary, as will be seen hereafter), they may be ground together with fine sand moistened with water.

Sensible from the beginning of the great importance of being absolutely master of the air which is admitted into the fire-place to feed the fire, so as to be able to admit more or less at pleasure, or to exclude it entirely, I took care, in all my fire-places, to close very exactly the passage into the ash-pit by a door carefully fitted to its frame, the air being admitted through a semicircular opening furnished with a register in the middle of this door. This contrivance (which admits of no further improvement) is indispensably necessary in all well-constructed fire-places, great or small. (See the Figures from Fig. 9 to Fig. 16, Plate II.)

Having occasion, in the course of my arrangements, to make use of a great number of boilers, and often of several boilers of the same dimensions, I availed myself of that circumstance to determine, by actual experiments, the best form for boilers, or that form which, with any given capacity, shall be best adapted for saving fuel.

Two or more boilers of the same capacity, but of different forms, constructed of sheet-copper of the same thickness, were placed in closed fire-places, constructed as nearly as possible upon the same principles, and were used for a length of time in the same culinary processes; and the quantity of fuel consumed by each being noted, the comparative advantages of their different forms were ascertained. Some of these boilers were made deep and narrow, others wide and shallow; there were some with flat bottoms, others of a globular form, and others again with their bottoms drawn inward like the bottom of a common glass bottle. The results of these inquiries were very curious, and led me to a most interesting discovery. They taught me not only what forms are best for boilers, but also (what is still more interesting) *why* one form is preferable to another. They gave me much new light with respect to the *manner* in which flame and hot vapour part with their heat; and suggested to me the idea of a very important improvement in the internal construction of fire-places, which I have since put in practice with great success.

But in order to be able to explain this matter in a clear and satisfactory manner, and to render it easier to be understood by those who have not been much conversant in inquiries of this kind, it will be necessary to go back a little, and to treat the subject under consideration in a more regular and scientific manner.

Though it was not my intention originally to write an elementary treatise on heat, yet, as the first or fundamental principles of that science are necessary to be known, in order to establish upon solid grounds the practical rules and directions relative to the management of heat which will hereafter be recommended, it will not, I trust, be deemed either improper or superfluous to take a more extensive view of the subject, and to treat it methodically, and at some length.

I have perhaps already exposed myself to criticism by

paying so little attention to method in this Essay, as to postpone so long the investigation of the elementary principles of the science I have undertaken to treat. It may be thought that the part of the subject I am now about to consider should have preceded all other investigation; that instead of occupying the middle of my book, it ought to have been discussed in the Introduction, or at least to have been treated in the beginning of the first chapter. But if I have been guilty of a fault in the arrangement of my subject, it has arisen not from inattention, but from an error of judgment. Desirous rather of writing a *useful book*, than of being the author of a *splendid performance*, I have not scrupled to transgress the established rules of elegant composition in all cases where I thought it would contribute to my main design, *public utility;* and well aware that my book, in order to its being really useful, must be read by many who have neither time nor patience to labour through an elementary treatise upon so abstruse a subject, I have endeavoured to *decoy* my reader into the situation in which I wish him to be placed, in order to his having a complete view of the prospect I have prepared for him, rather than to force him into it. If I have used art in doing this, he must forgive me; my design was not only innocent, but such as ought to entitle me to his thanks and to his esteem. I wished to entice him on as far as possible, without letting him perceive the difficulties of the road; and now that we have come on together so far, and are so near our journey's end, I hope and trust that he will not leave me. To proceed, therefore —

CHAPTER II.

Of the GENERATION OF HEAT *in the* COMBUSTION OF FUEL.—*Without knowing what Heat really is, the Laws of its Action may be investigated.*— *Probability that the Heat generated in the Combustion of Fuel is furnished by the Air, and not by the Fuel.*— *Effects of blowing a Fire explained.*— *Of Fire-places in which the Fire is made to blow itself.*— *Of Air-furnaces.*— *These Fire-places illustrated by a Lamp on* ARGAND'S *Principle.*— *Great Importance of being able to regulate the Quantity of Air which enters a closed Fire-place.*— *Utility of Dampers in the Chimneys of closed Fire-places.*— *General Rules and Directions for constructing closed Fire-places; with a full Explanation of the Principles on which these Rules are founded.*

WITHOUT entering into those abstruse and most difficult investigations respecting the nature of fire, which have employed the attention and divided the opinions of speculative philosophers in all ages; without even attempting to determine whether there be such a thing as an *igneous* fluid or not,— whether what we call *heat* be occasioned by the accumulation, or by the increased action of such a fluid, or whether it arises merely from an increased motion in the component particles of the body heated, or of some elastic fluid by which those particles are supposed to be surrounded, and upon which they are supposed to act, or by which they are supposed to be acted upon: in short, without bewildering myself and my reader in this endless labyrinth of darkness and uncertainty, I shall confine my inquiries to objects more useful, and which are clearly within the reach of human investigation; namely, the discovery of the sensible properties of heat, and of the most advantageous methods of generating it, and of directing it with certainty and effect in those various processes in which it is employed in the economy of human life.

Though I do not undertake to determine *what heat really is*, nor even to offer any opinions or conjectures relative to that subject; yet as heat is evidently something capable of being excited or generated, increased or accumulated, measured and transferred from one body to another,— in treating the subject I shall speak of it as being *generated, confined, directed, dispersed*, etc., it being necessary to use these terms in order to make myself understood.

Though it is not known exactly *how much* heat it is possible to produce in the combustion of any given quantity of any given kind of fuel, yet it is more than probable that the quantity depends in a great measure on the management of the fire. It is likewise probable — I might say certain — that the heat produced is furnished not merely by the fuel, but in a great measure, if not entirely, by the *air* by which the fire is fed and supported. It is well known that air is necessary to combustion; it is likewise known that the pure part of common atmospheric air, or that part of it (amounting to about $\frac{1}{4}$ of its whole volume) which alone is capable of supporting the combustion of inflammable bodies, undergoes a remarkable change, or is actually *decomposed* in that process; and as in this decomposition of pure air a great quantity of heat is known to be set loose, or to become redundant, it has been supposed by many (and with much appearance of probability) that by far the greater part, if not all the heat produced in the combustion of inflammable bodies, is derived from this source.

But whether it be the air or the fuel which furnishes the heat, it seems to be quite certain that the quantity furnished depends much upon *the management of the fire*, and that the quantity is greater as the combustion or decomposition of the fuel is more complete. In all probability, the decomposition of the air keeps pace with the decomposition of the fuel.

It is well known that the consumption of fuel is much accelerated, and the intensity of the heat augmented, by causing the air by which the combustion is excited to flow into the fire-place in a continued stream, and with a certain degree of velocity. Hence, blowing a fire, when the current of air is properly directed and when it is not too strong, serves to accelerate the combustion and to increase the heat; but when the blast is improperly directed, it will rather serve to derange and to impede the combustion than to forward it; and when it is too strong, it will blow the fire quite out, or totally extinguish it. There is no fire, however intense, but may be blown out by a blast of air, provided it be sufficiently strong, and that as infallibly as by a stream of cold water. Even gunpowder, the most inflammable perhaps of known substances, may be actually on fire at its surface, and yet the fire may be blown out and extinguished before the grain of powder has had time to be entirely consumed.

This fact, however extraordinary and incredible it may appear, I have proved by the most unexceptionable and conclusive experiments.

Fire-places may be so constructed that the fire may be made to blow itself, or — which is the same thing — to cause a current of air to flow into the fire; and this is an object to which the greatest attention ought to be paid in the construction of all fire-places where it is not intended to make use of an artificial blast from bellows for blowing the fire. Furnaces constructed upon this principle have been called *air-furnaces;* but every fire-place, and particularly every closed fire-place, ought to be an air-furnace, and that even were it intended to serve only for the smallest saucepan, otherwise it cannot be perfect.

An Argand's lamp is a fire-place upon this construction; for the glass tube which surrounds the wick (and which distinguishes this lamp from all others) serves merely as a blower. The circular form of the wick is not essential; for by applying a flatted glass tube as a blower to a lamp with a flat or riband wick, it may be made to give as much light as an Argand's lamp, or at least quite as much in proportion to the size of the wick, and to the quantity of oil consumed, as I have found by actual experiment.

But it is not the light alone that is increased in consequence of the application of these blowers: the heat also is rendered much more intense; and as the heat of any fire may be increased by a similar contrivance, on that account it is that I have had recourse to these lamps to assist me in explaining the subject under consideration. In these lamps the fire-place is closed on all sides, and the current of air which feeds the fire rises up perpendicularly from below the fire-place into the fire. By surrounding the fire on all sides by a wall, the cold atmosphere is prevented from rushing in laterally from all quarters to supply the place of the heated air or vapour, which, in consequence of its increased elasticity from the heat, continually rises from the fire, and this causes the current of air below (the only quarter from which it can with advantage flow into the fire) to be very strong.

But in order that a fire-place may be perfect, it should be so contrived that the combustion of the fuel and the generation of the heat may occasionally be accelerated or retarded, *without adding to or diminishing the quantity of fuel;* and, when the fire-place is closed, this may easily be done by means of a *register* in the door which closes the passage leading to the ash-pit; for, as the rapidity of the combustion depends upon the quantity of air by which the fire is fed, by opening the register more or less, more or less air will be admitted into the fire-place, and consequently more or less fuel will be consumed, and more or less heat generated in any given time, though the quantity of fuel in the fire-place be actually much greater than what otherwise would be sufficient. Fig. 9 shows the form of the register I commonly use for this purpose.

In order that this register may produce its proper effect, a valve, or a *damper*, as it is commonly called, should be placed in the chimney or canal by which the smoke is carried off; which damper should be opened more or less, as the quantity of air is greater or less which is admitted into the fire-place. This register and this damper will be found very useful in another respect, and that is, in putting out the fire when there is no longer an occasion for it; for, upon closing them both entirely, the fire will be immediately extinguished, and the half-consumed fuel, instead of being suffered to burn out to no purpose, will be saved.

Nearly the same effects as are produced by a damper may be produced without one, by causing the smoke, after it has quitted the fire-place, to descend several feet below the level of the grate on which the fuel is burned before it is permitted to go up the chimney.

There is another circumstance of much importance which must be attended to in the construction of fire-places, and that is, the proper disposition of the fuel; for in order that the combustion may go on well, it is necessary not only that the fuel be in its proper place, but also that it be properly disposed; that is to say, that the solid parts of the fuel be of a just size, and that they be not placed too near each other, so as to prevent the free passage of the air between them, nor too far asunder; and if the fire-place can be so contrived that solid pieces of the inflamed fuel, as they go on to be diminished in size as they burn, may naturally fall together in the centre of the fire-place without any assistance, it will be a great improvement, as I have found by experience. This may be done, in small fire-places (and in these it is more particularly necessary), by burning the fuel upon a grate in the form of a segment of a hollow sphere, or of a dish. (See the Figures 3 and 4, Plate I.) All those I now use, except it be for fire-places which are very large indeed, are of this form; and where wood is made use of for fuel, it is cut into small billets from 4 to 6 inches in length. Instead of a grate of iron, I have lately introduced grates, or rather hollow dishes or pans of earthen-ware, perforated with a great number of holes for giving a passage to the air.

These perforated earthen pans, which are made very thick and strong, are incomparably cheaper than iron grates; and judging from the experience I have had of them, I am inclined to think they answer even better than the grates; indeed it appears to me not difficult to assign a reason why they ought to be better.

For large fire-places I have sometimes used grates, the bars of which were common bricks placed edgewise, and these have been found to answer very well.

As only *that part of the air* which, entering the fire-place in a proper manner and in a just quantity, and coming into actual contact with the burning fuel, *is decomposed*, contributes to the generation of heat, it is evident that all the air that finds its way into the fire-place, *and out of it again*, without being decomposed, is a thief; that it not only *contributes nothing* to the heat, but being itself heated at the expense of the fire, and going off *hot* into the atmosphere by the chimney, occasions an actual loss of heat; and this loss is often very considerable, and the prevention of it is such an object, that too much attention cannot be paid to it in the construction of fire-places.

When the fire-place is closed on all sides by a wall, and when the opening by which the fuel is introduced is kept closed, no air can press in laterally upon the fire; but yet, when the grate is larger than the heap of burning fuel, which must often be the case, a great quantity of air may insinuate itself by the sides of the grate into the fire-place, without going through the fire. But when, instead of an iron grate, a perforated hollow earthen pan is used, by making the bottom of the pan of a certain thickness, 2, 3, or 4 inches, for instance, and making all the air-holes point to one common centre (to the focus or centre of the fire), this furtive entrance of cold air into the fire-place will in a great measure be prevented.

This evil may likewise be prevented when circular hollow iron grates are used, by narrowing the fire-place immediately under the grate in the form of an inverted, truncated, hollow cone, the opening or diameter of which above being equal to the internal diameter of the circular rim of the grate, and that below (by which the air rises to enter the fire-place) about *one third* of that diameter. (See the Figure 5, Plate I.) This opening below, through which the air rises, must be immediately under the centre of the grate, and as near to it as possible; care must be taken, however, that a small space be left between the outside or underside of the iron bars which form the hollow grate and the inside surface of this inverted hollow cone, in order that the ashes may slide down into the ash-pit.

As to the form and size of the ash-pit, these are matters of perfect indifference, provided, however, that it be large enough to give a free passage to the air necessary for feeding the fire, and that the only passage into it by which air can enter is closed by a good door furnished with a register. The necessity of being completely master of the passage by which the air enters the fire-place has already been sufficiently explained.

It is perhaps unnecessary for me to observe that, where perforated earthen pans are used instead of iron grates, the air-holes in the pans ought to be rather smaller above than below, in order that they may not be choked up by the small pieces of coal and the ashes which occasionally fall through them into the ash-pit.

One great advantage attending fire-places on the construction here proposed is, that they serve equally well for every kind of fuel. Wood, pit-coal, charcoal, turf, etc., may indifferently be used, and all of them with the same facility, and with the same advantages; or any two, or more, of these different kinds of fuel may be used at the same time without the smallest inconvenience; or the fire having been lighted with dry wood, or any other very inflammable material, the heat may afterwards be kept up by cheaper or more ordinary fuel of a more difficult and slow combustion. Some kinds of fuel will perhaps be found most advantageous for making the pot boil, and others for keeping it boiling; and a very considerable saving will probably be found to result from paying due attention to this circumstance. When the fire-place is so contrived as to serve equally well for all kinds of fuel, this may be done without the least difficulty or trouble.

I have just shown that narrowing that part of the fire-place which lies below the grate serves to make the air enter the fire in a more advantageous manner. This construction has another advantage, perhaps still more important: the heat which is projected downwards through the openings between the bars of the grate, instead of being permitted to escape into the ash-pit (where it would be lost), striking against the sides of this inverted hollow *cone*, it is there stopped, and afterwards rises into the fire-place again with the current of air which feeds the fire, or it is immediately reflected by this conical surface, and, after two or three bounds from side to side, is thrown up against the bottom of the boiler.

But in order to be able to form a clear and distinct idea upon this subject, it is necessary to examine with care all the circumstances attending the generation of heat in the combustion of inflammable bodies, and to see in what manner or under what form the heat generated manifests itself, and how it may be collected, accumulated, confined, and directed.

This opens a wide field for philosophical inquiry; but as these investigations are not only curious and entertaining, but also useful and important in a high degree, I trust my reader will pardon me for requesting his particular attention while I endeavour to do justice to this most interesting, but, at the same time, most abstruse and most difficult part of the subject I have undertaken to treat.

The heat generated in the combustion of fuel manifests itself in two ways; namely, in the hot vapour which rises from the fire, with which it may be said to be *combined*, and in the calorific rays which are thrown off from the fire in all directions. These rays may, with greater propriety, be said to be *calorific*, or *capable of generating heat*, in any body by which they are *stopped*, than to be called hot; for when they pass freely through any medium (as through a mass of air, for instance), they are not found to communicate any heat whatever to such medium; neither do they appear to excite any considerable degree of heat in bodies from whose surfaces they are reflected; and in these respects they bear a manifest resemblance to the rays emitted by the sun.

What proportion this *radiant heat* (if I may be allowed to use so inaccurate an expression) bears to that which goes off from burning bodies in the smoke and heated vapour, is not exactly known; it is certain, however, that the quantity of heat which goes off in the heated elastic fluids, visible and invisible, which rise from a fire, is much greater than that which all the calorific rays united would be capable of producing. But though the quantity of *radiant heat* is less than that existing in the hot vapour (and which, for the sake of distinction, may be called *combined heat*), the former is still much too considerable to be neglected.

That the heat generated, or excited, by the calorific rays which proceed from burning bodies is in fact considerable, is evident from the heat which is felt in a room warmed by a chimney fire; for as all the heat, combined with the smoke and hot vapour, goes up the chimney, it is certain that the increase of heat in the room, occasioned by the fire, is entirely owing to the calorific rays thrown into it from the burning fuel.

The activity of these rays may be shown in various ways, but in no way in a more striking manner than by the following simple experiment: When the fire burns bright upon the hearth, let the arm be extended in a straight line towards the centre of the fire, with the hand open, and all the fingers extended and pointing to the fire. If the hand is not nearer the fire than the distance of two or three yards, except the fire be very large indeed, the heat will scarcely be perceptible; but if, without moving the arm, the wrist be bent upwards so as to present the inside or flat of the hand perpendicular to the fire, the heat will not only be very sensibly felt, but if the fire be large, and if it burns clear and bright, it will be found to be so intense as to be quite insupportable.

It is not, however, burning bodies alone that emit calorific rays. All bodies — those which are fixed and incombustible as well as those which are inflammable, fluids as well as solids — are found to throw off these rays in great abundance, as soon as they are heated to that degree which is necessary to their becoming luminous in the dark, or till they are red-hot.

Bodies even which are heated to a less degree than that which is necessary to their emitting *visible* light send off calorific rays in all directions. This is a matter of fact, which has been proved by experiment. Do all bodies, at all temperatures, — freezing mercury as well as melting iron, — continually emit these rays in greater or less quantities, or with greater or less velocities? Are bodies cooled in consequence of their emitting these rays? Do these calorific rays always generate heat, even when the body by which they are stopped or absorbed is hotter than that from which the rays proceeded? But I forget that I promised not to involve myself in abstruse speculation. To return, then. Whatever may be the nature of the rays emitted by burning fuel, as *one* of their *known properties* is to generate heat, they ought certainly to be very particularly attended to in every arrangement in which the economy of heat, or of fuel, is a principal object in view.

As these calorific rays generate heat in the body by which they are *stopped or absorbed*, and not in the medium through which they pass, it is necessary to dispose those bodies which are designed for stopping them in such a manner that they may easily and *necessarily* communicate the heat they thus acquire to the body upon which it is intended that it should operate.

Of the Management of Fire

The closed fire-places which I have recommended, and which will hereafter be more particularly described, will answer this purpose completely. The fire being closed in these fire-places on every side, as well below the grate as laterally, and in short everywhere, except where the bottom of the boiler presents itself to the fire, none of these rays can possibly escape; and as the materials of which the fire-place is constructed (bricks and mortar) are bad conductors of heat, but a small part of the heat generated in the combustion of the fuel will be absorbed and transmitted by them into the interior parts of the wall, there to be dispersed and lost. But the confining of heat is a matter of sufficient importance to deserve being treated in a separate chapter.

CHAPTER III.

Of the Means of CONFINING HEAT, *and* DIRECTING ITS OPERATIONS. — *Of Conductors and Non-conductors of Heat.* — *Common Atmospheric Air a good Non-conductor of Heat, and may be employed with great Advantage for confining it; is employed by Nature for that Purpose, in many Instances; is the principal Cause of the Warmth of Natural and Artificial Clothing; is the sole Cause of the Warmth of Double Windows.* — *Great Utility of Double Windows and Double Walls: they are equally useful in Hot Countries as in Cold.* — ALL ELASTIC FLUIDS *Non-conductors of Heat.* — STEAM *proved by Experiment to be a Non-conductor of Heat.* — FLAME *is also a Non-conductor of Heat.*

THAT heat passes more freely through some bodies than through others, is a fact well known; but the cause of this difference in the conducting powers of bodies with respect to heat has not yet been discovered.

The utility of giving a wooden handle to a tea-pot or coffee-pot of metal, or of covering its metallic handle with leather, or with wood, is well known. But the difference in the conducting powers of various bodies with regard to heat may be shown by a great number of very simple experiments, such as are in the power of every one to make at all times and in all places, and almost without either trouble or expense.

If an iron nail and a pin of wood, of the same form and dimensions, be held successively in the flame of a candle, the difference in the conducting powers of the metal and of wood will manifest itself in a manner in which there will be no room left for doubt. As soon as the end of the nail which is exposed in the flame of the candle begins to be heated, the other end of it will grow so hot as to render it impossible to hold it in the hand without being burned; but the wood may be held any length of time in the same situation without the least inconvenience; and, even after it has taken fire, it may be held till it is almost entirely consumed, for the uninflamed wood will not grow hot, and, till the flame actually comes in contact with the fingers, they will not be burned. If a small slip or tube of glass be held in the flame of the candle in the same manner, the end of the glass by which it is held will be found to be more heated

than the wood, but incomparably less so than the pin or
nail of metal; and among all the various bodies that can
be tried in this manner, no two of them will be found to
give a passage to heat through their substances with
exactly the same degree of facility.*

To confine heat is nothing more than to prevent its
escape out of the hot body in which it exists, and in
which it is required to be retained; and this can only be
done by surrounding the hot body by some covering
composed of a substance through which heat cannot
pass, or through which it passes with great difficulty. If
a covering could be found perfectly impervious to heat,
there is reason to believe that a hot body, completely
surrounded by it, would remain hot for ever; but we are
acquainted with no such substance, nor is it probable
that any such exists.

Those bodies in which heat passes freely or rapidly
are called *conductors* of heat; those in which it makes
its way with great difficulty or very slowly, *non-conductors*, or bad conductors of heat. The epithets, good,
bad, indifferent, excellent, etc., are applied indifferently
to *conductors* and to *non-conductors*. A good conductor, for instance, is one in which heat passes very
freely; a good non-conductor is one in which it passes
with great difficulty; and an indifferent conductor may
likewise be called, without any impropriety, an indifferent
non-conductor.

* To show the relative conducting power of the different metals, Doctor
Ingenhous contrived a very pretty experiment. He took equal cylinders of the
different metals (being straight pieces of stout wire, drawn through the same
hole, and of the same length), and, dipping them into melted wax, covered them
with a thin coating of the wax. He then held one end of each of these cylinders in boiling water, and observed how far the coating of wax was melted by
the heat communicated through the metal, and with what celerity the heat
passed.

Those bodies which are the worst conductors, or rather the best non-conductors of heat, are best adapted for forming coverings for confining heat.

All the metals are remarkably good conductors of heat; wood, and in general all light, dry, and spongy bodies are non-conductors. Glass, though a very hard and compact body, is a non-conductor. Mercury, water, and liquids of all kinds, are conductors; but air, and in general all elastic fluids, *steam* even not excepted, are non-conductors.

Some experiments which I have lately made, and which have not yet been published, have induced me to suspect that water, mercury, and all other non-elastic fluids, do not permit heat to pass through them from particle to particle, as it undoubtedly passes through solid bodies, but that their apparent conducting powers depend essentially upon the extreme mobility of their parts; in short, that they rather *transport* heat than allow it a passage. But I will not anticipate a subject which I propose to treat more fully at some future period.

The conducting power of any solid body in one solid mass is much greater than that of the same body reduced to a powder, or divided into many smaller pieces. An iron bar, or an iron plate, for instance, is a much better conductor of heat than iron filings; and sawdust is a better non-conductor than wood. Dry wood-ashes is a better non-conductor than either; and very dry charcoal reduced to a fine powder is one of the best non-conductors known; and as charcoal is perfectly incombustible when confined in a space where fresh air can have no access, it is admirably well calculated for forming a barrier for confining heat, where the heat to be confined is intense.

But among all the various substances of which coverings may be formed for confining heat, none can be employed with greater advantage than common atmospheric air. It is what nature employs for that purpose; and we cannot do better than to imitate her.

The warmth of the wool and fur of beasts, and of the feathers of birds, is undoubtedly owing to the air in their interstices; which air, being strongly attracted by these substances, is confined, and forms a barrier which not only prevents the cold winds from approaching the body of the animal, but which opposes an almost insurmountable obstacle to the escape of the heat of the animal into the atmosphere. And in the same manner the air in snow serves to preserve the heat of the earth in winter. The warmth of all kinds of artificial clothing may be shown to depend on the same cause; and were this circumstance more generally known, and more attended to, very important improvements in the management of heat could not fail to result from it. A great part of our lives is spent in guarding ourselves against the extremes of heat and of cold, and in operations in which the use of fire is indispensable; and yet how little progress has been made in that most useful and most important of the arts, — the management of heat!

Double windows have been in use many years in most of the northern parts of Europe, and their great utility, in rendering the houses furnished with them warm and comfortable in winter, is universally acknowledged; but I have never heard that anybody has thought of employing them in hot countries to keep their apartments cool in summer; yet how easy and natural is this application of so simple and so useful an invention! If a double window can prevent the heat which is *in* a room from passing *out of it*, one would imagine it could require no great effort of genius to discover that it would be equally efficacious for preventing the heat *without* from coming *in*. But natural as this conclusion may appear, I believe it has never yet occurred to anybody; at least I am quite certain that I have never seen a double window either in Italy or in any other hot country I have had occasion to visit.*

But the utility of double windows and double walls, in hot as well as in cold countries, is a matter of so much importance that I shall take occasion to treat it more fully in another place. In the mean time, I shall only observe here that it is the *confined air* shut up between the two windows, and not the double glass plates, that renders the passage of heat through them so difficult. Were it owing to the increased thickness of the glass, a single pane of glass twice as thick would answer the same purpose; but the increased thickness of the glass of which a window is formed is not found to have any sensible effect in rendering a room warmer.

But air is not only a non-conductor of heat, but its non-conducting power may be greatly increased. To be able to form a just idea of the manner in which air may be rendered a worse conductor of heat, or, which is the same thing, a better non-conductor of it than it is in its natural unconfined state, it will be necessary to consider *the manner* in which heat passes through air.

---

* When double windows are used in hot countries to keep dwelling-houses cool, great care must be taken to screen those windows from the sun's direct rays, and even from the strong light of day, otherwise they will produce effects directly contrary to those intended. This may easily be done either by Venetian blinds or by awnings. In all cases where rooms are to be kept cool in hot weather, the less light that is permitted to enter them the cooler they will be.

Now it appears, from the result of a number of experiments which I made with a view to the investigation of this subject, and which are published in a paper read before the Royal Society,[*] that though the particles of air, *each particle for itself*, can receive heat from *other bodies*, or communicate it to them, yet there is no communication of heat *between one particle of air and another particle of air*. And from hence it follows that though air may, and certainly does, *carry off* heat and *transport it* from one place or from one body to another, yet a mass of air in a quiescent state, or with all its particles at rest, *could it remain in that state*, would be totally impervious to heat, or such a mass of air would be a perfect non-conductor.

Now if heat passes in a mass of air merely in consequence of the motion it occasions in that air; if it be *transported,—not suffered to pass,—*in that case, it is clear that whatever can obstruct and impede the internal motion of the air must tend to diminish its conducting power. And this I have found to be the case in fact. I found that a certain quantity of heat which was able to make its way through a wall, or rather a sheet of confined air, ½ an inch thick in 9⅝ minutes, required 21¾ minutes to make its way through the same wall, when the internal motion of this air was impeded by mixing with it 1/70 part of its bulk of eider-down, of very fine fur, or of fine silk, as spun by the worm.

But in mixing bodies with air, in order to impede its internal motion and render it more fit for confining heat, such bodies only must be chosen as are themselves non-conductors of heat, otherwise they will do more

---

[*] See the Philosophical Transactions, 1792. See also Vol. I., pp. 401 and following.

harm than good, as I have found by experience. When, instead of making use of eider-down, fur, or fine silk for impeding the internal motion of the confined air, I used an equal volume of exceedingly fine silver-wire flatted (being the ravellings of gold or silver lace), the passage of the heat through the barrier, so far from being impeded, was remarkably facilitated by this addition, — the heat passing through this compound of air and fine threads of metal much sooner than it would have made its way through the air alone.

Another circumstance to be attended to in the choice of a substance to be mixed with air, in order to form a covering or barrier for confining heat, is the fineness or subtilty of its parts; for the finer they are, the greater will be their surface in proportion to their solidity, and the more will they impede the motions of the particles of the air. Coarse horse-hair would be found to answer much worse for this purpose than the fine fur of a beaver, though it is not probable that there is any essential difference in the chemical properties of those two kinds of hair.

But it is not only the fineness of the parts of a substance, and its being a non-conductor, which render it proper to be employed in the formation of covering to confine heat; there is still another property, more occult, which seems to have great influence in rendering some substances better fitted for this use than others: and this is a certain attraction which subsists between certain bodies and air. The obstinacy with which air adheres to the fine fur of beasts and to the feathers of birds is well-known; and it may easily be proved that this attraction must assist very powerfully in preventing the motion of the air concealed in the interstices of those substances, and consequently in impeding the passage of heat through them.

Perhaps there may be another still more hidden cause which renders one substance better than another for confining heat. I have shown by a direct and unexceptionable experiment that heat can pass through the Torricellian vacuum,* though with rather more difficulty than in air (the conducting power of air being to that of a Torricellian vacuum as 1000 to 604, or as 10 to 6, very nearly); but if heat can pass where there is no air, it must in that case pass by a medium more subtile than air, — a medium which most probably pervades all solid bodies with the greatest facility, and which must certainly pervade either the glass or the mercury employed in making a Torricellian vacuum.

Now, if there exists a medium more subtile than air by which heat may be conducted, is it not possible that there may exist a certain affinity between that medium and sensible bodies? a certain attraction or cohesion, by means of which bodies in general, or some kinds of bodies in particular, may, somehow or other, impede this medium in its operations in conducting or transporting heat from one place to another? It appeared from the result of several of my experiments, of which I have given an account in detail in my paper before mentioned, published in the year 1786, in vol. lxxvi. of the Philosophical Transactions, that the conducting power of a Torricellian vacuum is to that of air as 604 to 1000; but I found by a subsequent experiment (see my second Paper on Heat, published in the Philosophical Transactions for the year 1792) that

* See my Experiments on Heat, published in the Philosophical Transactions, Vol. LXXVI.

55 parts in bulk of air, with 1 part of fine raw silk,
formed a covering for confining heat, the conducting
power of which was to that of air as 576 to 1284, or
as 448 to 1000. Now, from the result of this last-mentioned
experiment, it should seem that the introduction
into the space through which the heat passed of so small
a quantity of raw silk as $\frac{1}{56}$ part of the volume or capacity
of that space, rendered that space (which now contained
55 parts of air and 1 part of silk) more impervious
to heat than even a Torricellian vacuum. The silk must
therefore not only have completely destroyed the conducting
power of the air, but must also at the same time
have very sensibly impaired that of the ethereal fluid
which probably occupies the interstices of air, and which
serves to conduct heat through a Torricellian vacuum:
for a Torricellian vacuum was a better conductor of
heat than this medium, in the proportion of 604 to 448.
But I forbear to enlarge upon this subject, being sensible
of the danger of reasoning upon the properties of
a fluid whose existence even is doubtful, and feeling
that our knowledge of the nature of heat, and of the
manner in which it is communicated from one body to
another, is much too imperfect and obscure to enable us
to pursue these speculations with any prospect of success
or advantage.

Whatever may be the *manner* in which heat is communicated
from one body to another, I think it has been
sufficiently proved that it passes with great difficulty
through confined air; and the knowledge of this fact
is very important, as it enables us to take our measures
with certainty and with facility for confining heat, and
directing its operations to useful purposes.

But atmospheric air is not the only non-conductor of

heat. All kinds of air, artificial as well as natural, and in general all elastic fluids, *steam not excepted*, seem to possess this property in as high a degree of perfection as atmospheric air.

That steam is not a conductor of heat I proved by the following experiment: A large globular bottle being provided, of very thin and very transparent glass, with a narrow neck, and its bottom drawn inward so as to form a hollow hemisphere about 6 inches in diameter; this bottle, which was about 8 inches in diameter externally, being filled with cold water, was placed in a shallow dish, or rather plate, about 10 inches in diameter, with a flat bottom formed of very thin sheet brass, and raised upon a tripod, and which contained a small quantity (about $\frac{1}{10}$ of an inch in depth) of water; a spirit-lamp being then placed under the middle of this plate, in a very few minutes the water in the plate began to boil, and the hollow formed by the bottom of the bottle was filled with clouds of steam, which, after circulating in it with surprising rapidity 4 or 5 minutes, and after forcing out a good deal of air from under the bottle, began gradually to clear up. At the end of 8 or 10 minutes (when, as I supposed, the air remaining with the steam in the hollow cavity formed by the bottom of the bottle had acquired nearly the same temperature as that of the steam) these clouds totally disappeared; and though the water continued to boil with the utmost violence, the contents of this hollow cavity became so perfectly invisible, and so little appearance was there of steam, that had it not been for the streams of water which were continually running down its sides I should almost have been tempted to doubt whether any steam was actually generated.

Upon lifting up for an instant one side of the bottle, and letting in a smaller quantity of cold air, the clouds instantly returned, and continued circulating several minutes with great rapidity, and then gradually disappeared as before. This experiment was repeated several times, and always with the same result: the steam always becoming visible when cold air was mixed with it, and afterwards recovering its transparency when, part of this air being expelled, that which remained had acquired the temperature of the steam.

Finding that cold air introduced under the bottle caused the steam to be partially condensed, and clouds to be formed, I was desirous of seeing what visible effects would be produced by introducing a cold solid body under the bottle. I imagined that if steam was a conductor of heat, some part of the heat in the steam passing out of it into the cold body, clouds would of course be formed; but I thought if steam was a *non-conductor* of heat, — that is to say, *if one particle of steam could not communicate any part of its heat to its neighbouring particles*, — in that case, as the cold body could only affect the particles of steam *actually in contact with it*, no cloud would appear; and the result of the experiment showed that steam is in fact a *non-conductor of heat*. For, notwithstanding the cold body used in this experiment was very large and very cold, being a solid lump of ice nearly as large as a hen's egg, placed in the middle of the hollow cavity under the bottle, upon a small tripod or stand made of iron wire; yet as soon as the clouds which were formed in consequence of the unavoidable introduction of cold air in lifting up the bottle to introduce the ice were dissipated, which soon happened, the steam became so perfectly transparent and invisible that *not the smallest appearance of cloudiness was to be seen anywhere*, not even about the ice, which, as it went on to melt, appeared as clear and as transparent as a piece of the finest rock crystal.

This experiment, which I first made at Florence, in the month of November, 1793, was repeated several times in the presence of Lord Palmerston, who was then at Florence, and M. de Fontana.*

In these experiments the air was not entirely expelled from under the bottle; on the contrary, a considerable quantity of it remained mixed with the steam even after the clouds had totally disappeared, as I found by a particular experiment made with a view to ascertain that fact. But that circumstance does not render the result of this experiment less curious; on the contrary, I think it tends to make it more surprising. It should seem that neither the mass of steam, nor that of air, were at all cooled by the body of ice which they surrounded; for

---

* The bottle made use of in this experiment, though it appeared very large externally, contained but a very small quantity of water, owing to its bottom being very much drawn inwards. As the hollow cavity under the bottom of the bottle (which, as I just observed, was nearly in the form of a hemisphere, and 6 inches in diameter) served as a receiver for confining the steam which rose from the boiling water in the plate, it may perhaps be imagined that a common glass receiver in the form of a bell, such as are used in pneumatical experiments, might answer as well as this bottle; I thought so myself, but upon making the experiment I found my mistake. A common receiver will answer perfectly well for confining the steam, but the glass soon becomes so hot that the drops of water which are formed upon its internal surface, in consequence of the condensation of the steam, instead of running down the sides of the receiver in clear transparent streams, form blotches and streaks, which render the glass so opaque that nothing can be seen distinctly through it; and this of course completely frustrates the main design of the experiment. But cold water in the bottle keeping the glass cool, the condensation of the steam upon the sides of the hollow cavity formed by the bottom of the bottle goes on more regularly, and the streams of water which are continually running down the sides of the glass, uniting together, form one transparent sheet of water, by which means every thing that goes on under the bottle may be distinctly seen.

if the air had been cooled (in mass), it seems highly probable that the clouds would have returned.

The results of these experiments compared with those formerly alluded to, in which I had endeavoured to ascertain the most advantageous forms for boilers, opened to me an entirely new field for speculation and for improvement in the management of fire. They shewed me that not only cold air, but also hot air and hot steam, and hot mixtures of air and steam, are non-conductors of heat; consequently that the hot vapour which rises from burning fuel, and even the *flame itself, is a non-conductor of heat.*

This may be thought a bold assertion; but a little calm reflection, and a careful examination of the phenomena which attend the combustion of fuel, and the communication of heat by flame, will show it to be well-founded; and the advantages which may be derived from the knowledge of this fact are of very great importance indeed. But this subject deserves to be thoroughly investigated.

CHAPTER IV.

Of the MANNER *in which* HEAT *is* COMMUNICATED *by* FLAME *to other Bodies. — Flame acts on Bodies in the same Manner as a hot Wind. — The Effect of a Blowpipe in increasing the Activity of Flame explained, and illustrated by Experiments. — A Knowledge of the Manner in which Heat is communicated by Flame necessary in order to determine the most ad-*

vantageous Forms for Boilers. — General Principles on which Boilers of all Dimensions ought to be constructed.

IF flame be merely vapour, or a mixture of air and steam heated red-hot, as air and steam are both non-conductors of heat, there seems to be no difficulty in conceiving that flame may, notwithstanding its great degree of heat, still retain the properties of its component fluids, and remain *a non-conductor of heat*. The non-conducting power of air does not appear to be at all impaired by being heated to the temperature of boiling water; and I see no reason why that property in air, or in any other elastic fluid, should be impaired by any augmentation of temperature, however great. If steam, or if air, at the temperature of 212 degrees of Fahrenheit's thermometer, be a non-conductor of heat, why should it not remain a non-conductor at that of 1000 degrees, or when heated red-hot? I confess I do not see how a body *could* be deprived of a property so essential, without being at the same time totally changed; and I believe nobody will imagine that either air or steam undergoes any chemical change merely by being heated to the temperature of red-hot iron. But without insisting upon these reasonings, however conclusive I may think them, I shall endeavour to show, from experiment and observation, in short to *prove*, that flame is in fact a non-conductor of heat.

Taking it for granted — what I imagine will not be denied — that air is a non-conductor of heat, at least in the sense I have used that appellation, I shall endeavour to show that flame acts precisely in the same manner as a hot wind would do in communicating heat, and in no other way; and if I succeed in this, I fancy I may consider the proposition as sufficiently proved.

The effect of a blast of cold air in cooling any hot body exposed to it is well known, and the causes of this effect may easily be traced to that property of air which renders it a non-conductor of heat; for if the particles of cold air in contact with a hot body could, with perfect facility, give the heat they acquire from the hot body to other particles of air by which they are immediately surrounded, and these again to others, and so on, the heat would be carried off *as fast as the hot body could part with it*, and any motion of the particles of the air, any wind or blast, would not sensibly facilitate or hasten the cooling of the body; and by a parity of reasoning it may be shown that, if flame were in fact a perfect conductor of heat, any cold body plunged into it would always be heated *as fast as that body could receive heat;* and neither any motion of the internal parts of the flame, nor the velocity with which it impinged against the cold body, could have any sensible effect either to facilitate or accelerate the heating of the body. But if flame be a non-conductor of heat, its action will be exactly similar to that of a hot wind, and consequently much will depend upon the manner in which it is applied to any body intended to be heated by it. Those particles of it *only* which are in *actual contact* with the body will communicate heat to it; and the greater the number of different particles of the flame which are brought into contact with it, the greater will be the quantity of heat communicated. Hence the importance of causing the flame to impinge with force against the body to be heated, and to strike it in such

a manner that its current may be broken, and that
whirlpools may be formed in it; for the rapid motion
of the flame causes a quick succession of hot particles;
and, admitting our assumed principles to be true, it is
quite evident that every kind of internal motion among
the particles of the flame by which it can be agitated
must tend very powerfully to accelerate the communication of the heat.

The effect of a blowpipe is well known, but I do
not think that the *manner* in which it increases the
action of *flame* has ever been satisfactorily explained.
It has generally been imagined, I believe, that the current of fresh air which is forced through the flame by
a blowpipe actually increases the quantity of heat; I
rather suppose it does little more than direct the heat
actually existing in the flame to a given point. A current of air cannot *generate* heat without at the same
time being decomposed; and, in order to its being
decomposed in a fire, it must be brought into actual
contact with the burning fuel, or at least with the uninflamed inflammable vapour which rises from it. But
can it be supposed that there can be any thing inflammable, and not actually inflamed, in the clear, bright,
and perfectly transparent flame of a wax candle? A
blowpipe has however as sensible an effect, when
directed against the clear flame of a wax candle, as
when it is employed to increase the action of a common
glass-worker's lamp.

Conceiving that the discovery of the *manner* in
which the current of air from a blowpipe serves to
increase the intensity of the action of the flame could
not fail to throw much light upon the subject under
consideration, — namely, the investigation of *the man-*

ner in which heat is communicated to bodies by flame, — I made the following experiments, the results of which I conceive to be decisive.

Concluding that the current of air from a blowpipe, directed against the flame of any burning body, could tend to increase the intensity of the action of the flame only in one or both of these two ways, — namely, by increasing its *action* upon the body against which it is directed, or by actually increasing the *quantity* of heat generated in the combustion of the fuel, — a method occurred to me by which I thought it possible to determine, by actual experiment, to which of these causes the effect in question is owing, or how much each of them might contribute to it. To do this, I filled a large bladder, containing above a gallon, with *fixed air*, which, as is well known, is totally unfit for supporting the combustion of inflammable bodies, and which, of course, could not be suspected of *adding* any heat to a flame against which a current of it should be directed. I imagined therefore that if a blowpipe supplied with this air, on being directed against the flame of a candle, should be found to produce nearly the same effect as when common air is used for the same purpose, it would prove to a demonstration that the augmentation of the intensity of the action, or activity of the flame which arises from the use of a blowpipe, is owing to the agitation of the flame, to its being directed to a point, to the impetuosity with which it is made to strike against the body which is heated by it, and to the rapid succession of fresh particles of this hot vapour, and not to any *positive increase of heat*.

A blowpipe being attached to the bladder containing fixed air, the end of this pipe was directed to the clear brilliant flame of a wax candle, which had just been snuffed; and, by compressing the bladder, the flame was projected against a small tube of glass, which was very soon made red-hot, and even melted.

Having repeated this experiment several times, and having found how long it required to melt the tube when the flame of the candle was forced against it by a blast of *fixed air*, I now varied the experiment, by making use of common atmospheric air instead of fixed air; taking care to employ the same candle and the same blowpipe used in the former experiments, and even making use of the bladder, in order that, the experiments being exactly similar and differing only in the kinds of air made use of, the effect of that difference might be discovered and estimated.

The results of these experiments were most perfectly conclusive, and proved in a decisive manner that the effect of a blowpipe, *when applied to clear flame*, arises not from any real augmentation of heat, but merely from the increased activity of the flame, in consequence of its being impelled with force, and broken in eddies on the surface of the body against which it is made to act; the effect of the blowpipe on these experiments being to all appearance quite as great when fixed air was made use of (which *could not* increase the quantity of heat), as when atmospheric air was used.

But, conceiving the determination of this question relative to the manner in which flame communicates heat to be a matter of much importance, I did not rest my inquiries here. I repeated the experiments very often, and varied them in a great number of different ways, sometimes making use of fixed air, sometimes of atmospheric air, and at other times using dephlogisticated air, and common air rendered unfit for the support of animal life and of combustion, by burning a candle in it till the candle went out.

It would take up too much time to give an account in detail of all these experiments. I shall therefore content myself with merely observing that they all tended to show that the effect of a blowpipe *used in the manner here described* is owing to the direction and velocity it gives to the flame against which it is employed, and not to any real increase of heat.

It must be remembered that the principal object I had in view in these experiments was to discover the *manner* in which flame communicates heat to other bodies, and by what means that communication may be facilitated. Were it required to increase the intensity of the heat by *blowing the fire*, the current of air must be applied in such a manner as to expedite the combustion: it must be directed to the inflamed surface of the burning fuel, and not to the red-hot vapour or flame which rises from it, and in which the combustion is most probably already quite complete; and in this case there is no doubt but the effect produced by blowing would depend much upon the quality of the air made use of.

The results of the foregoing experiments with the blowpipe will, I am confident, be thought quite conclusive by those who will take the trouble to consider them attentively; and the advantages that may be derived from the knowledge of the fact established by them are very obvious. If flame, or the hot vapour which arises from burning bodies, be a non-conductor of heat; and if, in order to communicate its heat to any other body, it be necessary that its particles *individually* be brought into actual contact with that body, it is evident that the form of a boiler, and of its fire-place, must be matters of much importance; and that *that form* must be most advantageous which is best calculated to produce an internal motion in the flame, and to bring alternately as many of its particles as possible into contact with the body which is to be heated by it. The boiler must not only have as large a surface as possible, but it must be of such a form as to cause the flame which embraces it to impinge against it with force, to break against it, and to play over its surface in eddies and whirlpools.

It is therefore against the *bottom* of a boiler, and not against its sides, that the principal efforts of the flame must be directed; for when the flame, or hot vapour, is permitted to rise freely by the vertical sides of a boiler, it slides over its surface very rapidly, and, there being no obstacle in the way to break the flame into eddies and whirlpools, it glides quietly on like a stream of water in a smooth canal; and the same hot particles of this vapour which happen to be in immediate contact with the sides of the boiler at its bottom or lower extremity, being continually pressed against the surface of the boiler as they are forced upwards by the rising current, prevent other hot particles from approaching the boiler; so that by far the greatest part of the heat in the flame and hot vapour which rise from the fire, instead of entering the boiler, goes off into the atmosphere by the chimney, and is totally lost.

The amount of this loss of heat, arising from the faulty construction of boilers and their fire-places, may be estimated from the results of the experiments recorded in the following chapter.

CHAPTER V.

An Account of Experiments made with Boilers and Fire-places of various Forms and Dimensions; together with Remarks and Observations on their Results, and on the Improvements that may be derived from them. — An Account of some Experiments made on a very large Scale in a Brewhouse Boiler. — An Account of a Brewhouse Boiler constructed and fitted up on an improved Plan. — Results of several Experiments which were made with this new Boiler. — Of the Advantage in regard to the Economy of Fuel in boiling Liquids, which arises from performing that Process on a large Scale. — These Advantages are limited. — An Account of an Alteration which was made in the new Brewhouse Boiler, with a view to the SAVING OF TIME *in causing its Contents to boil. — Experiments showing the Effects produced by these Alterations. — An Estimate of the* RELATIVE QUANTITIES OF HEAT *producible from* COKES, PIT-COAL, CHARCOAL, *and* OAK. *— A Method of Estimating the Quantity of Pit-coal which would be necessary to perform any of the Processes mentioned in this Essay, in which Wood was used as Fuel. — An Estimate of the* TOTAL QUANTITIES *of Heat producible in the Combustion of different Kinds of Fuel; and of the real Quantities of Heat which are lost, under various Circumstances, in culinary Processes.*

WHAT has been said in the foregoing chapter will, I trust, be sufficient to give my reader a clear and distinct idea of the subject under consideration in all its various details and connections, and enable him to comprehend without the smallest difficulty every thing I have to add on this subject; and particularly to discover the different objects I had in view in the experiments of which I am now about to give an account, and to judge with facility and certainty of the conclusions I have drawn from their results.

These experiments, though they occupy so many pages in this Essay, are but a small part of those I have made, and caused to be made under my direction, on the subject of heat, during the last seven years. Were I to publish them all, with all their details as they are recorded in the register that has been kept of them, they would fill several volumes.

It was most fortunate for me that this register is very voluminous; for, had it not been so, I should in all probability have taken it with me to England last year, and in that case I should have lost it, with the rest of my papers, in the trunk of which I was robbed in passing through St. Paul's churchyard, on my arrival in London after an absence of eleven years.*

As I foresaw, when I first began my inquiries respecting heat, that I should have occasion to make many experiments on boiling liquids, to facilitate the registering of them I formed a table (which I had printed), in which, under various heads, every circumstance relative to any common experiment of the kind in question could be entered with much regularity, and with little trouble.

* I have many reasons to think that these papers are still in being. What an everlasting obligation should I be under to the person who would cause them to be returned to me!

As this table may be useful to others who may be engaged in similar pursuits, and as the publishing of it will also tend to give my reader a more perfect idea of the manner in which my experiments were conducted, I shall (as an example) give an account of one experiment *in the same form* in which it was registered in one of these printed tables.

These tables, as they are printed for use (on detached sheets), occupy one side of half a sheet of common folio writing paper.

Every thing in this table, except such figures and words as are printed between crotchets, is contained in the printed forms. Hence it is evident how much these tables tend to diminish the trouble of registering the results of experiments of this kind, and also to prevent mistakes.

The example I have here given is an account of an experiment in which a very large quantity of water, equal to 15,590 lbs. avoirdupois in weight, or 1866 wine gallons of 231 cubic inches each; but it is evident that these tables answer equally well for the small quantity contained by the smallest saucepan.

The height of the barometer is expressed in Paris inches; that of the thermometer, in degrees of Fahrenheit's scale. The other measures, as well of length as of capacity, are the common measures of the country (Bavaria); and the weight is expressed in Bavarian pounds, of which 100 make 123.84 lbs. avoirdupois.

What is entered under the head of GENERAL RESULTS OF THE EXPERIMENT requires no explanation; but what I have called the PRECISE RESULT must be explained.

Having frequent occasion to compare the results of

An Experiment on the Management of Fire in Boiling Liquids; made at [Munich] in [a Brewhouse belonging to the Elector] the [19th] of [April, 1795].

Time of the day.	Fuel put into the fire-place.		Temperature of the liquid	Contents of the boiler.			Height of the barometer, with inches of thermometer, 9T°.
	No. of pieces	In weight		Kind of liquid, &c.	Measure	In weight	
h m		lb.				lb.	Dimensions of the Boiler.
9 15	29	100	60°	[Water]	6984	12,508	Diameter { above ——— as long ——— 27 feet
30	6	50	70°				{ below ——— and wide ——— 8 feet
41	6	50	92°				Deep, 4 feet. We constructed it (copper), and weighed (not known). It consisted of staves, 8.75 measures, weighing 12,625 lbs.
10 35	7	50	105°				
46	7	50	120°				**Kind of Fuel used.**—[Pine wood, moderately dry, in lengths of 6 feet.]
0	7	50	130°				
11 15	7	50	145°				**General Results of the Experiment.**
20	8	50	155°				
43	7	50	165°				Time employed to make the liquid boil, {3 40}
12 50	7	50	173°				Fuel consumed to make the liquid boil, [800] lbs.
17	8	50	183°				
31	15	100	192°				Time the liquid continued to boil 2 13
38			[boiled]				Fuel added to keep the liquid boiling . . 100 lbs.
55	7	50					Quantity of the liquid evaporated [not observed].
2 30	7	50					
35							**Precise Result.**
38	1		[ceased boiling]				With the heat generated in the combustion of 1 lb. of the fuel, [13.23 lbs.] of ice-cold water was made to boil: or [339.80 lbs.] of boiling-hot water kept boiling 1 hour.

experiments made at different times and in different seasons of the year, as the temperature of the water in the boiler when the fire is lighted under it is seldom the same in any two experiments, and as the boiling heat varies with the variations of the pressure of the atmosphere, or of the height of the mercury in the barometer, it became necessary to make proper allowances for these differences. This I thought could best be done by determining, by computation, from the number of degrees the water was *actually heated*, and the quantity of fuel consumed in heating it that number of degrees, how much fuel would have been required to have it heated 180 degrees, or from the point of freezing to that of boiling water (the boiling point being taken equal to the temperature indicated by 212° of Fahrenheit's thermometer, which is the boiling point under the mean pressure of the atmosphere at the surface of the sea). Then, by dividing the weight of the water used in the experiment (expressed in pounds) by the weight of the fuel expressed in pounds necessary to heat it 180 degrees, or from the temperature of freezing to that of boiling water: this gives the number of pounds of ice-cold water which (according to the result of the given experiment) *might have been* made to boil, with the heat generated in the combustion of 1 lb. of the fuel, under the mean pressure of the atmosphere at the level of the surface of the sea.

The city of Munich, where all the experiments were made of which I am about to give an account, being situated almost in the centre of Germany, lies very high above the level of the sea. The mean height of the mercury in the barometer is only about 28 English inches, consequently water boils at Munich at a lower temperature than at London. The difference is even too considerable to be neglected: it amounts to 2½ degrees of Fahrenheit's scale, being 209½ degrees at a medium at Munich, and 212 degrees in all places situated near the level of the sea. To render the results of my experiments and computations more simple and more generally useful, I shall always make due allowance for this difference.

Having, from the actual result of each experiment, made a computation on the principles here described, showing what (for the want of a better expression) I have called the *precise result* of the experiment, it is evident that these computations show very accurately the comparative merit of the mechanical arrangements, and the management of the fire in conducting the experiments, in as far as relates to the economy of fuel; for the more ice-cold water that can be made to boil with the heat generated in the combustion of any given quantity (1 lb. for instance) of fuel, the more perfect of course (other things being equal) must be the construction of the fire-place.

Under the head of PRECISE RESULT I have sometimes added another computation, showing how much "*boiling-hot water*" might, according to the result of the given experiment, be *kept boiling* "*one hour*" with the heat generated in the combustion of "1 lb. of the fuel." Though I have called this a *precise result*, it is evident that in most cases it cannot be considered as being very exact, owing to the difficulty of estimating the quantity of fuel in the fire-place, which is *unconsumed at the moment when the water begins to boil.*

In the foregoing example, in making this computation I supposed that, when the water began to boil, there was wood enough in the fire-place *unconsumed* to keep the water boiling 43 minutes, and that the wood added afterwards (100 lbs.) kept the water boiling the remainder of the time it boiled, or just 2 hours.

In most cases, however, to save trouble in making these computations, I have supposed that all the wood employed in making the water boil is entirely consumed in that process, and that all the heat expended in *keeping the water boiling* is furnished by the fuel which is added *after the water had begun to boil.* This supposition is evidently erroneous; but, as the computation in question can at best give but an inaccurate and doubtful result, labour bestowed on it would be thrown away. But, imperfect as these rough estimates are, they will however in many cases be found useful.

In giving an account of the following experiments, I shall not place them exactly in the order in which they were made, but shall arrange them in such a manner as I shall think best, in order that the information derived from their results may appear in a clear point of view.

For greater convenience in referring to them, I shall number them all; and as I have already given numbers to the four I mentioned in the first chapter of this Essay, I shall proceed in regular order with the rest.

Experiment No. 5.— The first kitchen of the House of Industry at Munich has already been described in the first chapter of this Essay; and it was there mentioned that the daily expense of fuel in that kitchen, when food (peas-soup) was prepared for 1000 persons, amounted to 300 lbs. in weight of dry beech-wood.

Now as each portion of soup consisted of 1 lb., this gives 0.3 of a pound of wood for each pound of soup.

Experiment No. 6. — The first kitchen of the House of Industry having been pulled down, it was afterwards rebuilt on a different principle. Instead of copper boilers, iron boilers of a hemispherical form were now used, and each of these boilers had its own separate closed fire-place; the boiler being suspended by its rim in the brick-work, and room being left for the flame to play all round it. The smoke went off into the chimney by an horizontal canal, 5 inches wide and 5 inches high, which was concealed in the mass of brick-work, and which opened into the fire-place on the side opposite to the opening by which the fuel was introduced.

The fire was made on a flat iron grate placed directly under the boiler, and distant from its bottom about 12 inches. The ash-pit door was furnished with a register; but there was no damper to the canal by which the smoke went off into the chimney, which was a very great defect. The opening into the fire-place was closed by an iron door. Each of these iron boilers weighed about 148 lbs. avoirdupois, was ·25¾ English inches in diameter, and 14.935 inches deep, and contained 190¼ lbs. Bavarian weight of water, equal to 235.91 lbs. avoirdupois, or about 28¼ English wine-gallons.

From this account of the manner in which these iron boilers were fitted up, it is evident that the arrangement was not essentially different from that of kitchens for hospitals as they are commonly constructed.

From experiments made with care, and often repeated, I found that to prepare 89 portions (or 89 lbs.

Bavarian weight) of peas-soup in one of these boilers, 43 lbs. of *dry beech-wood* were required as fuel, and that the process lasted four hours and a half. This gives 0.483 of a pound of wood for each pound of the soup.

In the first arrangement of this kitchen, only 0.3 of a pound of wood was required to prepare 1 lb. of soup. Hence it appears that the kitchen had not been improved, considered with a view to the economy of fuel, by the alterations which had been made in it. This was what I expected; for the object I had in view in constructing this kitchen was not to save fuel, but to find out how much of it is wasted in culinary processes, as they are commonly performed on a large scale in hospitals and other institutions of public charity. Till I knew this, it was not in my power to estimate, with any degree of precision, the advantages of any improvements I might introduce in the construction of kitchen fire-places.

To determine in how far the quantity of fuel necessary in any given culinary process depends on the form of the *fire-place* (the boiler and every other circumstance remaining the same), I made the following experiments.

Experiments Nos. 7 and 8. — Two of the iron boilers in the kitchen of the House of Industry (which, as they were both cast from the same model, were as near alike as possible) being chosen for this experiment, one of them (No. 8) being taken out of the brick-work, its fire-place was altered and fitted up anew on improved principles. The grate was made circular and concave, and its diameter was reduced to 12 inches; the fire-place was made cylindrical above the grate, and only

12 inches in diameter; and the boiler being seated on the top of the wall of this cylindrical fire-place, the flame, passing through a small opening on one side of the fire-place, at the top of it, made one complete turn about the boiler before it was permitted to go off into the canal by which the smoke passed off into the chimney.

Though there was no damper in this canal, yet as its entrance or opening, where it joined the canal which went round the boiler, was considerably reduced in size, this answered (though imperfectly) the purpose of a damper. This fire-place being completed, and a small fire having been kept up in it for several days to dry the masonry, the experiment was made by preparing the same quantity of the same kind of soup in this and in a neighbouring boiler whose fire-place had not been altered.

The food cooked in each was 89 lbs. of peas-soup; and the experiment was begun and finished in both boilers at the same time.

The wood employed as fuel was pine; and it had been thoroughly dried in an oven the day before it was used.

The boilers were both kept constantly covered with their double covers, except only when the soup was stirred about to prevent its burning to the bottoms of the boilers.

The result of this interesting experiment was as follows:—

	Experiment No. 7.	Experiment No. 8.
	In the boiler No. 1.	In the boiler No. 8. with the improved fire-place.
Quantity of wood consumed in cooking 89 lbs. Bavarian weight of peas-soup ...	37 lbs.	14 lbs.

These experiments were made on the 7th of November, 1794. On repeating them the next day with pine-wood, which had not been previously dried in an oven, the result was as follows:—

Experiments Nos. 9 and 10.

	Experiment No. 9.	Experiment No. 10.
	In the Boiler No. 1.	In the Boiler No. 8. with the improved Fire-place.
Quantity of wood consumed in cooking 89 lbs. of peas-soup	39 lbs.	16 lbs.

The first remark I shall make on the results of these experiments is the proof they afford, by comparing them with that which preceded them (No. 6), of the important fact that pine-wood affords more heat in its combustion than beech. This fact is the more extraordinary, as it is directly contrary to the opinion generally entertained on that subject; and it is the more important, as the price of pine-wood is in most places only about half as high as that of beech, when the quantities, *estimated by weight*, are equal.

In the Experiment No. 6 it was found that 43 lbs. of dry beech-wood were necessary when used as fuel, to prepare 89 lbs. of peas-soup. In the Experiment No. 7, the same process was performed with 37 lbs., and in the Experiment No. 9 with 39 lbs., of dry pine. But I shall have occasion to treat this subject more at length in another place. In the mean time I would, however, just observe, that all my experiments have uniformly tended to confirm the fact that dry pine-wood affords more heat in combustion than dry beech. I have reason to think the difference is in fact greater than the experiments before us indicate; but the *apparent* amount of it will always depend in a great measure on the circumstances under which the fuel is consumed, or, in other words, on the construction of the fire-place; and it is no small advantage attending the fire-places I shall recommend, that they are so contrived as to increase as much as it is possible the superiority of the most common and cheapest fire-wood over that which is more scarce and costly.

By comparing the results of these two sets of Experiments (Nos. 7 and 8, Nos. 9 and 10), an estimate may be made of the advantage of using *very dry wood* for fuel, instead of making use of wood that has been less thoroughly dried; but, as I mean to take an opportunity of investigating that matter also more carefully hereafter, I shall not at present enlarge on it farther than just to observe that as the wood, which was dried in an oven, was weighed for use after it had been dried, and as it certainly weighed more before it was put into the oven, the real saving arising from using it in this dried state is not so great as the difference in the weights of the quantities of wood used in the two experiments. To estimate that saving with precision, the wood should be weighed before it is dried, or in the same state in which the other parcel of wood, which is used without being dried, is weighed.

But to proceed to the principal object I had in view in these experiments, — the determination of the effects of the difference in the construction of the two fire-places, — the difference in the quantity of fuel expended in the two fire-places, in performing the same process, shows, in a manner which does not stand in need of any illustration, how much had been gained by the improvements which had been introduced.

Conceiving it to be an object of great importance to ascertain by actual experiment, and with as much precision as possible, the real amount of the advantages, in regard to the economy of fuel, that may be derived from improvements in the forms of fire-places, I did not content myself with improving from time to time the kitchens I had constructed, but I took pains to determine how much I had gained by each alteration that was made. This was necessary, not only to furnish myself with more forcible arguments to induce others to adopt my improvements, but also to satisfy myself with regard to the progress I made in my investigations.

In the first arrangement of the kitchen of the Military Academy, the boilers were suspended by their rims in the brick-work in such a manner that the flame could pass freely all round them, and the smoke went off in horizontal canals which led to the chimney, but which were not furnished with dampers.

The fire was made on a flat square iron grate; and the internal diameter of the fire-place was 2 or 3 inches larger than the diameter of the boiler which belonged to it. The bottom of the boiler was from 6 to 10 or 12 inches (according to its size) above the level of the grate; and the door of the opening into the fire-place by which the fuel was introduced was kept constantly closed. The ash-pit door was furnished with a register, and the boilers were all furnished with double covers.

Having, in consequence of the progress I had made in my inquiries respecting the management of heat and the economy of fuel, come to a resolution to pull down this kitchen, and rebuild it on an improved principle; previous to its being demolished, I made several very accurate experiments to determine the real expense of fuel in the fire-places as they *then existed*, with all their faults; and when the new arrangement of the kitchen was completed, I repeated these experiments *with the same boilers*; and by comparing the results of these two sets of experiments, I was able to estimate with great precision the real amount of the saving of time as well as of fuel, which was derived from the improvements I had introduced.

After all that has been said (and perhaps already too often repeated in different parts of this Essay) on the construction of fire-places, my reader will be able to form a clear and just idea of the construction of those of which I am now speaking (those of the kitchen of the Military Academy, in its *present* improved state), when he is told that the fire burns on a circular concave iron grate, about half the diameter of the circular boiler which belongs to the fire-place; that the fire-place, properly so called, is a cylindrical cavity in the solid brick-work which supports the boiler, equal in diameter to the circular grate, and from 6 to 10 inches high, more or less according to the size of the boiler; that the boiler is *set down* on the top of the circular wall which forms this fire-place, — a small opening from 3 to 4 or 5 inches in length taken horizontally, and about 2 or 3 inches high, being left on one side of this wall at the top of it, that the flame which burns up under the middle of the bottom of the boiler may afterwards pass round (in a spiral canal constructed for that purpose) under that part of the bottom of the boiler which lies *without* the top of the wall of the fire-place on which the boiler reposes. The flame having made one complete turn *under* the boiler in this spiral canal, it rises upwards, and, going once *round the sides of the boiler*, goes off by a horizontal canal, furnished with a damper, into the chimney.

In order that the top of the circular wall of the fire-place on which the boiler is seated may not cover too much of the bottom of the boiler, its thickness is suddenly reduced *in that part* (that is to say, just where it touches the boiler) to about half an inch.

The opening by which the fuel is introduced into the fire-place is a conical hole in a piece of fire-stone, which hole is closed by a fit stopper made of the same kind of stone. The ash-pit door and its register are finished with so much nicety that, when they are quite closed, the fire almost instantaneously goes out.

The dimensions of the boiler, in which the experiments of which I am about to give an account were made, are as follows: —

$$\text{Diameter} \begin{cases} \text{above} & : 14.935 \\ \text{below} & : 13.39 \end{cases} \text{Inches, English measure.}$$
$$\text{Depth} \ . \ . \ . \ . \ : 14.52$$

78   *Of the Management of Fire*

It weighs 37 lbs. avoirdupois; and it contains, when quite full, about 73 lbs. avoirdupois, equal to 8¼ gallons (wine-measure) of water.

In two experiments with this boiler, which were both made by myself, and in which attention was paid to every circumstance that could tend to render them perfect, the results were as follows:—

	Experiment No. 11.	*Experiment No. 12.*
	The first fire-place.	The improved fire-place.
Quantity of water in the boiler, in *Bavarian pounds*	43.63 lbs.	43.63 lbs.
Temperature of the water in the boiler at the beginning of the experiment	59°	60°
Time employed in making the water boil	67 m.	30 m.
Wood consumed in making the water boil, in *Bavarian pounds*	9 lbs.	3 lbs.
Time the water continued boiling	2 h. 2 m.	3 h.
Wood added to keep the water boiling	5 lbs.	2¼ lbs.
Kind of wood used	Pine.	Pine.
Precise Results.		
Ice-cold water heated 180 degrees, or made to boil, with 1 lb. of wood	4.02 lbs.	11.93 lbs.
Boiling-hot water kept boiling 1 hour, with 1 lb. of wood	17.74 lbs.	52.36 lbs.

The following experiments were made with two copper boilers (Nos. 1 and 2) nearly of the same dimensions, in the kitchen of the Military Academy at Munich, in the present improved state of that kitchen. These boilers are round and deep, and weigh each about 62 lbs. avoirdupois. They belonged originally to the kitchen of the House of Industry, being two of the eight boilers which, in the first arrangement of that kitchen, were heated by the same fire.

Their exact dimensions, measured in English inches, are as follows: —

	The boiler No. 1.	The boiler No. 2.
	Inches.	Inches.
Diameter { above	22.66	22.66
{ below	19.82	20.85
Depth	24.72	22.04

At the beginning of each of the following experiments, each of these boilers contained just 95 measures (or *Bavarian maasse*) of water, weighing 187 lbs. Bavarian weight (equal to 232.58 lbs. avoirdupois), or a trifle less than 28 gallons.

The grate on which the fire was made under each of these boilers is circular and concave, and 11 inches in diameter; and their fire-places are in all respects similar to that just described (Experiment No. 11). Both boilers are furnished with double covers.

The experiments made with the boiler No. 1, and their results, were as follows:—

	Exp. No. 13.	Exp. No. 14.	Exp. No. 15.	Exp. No. 16.
Quantity of water in the boiler in the beginning of the experiment	lbs. 187	lbs. 187	lbs. 187	lbs. 187
Temperature of the water in the boiler at the beginning of the experiment	61°	59°	64°	55½°
Time employed in making the water boil	m. 78	m. 61	m. 61	m. 62
Wood consumed in making the water boil	lbs. 12	lbs. 11	lbs. 9	lbs. 8
Time the water continued to boil	m. 17	m. 28	m. 6	h. m. 2 19
Quantity of fuel added to keep it boiling this time	—	—	—	lbs. 4
Kind of wood used as fuel	Beech.	Beech.	Pine.	Pine.
Precise Results of the Experiments.				
Ice-cold water heated 180°, or made to boil with the heat generated in the combustion of 1 lb. of the fuel	lbs. 12.89	lbs. 14.15	lbs. 16.89	lbs. 20
Boiling water kept boiling one hour, with the heat generated in the combustion of 1 lb. of the wood	—	—	—	lbs. 108.40

All the foregoing experiments were made on the same day (the 13th of October, 1794), and in the same order in which they are numbered.

The following are the results of the experiments made with the boiler No. 2:—

	Exp. No. 17.	Exp. No. 18.	Exp. No. 19.	Exp. No. 20.	Exp. No. 21.
Quantity of water in the boiler at the beginning of the experiment, in Bavarian pounds . .	lbs. 187	lbs. 187	lbs. 187	lbs. 187	lbs. 187
Temperature of the water in the boiler at the beginning of the experiment	61°	58°	60°	55°	212°
Time employed in making the water boil. . . .	m. 75	m. 55	m. 57	m. 60	—
Wood consumed in making the water boil . .	lbs. 11	lbs. 11	lbs. 9	lbs. 8	—
Time the water continued to boil	m. 21	m. 17	m. 8	h. m. 2 29	h. m. 1 10
Wood added to keep the water boiling . . .	lb. 1	—	—	lbs. 3½	lbs. 1½
Kind of wood used . .	Beech.	Beech.	Pine.	Pine.	Beech.
Precise Results.					
Ice-cold water heated 180°, or made to boil, with 1 lb. of wood . .	lbs. 13.92	lbs. 14.33	lbs. 17.59	lbs. 20.10	—
Boiling-hot water kept boiling one hour with 1 lb. of wood	—	—	—	lbs. 132.68	lbs. 145.44

This set of experiments was made at the same time with the foregoing set, namely, on the 13th October, 1794, and they were made in the order in which they are here registered. In the last but one (No. 20), the economy of fuel in the process of heating water was carried farther than in any other experiment I have ever made.

In the following experiments, which were made in a large copper boiler fitted up on my most improved principles, belonging to the kitchen of the House of Industry, the economy of fuel was carried nearly as far.

This boiler, which is circular, is 42¼ English inches in diameter above, 42.17 inches in diameter below, and 18.54 inches deep. It weighs 78¼ lbs. avoirdupois; and contains, when quite full, 714 lbs. *Bavarian weight* (= 884 lbs. avoirdupois, or 106 gallons) of water, at the temperature of 55°.

It is surrounded above by a wooden ring about 2 inches in thickness, into which it is fitted; and in this ring, in a groove about ½ of an inch deep, is fitted a circular wooden flat cover. This cover is formed in three pieces, united by iron hinges; and one of these pieces being fastened down by hooks to the boiler, the other two are so contrived as to be folded back upon it occasionally. From the upper surface of the part of the cover which is fastened down on the boiler, a tin tube 2 inches in diameter, furnished with a damper, is fixed, by which the steam is carried off into a narrow wooden tube, which conducts it through an opening in the roof of the house into the open air.

To prevent still more effectually the escape of the heat through the wooden cover of the boiler, the upper surface of it is protected from the cold atmosphere by a thick circular blanket covered on both sides by strong canvas, which is occasionally thrown over it.

Though the diameter of this boiler below is more than 40 inches, the diameter of its fire-place (which is just under its centre) is only 11 inches; but as the flame makes two complete turns under the bottom of the boiler in a spiral canal, and one turn round it, the time required to heat it is not so great as, from the smallness of its fire-place, might have been expected.

It has ever been, and still continues to be, the decided favorite of the cook-maids.

and the Economy of Fuel. 83

The wood used as fuel in the following experiment was pine moderately dried. The billets were 6 inches long, and from 1 to 2 inches in diameter.

The following table shows the results of five experiments that were made with this boiler by myself, just after it was fitted up:—

	Exp. No. 11.	Exp. No. 13.	Exp. No. 14.	Exp. No. 15.	Exp. No. 16.
Quantity of water in the boiler, in Bavarian pounds	lbs. 508	lbs. 127	lbs. 254	lbs. 508	lbs. 508
Temperature of the water at the beginning of the experiment	48°	48°	96°	48°	48°
Time required to make the water boil	h. m. 2 4	m. 51	h. m. 1 15	h. m. 2 35	h. m. 3 1
Fuel employed to make the water boil	lbs. 24¼	lbs. 8¼	lbs. 12¼	lbs. 25	lbs. 24
Time the water continued boiling	h. 3	—	—	h. 3	—
Fuel added to keep the water boiling	lbs. 6¼¼	—	—	lbs. 4½	—
Precise Results of the Experiments.					
With the heat generated in the combustion of 1 lb. of the fuel, Ice-cold water heated 180°, or made to boil	lbs. 18.87	lbs. 12.74	lbs. 12.69	lbs. 17.48	lbs. 19.01
Or boiling-hot water kept boiling one hour	236.61	—	—	338.66	—

Without stopping to make any observations on the results of these experiments (though they afford matter for several of an interesting nature), I shall proceed to give a brief account of another set of experiments, on a much larger scale, which were made in the copper boiler of a brewery belonging to the Elector.

This boiler, which is rectangular, is 10 feet long, 8 feet wide, and 4 feet deep, *Bavarian measure,** and contains 8176 *Bavarian maasse*, or measures, equal to 1866 gallons wine-measure. On examining this boiler, I found its fire-place was constructed on very bad principles; and on inquiring respecting the quantity of fire-wood consumed in it, I found the waste of fuel to be very great.

This brewery is used for making small *white* beer (as from its pale colour it is called) from malt made of wheat; and as it is worked all the year round, the expense of fuel was very great, and the economy of it an object of considerable importance.

The quantity of fire-wood (pine) that had at an average been consumed daily in this brewery was rather more than four Bavarian *klafters*, or cords. On altering the fire-place of this brewery, and putting a (wooden) cover to the boiler, I reduced this expense to less than 1¼ klafters.

In the new fire-place which I caused to be constructed for this boiler, the cavity under the boiler is divided into three flues, by thin brick walls which run in the direction of the length of the boiler. The middle flue, which is twice as wide as one of the side flues, is occupied by the burning fuel, and is furnished with a grate 20 inches wide, and 6 inches long; and the opening by which the fuel is introduced into the fire-place is closed by two iron doors, placed one behind the other, at the distance of 8 inches. The grate, which is placed at the hither end of the fire-place, is horizontal; and it is situated about 20 inches below the bottom of the boiler. The air which serves to feed

* 100 Bavarian inches are equal to 95⅛ inches English measure.

the fire is let in under the grate through a register in the ash-pit door.

When the double doors which close the entrance into the fire-place are shut, the flame of the burning fuel first rises perpendicularly against the bottom of the boiler; it then passes along to the farther end of the (middle) flue, which constitutes the fire-place, where it separates, and returns in the two side flues; it then rises up into two horizontal flues (one situated over the other) which go all round the boiler; and, having made the circuit of the boiler, it goes off into separate canals (furnished with dampers) into the chimney.

Though the Figures 17 and 18, Plate III., are not drawings from the fire-place I am now describing, but of another which I shall soon have occasion to describe, yet an inspection of these figures will be found useful in forming an idea of the principles on which the fire-place in question was constructed, and on that account I shall occasionally refer to them.

The burning fuel being confined within a narrow compass, being well supplied with fresh air, and being surrounded on all sides by thin walls of brick (which are non-conductors), the heat of the fire is most intense, and the combustion of the fuel of course very complete. The flame, which is clear and vivid in the highest degree, and perfectly unmixed with smoke, runs rapidly along the bottom of the boiler (which forms the top of the flues), and from the resistance it meets with in its passage, from friction, and from the number of turns it is obliged to make, it is thrown into innumerable eddies and whirlpools, and really affords a most entertaining spectacle.

That I might be able to enjoy at my ease this amus-

ing sight, I caused a glass window to be made in the
front wall of the fire-place, through which I could look
into the fire when the fire-place doors were shut; and
I was well paid for the trouble and the trifling expense
I had in getting it executed.

Some may be tempted to smile at what they may
think a childish invention; but there are many others,
I am confident, and among these many grave philosophers, who would have been very glad to have shared
my amusement.

The window of which I am speaking is circular, and
only 6 inches in diameter; but as the hole in the wall
is conical, and much larger within than without, the
field of this window (if I may use the expression) is sufficiently large to afford a good view of what passes in
the fire-place.

This conical hole is represented in the Figures 18
and 21 by dotted lines. It is situated on the left hand
of the entrance into the fire-place. Into the opening of
the hole in the wall, on the outside of it, is fixed a short
tube of copper (about 6 inches in diameter, and 4 inches
long); and in this tube another short *movable* tube is
fitted, one end of which is closed by the circular plate
of glass which constitutes the window. As the wall of
the fire-place in front is thick, this pane of glass is at
a considerable distance from the burning fuel, and, as
there is no draught through the hole in the wall, the
glass does not grow very hot.

I have been the more particular in my description of
this little invention, as I think it may be useful. There
are many cases in which it would be very advantageous
to know exactly what is going on in a closed fire-place,
and this never can be known by opening the door; for

the instant the door is opened, the cold air rushing with impetuosity into the fire-place deranges entirely the whole economy of the fire. Besides this, it is frequently very disadvantageous to the process which is going on to open the door of a fire-place, and it is always attended with a certain loss of heat, and consequently should as much as possible be avoided.

I intimated that the window I have been describing afforded me amusement: it did still more, — it afforded me much useful information, it gave me an opportunity of *observing* the various internal motions into which flame may, by proper management of the machinery of a fire-place, be thrown, and of estimating with some degree of precision their different effects. In short, it made me better acquainted with the subject which had so long engaged my atteption, — fire; and with regard to *that* subject, nothing surely that is new can be uninteresting. But to return to the brewery. To the top of the boiler was fitted a curb of oak timber. The four straight beams of which this curb was constructed are each about 7 inches thick, and 15 inches wide; and the upper part of the boiler is fastened by large copper nails to the inside of the square frame formed by these four beams. From the top of this curb is raised a wooden building, like the roof of a house with a double slant or bevel, which serves as a cover to the boiler. This building, the sides of which are about 3 feet high inwards, and the top of which is covered in by a very flat roof, slanting on every side from the centre, is constructed of a light frame-work of timber (four-inch deal joists), which is covered within as well as without with thin deal boards, which are rabbeted into each other at their edges, to render the cover which this little edifice forms for the boiler as tight as possible.

From the top of this cover an open wooden tube (*m*, Fig. 17), about 12 inches in diameter, rises up perpendicularly, and going through the roof of the brewhouse ends in the open air. This tube, which is furnished with a wooden damper, is intended to carry off the steam.

On the side of this cover next the mashing-tub, as also on that opposite to it, by which the wort runs off into the coolers, there are large folding wooden doors (*i* and *k*, Fig. 17), which are occasionally lifted up by means of ropes which pass over pulleys fastened to the ceiling of the brewhouse.

There are likewise two glass windows (see Fig. 17) in two opposite sides of the cover, through which, as soon as in consequence of the boiling of the liquid the steam becomes transparent and *invisible* (which happens in a very few minutes after the liquid has begun to boil), the contents of the boiler may be distinctly seen and examined.

Whenever there is occasion during the boiling to open either a door or a window of the cover, it is necessary to begin by opening the damper of the steam-chimney, otherwise the hot steam, rushing out with violence, would expose the by-standers to the danger of being scalded; but when the damper of the steam-chimney is open, no steam comes into the brewhouse, though a door or window of the cover be wide open.

Another similar precaution is sometimes necessary in opening the door of the fire-place, which it may be useful to mention. When the dampers in the canals by which the smoke goes off into the chimney are nearly closed (which must frequently be done to confine and economize the heat), if, without altering the damper, or the register in the ash-pit door, the fire-place door be suddenly opened, it will frequently happen that smoke, and sometimes flame, will rush out of the fire-place by this passage. This accident may be easily and effectually prevented, either by opening the damper, or by closing the register of the ash-pit door, the moment before the fire-place door is opened. This precaution should be attended to in all fire-places of all dimensions, constructed on the principles I have recommended.

To economize the time and the *patience* of my reader as far as it is possible, without suppressing any thing essential relating to the subject under consideration, I shall give him, in a very small compass, the general results of a set of experiments which cost me more labour (or at least more *time*) than it would cost him to read all the Essays I have ever written. I believe I am sometimes too prolix for the taste of the age; but it should be remembered that the subjects I have undertaken to investigate are by no means indifferent to me; that I conceive them to be intimately connected with the comforts and enjoyments of mankind; and that a habit of revolving them in my mind, and reflecting on their extensive usefulness, has awakened my enthusiasm, and rendered it quite impossible for me to treat them with cold indifference, however indifferent or tiresome they may appear to those who have not been accustomed to view them in the same light.

I have already given an account, in all its various details, of one experiment which was made (on the 15th of April, 1795) with the boiler we have just been describing (see page 66). I shall now recapitulate the general results of that experiment, and compare them with the mean results of two other like experiments made with the same boiler.

	Experiment No. 27.	Experiment No. 28.
Quantity of water in the boiler	12,508 lbs.	12,508 lbs.
Temperature of the water in the boiler at the beginning of the experiment	60°	58°
Time required to make the water boil	3 h. 40 m.	3 h. 48 m.
Fuel employed to make the water boil	800 lbs.	825 lbs.
Time the water continued boiling	2 h. 43 m.	—
Fuel added to keep the water boiling	100 lbs.	—
Kind of fuel used	Pine-wood.	Pine-wood.
Precise Results of the Experiments.		
Quantity of *ice-cold water* which might be heated 180°, or made to boil, with the heat generated in the combustion of 1 lb. of the fuel	12.06 lbs.	12.70 lbs.
Time in which, according to the result of the experiment, *ice-cold water* might (at Munich) *be made to boil* with the given proportion of fuel	4 h. 20 m.	4 h. 20 m.
Quantity of *boiling hot water kept boiling one hour* with the heat generated in the combustion of 1 lb. of the fuel	339.80 lbs.	—

On comparing the results of these experiments with those made in the boilers of the kitchens of the House of Industry and Military Academy, I was led to imagine that either the boiler or the fire-place of the brewery, or both, were capable of great improvement; for, in some of the experiments with these small kitchen boilers, the economy of fuel had been carried so far that, with the heat generated in the combustion of 1 lb. of pine-wood, it appeared that 20 lbs. of ice-cold water might have been made to boil; but here, though the machinery was on a scale so much larger (and I had concluded, too rashly indeed, as will be shown hereafter, that the larger the boiler, the greater is of course the economy of fuel),

the results of these experiments indicated that not quite
13 lbs. of ice-cold water could have been made to boil
with the heat furnished in the combustion of 1 lb. of the
wood.

The Experiments No. 22, No. 25, and No. 26, which
were made with the largest of my kitchen boilers, had,
it is true, afforded grounds to suspect that, beyond certain
limits, an increase of size in a boiler does not tend
to diminish the expense of fuel in the process of heating
water; yet, as all my other experiments had tended to
confirm me in the opinion I had at an early period imbibed
on that subject, I was disposed to suspect any
other cause than the true one of having been instrumental
in producing the unexpected appearances I
observed.

I was much disappointed, I confess, at finding that
the brewhouse boiler, notwithstanding all the pains I
had taken to fit up its fire-place in the most perfect
manner, and notwithstanding its enormous dimensions,
when compared with the boilers I had hitherto used in
my experiments, so far from answering my expectations,
actually required considerably more fuel in proportion
to its contents than another boiler fitted up on the
same principles, which was not *one fiftieth* part of its
size.

This unexpected result puzzled me, and I must own
that it vexed me, though I ought perhaps to be ashamed
of my weakness; but it did not discourage me. Finding,
on examining the boiler, that its bottom was very
thick, compared with the thickness of the sheet copper
of which my kitchen boilers were constructed, it occurred
to me that possibly *that* might be the cause, or
at least *one of the causes*, which had made the consump-

tion of fuel so much greater than I expected; and as there was another brewhouse in the neighbourhood belonging to the Elector, which, luckily for me, stood in need of a new boiler, I availed myself of that opportunity to make an experiment, which not only decided the point in question, but also established a new fact with regard to heat, which I conceive to be of considerable importance.

Having obtained the Elector's permission to arrange the second brewhouse as I should think best, I determined to spare no pains to render it as perfect as possible in all respects, and particularly in every thing relating to the economy of fuel. As in brewing, in the manner that business is carried on in Bavaria, where the whole process, in as far as fire is employed in it, is begun and finished in the course of a day, *the saving of time* in heating the water and boiling the wort is an object of almost as much importance as that of economizing fuel, and consequently demanded particular attention.

The means I used for the attainment of both these objects will be evident from the following description of the boiler and its fire-place, which I caused to be constructed, and which are represented in all their details in the Plates III., IV., and V.

This boiler is 12 (Bavarian) feet long, 10 feet wide, and only 2 feet deep. The sheet copper of which it is made is uncommonly thin for a boiler of such large dimensions, being at a medium less than *one tenth* of an English inch in thickness. This boiler, when finished, weighed no more than 674 lbs. Bavarian weight, equal to 8341 lbs. avoirdupois, exclusive of 64 lbs. of copper nails used in riveting the sheets of copper together.

The top of the boiler is surrounded by a strong curb (*a, b*, Fig. 17) of oak timber, to which it is attached by strong copper nails, and over the boiler is built a roof, or standing cover (see Fig. 17), similar in all respects to that already described. The bottom of the boiler is flat, and reposes horizontally on the top of the thin brick walls by which the fire-place is divided into flues. (See Fig. 18.) These flues do not run in the direction of the length of the boiler, but from one side of it to the other; consequently the door of the fire-place is in the middle of one side of the boiler.

The sheets of copper, of which the bottom of the boiler was constructed, run in the direction of the flues; and they are just so wide that their seams or joinings (where they are united to each other by their sides) repose on the walls of the flues, except only in the middle flue, which, being about twice as wide as the others, one seam was necessarily left unsupported, at least a considerable part of its length. The sheets of copper used in constructing this part of the bottom of the boiler are rather thicker and stronger than the rest: they are just 0.118 of an English inch in thickness.

The fire is made under this boiler in the middle flue, which, as I have just observed, is a little more than twice as wide as one of the other flues. There are five flues under the boiler, namely, one in the middle 44 inches wide, above in the clear (which constitutes the fireplace), and two on each side of it, in which the flame circulates; one 20 inches wide, and the other 19 inches wide.

The side flues are each 14½ inches deep; but as the walls which separate them are much thicker below than above, where the bottom of the boiler reposes on them, the width of these flues below is only 13 inches. The walls of these flues are shown by dotted lines in Fig. 17.

The walls which separate the flues do not run quite from one side of the boiler to the other; an opening being left at one end of each of them, equal to the width of one of the narrow flues, for the passage of the flame from one flue into another, without its going from under the boiler.

The fire being made (on a circular grate) in the middle flue (see Fig. 18), the flame passes on in this flue to its farther end; and then, dividing to the right and left, comes forward in the two adjoining side-flues. Having arrived at the wall which supports the front of the boiler, it turns again to the right and left, and, entering the two outside flues, returns in them to the back of the boiler. Here it went out (before the fire-place was altered) at two openings left for that purpose in the wall which supports the back part of the boiler, and the two currents of flame uniting entered a canal 7 inches wide and 16 inches high, which goes all round the outside of the boiler. (See Fig. 20.) Having made the circuit of the boiler, it went off by a canal (furnished with a damper) into the chimney.

From this description of the fire-place, it appears that the flame and smoke generated in the combustion of the fuel, in passing through those different flues, made a circuit of above 70 feet in contact with the surface of the boiler, before they were permitted to escape into the chimney. This, I thought, must be sufficient to give these hot fluids an opportunity of communicating to the boiler all the heat they could part with, notwithstanding the difficulties which attend their getting rid of it; and I concluded that the communication of their heat to the boiler would be much facilitated and expedited by the various eddies and whirlpools produced in the flame in consequence of the number of abrupt turns and changes of direction it was obliged to make in passing under and round the boiler.

As the experiments which have been made with this boiler were conducted throughout with the utmost care and attention, and as their results are both curious and important in several respects, I have thought them deserving of being made known to the public in all their details.

An Account of three Experiments made at Munick, the 10th October, 1796, with the new Boiler in the Brewery called Neuheusel, belonging to HIS MOST SERENE HIGHNESS *the* ELECTOR. — *The weather being fair; the barometer standing at 28 English inches, and Fahrenheit's thermometer at 76°.*

Dimensions of the boiler, in English measure, as found by actual admeasurement.
- Length . . . 11 feet 6.02 inches.
- Width . . . 9 " 7.723 "
- Depth . . . 2 " 0.205 "

Contents of the boiler, when quite full to the brim, 14,163 lbs. *Bavarian weight* of water, at the temperature of 55°, equal to 17,540 lbs. avoirdupois, or 2099 wine-gallons.

The boiler actually contained of water, in the beginning of each of the two following experiments, *in Bavarian weight*, 8120 lbs., equal to 10,056 lbs. avoirdupois, or nearly 1204 wine-gallons.

The wood used in this and the following experiments was *pine*, which had been moderately seasoned; and the billets were 3 feet 4¼ inches, English measure, in length.

FIRST EXPERIMENT WITH THE NEW BOILER.

Experiment No. 29.

Time.		Quantity of fire-wood put into the fire-place.		Temperature of the water in the boiler.
h.	m.	No. of billets.	Quantity in weight. lbs.	In degrees of Fahrenheit's therm.
11	31 A. M.	10	50	50°
	46	15	25	54
12	0	5	25	64
	10 P. M.	5	25	67
	36	—	—	85
	40	4	25	—
	53	5	25	96
1	13	7	25	105
	21	10	50	110
	46	10	50	129
	58	40	50	—
2	17	46	50	156
	29			164
	34	10	50	—
	41	—	—	173
	49	—	—	180
	58	40	50	185
3	15	12	50	197
	26	20	25	205
3	35	—	—	The water boiled.

Time employed, 4 h. 4 m.   Wood consumed, 575 lbs.

The boiling water being let off, and it being replaced immediately with cold water, the experiment was repeated as follows:—

Experiment No. 30.

Time.	Quantity of firewood put into the fire-place.		Temperature of the water in the boiler.
	No of baskets.	Quantity in weight. lbs.	In degrees of Fahrenheit's therm.
h. m.			
4 41 P.M.	40	50	60°
50	40	50	72
5 4	10	50	86
16	10	50	99½
29	10	50	114
42	10	50	126
56	40	50	142
6 10	40	50	157
24	40	50	—
28	—	—	172
40	40	50	—
42½	—	—	185½
53	40	50	—
55	—	—	198
7 2	—	—	205
7 7	—	—	The water boiled.

Time employed, 2 h. 26 m. Wood consumed, 550 lbs.

This boiling water being let off, the boiler was again filled (immediately) with cold water; and in this third experiment the quantity of water was increased to 11,368 lbs. *Bavarian weight*, equal to 14,078 lbs. avoirdupois, or 1685 wine-gallons.

The results of this experiment were as follows:—

Experiment No. 31.

Time.	Quantity of fire-wood put into the fire-place.		Temperature of the water in the boiler.
	No. of billets.	Quantity in weight. lbs.	In degrees of Fahrenheit's therm.
h. m.			
8 51 P. M.	80	100	65½°
9 7	40	50	79
21	40	50	90
44	40	50	107
57	40	50	118
10 14	40	50	130
28	40	50	140
45	40	50	155
11 —	40	50	165
15	40	50	175
30	40	50	182
45	40	50	200
11 58	—	—	The water boiled.

Time employed, 3 h. 7 m. Wood consumed, 650 lbs.

Experiments Nos. 29, 30, 31.

	No. 29.	No. 30.	No. 31.
Quantity of water in the boiler at the beginning of the experiment, in *Bavarian pounds* . .	8120 lbs.	8120 lbs.	11,368 lbs.
Temperature of the water at the beginning of the experiment .	50°	60°	65½°
Time employed in making the water boil	4 h. 4 m.	2 h. 26 m.	3 h. 7 m.
Fuel (pine-wood) consumed in making the water boil, in *Bavarian pounds*	575 lbs.	550 lbs.	650 lbs.
Precise Results of the Experiments.			
Quantity of ice-cold water which might have been heated 180°, or made to boil with the heat generated in the combustion of 1 lb. of the fuel	12.54 lbs.	12.28 lbs.	14.59 lbs.
Time in which, according to the result of the experiment, ice-cold water might be made to boil at Munich with the given proportion of fuel	4 h. 31 m.	2 h. 59 m.	3 h. 35 m.

The foregoing table shows the result of these three experiments in a clear and satisfactory manner.

I was surprised, when I compared the results of these experiments with those made in the other brewhouse, to find how little in appearance I had gained by the alterations I had introduced. On a more careful examination of the matter, however, I found that I had gained much more than I at first imagined, both in respect to the economy of fuel and to that of time. The amount of these advantages will appear from the following comparison of the mean result of these two sets of experiments:—

Precise Results of the foregoing Experiments.	Quantity of ice-cold water made to boil with 1 lb. of the fuel.	Time required to make ice-cold water boil, according to the quantity of fire given in experiment.
First Set.	lbs.	h. m.
In the Experiment No. 27	12.06	4 20
In the Experiment No. 28	12.70	4 20
Sum	24.77	8 40
Means	12.384	4 20
Second Set.		
In the Experiment No. 29	12.54	4 31
In the Experiment No. 30	12.28	2 59
Sum	24.82	7 30
Means	12.41	3 45

The mean results of these two sets of experiments differ very little from each other in appearance; and from this circumstance I shall prove that the new boiler is better adapted for saving fuel than the old.

By comparing the results of the experiments made with the same boiler, but with different quantities of water, we shall constantly find that the expense of fuel was *less* in proportion as the quantity of water was *greater*. In the Experiment No. 23, when 127 lbs. of water were used, the result of the experiment indicated that no more than 12.74 lbs. of ice-cold water could be made to boil with the heat generated in the combustion of 1 lb. of the fuel used; but in the Experiment No. 26, made with the same boiler, but when 4 times as much water was used, or 508 lbs., it appeared from the result of the experiment that 19.01 lbs. of ice-cold water might be made to boil with 1 lb. of the fuel.

Now, in the first set of the experiments we are comparing, as the quantity of water used (12,508 lbs.) was much greater than that used in the second set (8120 lbs.), it is evident that, if the construction of the machinery and the management of the fire had been equally perfect in the two cases, the economy of fuel would have been greatest where the largest quantity of water was used, — that is to say, in the first set of experiments; but, as that was not the case, it is certain that the boiler used in the second set is better adapted to economize fuel than that used in the first.

But we need not go so far to search for proofs of that fact. The result of the Experiment No. 31 is alone sufficient to put the matter beyond doubt. In this experiment, in which the quantity of water (though still considerably short of that used in the former set of experiments) was augmented from 8120 lbs. to 11,368 lbs., the saving of fuel was so much increased as to show in a decisive manner the superiority of the new boiler.

The Precise Results	Quantity of ice-cold water made to boil with 1 lb. of the fuel.	Time required to make ice-cold water boil, according to the result of the experiment.
	lbs.	h. m.
Of this Experiment (No. 31) were as follows	14.59	3 37
In the Experiments Nos. 27 and 28, they were, at a medium	12.385	4 20

The difference in the expense of fuel in these experiments with these two boilers is by no means inconsiderable: it amounts to above 14 per cent, and would have amounted to more, if more time had been allowed for heating the water in the experiment with the new boiler; for it is easy to show (what indeed was clearly indicated by all the experiments) that, in causing liquids to boil, the quantity of fuel will be less in proportion as the time employed in that process is long, or, which is the same, as the fire is smaller; and the saving of fuel arising from any given prolongation of the process will be the greater, as the fire-place is more perfect, and as the means used for confining the heat are more effectual.

Though the general results of these two sets of experiments afforded abundant reason to conclude that the alterations I had introduced in arranging the new boiler were real improvements, yet, when I compared the quantity of fuel consumed in the experiments with this new boiler with the much smaller quantities, in proportion to the quantity of water, which were employed in some of my former experiments with kitchen boilers, I was for some time quite at a loss to account for this difference. In all my experiments with boilers of different sizes, from the smallest saucepan up to the largest kitchen boilers, I had invariably found that the *larger* the quantity of water was which was heated, the *less*, in proportion, was the quantity of fuel necessary to be employed in that process; and so entirely had that prejudice taken possession of my mind, that when the strongest reasons for doubt presented themselves, they were overlooked; and it was not till I had searched in vain on every side to discover some other cause to which I could attribute the unexpected appearance that embarrassed me, that I was induced — I may say, forced — to abandon my former opinion, and to be convinced that what I had too hastily considered as a general law does not in fact obtain but within narrow limits; that although in heating *certain quantities* of liquids there is an advantage, in point of the economy of fuel, in performing the process on a larger scale, in preference to a smaller one, yet when the liquid to be heated amounts to a certain quantity this advantage ceases; and, if it exceeds that quantity, it is attended with an expense of fuel proportionally greater than when the quantity is less.

What the size of a boiler must be, in order that the saving of fuel may be a *maximum*, I do not pretend to have determined. I think, however, that there are some reasons for suspecting that it would not be larger than some of the kitchen boilers used in my experiments. But I recollect to have promised my reader that I would not give him my opinion without laying before him at the same time the grounds of those opinions. In the present case they are as follows: —

In an experiment of which I have already given an account (No. 3), 7 11/16 lbs. of water, at the temperature of 58°, were made to boil in a saucepan fitted up in my best manner, in a closed fire-place; and the wood consumed was 1 lb. This gives, for the *precise result* of the experiment, 6.68 lbs. of ice-cold water made to boil with 1 lb. of the fuel.

In another experiment (No. 12) made with one of the small boilers belonging to the kitchen of the Military Academy, fitted up on the same principles, 43.63 lbs. of water, at the temperature of 60°, were made to boil with 3 lbs of wood. This gives 11.93 lbs. of ice-cold water made to boil with 1 lb. of the fuel.

Again, in the Experiment No. 20, which was made with a larger boiler belonging to the same kitchen, and fitted up in the same manner, 187 lbs. of water (equal to about 28 gallons), at the temperature of 55°, were made to boil with the combustion of 8 lbs. of fire-wood. This gives 20.10 lbs. of ice-cold water made to boil with 1 lb. of the wood; and farther than this I have not been able to push the economy of fuel.

In the Experiment No. 26, a boiler was used which had been constructed with the express view to see how far it was possible to carry the economy of fuel in culinary processes; and it was fitted up with the utmost care, and on the most approved principles. As I thought at that time that a large-sized boiler was essential to the economizing of fuel, this boiler was made to contain 106 gallons. In the experiment in question it actually contained 508 Bavarian pounds of water (or about 63 gallons), at the temperature of 48°; and, to make this water boil, 24 lbs. of wood were consumed. This gives 19.01 lbs. of ice-cold water made to boil with 1 lb. of fuel. Hence it appears that the expense of fuel was greater in this experiment than in that last-mentioned.

Again, in the Experiment No. 31, when no less than 11,368 lbs. or 1685 gallons of water were heated and made to boil in the new brewhouse boiler, the wood consumed amounted to 650 lbs., which (as the temperature of the water at the beginning of the experiment was $65\frac{1}{2}°$) gives for the *precise result* of the experiment 14.59 lbs. of ice-cold water made to boil with the heat generated in the combustion of 1 lb. of the fuel.

As the relative quantities of fuel expended in the experiments are inversely as the numbers expressing the quantities of ice-cold water, which, from the result of each experiment, it appears might have been heated 180°, or made to boil, under the mean pressure of the atmosphere at the level of the sea, with the heat generated in the combustion of 1 lb. of the fuel, it is evident that these numbers measure very accurately the different degrees to which the economy of fuel was carried in the different experiments. The economy of fuel in heating liquids, *depending on the quantity of the liquid*, as shown by the foregoing experiments, may therefore be expressed shortly in the following manner:—

	Quantity of water heated in the experiment, in Navy gallons lbs.	Degrees to which the economy of the fuel was carried.
	lbs.	lbs.
In the Experiment No. 3	7.93	6.68
No. 12	43.63	11.93
No. 16	187	20.10
No. 26	508	19.01
No. 31	11,368	14.59

Before I take my leave of this subject I would just remark that the cause of the appearances observed in the experiments may, I think, be traced to that property of flame from which it has been denominated a non-conductor of heat; for, if the different particles of flame give off their heat only to bodies with which they actually come into contact, the quantity of heat given off by it will be *not as its volume* (and consequently not as the quantity of fuel consumed), but rather *as its surface*. And as the surface of the flame, when fire-places are similar, is proportionally greater in small than in large fire-places, — the surfaces of similar bodies being as the *squares* of their corresponding sides, while their volumes are as the *cubes* of those sides, — it is evident that, on that account, less heat in proportion to the quantity generated in the combustion of the fuel, ought to be communicated to the boiler, when the fire-place and boiler are large, than when the process is carried on upon a smaller scale.

There are, however, several other circumstances to be taken into the account in determining the effects *of size* in the machinery necessary for boiling liquids; and one of them, which has great influence, is the heat absorbed by the masonry of the fire-place. This loss will most undoubtedly be the smaller, as the fire-place is larger; but to determine the exact point when, the saving on the one hand being just counterbalanced by the loss on the other, any augmentation or diminution of size in the machinery would be attended with a positive loss of heat is not easy to be ascertained. Provided however that proper attention be paid to the management of the fire, and that as much heat as possible be generated in the combustion of the fuel (which may always be done in the largest fire-place as well, if not better, than in smaller ones), as that part of the heat which goes off in the smoke is indubitably lost, a thermometer placed in the chimney would indicate, with a considerable degree of precision, the perfections or imperfections of the fire-place.

It is well known that the smoke which rises from the chimneys of the closed fire-places of very large boilers is much hotter than that which escapes from smaller fire-places; and I am surprised that this fact, which has long been known to me, should not have led me to suspect that the waste of fuel was proportionally greater in these large fire-places than in smaller ones.

Besides the experiments of which I have given an account, several others were made with the new brewhouse boiler; and, among others, four experiments were made on four succeeding days in brewing beer; and it was found that considerably less fuel was expended in these trials than was necessary in brewing the same quantity of beer in the other brewhouse, in which I first introduced my improvements. But though the alteration of form, diminution of the thickness of the metal, etc., which I had introduced in constructing the new boiler and also in the manner of fitting it up, had produced a considerable saving of fuel, yet it was not accompanied by a proportional saving of time. I had flattered myself that by making the boiler *very thin* and *very shallow*, I should bring its contents to boil in *a very short time;* but I did not consider how much time is necessary for the combustion of the fuel necessary for heating so large a quantity of water, otherwise my expectations on this head would have been less sanguine. The quantity of heat generated in any given time being as the quantity of fuel consumed, it must depend in a great measure on the size of the fire-place; and when it is required to heat a large quantity of water, or of any liquid, in a very short time, either the fire-place must be large, or (what in my opinion would be still better) a number of separate fire-places — two or three, for instance — must be made under the same boiler. The boiler should be made wide and shallow, in order to admit of a great number of flues, in which the flame and smoke of the different fires should be made to circulate separately *under its bottom.*

The combustion of the fuel, and consequently the generation and communication of the heat, may in the same fire-place be considerably accelerated by increasing the draught (as it is called) of the fire; which may be done by increasing the height of the chimney, or by enlarging the canal leading to the chimney, and keeping the damper open, when that passage is too small, or by shortening the length of the flues.

The master brewer having expressed a wish that some contrivance might be used by which the water might be made to boil a little sooner in the new boiler, I made an alteration in its fire-place which completely answered that purpose.

But, besides the desire I had to oblige the master brewer (who only thought how he could contrive to finish as early as possible his day's work), I had another and much more important object in view. Having had reason to suspect that flues which go round on the outside of large boilers do little more than prevent the escape of the heat by their sides, — which, with infinitely less trouble and less expense, may be prevented by other means, — I was desirous of finding out, by a decisive experiment, the real amount of the advantages gained by those flues, or the saving of fuel which they produce. And as I was confident that the suppression of the flue which went round the new boiler would increase the draught of the fire-place, and accelerate the combustion of the fuel, I concluded that, if my opinion was well founded with respect to the smallness of the advantages derived from these *side flues*, the increase of heat arising from the acceleration of the combustion occasioned by the increased draught on closing them up would more than counterbalance the loss of those advantages, and the time employed in heating the water would be found to be actually less than it was before.

The results of the following experiments show how far my suspicions were founded:—

Experiment No. 32.— The flue round the outside of the new brewhouse boiler having been closed up, and two canals (*a* and *b*, Fig. 21) formed from the end of the two outside flues of those situated *under* the boiler, by which two canals (which were both furnished with dampers) the smoke passed off from under the boiler directly into the chimney, the Experiment No. 31, which was made with the same boiler before the outside flues were closed up, was now repeated with the utmost care, in order to ascertain the effects which the closing up of those flues would produce. The quantity of water in the boiler, and its temperature at the beginning of the experiment, were the same; the wood used as fuel was taken from the same parcel, and it was put into the fire-place in the *same quantities*, and at the *same intervals of time*. In short, every circumstance was the same in the two experiments, excepting only the alterations which had been made in the fire-place. As the length of the flues through which the flame and smoke were obliged to pass to get into the chimney had been diminished more than half (or reduced from 70 to about 30 feet), the strength of the draught of the fire-place was much increased, as was evident not only from the increased violence of the combustion of the fuel, which was very apparent, but also from another circumstance, which I think it my duty to mention. Before the flue round the boiler was closed, if too much fuel was put into the fire-place at once, it not only did not burn with a clear flame, but frequently the smoke, and sometimes the flame, came out of the fire-place door, even when the damper in the chimney was wide open; but, after this flue was closed up, it was found to be hardly possible to overcharge the fire-place, and the fuel always burned with the utmost vivacity.

I ought to inform my reader that, though the entrance into the flue which went round the outside of the boiler was closed, and another and a shorter road opened for the flame and smoke to pass off into the chimney, yet the *cavity* of the flue remained; and, by means of openings (c, c, c, c, c, c, Fig. 21, Plate V.) about 6 inches square in the brick-work which separated this old road (which was now shut up) from the flues *under the boiler*, the flame was permitted to pass into this cavity, and to spread itself round the outside of the boiler. This contrivance (which I would recommend for all boilers) not only prevents the escape of the heat out of the boiler by its sides, but contributes something towards heating it; and, as the openings in the sides of the flues do not sensibly impede the motion of the flame, they can do no harm.

As the two experiments, the results of which I am about

to compare, were made with the greatest care, and as they are on several accounts uncommonly interesting, I shall place them in a conspicuous point of view.

A COMPARATIVE VIEW OF TWO EXPERIMENTS MADE WITH A NEW BREWHOUSE BOILER.

The time is reckoned from the beginning of the Experiment, and was the same in both Experiments.

Quantity of water in the boiler 11,368 lbs. Bavarian weight.

Time from the beginning of the experiment.		Fuel put into the fire-place.		Heat of the water in the boiler.	
h.	m.	Number of billets.	Quantity in weight.	Experiment No. 1. (outside flue open).	Experiment No. 2. (outside flue closed).
		No. 80	lbs. 100	Degrees 63½	Degrees 63½
0	16	40	50	79	82
0	30	40	50	90	94
0	53	40	50	107	110
1	6	40	50	118	122
1	53	40	50	130	135
1	37	40	50	140	147
1	54	40	50	155	160
2	9	40	50	165	171
2	24	40	50	175	182
2	39	40	50	183	191
2	54	40	50	200	—
2	59	—	—	—	Boiled.
3	7	—	—	Boiled.	—

Having found, by comparing the results of these two experiments, that I had lost nothing in respect to the economy of fuel by shutting up the outside flue of my boiler, I was now desirous of ascertaining how much I had gained in point of time, or how much the increased draught of the fire-place, in consequence of its flues being shortened, enabled me to abridge the time employed in causing the contents of the boiler to boil, in cases in which it should be advantageous to expedite that process at the expense of a small additional quantity of fuel.

By the following experiment, in which the combustion of the fuel was made as rapid as possible by keeping the fire-place full of wood, and the register in the ash-pit door and the damper in the chimney constantly quite open, may be seen how far I succeeded in the attainment of that object.

Experiment No. 33.—The boiler contained 11,368 lbs. Bavarian weight of water, at the temperature of 47°. The fuel used was pine-wood moderately seasoned, in billets 3 feet 4 inches long, and split into small pieces of about 1 lb. each, that it might burn the more rapidly.

This experiment was made the 29th of November, 1796, the barometer standing at 26 inches 8.7 lines, Paris measure, and Fahrenheit's thermometer at 33°.

Time.		Fuel put into the fire-place.	Temperature of the water in the copper.
h.	m.	lbs.	Degrees.
2	0	100	47
	14	100	58
	34	100	88
	51	100	100
3	9	100	123
	25	100	144
	39	100	151
4	0	100	—
	10	—	200
	17	—	Boiled.
Time employed, 2 17		Wood consumed, 800	

In the Experiment No. 32, the same quantity of water, at the temperature of 65½°, was made to boil in

2 hours 59 minutes, with the consumption of 625 lbs. of the same kind of wood. Had the water in this experiment been as cold as it was in the Experiment No. 33 (namely, at the temperature of 47°), instead of 625 lbs., 705 lbs. of the fuel would have been necessary; and the process, instead of lasting 2 hours and 59 minutes, would have lasted 3 hours and 22 minutes.

Hence we may conclude that to abridge 1 hour and 5 minutes of 3 hours and 22 minutes in the process of boiling 11,368 lbs. of water, this cannot be done at a less additional expense of fuel than that of 95 lbs. of pine-wood; or, to abridge the time *one third*, there must be an additional expense of about *one eighth* more fuel.

In some cases it will be most profitable to save time, in others to economize fuel; and it will always be desirable to be able to do either, as circumstances may render most expedient.

From a comparison of the quantities of fuel consumed, and consequently of heat generated, in the same time, with the quantities of heat actually communicated to the water in the Experiments Nos. 32 and 33 during this time, an idea may be formed of the great quantity of heat that may remain in flame and smoke after they have passed many feet in flues under the thin bottom of a boiler containing cold water; and this shows with how much difficulty these hot vapours part with their heat, and how important it is to be acquainted with that fact in order to take measures with certainty for economizing fuel.

I have been the more particular in my account of these experiments with large boilers, as I believe no experiments of the kind on so large a scale have been yet made; and, as they were all conducted with care, their results have intrinsic value independent of the particular uses to which I have applied them.

As, in the countries where this Essay is likely to be most read, pit-coals are more frequently used as fuel than wood, it will not only be satisfactory, but in many cases may be really useful, to my reader to know the relative quantities of heat producible from coals and from wood, in order to be able to compare the results of experiments in which coals are used as fuel, with those of which I have here given an account; or to determine the quantity of coals necessary in any process which it is known may be performed with a given quantity of wood.

It was my intention to have made a set of experiments on purpose to determine the relative quantities of heat producible from all the various kinds of combustible bodies which are used as fuel; and I made preparations for beginning them, but I have not yet been able to find leisure to attend to the subject.

The most satisfactory account I have been able to procure respecting the matter in question is one for which I am indebted to my friend Mr. Kirwan. By this account, which he tells me is founded on experiments made by M. Lavoisier, it appears that equal quantities of water, under equal surfaces, may be evaporated, and consequently equal heats produced —

In weight.	In measure,
By 403 lbs. of cokes,	By 17 of cokes,
600 „ of pit-coal,	10 of pit-coal,
600 „ of charcoal,	40 of charcoal,
1089 „ of oak;	33 of oak.

I wish I were at liberty to transcribe the ingenious and interesting observations which accompanied this estimate; but, as they make part of a work which I understand is preparing for the press, I dare not anticipate what Mr. Kirwan will himself soon lay before the public.

According to this estimate it appears that 1089 lbs. of oak produce as much heat in their combustion as 600 lbs. of pit-coal. Now, if we suppose that the pine-wood used in my experiments is capable of producing as much heat *per pound* as oak, — and I have reason to think it does not afford less, — from the quantity of pine-wood used in any of my experiments, it is easy to ascertain how much coal would have been necessary to generate the same quantity of heat; for the weight of the coal which would be required is to the weight of the wood actually consumed, as 600 to 1089.

In one of my experiments (No. 31), 11,368 lbs. of water, at the temperature of $65\frac{1}{2}°$, were made to boil with 650 lbs. of pine-wood. As when the experiment was made the mercury in the barometer stood at about 28 English inches, the temperature of the water when it boiled was only $209\frac{1}{2}°$, consequently its temperature was raised ($209\frac{1}{2} - 65\frac{1}{2}$) 144 degrees. Had the water been boiled in London, or in any other place nearly on a level with the surface of the sea, it must have been heated to 212° to have been made to boil, consequently its temperature must have been raised $146\frac{1}{2}°$; and to have done this, instead of 650 lbs. of wood, $661\frac{1}{2}$ lbs. would have been required (140° is to 650 lbs. as $146\frac{1}{2}°$ to $661\frac{1}{2}$ lbs.).

If pit-coal were used instead of wood, $363\frac{1}{4}$ lbs. of that kind of fuel would have been sufficient; for the quantities in weight of different kinds of fuel required to perform the same process being inversely as the quantities of heat which equal weights of the given kinds of fuel are capable of generating, or directly as the quantities of the kind of fuel in question, which are required to produce the same heat, it is 1089 to 600, as 661½ lbs. of wood to 363¾ lbs. of coal, supposing the foregoing estimate to be exact.

Whether it would be possible to cause so large a quantity of water (1681 wine-gallons), at the given temperature (65½°), to boil, with this small quantity of coal, I leave to those who are conversant in experiments of this kind to determine.

From the result of my 20th Experiment it appeared that $20\frac{1}{5}$ lbs. of ice-cold water might be heated 180 degrees, or made to boil under the mean pressure of the atmosphere at the level of the surface of the ocean, with the heat generated in the combustion of 1 lb. of pine-wood. Computing from the result of this experiment, and from the relative quantities of heat producible from pine-wood and from pit-coal, it appears that the heat generated in the combustion of 1 lb. of pit-coal would make $36\frac{1}{5}$ lbs. of ice-cold water boil.

Hence it appears that pit-coal should heat 36 times its weight of water, from the freezing point to that of boiling; and, as it has been found by experiments made with great care by Mr. Watt that nearly 5¼ times as much heat as is sufficient to heat any given quantity of ice-cold water to the boiling-point is required to reduce that same quantity of water, *already boiling-hot*, to steam, — according to this estimation, the heat generated in the combustion of 1 lb. of coal should be sufficient to reduce very nearly 7 lbs. of boiling-hot water to steam.

How far these estimates agree with the experiments that have been made with steam-engines, I know not;

but there seems to be much reason to suspect that the expense of fuel, in working those engines, is considerably greater than it ought to be, or than it would be, were the boilers and fire-places constructed on the best principles, and the fire properly managed.

In attempts to improve, it is always very desirable to know exactly what progress has been made,—to be able to measure the distance we have laid behind us in our advances, and also that which still remains between us and the object in view. The ground which has been gone over is easily measured; but to estimate that which still lies before us is frequently much more difficult.

The advances I have made in my attempts to improve fire-places, for the purpose of economizing fuel, may be estimated by the results of the experiments of which I have given an account in this Essay; but it would be satisfactory, no doubt, to know how much farther it is possible to push the economy of fuel.

In my 4th Experiment, $7\frac{18}{16}$ lbs. of water, at the temperature of 58°, were made to boil, at Munich, with 6 lbs. of wood. If, from the result of this experiment, we compute the quantity of ice-cold water which, with the heat generated in the combustion of 1 lb. of the fuel, might be heated 180°, or made to boil, it will turn out to be only $1\frac{1}{4}$ lb., or more exactly 1.11 lb.

According to the result of the Experiment No. 20, it appeared that no less than $20\frac{1}{8}$ lbs. of ice-cold water might have been made to boil with the heat generated in the combustion of 1 lb. of pine-wood.

It appears, therefore, that about *eighteen times* as much fuel, in proportion to the quantity of water heated, was expended in the Experiment No. 4, as in the No. 20; and hence we may conclude with the utmost certainty, that of the heat generated, or which with proper management might have been generated, in the combustion of the fuel used in the 4th Experiment, less than $\frac{1}{8}$ part was employed in heating the water, — the remainder, amounting to more than $\frac{7}{8}$ of the whole quantity, being dispersed and lost.

I ventured to give it as my opinion, in the beginning of this Essay, that " not less than *seven eighths* of the heat generated, or which with proper management might be generated, from the fuel actually consumed, is carried up into the atmosphere with the smoke, and totally lost." I will leave it to my reader to judge whether this opinion was not founded on good and sufficient grounds.

But though it be proved beyond the possibility of a doubt that the process of heating water was performed in the 20th Experiment with about $\frac{1}{8}$ part of the proportion of fuel which was actually expended in the 4th Experiment, yet neither of these experiments, nor any deductions that can be founded on their results, can give us any light with respect to the *real* loss of heat, or how much less fuel would be sufficient were there no loss whatever of heat. The experiments show that the loss of heat must have been at least *eighteen times* greater in one case than in the other; but they do not afford grounds to form even a probable conjecture respecting the amount of the loss of heat in the experiment in which the economy of fuel was carried the farthest, or the possibility of any farther improvements in the construction of fire-places. I shall, however, by availing myself of the labours of others, and comparing the results of their experiments with mine, endeavour to throw some light on this abstruse subject.

Dr. Crawford found, by an experiment contrived with much ingenuity, and which appears to have been executed with the utmost care, that the heat generated in the combustion of 30 grains of charcoal raised the temperature of 31 lbs. 7 oz. Troy (= 181,920 grains of water) 1$\frac{81}{100}$ degrees of Fahrenheit's thermometer, *when none of the heat generated was suffered to escape.*

But if 30 grains of charcoal are necessary to raise the temperature of 181,920 grains of water 1$\frac{81}{100}$ degrees, it would require 3157.9 grains of charcoal to raise the temperature of the same quantity of water 180 degrees, or from the point of freezing to that of boiling; for it is 1.71° to 30 grains, as 180° to 3157.9 grains. Consequently the heat generated in the combustion of 1 lb. of charcoal would be sufficient to heat 57.608 lbs. of ice-cold water 180°, or to make it boil; for 3157.9 grains of charcoal are to 181,920 grains of water as 1 lb. of charcoal to 57.608 lbs. of water.

From the results of M. Lavoisier's experiments, it appeared that the quantities of heat generated in the combustion of equal weights of charcoal and dry oak are as 1089 to 600. Hence we may conclude that equal quantities of heat are generated by 1 lb. of charcoal and 1.815 lbs. of oak; consequently that the heat generated in the combustion of 1.815 lbs. of oak would heat 57.608 lbs. of ice-cold water, — or 1 lb. of oak, 31.74 lbs of ice-cold water 180°, or cause it to boil, — *were no part of the heat generated in the combustion of the fuel lost.*

If now we suppose the quantities of heat producible from equal weights of dry oak and of dry pine-wood to be equal, — and there is reason to believe that this supposition cannot be far from the truth, — we can estimate the real loss of heat in each of the two experiments before mentioned (No. 4 and No. 20), as also in every other case in which the quantity of fuel consumed, and the effects produced by the heat, are known.

Thus, for instance, in the 20th Experiment, as the effects actually indicated that, with *that part* of the heat generated in the combustion of 1 lb. of the fuel which *entered the boiler*, $20\frac{1}{5}$ lbs. of ice-cold water might have been made to boil; as by the above estimate it appears that $31\frac{74}{100}$ lbs. of ice-cold water might be made to boil with *all* the heat generated in the combustion of 1 lb. of the fuel, it is evident that about *one third* of the heat generated was lost, or $\frac{20.1}{31.74}$ of it was saved.

This loss is certainly not greater than might reasonably have been expected, especially when we consider all the various causes which conspire in producing it; and I doubt whether the economy of fuel will ever be carried much farther.

In the Experiment No. 4, as the effects produced by the heat which entered the boiler indicated that no more than 1.14 lb. of ice-cold water could have been made to boil with 1 lb. of the fuel, it appears that in this experiment only about $\frac{1}{26}$th part of the heat generated was saved.

In all the experiments made on a very large scale, with brewhouse boilers, rather more than *one half* of the heat generated found its way up the chimney, and was lost.

CHAPTER VI.

A short Account of a Number of Kitchens, public and private, and Fire-places for various Uses, which have been constructed under the Direction of the Author, in different Places. — Of the Kitchen of the HOUSE *of* INDUSTRY *at* MUNICH; *of that of the* MILITARY ACADEMY; *of that of the* MILITARY MESS-HOUSE; *that of the* FARM-HOUSE, *and those belonging to the* INN *in the* ENGLISH GARDEN *at* MUNICH. — *Of the Kitchens of the Hospitals of* LA PIETÀ *and* LA MISERICORDIA *at* VERONA. — *Of a small Kitchen fitted up as a Model in the House of* SIR JOHN SINCLAIR, *Bart., in* LONDON. — *Of the Kitchen of the* FOUNDLING HOSPITAL *in* LONDON. — *Of a* MILITARY KITCHEN *for the Use of* TROOPS *in* CAMP. — *Of a* PORTABLE BOILER *for the Use of* TROOPS *on a* MARCH. — *Of a large* BOILER *fitted up as a Model for* BLEACHERS *at the* LINEN HALL *in* DUBLIN. — *Of a Fire-place for* COOKING, *and at the same Time* WARMING A LARGE HALL; *and of a* PERPETUAL OVEN, *both fitted up in the* HOUSE *of* INDUSTRY *at* DUBLIN. — *Of the* KITCHEN, LAUNDRY, CHIMNEY FIRE-PLACES, COTTAGE FIRE-PLACES, *and Model of a* LIME-KILN, *fitted up in* IRELAND *in the House of the* DUBLIN SOCIETY.

MY wish to give the most complete information possible with regard to the *grounds* on which the improvements I propose are founded has induced me to be very particular in my account of my experiments, and of the conclusions and practical inferences

I have thought myself authorized to draw from them; and as these investigations have frequently led me into abstruse philosophical disquisitions, which might not perhaps be very interesting to many of my readers, to whom a simple account of my fire-places, with directions for constructing them, might be really useful; in order to accommodate readers of all descriptions, I have thought it best to divide my subject, and to reserve what I have still to say on the mechanical part of it — the construction of kitchen fire-places — for a separate Essay. In the mean time, for the information of those who may have opportunities of examining any of the kitchens or fire-places, for other purposes, which have already been constructed on my principles, under my direction, I have annexed the following account of them, and of the particular merits and imperfections of each of them. This account, added to what has been said in the foregoing chapters of this Essay on the construction of fire-places, will, I flatter myself, be found sufficient to convey the fullest information respecting the subject under consideration, and enable those who may wish to adopt the proposed improvements to construct fire-places of all kinds on the principles recommended, without any farther assistance.

Those who may not have leisure to enter into these scientific investigations, and who, notwithstanding, may wish to imitate these inventions, will find all the information they can want in my next Essay.

An Account of the Kitchen of the House of Industry at Munich, in its present State.

The large circular copper boiler (which is situated in a small room adjoining to the great kitchen) is fitted up in a very complete manner; its (wooden) cover is cheap, simple, and durable, and answers perfectly well for confining the heat; the steam tube (or steam chimney as I have called it) is very useful, as it carries off all the steam generated in cooking, and keeps the air of the kitchen dry and wholesome. To carry off the steam which rises from the hot soup when it is served up, there is a steam-chimney of wood (furnished with a valve), the opening of which is situated at the highest part of the kitchen. To prevent the cold air from coming down by this passage into the kitchen, its damper (which is opened and shut by a cord which goes over a pulley) is, in winter, kept constantly shut, except just when it is necessary to open it for a moment to let out the steam.

The only alteration I would make, were I to fit up this boiler again, would be to leave openings by which the flues might be cleaned occasionally, without lifting the boiler out of its place. This should be done in the fire-places of all large boilers. This boiler, which is used every day, requires to have its flues cleaned, and its bottom and sides scrubbed with a broom, to free them of soot, once in six weeks.

Over against this boiler is a machine for drying potatoes, which has been found to answer perfectly well the end for which it was contrived. Potatoes first moderately boiled, and then skinned and cut into thin slices, and dried in this machine, may be kept good for many years.

The eight iron boilers in the *great kitchen* are fitted up on good principles; and the oven, which is heated by the smoke from the fire-places of two of these boilers, which oven is destined for drying the wood for the use of this kitchen, is deserving of attention.

The wooden covers of these eight boilers, and the horizontal tubes, constructed of wood wound round with canvas and painted with oil colours, by which the steam is carried off, have been found to answer very well the purposes for which they were contrived.

The Kitchen of the Military Academy at Munich.

This kitchen in its present state is so perfect in all its parts, that I do not think it capable of any considerable improvement. The *roaster*, which has been in daily use *seven years*, is still in good condition, and bids fair to last *twenty years* longer. It is large and roomy, and has been found to be extremely useful. Though the different parts of this kitchen are not distributed with so much symmetry as could have been wished, owing to local circumstances, yet it is very complete in its various details, and all the various processes of cookery are performed in it with little labour, and with a very small expense indeed of fuel. Two large boilers and three large saucepans, which are fitted up in a detached mass of brick-work in a corner of the room (on the right hand on going into it), I can recommend as perfect models for imitation. In short, I know of nothing which I could wish to alter in this kitchen. To say the truth, it has already undergone a sufficient number of changes and alterations.

The Kitchen in the Military Hall or Officers' Mess-House in the English Garden at Munich.

This kitchen is much less perfect in its details than that just mentioned. It was built in the spring of the year 1790, and has since undergone only a few trifling alterations. It has three roasters, which are made small on purpose to serve as models for private families; and I have had the pleasure to know that they have often been imitated.

The Kitchen in the Farm-House in the English Garden.

This kitchen is well contrived for the use for which it was designed, and I can recommend it as a very good model for the kitchens of farm-houses, for families consisting of eighteen or twenty persons. One of the boilers, which is destined for warming water for the use of the kitchen and the stables, is in winter heated by the smoke of a German stove, which is situated in an adjoining room, — that inhabited by the overseer of the farm.

The great Kitchen of the Inn in the Garden.

This kitchen, which is adjoining to the farm-house, is contrived almost for the sole purpose of roasting chickens before an open fire, a kind of food of which the Bavarians are extravagantly fond. It has three open fire-places, constructed on the principles recommended in my Essay on Chimney Fire-places, fronting different sides of the kitchen, and all opening into the same chimney, which chimney is built nearly in the middle of the room. This kitchen was built before my roasters were come into use.

The small Kitchen belonging to the Inn.

This kitchen has nothing belonging to it which deserves attention, or which I would recommend for imitation. It was originally designed merely for making coffee, chocolate, etc.

A kitchen which has lately been fitted up on my principles, in the new hospital for the infirm and helpless poor, which is situated on the height called the *Gasteig*, on the side of the river opposite to the town of Munich, is much more interesting, and is a good model for imitation.

The Kitchen of the Hospital of La Pietà at Verona

Is peculiarly interesting, on account of its convenient form and the perfect symmetry of its parts.

The mass of brick-work in which the boilers are fixed occupies the middle of one side of a large high room, which is plastered and white-washed, and neatly paved. The covers of the large boilers are lifted up by ropes which go over pulleys fixed to the ceiling of the top of the room; but were I to build the kitchen again, I should substitute wooden covers with steam-chimneys instead of them, such in all respects as that belonging to the large round copper boiler in the kitchen of the House of Industry at Munich. When the covers are so large that they cannot conveniently be lifted on and off with the hand, they should, in my opinion, always be made of wood, and divided into parts, united by hinges. When they are designed for confining the steam *entirely*, they should be made on a peculiar construction, which will hereafter be described. The covers for small boilers, and those for saucepans, should always be of tin, and double.

The grates on which the fires are made under the boilers in the kitchen of the Hospital of *La Pietà* are circular; but they are not hollow, or dishing, as that improvement did not occur to me till after that kitchen was finished. The spiral flues under the boilers are also wanting, and for the same reason. In all other respects this kitchen is, I believe, quite perfect.

The Kitchen of the Hospital of La Misericordia at Verona

Is constructed on the same principles as that of *La Pietà*. The only difference between them is in the distribution of the boilers. That of *La Misericordia* is built round two sides of the room. In many cases, this manner of disposing of the boilers will be found more convenient than any other; but in all cases where this method of placing them is preferred, care must be taken to place the largest boilers farthest from the chimney, and the smaller ones nearer to it, and in regular succession as their sizes diminish. This is necessary, in order that in the mass of brick-work in which the boilers are fixed there may be room behind the smaller boilers for the canals which carry off the smoke from the large ones into the chimney.

This circumstance was attended to in constructing the small kitchen which I fitted up last spring in the house of Sir John Sinclair, Bart., President of the Board of Agriculture, Whitehall, London. This kitchen (which was intended to serve as a model, and is open to the public view at all hours) is by no means as perfect as I wished it to be. Having been built during my journey to Ireland, several mistakes were made by the workmen I employed, who, though they have great merit in their different lines of business, had not *then* had sufficient experience in constructing kitchens on my principles, to be able to execute such a job in my absence without committing some faults. Those which were most essential I corrected; but my stay in England, after my return from Ireland, was too short, and my time too much taken up with other matters, to rebuild the kitchen from the foundation, which I was very desirous of doing, and which, with the permission of the proprietor, I shall certainly do when I come to England again. The greatest fault of the kitchen is the want of dampers to the canals by which the smoke is carried off from the closed fire-places of the boilers and saucepans into the chimney. These dampers should never be omitted in any fire-place, however small. They are necessary even in fire-places for the smallest saucepans, and no large boiler should on any account be without one. Some experiments I have lately made (since my return to Bavaria) have showed me how very necessary these dampers are; and I consider it as my duty to the public to lose no time in recommending the general use of them. The flattering attention which has been paid by the public to the various improvements I have taken the liberty to propose, not only demands my warmest gratitude, but lays me under an indispensable obligation to exert myself to the utmost to deserve their esteem, and to merit the distinguished marks of their confidence with which on so many occasions I have been honoured.

But to return to the kitchen in the house of Sir John Sinclair (the place where the meetings of the Board of Agriculture are held, and where of course there is a great concourse of ingenious men from all parts of the kingdom,—of men zealous for the progress of useful improvements). As the room is very small, it was not possible to do more in it than just to fit up a few small boilers and saucepans, and one middling-sized roaster, such as might serve for a small family; which last is a machine so very useful that I cannot help flattering myself that it will soon come into general use. The saving of fuel which it occasions is almost incredible, and the meat roasted in it is remarkably well-tasted and high-flavoured.

One of these roasters, on a large scale, was put up, under my direction, in the kitchen of the Foundling Hospital in London; and though I could not stay in England to see it finished, I have had the satisfaction to learn, since my arrival at Munich, from my friend, Mr. Bernard (who is treasurer to the hospital), that it has answered even beyond his expectations. He informs me, that when 112 lbs. of beef are roasted in it at once, the expense for fuel amounts to no more than *four pence* sterling; and this when the coals are reckoned at an uncommonly high price, namely, at 1s. 4d. the bushel.

In the roaster belonging to the kitchen of the Military Academy at Munich I caused 100 lbs. Bavarian weight (equal to 123.84 lbs. avoirdupois) of veal, in *six large pieces*, to be roasted at once, as an experiment; the fuel consumed was 33 lbs. Bavarian weight of dry pine-wood (equal to 40.86 lbs. avoirdupois), which (at 4½ florins the *klafter*, weighing 2967 lbs. Bavarian weight) cost 3 kreutzers, or about *one penny* sterling.

This experiment was made in the year 1792. Happening to mention the result of it in a large company in London, soon after my arrival there in the autumn of the year 1795, I had the mortification to perceive very plainly by the countenances of my hearers how dangerous it is to promulgate very extraordinary truths. I afterwards grew more cautious, and should not now have ventured to publish this account, had not the results of experiments equally surprising, which have been made with the roaster in the kitchen of the Foundling Hospital, been made known to the public.

Not only the roaster, but the boilers also which have been put up under my direction in the kitchen of the Foundling Hospital, have been found to answer very well; and I am informed that several other great hospitals are about to imitate them. As I left London before the kitchen of the Foundling Hospital was entirely finished, I do not know whether there are dampers to the canals by which the smoke goes off from the fire-places of the boilers, and from that of the roaster to the chimney. If there are not, I could wish they might still be added; and I would strongly recommend it to those who may be engaged in constructing kitchen fire-places on my principles, never to omit them.

Oval grates of cast-iron in the form of a dish, such as I have described in the foregoing chapters of this Essay, were tried in the kitchen of the Foundling Hospital; but the heat was found to be so intense that they were soon melted and destroyed; and we were obliged to have recourse to common flat grates, composed of strong bars of cast-iron. Perhaps the heat generated in the combustion of pit-coal is so intense, when completely confined (as it ought always to be in closed fire-places), that it will not be possible, where coals are used as fuel, to use the hollow dishing grates I have introduced in the public kitchens at Munich, and which have been described and recommended in this Essay.

Since my return to Bavaria, I have made several experiments with grates composed of common bricks, placed edgewise, and I find that they answer for that use full as well, if not better, than iron bars. By making bricks *on purpose* for this use, of proper forms and dimensions, and composed of the best clay mixed with broken crucibles beaten to a coarse powder, kitchen fire-places might be fitted up with them, which would be both cheap and durable, and as perfect in all other respects as any that could possibly be made, even were the most costly materials to be used in their construction.

To diminish still farther the expense attending the construction of closed kitchen fire-places designed for the use of poor families, the opening by which fuel is introduced might be closed with a brick, or with a flat stone; another brick or stone might be made to serve at the same time as a register and a door to the ash-pit, and a third as a damper to the chimney or canal for carrying off the smoke from the fire-place.

I lately had an opportunity of fitting up a kitchen on these principles, in the construction of which there was not a particle of iron used, or of any other metal, except for the boiler. On the approach of the French army under General Moreau in August last, the Bavarian troops being assembled at Munich (under my command) for the defence of the capital, the town was so full of soldiers that several regiments were obliged to be quartered in public buildings, and encamped on the ramparts, where they had no conveniences for cooking. For the accommodation of a part of them, four large oblong square boilers, composed of very thin sheet coppers well tinned, were fitted up in a mass of brickwork in the form of a cross; each boiler with its separate fire-place, communicating by double canals, furnished with dampers, with one common chimney which stands in the centre of the cross. The dampers are thin flat tiles; the grates on which the fuel is burned are composed of common bricks, placed edgewise; and the passages leading to the fire-place, and to the ash-pit, are closed by bricks which are made to slide in grooves.

Under the bottom of each boiler, which is quite flat, there are three flues, in the direction of its length; that in the middle, which is as wide as both the others, being occupied by the burning fuel. The opening by which the fuel is introduced is at the end of the boiler *farthest from the chimney;* and the flame, running along the middle flue to the end of it, divides there, and returning in the two side flues to the hither end of the boiler, there rises up into two other flues, in which it passes along the outside of the boiler into the chimney. The boilers are furnished with wooden covers divided into two equal parts, united by hinges. In order that the four boilers may be transported with greater facility from place to place (from one camp to another for instance), they are not all precisely of the same size, but one is so much less than the other, that they may be packed one in the other. The largest of them, which contains the three others, is packed in a wooden chest, which is made just large enough to receive it. In the smallest may be packed a circular tent, sufficiently large to cover them all. In the middle of the tent there must be a hole through which the chimney must pass. The four boilers, together with the tent, and all the apparatus and utensils necessary for a kitchen on this construction for a regiment consisting of 1000 men, might easily be transported from place to place on an Irish car drawn by a single horse.

I have been the more particular in my account of this

portable kitchen, as I think it would be found very useful for troops in camp. The Right Honourable Mr. Thomas Pelham made a trial of one of them last summer for his regiment (the Sussex militia), and found it to be very useful. The saving of fuel was very considerable indeed; and the saving of trouble in cooking not less important. The first experiment we made together in a single boiler, fitted up for the purpose in the open air, in the middle of the court-yard of Lord Pelham's house in London.

I ought, perhaps, to have reserved what I have here said on the subject of these military portable kitchens for my next Essay, where it would more naturally have found its place; but being persuaded of the great advantages that may be derived from them, I am unwilling to lose a moment in recommending them to the attention of those who have it in their power to bring them into use.

Those who wish to know more about them may, I am confident, procure every information they can desire respecting them, by applying to Mr. Pelham, or to any of the officers of the Sussex militia who were in camp with the regiment last summer.

There is one more invention for the use of armies in the field which I wish to recommend, and that is a *portable boiler* of a light and cheap construction, in which victuals may be cooked *on a march*. There are so many occasions when it would be very desirable to be able to give soldiers, harassed and fatigued with severe service, a warm meal, when it is impossible to stop to light fires and boil the pot, that I cannot help flattering myself that a contrivance, by which the pot *actually boiling* may be made to keep pace with the troops as they advance, will be an acceptable present to every humane officer and wise and prudent general. Many a battle has undoubtedly been lost for the want of a good comfortable meal of warm victuals to recruit the strength and raise the spirits of troops fainting with hunger and excessive fatigue.

But to return from this digression. The form of the two principal boilers in the kitchen of the Foundling Hospital is that of an oblong square; that form which, on several accounts, I have reason to think preferable to all others for large boilers, but especially on account of the facility of fitting them up with square bricks, and of cleaning their flues, I first introduced in Ireland in several fire-places designed for different uses, which I fitted up as models, in Dublin, during the visit I made last spring to that country on the invitation of my friend Mr. Secretary Pelham.

The first of these oblong square boilers is that which is fitted up in the court-yard of the Linen-hall at Dublin, *as a model for bleachers*. It is 8 feet wide, 10 feet long, and 2 feet deep; and it is furnished with a wooden cover, which shutting down in a groove in which there is a small quantity of water, the steam is by these means confined in the boiler. This cover is movable on its hinges, which are placed at the end of the boiler farthest from the door of the fire-place; and it is occasionally lifted up by means of a rope, which goes over a compound pulley which is fixed over the boiler at the top or ceiling of the room.

Under this boiler there are five flues which run in the direction of its length, and are arranged and constructed in the same manner as the flues of the new brewhouse boiler which I lately fitted up at Munich. (See Fig. 21, Plate V.) There are no flues round the outside of this boiler; but the brick walls by which they are defended from the cold air are double, and the space between them is filled with charcoal dust.

The fuel burns at the hither end of the middle flue, in an oval dish-grate; and the flame running along in this flue under the middle of the boiler to the farther end of it, there divides, and returns in the two adjoining flues. It then turns to the right and left, and, going back again in the two outside flues to the farther end of the boiler, goes out from under it there in two canals, which, sloping upwards, conduct it to the flues of a *second boiler* of equal dimensions with the first, where it circulates, and warms the water which is designed for refilling the first boiler.

As these boilers are made of exceedingly thin sheet-copper, and *thin boilers* are stronger to resist the effects of the fire, and consequently more durable than very thick ones, they both together cost much less than one single boiler on the common construction; and Mr. Duffin, secretary to the Linen Board, who is a very active, intelligent man, and is himself engaged in a large concern in the bleaching business, showed me a computation, founded on actual experiments which he himself made with this new boiler, by which he proved that the saving of fuel which will result from the general introduction of these boilers in the bleaching trade throughout Ireland will amount to at least fifty thousand pounds sterling a year.

In a laundry which I fitted up in the house belonging to the Dublin Society (and which is designed to serve as a model for laundries for private gentlemen's families), there are also two oblong square boilers, the one heated by the fire, and the other by the smoke; and this smoke, after having circulated in the flues under the second boiler, passes through a long flue (constructed like hothouse flues), which goes round two sides of the *drying-room* (which is adjoining to the *washing-room*), and then, passing through the wall of the drying-room into the ironing-room, it goes off into an open chimney. As the bottom of the second boiler lies on a level with the top of the first, the warm water runs out of the second to refill the first, by a tube furnished with a brass cock, which greatly facilitates the filling of the principal boiler. The wooden covers of these boilers, which are double and movable on hinges, are shut down in grooves in which there is water; and the steam, being by these means confined, is forced to pass off by a wooden tube, which, standing on a part of the cover which is fastened down to the boiler with hooks, carries the steam upwards to the height of seven or eight feet, where it goes off laterally by another (horizontal) wooden tube, through the wall into the drying-room. As soon as this horizontal wooden tube has passed through the wall into the drying-room, it ends in a copper tube, about 3 inches in diameter, which, lying nearly in a horizontal position, conducts the steam through the middle of the drying-room in the direction of its length, and through a hole in a window at the end of the room into the open air.

The steam, in passing through the drying-room in a metallic tube (which is a good conductor of heat), gives off its heat through the sides of the tube to the air of the room, and the water which is condensed runs off through the tube. By sloping the tube *upwards*, instead of downwards, as by accident it was sloped, the condensed water, which is always nearly boiling hot, when it is condensed might be made to return into the boiler, which would be attended with a saving of heat, and consequently of fuel.

The furnace for heating the irons used in smoothing the linen (or ironing, as it is called) is a kind of oven built of bricks and mortar, the bottom of which is a shallow pan of cast iron, 18 inches square and about 3 inches deep, which is nearly filled with fine sand. The fire being made under this pan in a closed fire-place, as the sand defends the upper surface of the pan from the cold air of the atmosphere, the pan is commonly red-hot; and the irons, being shoved down through the sand and placed in contact with this plate of red-hot metal, are heated in a very short time, and at a small expense of fuel.

This contrivance might be used with great success for covering the *hot plates* on which saucepans are made to boil in many private kitchens.

This stove, or oven, for heating the smoothing-irons, projects into the drying-room; but the door by which the irons are introduced, as well as that leading to the fire-place, and that leading to the ash-pit, all open into the ironing-room.

The smoke goes off through the drying-room in an iron tube, and assists in warming the room and in drying the linen.

As it may sometimes be necessary to heat the drying-room when neither the wash-house boilers nor the stove for heating the smoothing-irons are heated, provision is made for that, by constructing a small closed fire-place, designed merely for that purpose, which opens into the flue, by which the smoke from the boilers is carried round the drying-room. This fire-place (which is never used but when it is wanted for drying the linen) is situated just without the drying-room, under the end of the flue where it joins the second boiler. The opening at the top of its fire-place, by which the flame of the burning fuel enters the under part of the flue, is kept closed by a sliding plate of iron, or damper, when this fire-place is not used; and when it is used, the door which closes the opening into the fire-place of the first or principal boiler, and the register in its ash-pit door, are kept shut.

That the top of the principal boiler might not be too high above the pavement of the wash-house for the laundresses to work in the boiler without being obliged to go up steps or stairs, the grate and the bottom of the flues under the boiler are nearly on a level with the pavement, and the ash-pit is sunk into the ground; and, to render the approach to the opening into the fire-place more convenient in introducing the fuel and lighting and managing the fire, there is an area before the fire-place, about 3 feet square and 2 feet deep, sunk in the ground, and walled up on its sides, into which there is a descent by steps. In two of the sides of these vertical walls (those on the right and left when you stand fronting the fire-place) there are vaults for containing fuel, which extend several feet under the pavement. The steps which descend into this area are on the side of it, opposite the fire-place.

Areas of this kind are very necessary for all fire-places for large boilers, otherwise the top of the boiler will necessarily be raised too high above the level of the pavement to be approached with facility and convenience. Steps may be made, it is true, for approaching boilers which are placed higher; but these are always inconvenient, and take up more room, and cost more than the execution of the plan here proposed for rendering them unnecessary.

The areas before the fire-place door of the large boilers in the kitchen of the Foundling Hospital are occasionally closed by trap-doors. As often as this is done there must be a number of small holes bored in the door to permit the air necessary for feeding the fire to descend into the ash-pit; and when the bottom of the passage leading into the fire-place happens to lie above the level of the upper surface of this trap-door, the part of the door immediately under this opening should, to prevent accidents from live coals which may occasionally fall out of the fire-place, be covered with a thin plate of sheet iron.

When large boilers are fitted up in situations where it is not possible to sink an area in front of the fire-place, the mass of brick-work in which the boiler is set must be raised, and steps must be made to approach it. When this is done, the upper step should be made very wide (at least 2 feet), in order that there may be room to stand and work in the boiler; and, for still greater convenience, the steps should be continued round three sides of the boiler, when the boiler stands in a detached mass of brick-work. The bottom of the door of the fire-place should, if possible, be above the upper flat surface of the upper step; and, to preserve the symmetry of the whole, the ash-pit door may be in the front of the upper step, and the passage into the ash-pit (which will be long of course) may descend in a gentle slope. In this manner the kitchen of the Hospital of *La Pietà* at Verona was constructed.

No inconvenience whatever attends the increase of the length of the passage into the ash-pit, except it be that very trifling one,—which surely does not deserve to be mentioned,—the increase of labour attending the removal of the ashes; but the inconvenience would be very considerable which would unavoidably attend the discontinuation or breaking off of the steps round the hither end or front of the boiler, which would be necessary in order to be able to place the ash-pit door *directly under* the fire-place door, and to make a way to approach it.

The flues under the principal boiler of the laundry in the house of the Dublin Society are not contrived so as to divide the flame and cause it to circulate in *two* currents. They run from side to side under it: the door of the fire-place is not in the middle, but on one side of the boiler, and near one end of it. The flame, passing and returning under the boiler twice from its front to its opposite side, goes off at its end (that farthest from the fire-place) into a canal furnished with a damper, which canal, rising upward at an angle of about 45 degrees, leads to the flues under the second boiler. The bottom of the flues of the principal boiler are just on a level with the pavement of the wash-house; and in order that they may easily be cleaned out, and the bottom of the boiler scrubbed with a broom to free it from soot, the ends of the flues are, in building the fire-place, left open, and afterwards, when the boiler is set, they are closed by temporary (double) walls of dry bricks. To make these walls tight, the joinings of the bricks are plastered on the outside with moist clay.

The sides of the boilers are defended from the cold air by thin walls of bricks covered with wainscot, and by filling the space between these walls and the boiler with pounded charcoal. Were I to fit up these boilers again, I should leave this space void, or filled merely with air, forming several small openings below, through which the flame and hot vapour from the flues might ascend and surround the boiler. In the large boiler fitted up in the Linen-hall as a model for bleachers, this alteration is also necessary to render it complete; and as it might be made in a few hours, and almost without any expense, I cannot help expressing a wish that it might still be done.

The ardent zeal for the prosperity of his country, and indefatigable attention to every thing that tends to promote useful improvement, which so eminently distinguish that enlightened patriot and most respectable statesman, to whom the manufactures and commerce of Ireland, and the linen trade in particular, are so much indebted, encourage me to hope that he will take pleasure in giving his assistance to render the models for improving fire-places and saving fuel, which I have had the satisfaction of leaving in Ireland, as free from faults as they can possibly be made.

Though my stay in Ireland was too short to construct models of all the improvements I wished to have introduced in that delightful and most interesting island, yet the liberality with which my various proposals were received, and the generous assistance I met with from all quarters, enabled me to do more in two months than I probably should have been able to have effected in as many years in some other older countries, where the progress of wealth and of refinements has rendered it extremely difficult to get people to attend to useful improvements.

I wished much to have been able to have fitted up

the great kitchen in the House of Industry at Dublin, as the expense of fuel is very considerable in that extensive establishment, where more than 1500 persons are fed daily, at an average; but, not having time to finish so considerable an undertaking, I thought it most prudent not to begin it. I fitted up one large boiler as a model at one end of one of the working-halls; but this was designed principally to show how a large hall might be heated from a kitchen fire-place, and from the very same fire which is used for cooking.* The smoke from the fire-place is carried along horizontally on one side of the hall from one end of it to the other; and the boiler being closed by a cover which is steam-tight, the steam from the boiler is also forced along from one end of the hall to the other, in a horizontal leaden pipe, which runs parallel to the flue occupied by the smoke, and lies immediately over it. In warm weather, when the hall does not require to be heated, the smoke and steam go off immediately into the atmosphere by a chimney adjoining the fire-place, without passing through the hall.

To be able to equalize the heat in the hall (which is very long and narrow), or to render it as warm at the end of it which is farthest from the fire-place as at that next the fire, I directed clothing for the steam tube of warm blanketing to be made in lengths of three or four feet, to be occasionally put round it and fastened by buttons.

By clothing or covering the steam tube more or less, as may be found necessary in those parts of the hall

---

* This contrivance might easily be applied to the heating of hothouses, even though the hothouse should happen to be situated at a considerable distance from the kitchen.

where the heat is greatest, the steam, being by this covering prevented from giving off its heat to the air through the tube, will go on farther and warm those parts of the hall which otherwise would be not sufficiently heated. The steam tube, which is constructed of very thin sheet lead, is about 3 inches in diameter, and, instead of being laid exactly in a horizontal position, slopes a little upwards, just so much that the water which results from the condensation of the steam may return into the boiler.*

The horizontal flue through which the smoke passes is a round tube of sheet iron, about 7 inches in diameter, divided, for the facility of cleaning it, in lengths of 12 or 15 feet, fixed nearly horizontally at different heights from the floor, or, in an interrupted line, in hollow pilasters or square columns of brick-work. A common hothouse flue constructed of bricks and mortar would have answered equally well for warming the hall, but would have taken up too much room, which is the only reason it was not preferred to these iron tubes.

---

* I contrived a fire-place for heating one of the principal churches in Dublin on these principles with steam (but without making use of the smoke); and I promised to give a plan (which, I am ashamed to say, I have not yet been able to finish) for heating the superb new building destined for the meeting of the Irish House of Commons.

One of the two chimney fire-places, which I fitted up in the hall in which the meetings of the Royal Irish Academy are held, will, I imagine, be found to answer very well for heating high rooms and large halls in private houses. In this fire-place I have endeavoured, and I believe successfully, to unite the advantages of an open fire with those of a German stove. The grate used in fitting up this fire-place, and which is of cast iron, and far from being unelegant in its form, and which cost only *seven shillings and sixpence sterling*, is decidedly the best adapted for open chimney fire-places, where coals are used as fuel, of any I have yet seen. By a letter I lately received from a friend in Ireland, I had the satisfaction to learn that these grates are coming very fast into general use in that country.

In constructing the boiler (which is of thin sheet iron), I made an experiment which succeeded even beyond my expectation. The flues under the boiler (and there are none round it) are projections from the bottom of the boiler: they are hollow walls of sheet iron, about 9 inches high and an inch and three-quarters thick, into which the liquid in the boiler descends, and which in fact constitute a part of the boiler. By this contrivance the flame is surrounded on all sides, except at the bottom of the flues (where the heat has little or no tendency to pass), by the liquid which is heated, and the fire-place is merely a flat mass of brick-work. The grate is even with the upper surface of this mass of brick-work, and the ash-pit is the only cavity in it.

In constructing the boiler, provision was made, by omitting or interrupting the hollow walls or divisions of the flues, in the proper places, to leave room for introducing the fuel, for the passage of the flame from one flue to another, and from the last flue into the canal by which the smoke goes off into the chimney, or into the iron tubes by which the hall is occasionally warmed.

One principal object which I had in view in this experiment was to see if I could not contrive a boiler, which, being suspended under a wagon or other wheel-carriage, might serve for cooking for troops on a march; or which, being merely set down on the ground, a fire might be immediately kindled under it.

Those who will take the trouble to examine the boiler in question will find that the principle on which it is constructed may easily be applied to the objects here mentioned. But it is not merely for portable boilers that this construction would be found useful: I am convinced that it would be very advantageous for the boilers of steam engines, for distilleries, and for various other purposes. As the escape of heat into the brick-work is almost entirely prevented, and as the surface of the boiler on which the heat is made to act is greatly increased by means of the hollow walls, the liquid in the boiler is heated in a very short time, and with a small quantity of fuel.

There is still another advantage attending this construction, which renders it highly deserving the attention of distillers. By making the tops of the flues arched instead of flat (which may easily be done, and which is actually done in the boiler in question), or in the form of the roof of a house, as the hottest part of the flame will, of course, always occupy the upper part of the flues, and as the thick or viscous part of the liquor in the boiler — that which is in most danger of being burned to the bottom of the boiler, and giving a bad taste to the spirit which comes over — cannot well lie on the convex or sloping surface of these flues, there will be less danger of an accident which distillers have hitherto found it extremely difficult to prevent.

In constructing boilers on these principles for distillers, it will probably be found necessary to increase very much the thickness of the hollow walls of the flues, and perhaps to make them even deeper than the level of the bottom of the flues, in order more effectually to prevent the thick matter which will naturally settle in those cavities from being exposed to too great a heat.

A similar advantage will attend large boilers constructed on these principles for making thick soups for hospitals; these soups being very apt to burn to the bottoms of the boilers in which they are prepared.

I made another experiment in the House of Industry

in Dublin, which I wished much to have had time to have prosecuted farther. Finding that the expense for wheaten bread for the House was very great (amounting, in the year 1795, to no less than 3841*l.* sterling), I saw that a very considerable saving might be made by furnishing those who were fed at the public expense with oaten cakes (a kind of bread to which they had always been used), instead of rendering them dainty and spoiling them by giving them the best wheaten bread that could be procured, as I found had hitherto been done. But to be able to furnish oaten cakes in sufficient quantities to feed 1500 persons, some more convenient method of baking them than that commonly practised was necessary, and one in which the expense of fuel might be greatly lessened.

With a view to facilitate this important change in the mode of feeding the numerous objects of charity and of *correction*, who were shut up together within the walls of that extensive establishment, I constructed what I would call a *perpetual oven*.

In the centre of a circular, or rather cylindrical mass of brick-work, about 8 feet in diameter, which occupies the middle of a large room on the ground floor, I constructed a small, circular, closed fire-place for burning either wood, peat, turf, or coals. The diameter of the fire-place is about 11 inches, the grate being placed about 10 inches above the floor, and the top of the fire-place is contracted to about 4 inches. Immediately above this narrow throat, six separate canals (each furnished with a damper, by means of which its opening can be contracted more or less, or entirely closed) go off horizontally, by which the flame is conducted into six separate sets of flues, under six large plates of cast iron, which form the bottoms of six ovens on the same level, and joining each other by their sides, which are concealed in the cylindrical mass of the brick-work. Each of these plates of cast iron being in the form of an equilateral triangle, they all unite in the centre of the cylindrical mass of brick-work; consequently the two sides of each unite in a point at the bottom of it, forming an angle of 60 degrees.

The flame, after circulating under the bottoms of these ovens, rises up in two canals concealed in the front wall of each oven, and situated on the right and left of its mouth, and after circulating again in similar flues on the upper flat surface of another triangular plate of cast iron, which forms the top of the oven, goes off upwards by a canal furnished with a damper into a hollow place, situated on the top of the cylindrical mass of the brick-work, from which it passes off in a horizontal iron tube, about 7 inches in diameter, suspended near the ceiling of the room, into a chimney situated on one side of the room.

These six ovens which are contiguous to each other in this mass of brick-work are united by their sides by thin walls made of tiles, about $1\frac{1}{2}$ inches thick and 10 inches square, placed edgewise; and each oven having its separate canal, furnished with a register communicating with the fire-place, any one or more of them may be heated without heating the others, or the heat may be turned off from one of them to the other in continual succession; and, by managing matters properly, the process of baking may be *uninterrupted*. As soon as the bread is drawn out of one of the ovens, the fire may immediately be turned under it to heat it again, while that from under which the fire is taken is filled with unbaked loaves, and closed up.

A principal object which I had in view in constructing

this oven was to prevent the great loss of heat which is occasioned in large ovens, by keeping the mouth of the oven open for so considerable a length of time as is necessary for putting in and drawing out the bread. As one of these small ovens contains only five large loaves, or cakes, it may be charged, or the bread when baked may be drawn, in a moment; and during this time the other five ovens are kept closed, and consequently are not losing heat; *one* of them is heating, while the other *four* are filled with bread in different stages of the process of baking.

When I constructed this oven, though I had no doubt of its being perfectly well calculated for the use for which it was principally designed,— baking oaten cakes, which are commonly baked on heated iron plates,— yet I was by no means sure it would answer for baking common bread in large thick loaves. I had not made the experiment. And though I could not conceive that any thing more could be necessary in the process of baking than *heat*,— and here I was absolutely master of every degree of it that could possibly be wanted, and could even regulate the succession of different degrees of it at pleasure, — I thought it probable that some particular management might be required in baking bread in these metallic ovens, a knowledge of which could only be acquired by experience.

What served to strengthen these suspicions was a discovery which had accidentally been made by the cook of the Military Academy. In the course of *his* experiments, he found that my roaster is admirably well calculated for baking pies, puddings, and pastry of all kinds: provided, however, that the fire be managed *in a certain way;* for when the fire is managed in the same manner in which it ought to be managed in roasting meat, pies and pastry will absolutely be spoiled. After repeated failures and disappointments, and after having lost all hopes of ever being able to succeed in his attempts, the cook (by mere accident, as he assured me) discovered the important secret; and important he certainly considers it to be, and feels no small degree of satisfaction, not to say pride, in having been so fortunate as to make the discovery. He must pardon me if I take the liberty, even without his permission, to publish it to the world for the good of mankind.

The roaster must be well heated before the pies or pastry are put into it, and the blowers must never be quite closed during the process.

I have lately found that, by using similar precautions, bread may be perfectly well baked in metallic ovens, similar to that in the House of Industry in Dublin.

Thinking it more than probable that means might be devised for managing the heat in such a manner as to perform that process in ovens constructed on these principles, and heated *from without;* and conceiving that not only a great saving of fuel, but also several other very important advantages, could not fail to be derived from that discovery, on my return to Munich from England, in August last, I immediately set about making experiments, with a view to the investigation of that subject; and I have so far succeeded in them that, for these last four months, my table has been supplied entirely with bread baked in my own house, by my cook, in an oven constructed of thin sheet iron, which is heated (like my roasters) from without; and I will venture to add that I never tasted better bread. All those who have eaten of it have unanimously expressed the same opinion of it. It is very light, most thoroughly baked without being too much dried, and I think remarkably well-tasted. The loaves, which are made small in order that they may have a greater proportion of crust (which, when the bread is baked in this way, is singularly delicate), are placed in the oven on circular plates of thin sheet iron, raised about an inch on slender iron feet. Were the loaf placed on the bottom of the oven, the under crust would presently be burned to a coal, and the bread spoiled. A precaution absolutely necessary in baking bread in the manner here recommended is to leave a passage for the steam generated in the process of baking to escape. This may be done either by constructing a steam chimney for that purpose, furnished with a damper, or simply by making a register in the door of the oven.

As this is not the proper place to enlarge on this subject, I shall leave it for the present; but I cannot help expressing a wish that what I have here advanced may induce others, especially *bakers*, who may find their own advantage in the prosecution of these interesting and important investigations, to turn their attention to them.

How exceedingly useful would my roasters be, and ovens constructed on the principles here recommended, on shipboard! Having served a campaign (as a volunteer) in a large fleet (that commanded by Admiral Sir Charles Hardy, in the year 1779), and having made several long sea voyages, I have had frequent opportunities of seeing how difficult it is in bad weather to cook at sea; and it is easy to imagine how much it would contribute to the comfort of seafaring people, especially at times when they are exposed to the greatest fatigues and hardships, to enable them to have their tables well supplied with warm victuals.

In order that the motion of the vessel might not derange any part of the apparatus used in the process of cooking at sea in my roasters, the form of the roaster should be that of a perfect cylinder; and the dripping-pan in which the meat is placed should be a longitudinal section of another cylinder, less in diameter than the roaster by about an inch, and suspended on two pivots in the axis of the roaster, in such a manner that the dripping-pan may swing freely in the roaster without touching its sides. The roaster should be placed in the brick-work, with its axis in the direction of the length of the ship; and, to prevent the gravy from being thrown out of the dripping-pan when the vessel pitches, its hollow cavity should be divided into a number of compartments, by partitions running across it from side to side.

It remains for me to give some account of the kitchen which I fitted up in the house of the Dublin Society, as a model for private families; and also of a cottage fire-place, and a lime-kiln, which I constructed as models for imitation, in the courtyard of that public building.

With regard to the kitchen, it is necessary that I should remark, at setting out, that it was not intended so much to serve as a complete model of a convenient kitchen for a private family, as to display a variety of useful inventions, all or any of which may at pleasure be easily adopted, in kitchens of all kinds and of all dimensions. I thought this would be more useful than any simple model of a kitchen I could contrive.

It is, however, a very complete kitchen; and though there are some contrivances belonging to it which might have been omitted, yet they will all, I am confident, be found useful for the different purposes for which they were particularly designed, and in a kitchen for a large family would often come into use.

The general disposition of the various parts of this kitchen I consider as being quite perfect. It is the same as that of the Hospital of *La Pietà* at *Verona*, and of a very complete private kitchen which was built about two years ago at Munich, under my direction, in the house of Baron Lerchenfeld, steward of the household to his Most Serene Highness the Elector. In my next Essay, which will treat exclusively of the construction of kitchen fire-places and of kitchen utensils, I shall give a particular detailed account of the manner in which the various boilers — steam-boilers, saucepans, oven, roasters, etc. — are disposed and connected in the mass of brick-work in these kitchens, and shall accompany these descriptions with a sufficient number of Plates to render them perfectly intelligible.

Cottage Fire-place and Iron Pot, for cooking for the Poor.

The cottage fire-place which I fitted up as a model, in the courtyard of the house of the Dublin Society, was not quite finished when I left Ireland; but an idea may be formed from what was done of the general principles on which such fire-places may be constructed. On each side of the open chimney fire-place (which, being small, was built in the middle of one much larger, which was constructed to represent a large open fireplace, such as are now general in cottages) I fitted up an iron pot on a peculiar construction, cast by Mr. Jackson of Dublin, and designed for the use of a poor family in cooking their victuals. This pot is nearly of a cylindrical form, about 16 inches in diameter, and

8 inches deep; and under its bottom, which is quite flat, there is a thin spiral projection, which was cast with the pot, and serves instead of feet to it, the turns of which, when the pot is set down on a flat surface, form a spiral flue in which the flame circulates under the bottom of the pot. This projection, which is near half an inch thick where it is united with the bottom of the pot, and less than a quarter of an inch below where its lower edge rests on the ground, is about 4 inches wide, or rather deep. This projection was made tapering, in order to its being more easily cast. To defend the outside of this pot from the cold air, the pot is enclosed in a cylinder of thin sheet iron, equal in diameter to the extreme width of the pot at its brim, just as high as the depth of the pot and of its spiral flues taken together. The pot is fastened to this cylindrical case by being driven into it with force, a rim in the form of a flat hoop, about an inch and a half deep and a little tapering, being cast on the outside of the pot at its brim, the external surface of which was fitted exactly into the top of this cylinder. This projection is useful, not only in uniting the pot to its cylindrical case, but also to keep this cylindrical case at some small distance from the sides of the pot, by which means the heat is more effectually confined.

To be able to move about this pot from place to place, it has two handles which are riveted to the outside of its cylindrical case; and it is provided with a wooden cover.

I am sensible that I often expose myself to criticism by anticipating what would more naturally find its place elsewhere. But what I have here said in regard to this iron pot is intended merely as hints to awaken the curiosity and excite the attention of ingenious men, — of such as take pleasure in exercising their ingenuity in contriving and perfecting useful inventions, and who delight in contemplating the progress of human industry.

Model of a perpetual Lime-kiln.

The particular objects principally had in view in the construction of this lime-kiln (which stands in the courtyard of the Dublin Society) were, *first*, to cause the fuel to burn in such a manner as to consume the smoke, which was done by obliging the smoke to descend and pass through the fire, in order that as much heat as possible might be generated. Secondly, to cause the flame and hot vapour which rise from the fire to come into contact with the limestone by a very large surface, in order to economize the heat and prevent its going off into the atmosphere, which was done by making the body of the kiln in the form of a hollow truncated cone, and very high in proportion to its diameter; and by filling it quite up to the top with limestone, the fire being made to enter near the bottom of the cone. Thirdly, to make the process of burning lime *perpetual*, in order to prevent the waste of heat which unavoidably attends the cooling of the kiln in emptying and filling it, when, to perform that operation, it is necessary to put out the fire. And, fourthly, to contrive matters so that the lime in which the process of burning is *just finished*, and which of course is still *intensely hot*, may, in *cooling*, be made to give off its heat in such a manner as to assist in heating the fresh quantity of cold limestone with which the kiln is replenished as often as a portion of lime is taken out of it.

To effectuate these purposes, the fuel is not mixed with the limestone, but is burned in a closed fire-place, which opens into one side of the kiln, some distance above the bottom of it. For large lime-kilns on these principles there may be several fire-places, all opening into the same cone, and situated on different sides of it; which fire-places may be constructed and regulated like the fire-places of the furnaces used for burning porcelain.

At the bottom of the kiln there is a door, which is occasionally opened to take out the lime.

When, in consequence of a portion of lime being drawn out of the kiln, its contents settle down or subside, the empty space in the upper part of the kiln, which is occasioned by this subtraction of the burned lime, is immediately filled up with fresh limestone.

As soon as a portion of lime is taken away, the door by which it is removed must be immediately shut, and the joinings well closed with moist clay, to prevent a draught of cold air through the kiln. A small opening, however, must be left, for reasons which I shall presently explain.

As the fire enters the kiln at some distance from the bottom of it, and as the flame *rises* as soon as it comes into this cavity, the lower part of the kiln (that below the level of the bottom of the fire-place) is occupied by lime already burned; and as this lime is intensely hot when, on a portion of lime from below being removed, it descends into this part of the kiln, and as the air in the kiln to which it communicates its heat must *rise upwards* in consequence of its being heated, and pass off through the top of the kiln, this lime in cooling is, by this contrivance, made to assist in heating the fresh portion of cold limestone with which the kiln is charged. To facilitate this communication of heat from the red-hot lime just burned to the limestone above in the upper part of the kiln, a gentle draught of air through the kiln from the bottom to the top of it must be established by leaving an opening in the door below, by which the cold air from without may be suffered to enter the kiln. This opening (which should be furnished with some kind of a register) must be very small, otherwise it will occasion too strong a draught of cold air into the kiln, and do more harm than good; and it will probably be found to be best to close it entirely, after the lime in the lower part of the kiln has parted with a certain proportion of its heat.

Conceiving the improvement of lime-kilns to be a matter of very great national importance, especially since the use of lime as manure has become so general, I intend to devote the first leisure time I can spare to a thorough investigation of that subject. In the mean time, I have here thrown out the loose ideas I have formed respecting it, in order that they may be examined, corrected, and improved upon by others who may be engaged in the same pursuits.

The model I caused to be constructed in the courtyard of the Dublin Society is, I am sensible, very imperfect. It was built in a great hurry, being begun and finished the same day, — the day but one before I left Ireland; but I am now engaged in constructing a lime-kiln on the same principles (for the use of the farm in the English Garden at Munich), which I shall take pains to make as perfect as possible; and, should it be found to answer as well as I have reason to hope it will, I shall not fail to give a particular account of it to the public, accompanied with drawings, and all the details that shall be necessary in order to give the most satisfactory account of the result of the experiment.

These investigations will be the more interesting, and their results more generally useful, as the discovery of a mine of pit-coal in the neighbourhood of Munich, which is now worked with success, has put it in my power to use coal as fuel, as well as wood and turf, in the experiments I shall make in burning lime in this kiln.

For the information of those who may be disposed to engage in these pursuits, I have published the annexed sketch of the lime-kiln in question, which is now actually building (see Plate VI.). I thought it right to do this, that we might start fair; and I can assure my competitors in this race, that I shall feel no ill-will on seeing them get before me.

If I do not deceive myself, the laudable exertions of others afford me almost as much pleasure as my own pursuits; at least I am quite certain that when I can flatter myself that I have had any — even the smallest — share in *exciting* those exertions, the satisfaction I feel in contemplating them is inexpressible.

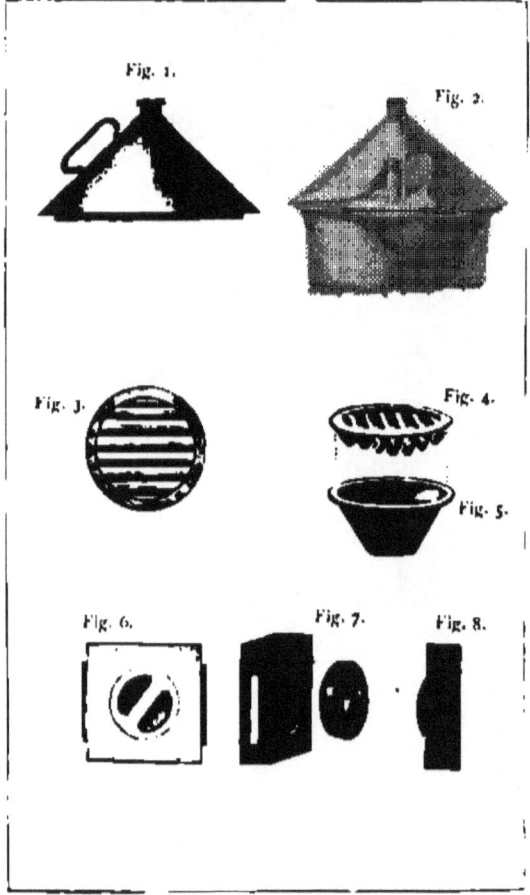

PLATE L

DESCRIPTION OF THE PLATES.

PLATE I.

Fig. 1. A view of a double cover for a boiler or saucepan. In this design the rim is seen which enters the boiler, and the tube by which the steam goes off is seen in part (above), and is in part indicated by dotted lines. (See page 15.)

Fig. 2 shows this cover placed on its boiler. Part of the side of the cover is represented as wanting, in order that the steam tube might be better seen. The height of this cover is represented as being equal to *one half* its diameter; but I have found *one third* of its diameter quite sufficient for its height.

Fig. 3 and Fig. 4 are views of my circular dishing-grates for closed kitchen fire-places. They may be made of any size, from 5 inches to 18 inches in diameter, according to the size of the boiler. The rules I have in general followed, in determining the size proper for the grate for any (circular) boiler, has been to make its diameter equal to half the diameter of the boiler at the brim. (See page 35.)

Fig. 5 is an inverted hollow cone of thin sheet iron, which is placed immediately under the grate, its brim being made to receive the circular rim of the grate. When the fire-place is large, this inverted cone may be made of fire-stone, or constructed of bricks and mortar. For small fire-places it may be made of earthen-ware, which is, perhaps, the very best material for it that can be found. (See page 37.)

Fig. 6, Fig. 7, and Fig. 8, are views and sections of a perforated tile, with its stopper, such as are used for closing the entrance by which the fuel is introduced into closed kitchen fire-places. The diameter of the circular opening, or hole in the tile, may be from 6 to 7 inches. (See page 26.)

PLATE II.

The various figures, from No. 9 to No. 16 of this plate, show the construction of an ash-pit door, with its register. (See page 27.)

Fig. 9 is a front view of the door with its register. The whole is constructed of sheet iron, except the four narrow pieces at the four corners, which hold down in its place the circular plate of the register, and the small circular plate (as large as a half-crown) in the centre of the register, which are made of brass, on account of that metal not being so liable to rust as iron.

Fig. 10 is a side view of the back-side of the door, fixed in its frame, in which the manner of its being shut in its frame is seen; and the iron straps, $a, b, c, d,$ are seen, by which the frame is fastened in the brick-work.

Fig. 11 is a horizontal section through the middle of the door and its frame, and through the button which serves for shutting the door.

Fig. 12 is a section of this button, on an enlarged scale, showing the manner in which it is constructed.

Fig. 13 is the plate of sheet iron which forms the front of the door, with the holes in it by which the other parts of the machinery are fixed to it.

Fig. 14 is the circular plate which forms the register. To this plate is fixed a projecting knob, or button (represented in the figure), by which it is turned about.

PLATE II.

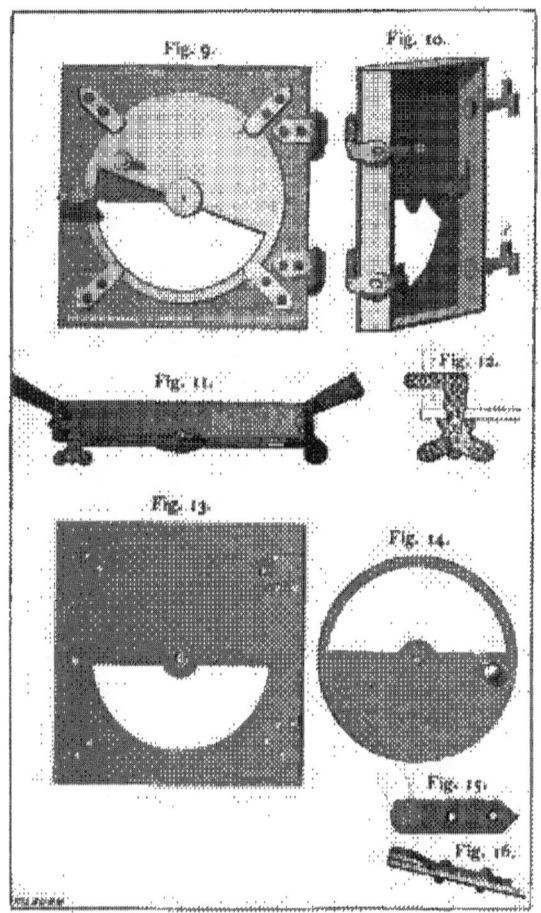

Scale 3 inches to the inch.

Fig. 15 and Fig. 16 show, on an enlarged scale, one of the four pieces of brass by which the circular plate of the register is kept down in its place.

In constructing these register doors, and in general all iron doors for fire-places, great and small, the door should never shut in a rabbet or groove in the frame, but should merely *shut down on the front edge of the frame*, which edge, by grinding it on the flat surface of a large flat stone, should be made quite level to receive it. If this be done, and if the plate of iron which constitutes the door be made quite flat, and if it be properly fixed on its hinges, the door will always shut with facility and close the opening with precision, notwithstanding the effects of the expansion of the metal by heat; but this cannot be the case when the doors of fire-places are fitted in grooves and rabbets.

Where the heat is very intense, the frame of the door should be made of fire-stone; and that part of the door which is exposed naked to the fire should be covered either with a fit piece of fire-stone, fastened to it with clamps of iron, or a sufficient number of strong nails with long necks and flat heads, or of staples, being driven into that side of the plate of iron which forms the door which is exposed, should be covered with a body about two inches thick of strong clay mixed with a due portion of coarse powder of broken crucibles, which mass will be held in its place by the heads of the nails and by the projecting staples. This mass being put on wet, and gently dried, the cracks being carefully filled up as they appear, and the whole well beaten together into a solid mass, will, when properly burned on by the heat of the fire, form a covering for the door which will effectually defend it from all injury from the fire; and the door so defended will last ten times longer than it would last without this defence.

The inside doors of the two brewhouse fire-places which I have fitted up at Munich are both defended from the heat in this manner; and the contrivance, which has answered perfectly all that was expected from it, has not been found to be attended with any inconvenience whatever.

PLATE III.

Fig. 17 is a front view of the new boiler of the brewhouse called Neuheusel, or rather of its fire-place and cover (the boiler being concealed in the brick-work). The inside door of the fire-place is here represented shut; and, in order that it might appear, the outside door is taken off its hinges, and is not shown. The two vaulted galleries, A, B, in the solid mass of brickwork, on the right and left of the fire-place (which were made to save bricks), serve for holding firewood. The partition walls of the fire-place and the different flues, as also a section of the boiler, are represented by dotted lines. The small circular hole on the left of the fire-place door is the window opening into the fire-place, by which the burning fuel may be seen.

a, b, is the wooden curb of the boiler; c, d, a platform on which the men stand when they work in emptying the boiler, etc.; e, f, is a platform which serves as a passage from one side of the boiler to the other. This platform, which is about 18 inches wide, is 12 inches higher than the other platforms, in order that the openings g and h, into the flues, may remain free. These openings, which are opened only occasionally, — that is to say, when the flues want cleaning, — are kept closed

PLATE III.

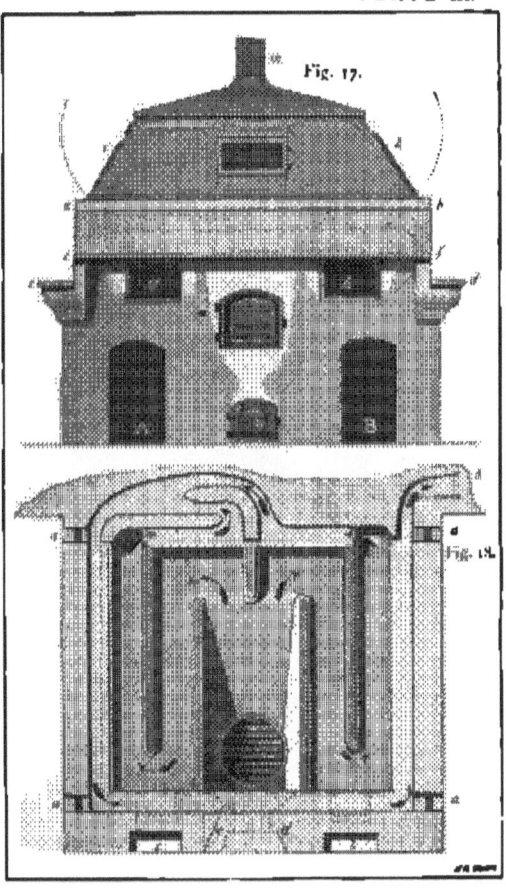

Fig. 17.

Fig. 18.

Scale 6 feet to the Inch.

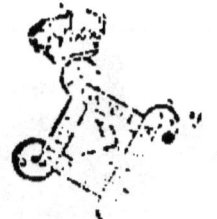

PLATE IV.

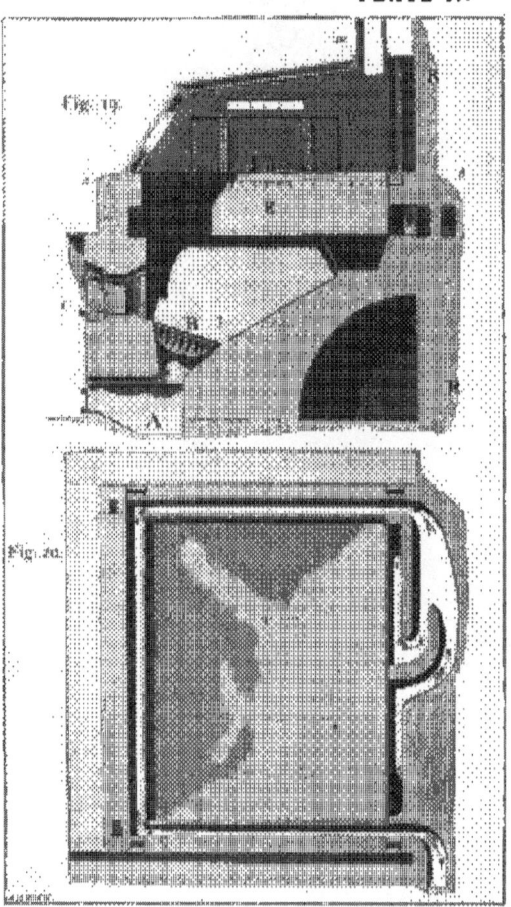

by double brick walls. These walls are expressed in the following figure.

Fig. 18. This is a horizontal section of the fire-place at a level with the bottom of the boiler. *a, a, a, a*, are four openings by which the flues which, in the first arrangement of this fire-place, went round the outside of the boiler, were occasionally cleaned; *b* is the canal by which the smoke went off into the chimney.

. The entrance into the fire-place, and the conical perforation in the wall of the fire-place which serves as a window for observing the fire, are marked by dotted lines. The position of the inside door of the fire-place is marked by a dotted line, *c, d*. The circular dishing-grate is seen in its place; and the walls of the flues under the boiler are all seen. The crooked arrows in the flues show the direction of the flame. (See page 92.)

PLATE IV.

Fig. 19 is a vertical section of the boiler represented in the foregoing plate (Fig. 17). This section is taken through the middle of the boiler, of the fire-place, and of the cover of the boiler. A is the ash-pit, with a section of its register door; B is the fire-place, and its circular dishing-grate; C is the entrance by which the fuel is introduced, with sections of its two doors; D is a space left void to save bricks; E is the boiler, and F its wooden cover; *m* is the steam chimney, which is furnished with a damper; R, R, is the vertical wall of the house against which the brick-work in which the boiler is fixed is placed; *a, b*, is the curb of timber in which the boiler is set.

The manner in which the cover of the boiler is constructed, as well as its form, and the door and windows which belong to it, are all seen distinctly in this figure.

Fig. 20 is a horizontal section of this fire-place taken on a level with the bottom of the flue which goes round the outside of the boiler, in which flue, before the fire-place was altered, the flame circulated. The flues under the boiler are, in this figure, indicated by dotted lines.

PLATE V.

Fig. 21 is a horizontal section of the fire-place of the brewhouse boiler, at a level with the top of the flues under the boiler, *after the flue round the outside of the boiler had been stopped up*, or rather the flame prevented from circulating in it. This figure shows the actual state of the fire-place at the present time. (See page 108.)

The crooked arrows show the direction of the flame in the flues; *a, b,* are the two canals (each of which is furnished with a damper) by which the smoke goes off into the chimney; and *c, c, c, c, c, c,* are six small openings communicating with the flues, by which the flame and hot vapour can pass up into the cavity on the outside of the boiler which formerly served as a flue.

Fig. 22 is a front view of the ash-pit door of this brewhouse fire-place, with its register. This door is closed by means of a latch of a particular construction, which is shown in the figure.

Fig. 23 is the door without its register; and

Fig. 24 the circular plate of the register represented alone.

This ash-pit door shuts against the front edge of its frame, and not into it. The reasons for preferring this

PLATE V.

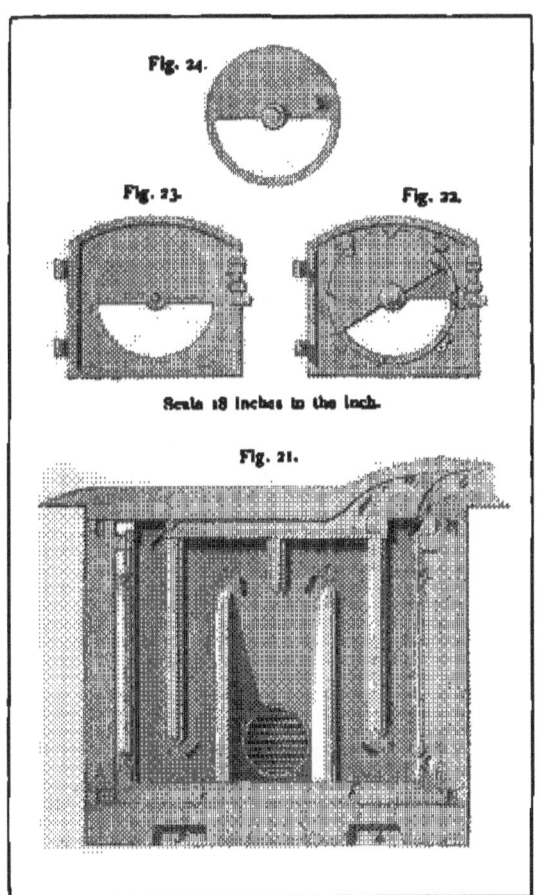

Fig. 24.
Fig. 23.   Fig. 22.
Scale 18 inches to the inch.
Fig. 21.

PLATE VI.

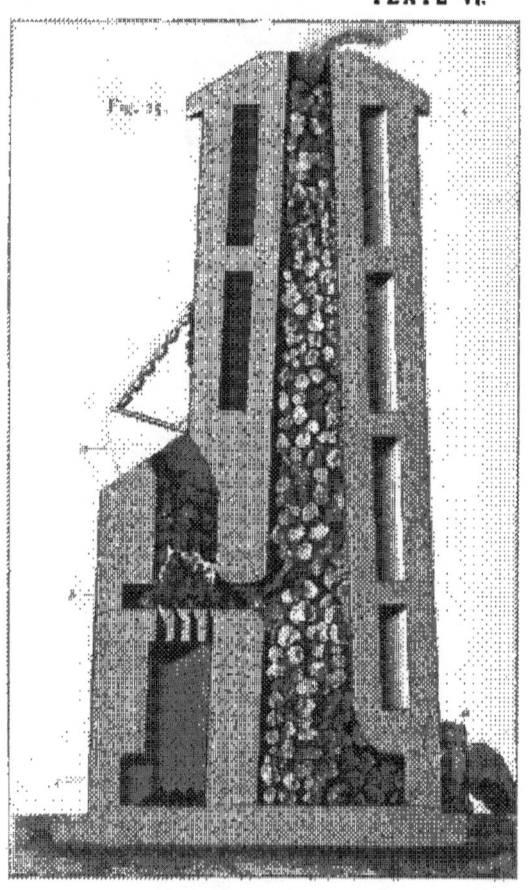

method of fitting the door to its frame have already been explained. (See descriptions of the Plate II.)

PLATE VI.

Fig. 25 is a section of a small lime-kiln, built, or rather now building, at Munich, for the purpose of making experiments. The height of the kiln is 15 feet; its internal diameter below, 2 feet; and above, 9 inches. In order more effectually to confine the heat, its walls, which are of bricks and very thin, are double, and the cavity between them is filled with dry wood ashes. To give greater strength to the fabric, these two walls are connected in different places by horizontal layers of bricks which unite them firmly.

a is the opening by which the fuel is put into the fire-place. Through this opening the air *descends* which feeds the fire. The fire-place is represented nearly full of coals, and the flame passing off laterally into the cavity of the kiln, by an opening made for that purpose at the bottom of the fire-place.

The opening above, by which the fuel is introduced into the fire-place, is covered by a plate of iron, movable on hinges; which plate, by being lifted up more or less by means of a chain, serves as a register for regulating the fire.

A section of this plate, and of the chain by which it is supported, are shown in the figure.

b is an opening in the front wall of the fire-place, which serves occasionally for cleaning out the fire-place and the opening by which the flame passes from the fire-place into the kiln. This opening, which must never be quite closed, serves likewise for admitting a small quantity of air to pass horizontally into the fire-place. A small proportion of air admitted in this manner has been found to be useful, and even necessary, in fire-places in which, in order to consume the smoke, the flame is made to descend. Several small holes for this purpose, fitted with conical stoppers, may be made in different parts of the front wall of the fire-place.

The bottom of the fire-place is a grate constructed of bricks placed edgewise, and under this grate there is an ash-pit; but, as no air must be permitted to pass up through this grate into the fire-place, the ash-pit door, *c*, is kept constantly closed, being only opened occasionally to remove the ashes.

d is the opening by which the lime is taken out of the kiln; which opening must be kept well closed, in order to prevent a draught of cold air through the kiln.

As only as much lime must be removed at once as is contained in that part of the kiln which lies below the level of the bottom of the fire-place, to be able to ascertain when the proper quantity is taken away, the lime as it comes out of the kiln may be directed into a pit sunk in the ground in front of the opening by which the lime is removed, this pit being made of proper size to serve as a measure.

While the lime is removing from the bottom of the kiln, fresh limestone should be put into it above; and during this operation the fire may be damped by closing the top of the fire-place with its iron plate.

Should it be found necessary, the fire and the distribution of the heat may, in burning the lime, be farther regulated by closing more or less the opening at the top of the lime-kiln with a flat piece of fire-stone, or a plate of cast iron.

The double walls of the kiln, and the void space between them, as also the horizontal layers of bricks by which they are united, are clearly and distinctly expressed in the figure. The kiln is represented as being nearly filled with small round stones, such as are used at Munich in burning lime. These stones are brought down from the calcareous mountains on our frontiers, by the river (the Isar), and are rounded by rubbing against each other as they are rolled along by the impetuosity of the torrent.

[This paper is printed from the English edition of Rumford's Essays, Vol. II., pp. 1-196.]

ON THE

CONSTRUCTION OF KITCHEN FIRE-PLACES

AND KITCHEN UTENSILS;

TOGETHER WITH

REMARKS AND OBSERVATIONS RELATING TO THE VARIOUS PROCESSES OF COOKERY,

AND

PROPOSALS FOR IMPROVING THAT MOST USEFUL ART.

ADVERTISEMENT.

ALMOST four years have elapsed since this Essay was announced to the public; and although a considerable part of the manuscript was then ready, yet, from a variety of considerations, I have been induced to defer sending it to the press, and even now the first part only of the Essay is laid before the public.

Among the motives which have operated most powerfully to induce me to postpone the publication of this work was a desire to make it as free of faults as possible, and to accommodate it as much as possible to the actual state of opinions and practices in this country.

In proportion as my exertions to promote useful improvements have been favourably received by the public, and my writings have obtained an extensive circulation, my anxiety has been increased to deserve that confidence which is essential to my success. I feel it to be more and more my duty to proceed slowly, and to use every precaution in investigating the subjects I have undertaken to treat, and in explaining what I recommend, in order that others may not be led into errors, either by mistakes in principle or inaccuracy in description.

I have, indeed, of late seen but too many proofs of the necessity of adopting this cautious method of proceeding.

On my return to England from Bavaria last autumn (1798), after an absence of two years, I was not a little gratified to learn that several improvements recommended in my Essays, and particularly the alterations in the construction of chimney fire-places, that were proposed in my fourth Essay, had been adopted in many places, and that they had in general been found to answer very well; but the satisfaction which this information naturally afforded me has since been, I believe I may say, more than counterbalanced by the pain I have experienced on discovering, on a nearer examination, the numerous mistakes that have been committed by those who have undertaken to put my plans in execution; not to mention the unjustifiable use that has in some instances been made of my name in bringing forward for sale inventions which I never recommended, and of which I never can approve without abandoning all the fundamental principles relative to the combustion of fuel, and the management and direction of heat, which, after a long and patient investigation, I have been induced to adopt.

It would be foolish for me to imagine, and ridiculous to pretend, that the plans I have proposed are so perfect as to be incapable of farther improvement. I am far, very far, from being of that opinion, and I can say with truth that I shall at all times rejoice when farther improvements are made in them; but still I may be permitted to add that it would be a great satisfaction to me if those who, from an opinion of their utility or from a desire to give the experiment a fair trial, should be disposed to adopt any of the plans I have recommended, would take the trouble to examine whether the workmen they employ really understand and are disposed to follow the directions I have given; or whether they are not, perhaps, prepossessed with some favourite contrivance and imaginary improvement of their own; or whether there is no danger of their introducing alterations for the purpose of enhancing the price of their work, or of the articles they furnish.

These are dangers of which those who have the smallest acquaintance with mankind must be perfectly sensible; and it would be unwise, and I had almost said unjust, not to attend to them, at least to a certain degree.

All I ask is that a *fair trial* may be given to the plans I propose, when *any* trial is given them; and this request will not, I trust, be thought unreasonable. And as I never presume to recommend to the public any new invention or improvement that I have not previously and repeatedly tried, and found *by experience* to be useful, it would perhaps be thought excusable were I to express a wish that my proposals might not be condemned nor neglected merely in consequence of the failure of contrivances announced as *improvements* of my plans.

The reader will not be surprised at my extreme anxiety to remove those obstacles which appear to me most powerfully to obstruct and retard the general introduction of the improvements I am labouring to introduce; for anxiety for the success of an undertaking naturally flows from a conviction of its importance, and is always connected with that fervent zeal which important undertakings are so eminently calculated to inspire.

To this second edition of the first part of my tenth Essay I beg leave to add a few words respecting the soup establishments that have lately been formed in London and in other places for feeding the poor.

Many persons in this country are of opinion that a great deal of meat is necessary in order to make a good and wholesome soup; but this is far from being the case in fact. Some of the most savoury and most nourishing soups are made without any meat; and in providing food for the poor it is necessary, on many accounts, to be very sparing in the use of it.

When the poor are fed from a public kitchen, care should be taken to supply them with the cheapest kinds of food, and particularly with such as they can afterwards provide for themselves, at their own dwellings, at a small expense; otherwise the temporary relief that is afforded them in times of scarcity, by selling to them rich and expensive meat soups at reduced prices, will operate as a great and permanent evil to themselves and to society.

The most palatable and the most nourishing soups may, with a little care and ingenuity, be composed with very cheap materials, as has been proved of late by a great number of decisive experiments made upon a large scale in different countries. The soup establishments that have been formed at Hamburg, at Geneva, at Lausanne, and other parts of Switzerland, at Marseilles, and lately at Paris, have all succeeded; and at most of these places the kind of soup that was provided for the poor at Munich has been adopted with but little variation. In some cases a small quantity of salt meat has been used, but this has been merely as a seasoning. The basis of these soups has uniformly been barley, potatoes, and peas or beans; and a small quantity of bread has in all cases been added to the soup when it has been served out.

No ingredient is, in my opinion, so indispensably necessary in the soups that are furnished to the poor as *bread*. It should never be omitted, and certainly not in times of scarcity, because there is no way in which bread will go so far as when it is eaten in soups: for every ounce so used, I am confident that four ounces that would otherwise be eaten by the poor at their homes would be saved. And to this we may add that oaten cakes, and other bread of inferior quality, will answer very well in soups, particularly if it be toasted or fried, and broken or cut into small pieces. If the soup be well seasoned, its taste will predominate, and the taste peculiar to the bread will not be perceived.

A great variety of the most agreeable tastes may be given to soups, at a very small expense; and, if bread be mixed with the soup, mastication will be rendered necessary, and the pleasure that is enjoyed in eating a good meal of it will be greatly prolonged and increased.

It is by no means surprising that prejudices should be strong against soups, in those countries where soups and broths are considered as being merely thin wash, without taste or substance, a pint of which might as easily be swallowed down at a breath as so much water; but these prejudices will vanish when the false impressions which gave rise to them are removed.

Soups may, it is true, be made thick and substantial with meat. But, when this is done, they are neither palatable nor wholesome: they appall and load the stomach, weaken the powers of digestion, and instead of affording wholesome nourishment, strength, and refreshment, are the cause of many disorders. They are, moreover, very expensive. But this is not the case with soups made thick and substantial with farinaceous matter, and other vegetable substances, and seasoned and rendered palatable with salt, pepper, onions, and a little salted herrings, hung beef, bacon, or cheese, and eaten with a due proportion of bread.

I am the more anxious to recall the attention of the public to this subject at the present time, as the utility of the public kitchens for feeding the poor, which have lately been formed, and are now forming in various parts of the kingdom, must depend very much on the choice of the ingredients used in preparing food, and the manner of combining them which is adopted by those who have the direction of these interesting establishments. The share I have had in bringing these establishments into use, the opinion I entertain of their importance to society, and the anxiety I must naturally feel for their success, will, I flatter myself, be considered as a sufficient excuse for my solicitude in watching over their progress, and for the liberty I may take in pointing out any mistakes in the management of them that might tend to bring them into disrepute.

ON THE CONSTRUCTION OF KITCHEN FIRE-PLACES AND KITCHEN UTENSILS.

INTRODUCTION.

IN contriving machinery for any purpose, it is indispensably necessary to be acquainted with the nature of the mechanical operation to be performed; and though the processes of cookery appear to be so simple and easy to be understood, that any attempt to explain and illustrate them might perhaps be thought not only superfluous, but even frivolous, yet when we examine the matter attentively we shall find their investigation to be of serious importance. I say of *serious* importance; for surely those inquiries which lead to improvements by which the providing of *food* may be facilitated are matters of the highest concern to mankind in every state of society.

The process by which food is most commonly prepared for the table — boiling — is so familiar to every one, and its effects are so uniform, and apparently so simple, that few, I believe, have taken the trouble to inquire *how* or in *what manner* those effects are produced; and whether any and what improvements in that branch of cookery are possible. So little has this matter been an object of inquiry, that few, very few indeed, I believe, among the *millions of persons* who for so many ages have been *daily* employed in this process, have ever given themselves the trouble to bestow one serious thought on the subject.

The cook knows, *from experience*, that if his joint of meat be kept a certain time immersed in boiling water it will be *done*, as it is called in the language of the kitchen; but if he be asked *what* is done to it, or *how* or *by what agency* the change it has undergone has been effected, if he understands the question, it is ten to one but he will be embarrassed; if he does not understand it, he will probably answer, without hesitation, that "*the meat is made tender and eatable by being boiled*." Ask him if the boiling of the water be essential to the success of the process, he will answer, "*Without doubt*." Push him a little farther, by asking him whether, *were it possible* to keep the water *equally hot* without boiling, the meat would not be cooked *as soon* and *as well* as if the water were made to boil. Here it is probable that he will make the first step towards acquiring knowledge, *by learning to doubt*.

When you have brought him to see the matter in its true light, and to confess that, *in this view of it*, the subject is new to him, you may then venture to tell him (and to prove to him, if you happen to have a thermometer at hand) that water which *just boils* is as hot as it can possibly be made *in an open vessel*. That all the fuel which is used in making it boil with violence is wasted, without adding a single degree to the heat of the water, or expediting or shortening the process of cooking a single instant. That it is by *the heat*, its *intensity* and the *time of its duration*, that the food is cooked, and not by the *boiling* or *ebullition*, or bubbling up of the water, which has *no part whatever* in that operation.

Should any doubts still remain in his mind with respect to the inefficacy and inutility of boiling, in culinary processes, where *the same degree of heat* may be had and be *kept up* without it, let a piece of meat be cooked in a Papin's digester, which, as is well known, is a boiler whose cover (which is fastened down with screws) shuts with so much nicety that no steam can escape out of it. In such a *closed* vessel, boiling (which is nothing else but the escape of steam in bubbles from the hot liquid) is absolutely impossible; yet, if the heat applied to the digester be such as would cause an equal quantity of water in an open vessel to boil, the meat will not only be *done*, but it will be found to be dressed in a shorter time, and to be much tenderer than if it had been boiled in an open boiler. By applying a still greater degree of heat to the digester, the meat may be so much done in a very few minutes as actually to fall to pieces; and even the very bones may be made soft.

Were it a question of mere idle curiosity, whether it be the *boiling* of water, or simply the *degree of heat* which exists in boiling water, by which food is cooked, it would doubtless be folly to throw away time in its investigation; but this is far from being the case, for *boiling* cannot be carried on without a very great expense of fuel; but any boiling-hot liquid (by using proper means for confining the heat) may be kept *boiling-hot* for any length of time almost without any expense of fuel at all.

The waste of fuel in culinary processes, which arises from making liquids boil *unnecessarily*, or when nothing more would be necessary than to keep them *boiling-hot*, is enormous. I have not a doubt but that much more than half the fuel used in all the kitchens, public and private, in the whole world, is wasted precisely in this manner.

But the evil does not stop here. This unscientific and slovenly manner of cooking renders the process much more laborious and troublesome than otherwise it would be; and (what by many will be considered of more importance than either the waste of fuel or the increase of labour to the cook) the food is rendered less savoury, and very probably less nourishing and less wholesome.

It is natural to suppose that many of the finer and more volatile parts of food (those which are best calculated to act on the organs of taste) must be carried off with the steam when the boiling is violent; but the fact does not rest on these reasonings. It is *proved* to a demonstration, not only by the agreeable fragrance of the steam which rises from vessels in which meat is boiled, but also from the strong flavour and superior quality of soups which are prepared by a long process over a very gentle fire.

In many countries, where soups constitute the principal part of the food of the inhabitants, the process of cooking lasts from one meal-time to another, and is performed almost without either trouble or expense. As soon as the soup is served up, the ingredients for the next meal are put into the pot (which is never suffered to cool, and does not require scouring); and this pot, — which is of cast iron or of earthen-ware, — being well closed with its thick wooden cover, is placed *by the side of the fire*, where its contents are kept simmering for many hours, but are seldom made to boil, and never but in the gentlest manner possible.

Were the pot placed in a closed fire-place (which might easily be constructed, even with the rudest materials, with a few bricks or stone, or even with sods, like a camp-kitchen), no arrangement for cooking could well be imagined more economical or more convenient.

Soups prepared in this way are uncommonly savoury; and I am convinced that the true reason why nourishing soups and broths are not more in use among the common people in Great Britain and Ireland is because they do not know how good they really are, nor how to prepare them; in short, because they are not acquainted with them.

But to return from this digression. It is most certain not only that meat and vegetables of all kinds may be cooked in water which is kept *boiling-hot* without actually boiling, but also that they may even be cooked with a degree of heat *below* the boiling point.

It is well known that the heat of boiling water is not the same in all situations, — that it depends on the pressure of the atmosphere, and consequently is considerably greater at the level of the surface of the sea than inland countries, and on the tops of high mountains; but I never heard that any difficulty was found to attend the process of dressing food by boiling, even in the highest situations. Water boils at London (and at all other places on the same level) at the temperature of 212 degrees of Fahrenheit's thermometer; but it would be absolutely impossible to communicate that degree of heat to water in an open boiler in Bavaria. The boiling-point at Munich, under the mean pressure of the atmosphere at that place, is about $209\frac{1}{2}$ degrees of Fahrenheit's thermometer; yet nobody, I believe, ever perceived that boiled meat was *less thoroughly done* at Munich than at London. But if meat may, without the least difficulty, be cooked with the heat of $209\frac{1}{2}$ degrees of Fahrenheit at Munich, why should it not be possible to cook it with the same degree of heat in London? If this can be done (which I think can hardly admit of a doubt), then it is evident that the process of cookery, which is called *boiling*, may be performed in water which is not boiling-hot.

I well know, from my own experience, how difficult it is to persuade cooks of this truth; but it is so important, that no pains should be spared in endeavouring to remove their prejudices and enlighten their understandings. This may be done most effectually in the case before us by a method I have several times put in practice with complete success. It is as follows: Take two equal boilers, containing equal quantities of *boiling-hot water*, and put into them two equal pieces of meat taken from the same carcass,—two legs of mutton, for instance,—and boil them during the same time. Under one of the boilers make a *small fire*, just barely sufficient to keep the water *boiling-hot*, or rather just *beginning to boil;* under the other make *as vehement a fire as possible*, and keep the water boiling the whole time with the utmost violence.

The meat in the boiler in which the water has been kept *only just boiling-hot* will be found to be quite as well done as that in the other,* under which so much fuel has been wasted in making the water boil violently to no useful purpose. It will even be more done; for, as a great deal of water will be boiled away (evaporated) during the process in the boiler under which a great fire is kept up, this boiler must often be filled up; and, if the water with which it is from time to time replenished be cold, this will of course retard the process of cooking the meat.

* It will even be found to be much better cooked; that is to say, tenderer, more juicy, and much higher flavoured.

To form a just idea of the enormous waste of fuel that arises from making water boil, and *evaporate* unnecessarily in culinary processes, we have only to consider how much heat is expended in the formation of steam. Now it has been proved by the most decisive and unexceptionable experiments that have ever been made by experimental philosophers that, if it were possible that the heat which actually combines with water in forming steam (and which gives it wings to fly up into the atmosphere) could exist in the water without changing it from a dense liquid to a rare elastic vapour, this water would be heated by it to the temperature of red-hot iron.

From the same *data* it is easy to show by computation that, if any given quantity of ice-cold water can be made to boil with the heat generated in the combustion of a certain quantity of any given kind of fuel, it will require more than *five times* that quantity of fuel to reduce that same quantity of water — already boiling-hot — to steam.

Hence it appears that, in the formation of steam, there is a great and unavoidable *expense* of heat; but it does not seem probable that heat is *expended* or *combined* in any of those processes by which food is prepared for the table, except it be, perhaps, in baking; and as heat is *immortal*, — that is to say, as it never dies or ceases to exist, and as its dispersion may be prevented, or at least greatly *retarded*, by various simple contrivances, — it is not surprising, when we consider the matter attentively, that most of those processes (in which nothing more seems to be necessary than that the food to be cooked should be exposed a certain time in a medium at a certain temperature) should be capable of being performed with *a very small expense of fuel.*

The quantity of heat, or rather the quantity of fuel, by which any given culinary process may be performed, may be determined with much certainty and precision from the results of experiments which have already been made.

Suppose, for instance, it were required to compute the quantity of dry pine-wood (what, in England, is called deal) used as fuel, and burned in a closed fire-place, constructed on the most approved principles, to boil 100 lbs. of beef. And, first, we will suppose this beef to be in such large pieces that 3 hours of boiling, after it has been made boiling-hot, are necessary to make it sufficiently tender to be fit for the table; and we will suppose, farther, that 3 lbs. of water are necessary to each pound of beef, and that both the water and the beef are at the temperature of 55° of Fahrenheit's thermometer (the mean temperature of the atmosphere in England) at the beginning of the experiment.

The first thing to be ascertained is how much fuel would be required to heat the water and the beef *boiling-hot*; and then to see how much more would be required to *keep them boiling-hot* three hours.

And, first, for *heating the water*. It has been shown by one of my experiments (No. 20, see page 81) that $20\frac{1}{5}$ lbs. of water may be heated 180 degrees of Fahrenheit's thermometer with the heat generated in the combustion of 1 lb. of dry pine-wood.

But it is required to heat the water in question only 157 degrees; for its temperature being that of 55°, and the boiling-point 212°, it is 212° − 55° = 157°; and if 1 lb. of the fuel be sufficient for heating $20\frac{1}{5}$ lbs. of

Fire-places and Kitchen Utensils. 183

water 180 degrees, it must be sufficient for heating 23 lbs. of water 157 degrees, for 157° is to 180° as 20$\frac{1}{6}$ lbs. to 23 lbs.

But if 23 lbs. of water, at the temperature of 55°, require 1 lb. of dry pine-wood, as fuel, to make it boil, then 300 lbs. of water (the quantity required in the process in question) would require 12$\frac{6}{6}$ lbs. of the wood to heat it boiling-hot.

To this quantity of fuel must be added that which would be required to heat the meat (100 lbs. weight) boiling-hot. Now it has been found by actual experiment by the late ingenious Doctor Crawford (see his Treatise on Animal Heat, second edition, page 490) that the flesh of an ox requires less heat to heat it than water, in the proportion of 74 to 100; consequently the quantity of beef in question (100 lbs.) might be made boiling-hot with precisely the same quantity of fuel as would be required to heat 74 lbs. of water at the same temperature to the boiling-point. And this quantity in the case in question would amount to 3$\frac{1}{4}$ lbs., as will be found on making the computation.

This quantity (3$\frac{1}{4}$ lbs.) added to that before found, which would be required to heat the water alone (= 23 lbs.), gives 26$\frac{1}{4}$ lbs. of dry pine-wood for the quantity required to heat 300 lbs. of water and 100 lbs. beef (both at the temperature of 55°) boiling-hot.

To estimate the quantity of fuel which would be necessary to keep this water and beef boiling-hot 3 hours, we may have recourse to the results of my experiments. In the Experiment No. 25 (see page 83), 508 lbs. of boiling-hot water were kept actually boiling — not merely kept boiling-hot — 3 hours with the heat generated in the combustion of 4$\frac{1}{2}$ lbs. of dry pine-wood:

this gives 338¼ lbs. of boiling-hot water kept boiling 1 hour with 1 lb. of the fuel; and computing from these data, and supposing, farther, that a pound of beef requires as much heat to keep it boiling-hot any given time as a pound of water, it appears that 3⅜ lbs. of pine-wood, used as fuel, would be sufficient to keep the 300 lbs. of water, with the 100 lbs. of beef in it, boiling 3 hours. This quantity of fuel (= 3⅜ lbs.), added to that required to heat the water and the meat boiling-hot (= 26¼ lbs.), gives 29⅝ lbs. of pine-wood for the quantity of fuel required to cook 100 lbs. of boiled beef.

This quantity of fuel, which is just about equal in effect to 16 lbs., or ⅘ of a peck of pit-coal, will doubtless be thought a small allowance for boiling 100 lbs. of beef; but it is in fact much more than would be necessary *merely for that purpose*, could all the heat generated in the combustion of the fuel be applied *immediately* to the cooking of the meat, and *to that purpose alone*. Much the greatest part of that which is generated is expended in heating the water in which the meat is boiled, and as it remains in the water after the process is ended it must be considered as lost.

This loss may, however, be prevented in a great measure; and, when that is done, the expense of fuel in boiling meat will be reduced almost to nothing. We have just seen that 100 lbs. of meat, at the mean temperature of the atmosphere in England (55°), may be made boiling-hot with the heat generated in the combustion of 3¼ lbs. of pine-wood; and there is no doubt but, with the use of proper means for confining the heat, this meat might be kept boiling-hot 3 hours, and consequently be thoroughly done, with the addition of ⅞ of a pound of the fuel, making in all 4 lbs. of pine-wood, equal in effect to about 2¼ lbs. of pit-coal; which, according to this estimate, is all the fuel that would be *absolutely necessary* for cooking 100 lbs. of beef.

This quantity of fuel would cost in London less than *one farthing and a half*, when the chaldron of coals weighing 28 cwt. is sold at 40 shillings. This, however, is the *extreme* or *utmost limit* of the economy of fuel, beyond which it is absolutely impossible to go. It is even impossible, in practice, to arrive at this limit, for the containing vessel must be heated, and kept hot, as well as the meat; but very considerable advances may be made towards it, as I shall show hereafter.

If we suppose the meat to be boiled in the usual manner, and that 300 lbs. of cold water are heated expressly for that purpose, in that case the fuel required, amounting to 16 lbs. of coal, would cost in London (the chaldron reckoned as above) just 2 *pence* 1¾ *farthings*. But all this expense ought not to be placed to the account of the cooking of the meat. By adding a few pounds of barley meal, some greens, roots, and seasoning to the water, it may be changed into a good and wholesome soup, at the same time that the meat is boiled; and the expense for fuel (2 pence 1¾ farthings) may be divided between the meat boiled (100 lbs.) and 300 lbs., or 37½ gallons, of soup.

I am aware of the danger to which I expose myself by entertaining the public with accounts of facts, and of deductions from them, which are certainly much too new and extraordinary to be credited but on the strongest proofs, while many of the arguments and computations I offer in their support — however conclusive they may, and certainly *must*, appear to natural philosophers and mathematicians — are such as the generality of readers will be tempted to pass over without examination; but, deeply impressed with the importance of the object I have in view, I am determined to pursue it at all hazards.

My principal design in publishing these computations is to *awaken the curiosity of my readers*, and fix their attention on a subject which, however low and vulgar it has hitherto generally been thought to be, is in fact highly interesting, and deserving of the most serious consideration. I wish they may serve to inspire cooks with a just idea of the importance of their art, and of the intimate connection there is between the various processes in which they are daily concerned, and many of the most beautiful discoveries that have been made by experimental philosophers in the present age.

The advantage that would result from an application of the late brilliant discoveries in philosophical chemistry, and other branches of natural philosophy and mechanics, to the improvement of the art of cookery, are so evident and so very important that I cannot help flattering myself that we shall soon see some enlightened and liberal-minded person of the profession take up the matter in earnest, and give it a thoroughly *scientific* investigation.

In what art or science could improvements be made that would more powerfully contribute to increase the comforts and enjoyments of mankind?

And it must not be imagined that the saving of fuel is the only or even the most important advantage that would result from these inquiries: others of still greater magnitude, respecting the *manner* of preparing food for the table, would probably be derived from them.

The heat of boiling water, continued for a shorter or a longer time, having been found by experience to be sufficient for cooking all those kinds of animal and vegetable substances that are commonly used as food; and *that degree* of heat being easily procured, and easily kept up, in all places and in all seasons; and as all the utensils used in cookery are contrived for that kind of heat, few experiments have been made to determine the effects of using *other degrees of heat*, and *other mediums* for conveying it to the substance to be acted upon in culinary processes. The effects of different degrees of heat in the same body are, however, sometimes very striking; and the taste of the same kind of food is often so much altered by a trifling difference in the manner of cooking it, that it would no longer be taken for the same thing. What a surprising difference, for instance, does the manner of performing that most simple of all culinary processes, *boiling in water*, make on potatoes! Those who have never tasted potatoes *boiled in Ireland*, or cooked according to the Irish method, can have no idea what delicious food these roots afford when they are properly prepared. But it is not merely the *taste* of food that depends on the manner of cooking it: its nutritiousness also, and its wholesomeness, — qualities still more essential if possible than taste, — are, no doubt, very nearly connected with it.

Many kinds of food are known to be most delicate and savoury when cooked in a degree of heat considerably below that of boiling water; and it is more than probable that there are others which would be improved by being exposed in a heat greater than that of boiling water.

In the seaport towns of the New England States in North America, it has been a custom, time immemorial, among people of fashion, to dine one day in the week (Saturday) on *salt-fish;* and a long habit of preparing the same dish has, as might have been expected, led to very considerable improvements in the art of cooking it. I have often heard foreigners, who have assisted at these dinners, declare that they never tasted salt-fish dressed in such perfection; and I well remember that the secret of cooking it is to keep it a great many hours in water that is *just scalding-hot*, but which is never made actually to boil.

I had long suspected that it could hardly be possible that *precisely* the temperature of 212 degrees of Fahrenheit's thermometer (that of boiling water) should be that which is best adapted for cooking *all sorts of food;* but it was the unexpected result of an experiment that I made with another view which made me particularly attentive to this subject. Desirous of finding out whether it would be possible to roast meat in a machine I had contrived for drying potatoes, and fitted up in the kitchen of the House of Industry at Munich, I put a shoulder of mutton into it, and after attending to the experiment three hours, and finding it showed no signs of being done, I concluded that the heat was not sufficiently intense; and, despairing of success, I went home rather out of humour at my ill success, and abandoned my shoulder of mutton to the cook-maids.

It being late in the evening, and the cook-maids thinking, perhaps, that the meat would be as safe in the drying-machine as anywhere else, left it there all night. When they came in the morning to take it away, intending to cook it for their dinner, they were much surprised to find it *already cooked*, and not merely eatable, but perfectly done, and most singularly well-tasted. This appeared to them the more miraculous, as the fire under the machine was gone quite out before they left the kitchen in the evening to go to bed, and as they had locked up the kitchen when they left it and taken away the key.

This wonderful shoulder of mutton was immediately brought to me in triumph, and though I was at no great loss to account for what had happened, yet it certainly was quite unexpected; and when I tasted the meat I was very much surprised indeed to find it very different, both in taste and flavour, from any I had ever tasted. It was perfectly tender; but, though it was so much done, it did not appear to be in the least sodden or insipid, — on the contrary, it was uncommonly savoury and high flavoured. It was neither boiled nor roasted nor baked. Its taste seemed to indicate the manner in which it had been prepared; that the gentle heat, to which it had for so long a time been exposed, had by degrees loosened the cohesion of its fibres, and concocted its juices, without driving off their fine and more volatile parts, and without washing away or burning and rendering rancid and empyreumatic its oils.

Those who are most likely to give their attention to this little history will perceive what a wide field it opens for speculation and curious experiment. The circumstances I have related, however trifling and uninteresting they may appear to many, struck me very forcibly, and recalled to my mind several things of a similar nature which had almost escaped my memory. They recalled to my recollection the manner just described in which salt-fish is cooked in America; and also the manner in which *samp* is prepared in the same country. (See my Essay on Food.) This substance, which is exceedingly palatable and nourishing food when properly cooked, *is not eatable* when simply boiled. How many cheap articles may there be of which the most delicate and wholesome food might be prepared, were the art and the *science* of cooking them better understood. But I beg my reader's pardon for detaining him so long with speculations which he may perhaps consider as foreign to the subject I promised to treat in this Essay. To proceed, therefore, to those investigations which are more immediately connected with the construction of kitchen fire-places.

PART I.

CHAPTER I.

Of the Imperfections of the Kitchen Fire-places now in common Use.—Objects particularly to be had in View in Attempts to improve them.—Of the Distribution of the various Parts of the Machinery of a Kitchen.—Of the Method to be observed in forming the Plan of a Kitchen that is to be fitted up, and in laying out the Work.

AS the principal object of this publication is to convey such plain and simple directions for constructing kitchen fire-places and kitchen utensils as may easily be understood, even by those who are not versed in philosophical inquiries, and who have not had leisure to examine scientifically the principles on which the proposed improvements are founded, I shall endeavour, in treating the subject, to make use of the plainest language, and to avoid as much as possible all abstruse and difficult investigation.

It will be proper to begin by taking a cursory view of kitchen fire-places, as they are now commonly constructed, and to point out their defects, and show what the objects are which ought principally to be had in view in attempts to improve them.

Of the Imperfections of the Kitchen Fire-places now in common Use.

The great fault in the construction and arrangement of the kitchens of private families now in common use in most countries, and particularly in Great Britain and Ireland (a fault from which all their other imperfections arise), is that they are not *closed*. The fuel is burned in a long open grate called a *kitchen range*, over which the pots and kettles are freely suspended, or placed on stands; or fires are made with charcoal in square holes, called *stoves* in a solid mass of brick-work, and connected with no flue to carry off the smoke, over which holes stewpans or saucepans are placed on tripods, or on bars of iron, exposed on every side to the cold air of the atmosphere.

The loss of heat and waste of fuel in these kitchens is altogether incredible; but there are other evils attending them, which are, perhaps, still more important. All the various processes in which fire is used in preparing food for the table are extremely unpleasant and troublesome in these kitchens, not only on account of the excessive heat to which those are exposed who are employed in them, but also and more especially on account of the *noxious exhalations* from the burning charcoal, and the *currents of cold air* in the kitchen, which are occasioned by the strong draught up the chimney.

It is sufficient to have once been in a kitchen when dinner was preparing for a large company, or even merely to have met the cook coming sweltering out of it, to be convinced that the business of cooking, as it is now performed, is both disagreeable and unwholesome;

and it appears to me that it would be no small addition to the enjoyments of those who are fond of the pleasures of the table to know that they were procured with less trouble and with less injury to the health of those who are employed in preparing them.

Another inconvenience attending open chimney fireplaces, as they are now constructed, is the great difficulty of preventing their smoking. In order that there may be room for all the pots and kettles which are placed over the fire, the grate, or *kitchen range*, as it is called, must be very long; and in order that the cook may be able to approach these pots, etc., the mantel of the chimney is made very high: consequently the throat of the chimney is not only enormously large, but it is situated very high above the burning fuel, both of which circumstances tend very much to make a chimney smoke, as I have shown in my Essay on Open Chimney Fire-places; and there does not appear to be any effectual remedy for the evil, without altering entirely the construction of such fire-places.

Of the Objects particularly to be had in View in Attempts to improve Kitchen Fire-places.

The objects which ought principally to be attended to in the arrangement of a kitchen are the following: —

1*st*, Each boiler, kettle, and stewpan should have its separate closed fire-place.

2*dly*, Each fire-place should have its grate, on which the fuel must be placed, and its separate ash-pit, which must be closed by a door well fitted to its frame, and furnished with a register for regulating the quantity of air admitted into the fire-place through the grate. It should also have its separate canal for carrying off the smoke into the chimney, which canal should be furnished with a damper. By means of this damper and of the ash-pit door register, the rapidity of the combustion of the fuel in the fire-place, and consequently the rapidity of the generation of the heat, may be regulated at pleasure. The economy of fuel will depend principally on the proper management of these two registers.

3*dly*, In the fire-places for all boilers and stewpans which are more than 8 or 10 inches in diameter, or which are too large to be easily removed with their contents *with the strength of one hand*, a horizontal opening just above the level of the grate must be made for introducing the fuel into the fire-place, which opening must be nicely closed by a fit stopper or by a double door. In the fire-places which are constructed for smaller stewpans this opening may be omitted, and the fuel may be introduced through the same opening into which the stewpan is fitted, by removing the stewpan occasionally for a moment for that purpose.

4*thly*, All portable boilers and stewpans, and especially such as must often be removed from their fire-places, should be circular, and they should be suspended in their fire-places by their circular rims; but the best form for all fixed boilers, and especially such as are very large, is that of an oblong square, and all boilers, great and small, should rather be broad and shallow than narrow and deep.

A circular form is best for portable boilers, on account of the facility of fitting them to their fire-places; and an oblong square form is best for large fixed boilers, on account of the facility of constructing and repairing the straight horizontal flues under them and round them, in which the flame and smoke by which they are heated are made to circulate.

When large boilers are shallow, and when their bottoms are supported on the tops of narrow flues, the pressure or weight of their contents being supported by the walls of the flues, the metal of which the boiler is constructed may be very thin, which will not only diminish very much the first cost of the boiler, but will also greatly contribute to its durability; for the thinner the bottom of a boiler is, the less it is fatigued and injured by the action of the fire, and the longer, of course, it will last; which is a curious fact, that has hitherto been too little known, or not enough attended to, in the construction of large boilers.

5*thly*, All boilers, great and small, should be furnished with covers, which covers should be constructed in such a manner and of such materials as to render them well adapted for confining heat. Those who have never examined the matter with attention would be astonished on making the experiment to find how much heat is carried off by the cold air of the atmosphere from the surface of hot liquids, when they are exposed naked to it, in boilers without covers. But in culinary processes it is not merely the loss of heat which is to be considered: a great proportion of the finer and more rich and savoury particles of the food are also carried off at the same time, and lost, which renders it an object of serious importance to apply an effectual remedy to this evil.

As heat makes its way through wood with great difficulty, and very slowly, there would perhaps be no substance better adapted for constructing covers for boilers than it, were it not for the perpetual changes in its form and dimensions which are occasioned by alternate changes of dryness and moisture; but these alterations are so considerable, and their effects so difficult to be counteracted, especially when the form of the cover is circular, that, for portable boilers and for stewpans and saucepans, I should prefer covers made of thin sheets of tinned iron, or of tin, as it is commonly called. These covers (which must always be made double) have already been particularly described in my sixth Essay.

Though boilers and stewpans should never be used naked over an open fire, or otherwise than in closed fire-places, yet it is not necessary in fitting up a kitchen to build as many separate fire-places as it may be proper to have boilers, stewpans, and saucepans; for the same fire-place may be made to serve occasionally for several boilers or stewpans. Those, however, that are used in the same closed fire-place must be all of the same diameter; and, in order that their capacities may be different, they may be made of different depths.

As, in the hurry of business in the kitchen, one stewpan or boiler might easily be taken for another, were their diameters to vary by only a small difference, and were they not distinguished by marks or numbers, — to prevent these mistakes, their diameters, expressed in inches, should be marked on some conspicuous part, — on their handles for instance, or on their brims, and also on their covers; and their fire-places should be marked with the same number.

To guard still more effectually against all mistakes respecting the sizes of these utensils, and the fire-places to which they belong, the difference of the diameters of two boilers or stewpans should never be less than one whole inch. In several private kitchens that have been constructed on my principles, their diameters have been made to vary by two inches, — that is to say, they have been made of 6, 8, 10, 12, and 14 inches in diameter; and, in order that those of the same diameter might be of different capacities, they were made of three different depths, namely, ¼, ½, and ¾ their diameter in depth. Not only the numbers which show their diameters, but the fractions also which express their depths, are marked on their handles, or on their brims.

The size of a private kitchen, or the number and size of its separate closed fire-places, and of its boilers and stewpans, must be regulated by the size of the family, or rather by the style of living; for, where sumptuous entertainments are occasionally provided for large companies, the kitchen must be spacious and its arrangement complete, however small the family may be, or however moderate the expenses of their table may be in their ordinary course of living in private.

Yet when kitchens are fitted up on the principles I am desirous of recommending, neither the size of the kitchen, nor the number or dimensions of its utensils, will occasion any addition to the table expenses of the family in their ordinary course of living when they have no company, which is an important advantage that these kitchens have over those on the common construction.

In large kitchens with open fire-places, the kitchen range being wide and very roomy, an enormous quantity of fuel is swallowed up by it, even when only a very small quantity of food is provided; but this unnecessary waste is completely prevented by cooking in boilers and stewpans properly fitted into separate closed fire-places.

More fuel is frequently consumed in a kitchen range to boil a tea-kettle than, with proper management, would be sufficient to cook a dinner for fifty men.

Of the Distribution of the various Parts of the Machinery of a Kitchen.

Though the internal construction of the fire-places, and the means employed for confining and directing the heat generated in the combustion of the fuel (subjects which have been thoroughly investigated in my sixth Essay), are matters of the first concern in the fitting up of a kitchen, yet these are not all that require attention. The distribution of the various parts of the machinery is a matter of considerable importance, for a good arrangement of the different instruments and utensils — of the boilers, ovens, roasters, etc. — will tend very much to facilitate the business of cooking, and consequently *to put the cook in good humour*, which is certainly a matter of serious importance.

Cooks in general are averse to all new inventions, and this is not surprising, and ought by no means to be imputed to them as a fault. Accustomed *to work with their own tools*, they naturally feel awkward and embarrassed when others are put into their hands; and to this we may add that there is always a degree of humiliation felt by those who, after having been accustomed to consider themselves, and to be considered by others, as masters of their profession, are required to learn any thing new, or to do any thing in any other manner than that in which they have always been accustomed to do it, and in the performance of which they have always acquired praise. It will not, however, be difficult to convince those of the profession who are possessed of a good understanding, and are above low and vulgar prejudices, that the alterations proposed will most certainly meet with their approbation *when they become better acquainted with them.*

The distribution of the parts of a kitchen must always depend so much on local circumstances that general rules can hardly be given respecting it: the principles, however, on which this distribution ought in all cases to be made — viz., convenience to the cook, cleanliness, and symmetry — are simple, and easy to be understood; and, in the application of them, the architect will have a good opportunity of displaying his ingenuity and showing his taste.

Should he condescend to consult the cook in making these arrangements, he will do wisely, on more accounts than one.

Though the smoke from the fire-places of the boilers may be conveyed almost to any distance in horizontal canals, yet it will in most cases be advisable to place the boilers near the chimney; and it will in general, though not always, be best to place them all in one range, or rather in one mass of brick-work.

Of the Method of forming a Plan of a Kitchen that is to be fitted up, and of laying out the Work.

Before the plan of a kitchen which it is intended to fit up is made, an exact plan must be procured of the room in which it is to be constructed, in which plan all the doors and windows must be distinctly marked, and also the fire-place, if there be one in the room, and the chimney. The number and the dimensions must likewise be known of all the boilers and saucepans which are to be fitted up in the brick-work.

The readiest way of proceeding in making a plan or drawing of the machinery of a kitchen is to form it on the plan of the room; and in doing this the work will be much facilitated by the following very simple contrivance.

Cut out of thick pasteboard detached pieces to represent the boilers, saucepans, roasters, ovens, etc., which are to be fitted up in the brick-work, and placing these in different ways on the plan of the room, see in what manner they can best be disposed or arranged. As these models (which must be drawn to the same scale as that used in drawing the plan of the room) may be moved about at pleasure, and placed in an infinite variety of different positions in regard to each other, and to the different parts of the room; the effect of any proposed arrangement may be tried in a few moments, in a very satisfactory manner, without expense, and almost without any trouble.

To facilitate still more these preliminary trials with these models of the boilers, etc., several slips of pasteboard, equal in width to the distance at which one boiler ought to be placed from the other in the brick-work, measured on the scale of the plan, should be provided and used in placing the models of the boilers at proper distances from each other. This distance in fitting up or setting kitchen boilers and saucepans I have commonly taken at the width of a brick, or $4\frac{1}{2}$ inches; and I have allowed the same space ($4\frac{1}{2}$ inches) for the distance of the side of the boiler from the outside or front of the mass of the brick-work in which it is set. When this point is settled (that respecting the distance which should be left between the boilers), the arranging of the pasteboard models of the boilers on the plan will be perfectly easy.

As soon as the distribution of the various boilers,

etc., is finally settled, a ground plan of the whole of the machinery should be traced on the plan of the room; and a sufficient number of sections and elevations should be drawn to show the situations, forms, and dimensions of the fire-places, and of all the other parts of the apparatus.

When this is done, and when the boilers and the materials for building are provided, and every thing else that can be wanted in fitting up the kitchen is in readiness, the architect or amateur may proceed to the laying out of the work.

As this will not be found to be difficult, and as it is really a most amusing occupation, I cannot help recommending it very earnestly to gentlemen, and even to ladies, to superintend and direct these works.

I don't know what opinion others may entertain of these amusements, but with regard to myself I own that I know of nothing more interesting than the planning and executing of machinery, by which the powers of Nature are made subservient to my views, by which the very elements are bound as it were in chains, and made to obey my despotic commands; and not my commands alone, but those of all the human race, to whose necessities and comforts they are made the faithful and obedient ministers.

The first thing to be done in laying out the work when a kitchen is to be fitted up is to draw with red or white chalk, or with a coal, a ground plan of the brickwork, of the full size, on the floor or pavement of the room. When the kitchen is neither paved nor floored, this drawing must, of course, be made on the ground. In this drawing, the ash-pits and the passages leading to them must be marked; and, when the ash-pit is to be sunk into the ground, that is the first thing that must be executed.

As soon as this ground plan is sketched out, the ash-pit doors should all be placed, and the foundations of the brick-work laid.

To assist the bricklayer, and prevent his making mistakes, several sections of the brick-work of the full size, and particularly sections of all the boilers, represented as fixed in their fire-places, should be drawn on wide boards, or on very large sheets of paper, or they may be drawn with charcoal or red chalk on the sides of the room. These sections of the full size, where the bricklayer can readily take measure of the various parts of the work to be performed, will be found very useful.

Before I proceed to give a more particular and minute description of the various kitchen utensils and other machinery which will be recommended, I shall lay before my reader an account, illustrated by drawings, of several complete kitchens that have already been constructed under my direction. I have been induced to adopt this method in treating my subject, from an opinion that the directions which still remain to be given respecting the construction of kitchen fire-places and of kitchen utensils will more easily be understood when a general idea shall have been formed of some of those kitchens which have already been constructed on the principles recommended.

PLATE VII.

Fig. 1.

CHAPTER II.

Detailed Accounts, illustrated by correct Plans, of various Kitchens, public and private, that have already been constructed on the Author's Principles, and under his immediate Direction.

ONE of the most complete kitchens I have ever yet caused to be constructed is, in my opinion, that belonging to Baron de Lerchenfeld at Munich, and although its general form and the distribution of the machinery are very different from any thing that has been seen in this country,—so different that I should, perhaps, doubt whether it would be prudent at the first outset to recommend their adoption and exact imitation,—yet as this kitchen has been found to answer remarkably well,—even to the entire satisfaction of the cook, who began, however, by entering his formal protest against it,—I have thought it right to lay the following description of it before my readers. Those who are alarmed at the novelty of its appearance will be so good as to recollect that much may be done, as will hereafter be shown, by way of accommodating the plan to the idea of those to whom it is too new not to appear extraordinary and uncouth.

Description of a Kitchen in the House of Baron de Lerchenfeld at Munich.

PLATE VII.

Fig. 1. This plate shows a perspective view of the kitchen fire-place seen nearly in front. The mass of brick-work in which the boilers and saucepans are set projects out into the room, and the smoke is carried off by flues that are concealed in this mass of brick-work, and in the thick walls of an open chimney fire-place which, standing on it, on the farther side of it, where it joins to the side of the room, is built up perpendicularly to the ceiling of the room. At the height of about 12 or 15 inches above the level of the mantel of this open chimney fire-place, the separate canals for the smoke concealed in its walls end in the larger canal of this fire-place, which last-mentioned larger canal, sloping backwards, ends in a neighbouring chimney which carries off the smoke through the roof of the house into the atmosphere.

A horizontal section of this open chimney fire-place, at the level of the upper surface of the mass of brick-work on which it stands, may be seen Plate IX., Fig. 5. In this section the vertical canals are distinctly marked, which carry off the smoke from the boilers into the chimney, as also the stoppers which are occasionally taken away to remove the soot, when these canals are cleaned. These stoppers, which are made of earthenware burnt like a brick or tile, are 8 inches long, 6 inches wide, and 3 inches thick, and on their outsides they have two deep grooves that form a kind of handle for taking hold of them. When they are fixed in their places, their joinings with the door-way into which they are fitted are made tight by filling up the crevices with moist clay. The canals are cleaned by means of a strong cylindrical brush, made of hogs' bristles fixed to a long flexible handle of twisted iron wire.

The open chimney fire-place was constructed in order that an open fire might be made on its hearth (which, as appears by the plan, is on a level with or is a continuation of the top or upper surface of the mass of brick-work in which the boilers are set), should any such fire be wanted; but the fact is that, although this kitchen has been in daily use more than five years, it has not yet been found necessary to light a fire in this place. When any thing is to be fried or broiled, the cook finds it very convenient to perform these processes of cookery over the two large stoves that are placed in the front of this open fire-place, as the disagreeable vapour that rises from the frying-pan or from the gridiron goes off immediately by the open chimney; and these stoves serve likewise occasionally for warming heaters for ironing, and also for burning wood to obtain live coals for warming beds, or for keeping up a small fire for boiling a tea-kettle, or for warming any thing that is wanted in the family. When this fire is not wanted, the register in the ash-pit door is nearly closed, and the top of the stove is covered with a fit cover of earthen-ware, by which means the fire is kept alive for a great length of time, almost without any consumption of fuel; and may at any time be revived and made to burn briskly in less than half a minute, merely by admitting a larger current of fresh air.

The convenience in a family of being able to have a brisk fire in the kitchen in a moment, when wanted, and to check the combustion in an instant, without extinguishing the fire, and without even cooling the fire-place, when the fire is no longer wanted, can hardly be conceived by those who have not been used to any other methods of making and keeping up kitchen fires than those commonly used in the kitchens in Great Britain.

It will certainly be confessed that neither science nor art has done much either for saving labour or for saving expense, either for convenience, comfort, cleanliness, or economy in the invention and management of a *kitchen range*.

Before I proceed to explain more minutely the different parts of this kitchen, it may be useful to give a general idea of the whole of it, taken together.

PLATE VIII.

Fig. 2. This figure shows a front view, or, more strictly speaking, an elevation of this kitchen. In this plan the ash-pit doors with their registers are distinctly seen; and also the ends of the earthen stoppers which close the openings into the fire-places* of four of the principal boilers. The covers of the principal boilers,† as also of several of the stewpans, are seen above the level of the upper surface of the mass of brick-work.

The height of this mass of brick-work, *a b*, measured from the floor or pavement of the kitchen, is just 3 feet.

Fig. 3. This figure shows a horizontal section of the mass of brick-work in which the boilers, etc., are set, taken at the level of the horizontal flues, that carry off the smoke from the boilers, stewpans, and saucepans, into the vertical canals which convey it into the chimney.

The smoke from three of the principal boilers, situated on the left hand, is carried by separate canals to a circular cavity, over which a large shallow boiler is placed, in which water is heated (by this smoke) for the use of the kitchen, and more especially for washing the plates and

---

* For a particular account of these stoppers, see pp. 26-158, and Plate I., Figs. 6, 7, and 8.

† For an account of these covers, see pp. 15-157, and Plate I, Figs. 1 and 2.

Fig. 2. PLATE VIII.

Fig. 3.

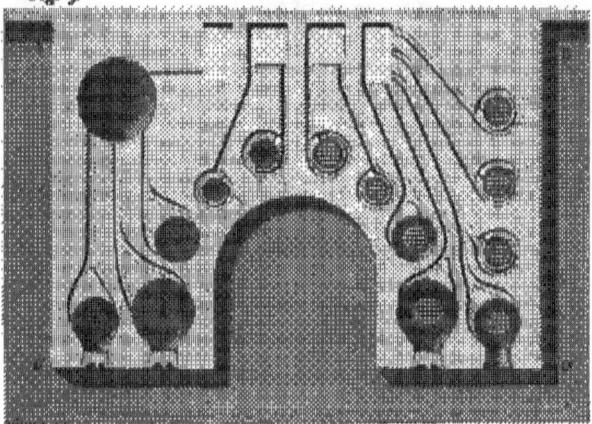

Scale 40 inches to the inch.

dishes. This boiler is distinctly seen with its wooden cover (consisting of three pieces of deal united by two pairs of hinges) in the Fig. 5, Plate IX.

The five fire-places on the left-hand side of the mass of brick-work are represented without their circular grates, and the eight fire-places that are situated on the right hand are shown with their circular grates in their places.[*]

The fire-places of the four largest boilers, which are situated in front of the brick-work, have doors or openings, closed with stoppers, for introducing fuel into these fire-places, and three of these openings are represented in the plan as being closed by their stoppers; while the fourth (that situated on the right hand) is shown open, or without its stopper.

As all the rest of the fire-places (or stoves, as they would be called in this country) are without any lateral opening for introducing the fuel, when any fuel is to be introduced into one of these fire-places, the stewpan or saucepan must be removed for a moment for that purpose.

It will be observed that several of the horizontal canals that carry off the smoke from the boilers are divided into two branches, which unite at a little distance from their fire-places. This contrivance is very useful, especially for closed fire-places that are without flues under the boilers, as it occasions the flame to divide under the bottom of the boiler, and to play over every part of it in a thin sheet.

The reason why flues were not made under these boilers was to render it possible to use occasionally

---

[*] For a particular account of these circular grates, see pp. 35-157, and Plate I., Figs. 3 and 4. In Great Britain these grates may be made very cheap of cast iron.

several boilers of different depths in the same fire-place; a convenience of no small importance in the kitchen of a private gentleman, who occasionally gives dinners to large companies.

It will be perceived that, in the fire-places of all the stewpans and saucepans, there are circular flues which oblige the flame to make one complete turn round the sides of the vessel, before it goes off into the horizontal canal; but I am far from being sure that the saving of fuel arising from this peculiar arrangement is sufficient to counterbalance the loss of that great convenience that results from being able to use indifferently stewpans and saucepans of different depths in the same stove, which cannot be obtained while these circular flues remain.

They will, indeed, be rendered unnecessary, provided that the flame be made to divide under the bottom of the vessel (which may be done by causing it to enter the horizontal canal by two opposite openings), and provided that this canal be furnished with a good damper, *which ought never to be omitted*. Although, to avoid the confusion that is apt to result from the delineation of a multitude of different objects in the same drawing, the dampers to the canals are all omitted in these plans, they must on no account be left out in practice, for they are of such importance that there is no possibility of managing fires properly without them; and as it is of very little importance whether they be placed near the fire or far from it, or what is their form, provided they be so constructed as to diminish at pleasure, and occasionally to close entirely the canal by which the smoke makes its escape, it is not necessary for me to give any particular directions how they are to be made; indeed, their construction is so very simple, and so

Fig. 4. PLATE IX.

Fig. 5.

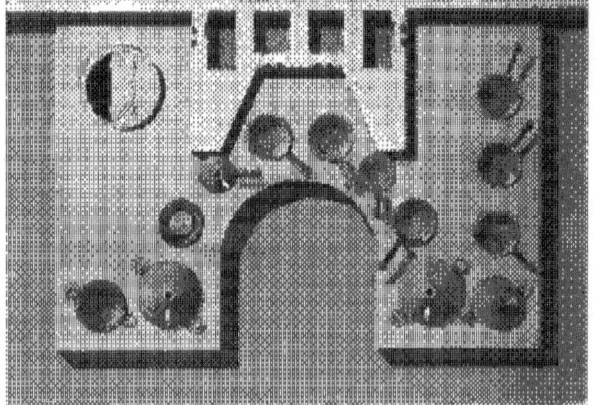

generally known, that it would be quite superfluous for me to enlarge on that subject.

The dotted lines leading from the front of the brick-work to the fire-places show the position and dimensions of the ash-pits.

The whole length of the mass of brick-work from A to B is 11 feet, and its width from A to C is 7 feet 4 inches. The space it occupies on the ground may be conceived to consist of six equal squares of 44 inches each, placed in two rows of three squares each; these two rows being joined to each other by their sides, and forming together a parallelogram. And, in laying out the work when a kitchen is to be fitted up on the plan here described, it will always be best to begin by actually drawing these six squares on the floor of the kitchen. Nearly the whole of the middle square of the back row is occupied by the open chimney fire-place, and by its thick hollow walls; and the greater part of the middle square of the front row is left as a passage for the cook to come to the open chimney fire-place, or rather to the stoves that are situated near it.

PLATE IX.

Fig. 4. This figure, which represents a vertical section of the mass of brick-work through the centres of the fire-places of the four principal boilers, is chiefly designed to show the construction of those fire-places, and also that of the boilers. Sections of the circular grates on which the fires are made to burn under the boilers are here represented, and also sections of the ash-pits, and of the contractions of the fire-places immediately below the grates;*

* For an account of the utility of these contractions, see page 37.

and in one of the fire-places, which is shown without its boiler, the openings of the branched canal by which the smoke goes off horizontally towards the chimney are also marked.

Fig. 5. This figure shows a bird's-eye view of the upper surface of the brick-work, with all the boilers and saucepans in their places, except one; three of the principal boilers and one saucepan with their covers on; and the rest of them without their covers. It likewise represents a horizontal section of the open chimney fire-place, 4 inches above the level of the top of the mass of brick-work in which the boilers and saucepans are set.

It is to be observed that all the boilers, stewpans, and saucepans are fitted into circular rings of iron, which are firmly fixed to the brick-work; and that they are suspended in their fire-places by their circular rims. All the stewpans and saucepans, that are not too large to be lifted with their contents in and out of their fire-places with the strength of one hand, have iron handles attached to their circular rims; but the four principal boilers, which are too large to be managed with one hand, have each two rings fitted to their rims. These handles and rings are so constructed that they do not prevent the saucepans and boilers from fitting the circular openings of their fire-places; neither do they prevent their being fitted by their own circular covers.

It will, doubtless, be observed that the four principal boilers shown in Fig. 4, belonging to the kitchen I am now describing, differ but very little in form from the boilers in common use, and consequently that they are considerably deeper in proportion to their width than they ought to be, in order that the heat generated in the combustion of the fuel might act upon them to the greatest advantage; but it is to be remembered that to each of these fire-places there are other shallower boilers that are used occasionally, which do not appear in these plans. There is, however, one advantage attending deep boilers, to which it may in some cases be useful to pay attention; and that is, that they economize *space* in a kitchen. And when their fire-places are properly constructed, and, above all, when they are furnished with good registers and dampers, the additional quantity of fuel they will require will be too trifling to be considered. The walls of their fire-places will absorb more heat in the beginning; but who knows but that the greater part of this heat may not afterwards be emitted in rays, and at last find its way into the boiler? I could mention several facts that have lately fallen under my observation, which seem to render this supposition extremely probable. This, however, is not the proper place to give an account of them.

As I have said that no fire has yet been made in the open chimney fire-place of the kitchen I am describing, it may, perhaps, be asked how this kitchen is warmed in cold weather. To this I answer, that it has been found that the mass of brick-work is made sufficiently hot by the fires that are kept up in it when cooking is going on every day to keep the room comfortably warm in the coldest weather.

This answer will probably give rise to another question, which is, how we contrive to prevent the room from being much too warm in summer. By opening one of the windows a very little, and by opening at the same time the register of a wooden tube or steam-chimney, which, rising from the ceiling of the room, ends in the open air; and which is always opened to clear the room of vapour when it is found necessary, and especially when the victuals are taken out of the boilers, or when any other operation is going on that occasions the diffusion of a considerable quantity of steam. The oblong opening of this steam-chimney may be seen Plate VII., Fig. 1, in the ceiling, at the right-hand corner of the room.

Near this corner of the room may likewise be seen a front view of the hither end of one large roaster, and part of the front view of a smaller one situated by the side of it, both with their separate fire-place doors.

The fire-place door of the larger roaster, as also both its blowpipes, are represented as being open; but the ash-pit door of this roaster is hid by the mass of brick-work in which the boilers are set. A particular account of these roasters will be given hereafter.

The dimensions of the boilers in this kitchen are as follows:—

	Wide at the brim. Inches.	Deep. Inches.
One large boiler heated by smoke	20	8
Two large boilers	16	16
Two ditto, used occasionally in the fire-places of the two boilers last mentioned	16	8
Two smaller boilers	12	12
Two ditto, fitted to the same fire-places	12	6

The diameters of the stewpans and saucepans are 12, 10, and 8 inches; and their depth is made equal to half their diameters.

The fuel burnt in this kitchen is wood; and the billets used are cut into lengths of about 6 inches.

Common bricks were used in the construction of the fire-places, but care was taken to lay them in mortar

Fig. 6.   PLATE X.

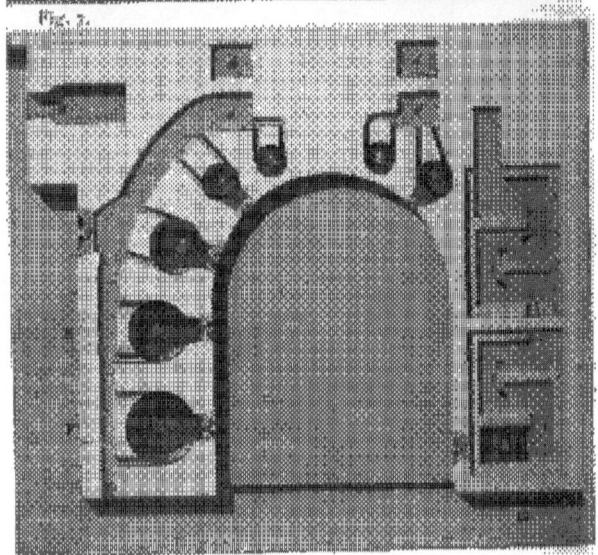

Scale 40 inches to the inch.

composed of clay and brickdust, without any sand, with only a very small proportion of lime.

In this kitchen, as also in that which I am now about to describe, the mass of brick-work in which the boilers are set projects into the room from the middle of one side of it.

Description of the Kitchen of the Hospital of La Pietà at Verona.

PLATE X.

Fig. 6. This figure represents the ground plan of the mass of brick-work in which the boilers are fixed, and the canals by which the smoke is carried off from the fire-places into the chimney. The ground covered by this mass of brick-work, and by the area (y) between the boilers, may be conceived to be divided into six equal squares, of 43 inches, placed in two rows of three squares each. In the centres of four of these squares — namely, of those which are situated at the ends of the rows — are placed four large circular boilers. The middle square of the front row is chiefly occupied by the area which is left between the two front boilers; and one half of the middle square of the back row is occupied by an open chimney fire-place, in the thick walls of which no less than six vertical flues are concealed, which carry off the smoke from the boilers and stewpans into the chimney.

The smoke from the fire which heats the large boiler P (which boiler is 32½ inches in diameter), on quitting its fire-place, goes off in four separate branches, which soon unite and form one canal, rises up under the middle of the bottom of the neighbouring large boiler Q, makes one complete turn under that boiler, and, passing from thence towards the centre of the mass of brick-work, circulates in canals divided into several branches under an iron plate that forms the bottom of an oven, which is situated under the hearth of the open chimney fire-place. From under the bottom of this oven this smoke goes off obliquely, and, entering the bottom of the vertical canal p, goes off into the chimney. The principal use of this oven is to dry the wood that is used as fuel in the kitchen. The large boiler Q, that is heated by this smoke, is designed for warming water for the use of the kitchen, and for various other purposes for which hot water is occasionally used in the hospital.

The boiler P is principally used in preparing food for the children in the hospital.

The smoke from the fire which heats the boiler R, passing off in a canal which leads to the boiler S, there separates, and passing round the sides of the boiler S, and under a small part of its bottom, unites again, and passes off into the chimney by the vertical canal r. The heat in this smoke, though it is sufficient to *warm* the water in the boiler S, is not sufficient to make it boil. In order that the contents of this boiler may occasionally be made boiling-hot, the boiler has a small fire-place of its own, situated immediately under the middle of its bottom; and when the water in the boiler has been previously made warm by the smoke from the boiler R, a very small fire made under it, in its own separate fire-place, will make it boil. The smoke from this fire-place goes off by its own separate canal into the vertical canal s, so that it does not interfere at all with the smoke from the fire-place of the boiler R; and, in consequence of this arrangement, the heating of the boiler S, by the smoke from this neighbouring fire-place and by its own fire, may be going on at the same time.

The smoke from the small boiler T, and from the stewpans U and W, goes off immediately by separate horizontal canals into their separate vertical canals (*t*, *u*, and *w*) that open into the chimney, at the height of about 15 inches above the mantel of the open chimney fire-place; and all the vertical canals, by which the smoke goes into the chimney, are furnished with dampers.

The side *b c* of the mass of brick-work is placed against the middle of one side of the kitchen, which is a large room; and the walls of the open chimney fire-place *g h i k* are carried up perpendicularly to the ceiling of the room. The hearth *l m n o* is on a level with the top of the brick-work in which the boilers are set.

As the principal boilers are deep, in order to provide sufficient room for them and a sufficient depth for their ash-pits, the foundation of the quadrangular mass of brick-work *a b c d* was raised 16 inches above the pavement of the kitchen; and on the three sides of the mass of brick-work *a b*, *a d*, and *d c*, which project into the room, there are two steps, 8 inches in height each, which extend the whole length of each of those sides; and for greater convenience in approaching the boilers the uppermost step is made 2 feet wide, and the area *y* is on a level with the top of this wide step. The ash-pit doors of the principal boilers are placed in the front of this step, and the bottoms of the passages or door-ways into their fire-places, by which the fuel is introduced, are situated just on a level with its upper surface.

The mass of brick-work in which the boilers are placed is 10 feet 9 inches long, and 8 feet 2 inches wide; and it is elevated to the height of about 3 feet 2 inches above the top of the upper broad step, by which it is surrounded on three sides, and on which it appears to stand.

Description of the Kitchen of the House of Correction at Munich.

Plate X., Fig. 7, and Plate XI., Figs. 8 and 9, represent the plans and sections of this kitchen.

Fig. 7 represents the ground plan of the brick-work in which the boilers, etc., are set, or rather a horizontal section of the brick-work at the level of the fire-places, and of the canals for carrying off the smoke. In this kitchen the fires are not made on circular iron grates, as in that just described, but the fuel is burned on grates or bars composed of bricks set edgewise, as may be seen by the plans. (See *b, b, b*, etc., Fig. 7.)

The two principal boilers (*l, l*, Fig. 9) are quadrangular, each being 3 feet long, 2 feet wide, and 15 inches deep, furnished with wooden covers movable on hinges; and they are both heated by one fire. That which is situated in the front of the brick-work, and immediately over the fire, is used for making soup; while the other, which is placed very near it, and on the same level, is used for boiling meat, potatoes, greens, etc., in steam. A small quantity of water (about an inch in depth) being put into the second boiler, the smoke from the first, which passes in flues under the second, soon causes this water to boil, and fills the boiler with hot steam. The steam from the first boiler is also carried into the second by means of a tube about $\frac{3}{4}$ of an inch in diameter, furnished with a cock, which forms a communication between the two boilers just below the level of their brims. This tube of communication is not expressed in the plates.

The smoke, having quitted the second boiler, rises up obliquely to the level of the top of the mass of brick-work

Fig. 8.   PLATE XI.

Fig. 9.

Scale 40 inches to the inch.

in which the before-mentioned boilers are set, and then circulates under a quadrangular copper vessel (expressed by dotted lines at A, Fig. 8), 27 inches long, 19 inches wide, and 20 inches deep, destined for containing warm water for the use of the kitchen. As this vessel stands higher than the tops of the boilers, it is found to be very convenient for filling them with water; and, as this water is kept warm by the smoke, this arrangement produces a considerable economy of fuel as well as of time. The water is drawn off from this vessel for use by means of a brass cock, which is not expressed in the drawing; and it is supplied with water from a neighbouring reservoir, the entrance of the water being regulated by a regulating cock or valve, furnished with a swimming ball.

The smoke, after it has circulated in flues under this vessel, goes off into a vertical canal which conducts it into the chimney. This vertical canal, together with three others designed for a similar use (see *d, d, d, d*, Fig. 7, and Fig. 9), are situated in the thick walls of an open chimney fire-place (*n*, Fig. 8), the hearth of which is on a level with the top of the mass of brick-work in which the boilers are set. A horizontal section of these four vertical flues, taken at the height of 3 inches above the level of the hearth, and also a horizontal section of the brick-work of a roasting-machine (B, Figs. 8 and 9), situated on the left of this open chimney fire-place, are distinctly represented in the Fig. 9.

Under the hearth of the fire-place there is an open vault which serves as a magazine for fuel; and in the front wall of the fire-place, above the mantel, just under the ceiling of the room, there are two openings into the chimney, by which the steam that rises from the boilers escapes into the chimney, and goes off with the smoke.

The manner in which the flues are constructed under the different boilers, and the horizontal canal for carrying off the smoke from the round boilers into the chimney, are shown in the Fig. 7. The ash-pit doors to the two principal round boilers, which are expressed by dotted lines, are opposite to E and F, Fig. 7.

The ash-pit door belonging to the fire-place of the large quadrangular boilers is situated opposite to G, Fig. 7. The reason why these ash-pit doors were not placed immediately under their fire-place doors is because there was not room for them in that situation, owing to the pavement of the area between the boilers being raised one step higher than the floor of the kitchen, which was done for the convenience of the cook.

The openings for introducing the fuel into the fire-places are conical holes in square tiles, closed with earthen stoppers (see page 26). Though these tiles are not particularly distinguished in these plates, the stoppers which close their conical openings are shown. As these tiles are so worked into the mass of the brick-work as to make a part of it, and as they are plastered and white-washed in front, it is not easy to distinguish them from the bricks when the work is finished. Their joinings with the bricks in front could not therefore with propriety be marked in any of these plans.

Although the roaster belonging to the kitchen we are describing is not seen, yet the mass of brick-work in which it is fitted up appears on the left-hand side of the open chimney fire-place in Fig. 8; and a bird's-eye view of its fire-place, and of the projecting edges of the bricks on which it rests, is seen in the Fig. 9.

PLATE XII.

Fig. 11.

Fig. 10.

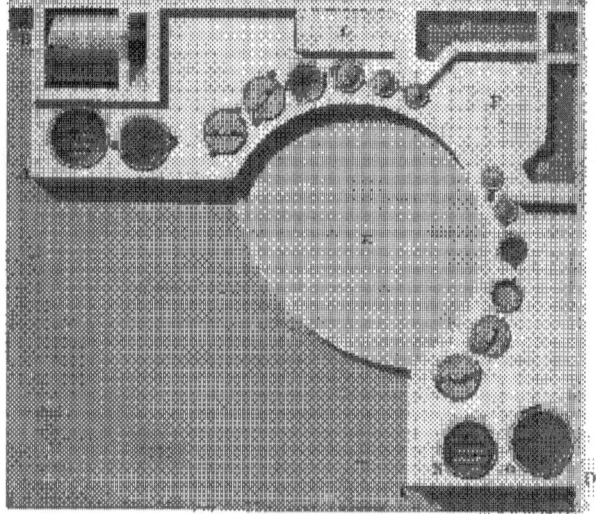

Description of the new Kitchen in the Military Hospital at Munich.

PLATE XII., FIGS. 10 AND 11, AND PLATE XIII., FIG. 12.

The mass of brick-work in which the boilers, the roaster, the stewpans, etc., are set, occupies one corner of the kitchen, extending 11¼ feet on one side of the room, and 13 feet 7 inches on the other. The greatest width of the mass of brick-work (from A to B, or from C to D) is 50¾ inches, and its height from the floor 36 inches. The circular area (E, Figs. 9 and 10) in the angle of the mass of brick-work is 6 feet 8½ inches in diameter; and it is raised one easy step, or about 5 inches, above the level of the floor of the room. There is an open chimney fire-place of a peculiar form (F, Fig. 10) in the corner of this kitchen, the hearth of which is on a level with, or rather makes a part of the upper surface of, the mass of brick-work. The side-walls of this open chimney fire-place are hollow (see G and H, Fig. 10), and serve as canals for carrying off the smoke from the boilers into a chimney, which is situated quite in the corner of the room. These canals open into the chimney about 15 inches above the level of the mantel.

The smoke goes off from each fire-place by two separate and very narrow horizontal canals into larger common canals (see I and K, Fig. 9), which conducts it to the chimney; and the openings of these narrow canals are occasionally closed more or less by means of small pieces of brick or of earthen-ware, which serve instead of dampers, but which are not expressed in the plates. The fires all burn on flat grates, composed of bricks or thin tiles set edgewise. To save expense, the covers of the boilers and stewpans were all made of wood. The oblong quadrangular vessel (see L, Figs. 10 and 11), which is made of copper, and has a door above movable on hinges, is destined for containing warm water for the use of the kitchen, and is heated by the smoke from all the neighbouring closed fire-places.

The fire-place of the roaster is seen in Fig. 9 (M); a bird's-eye view of the top of the roaster appears in Fig. 10, and a vertical section of it and of its flues are faintly marked by dotted lines in Fig. 11.

The two large shallow stewpans (N, O, Fig. 10), vertical sections of which and of their fire-places are faintly marked by dotted lines in Fig. 11, are constructed of hammered iron, and are used principally for cooking steam dumplings (*dampf-nudels*), a kind of food in great repute in Bavaria.

When any thing is to be fried or broiled, a fire is made on the hearth of the open chimney fire-place. Under this hearth there is a small vault which serves for holding the wood that is wanted for fuel; but it would have been much better if that space had been occupied by two circular closed fire-places, so constructed as to be used occasionally for a frying-pan or a gridiron.

Description of a detached Part of the Kitchen of the Military Academy at Munich.

PLATE XIII.

Fig. 13. This figure is the ground plan of a mass of brick-work occupying a space about 6 feet 9 inches square, measured on the floor, in one corner of the

PLATE XIII.

Fig. 13.

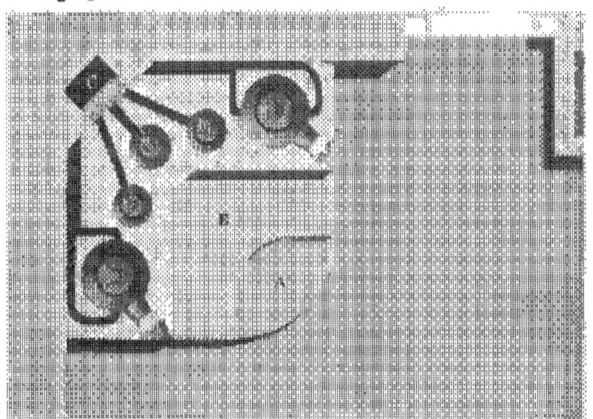

Fig. 12.

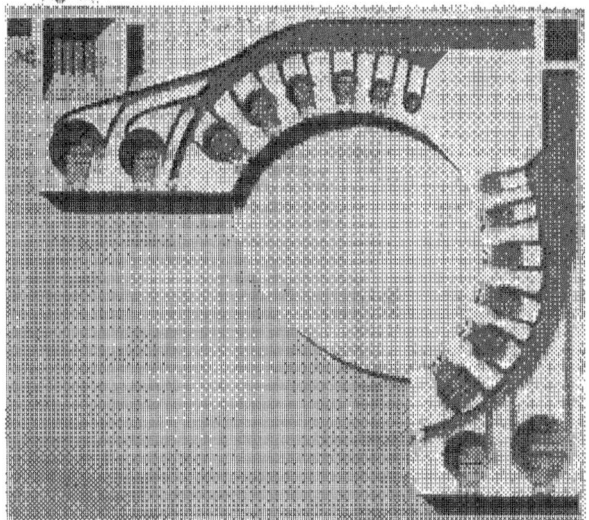

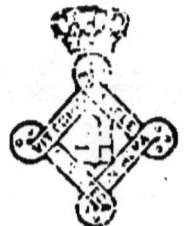

room, in which two of the principal boilers belonging to the kitchen, and three large stewpans, are fixed.

A and B are two steps, each 8 inches high, and the upper (flat) surface of the mass of brick-work, in which the boilers are set, and which is 45 inches wide, is just 30 inches above the level of the upper surface of the step B.

Neither the boilers nor stewpans are shown in this plan, but their circular fire-places are represented, as also their circular dishing iron grates, on which the fuel is burned, and the horizontal canals by which the smoke passes off into the chimney.

The smoke divides under each of the two principal boilers, and passes off in two canals situated on opposite sides of the fire-place; which canals, however, unite and form one single canal at a small distance from the boiler. In the fire-places of the stewpans the smoke does not divide in this manner; but the fire-place is so constructed that the flame makes one complete turn round the stewpan before it goes off into the horizontal canal leading to the chimney.

The opening by which the fuel is introduced into the fire-place of each of the two large boilers is closed by a conical stopper (constructed of fire-stone), represented in the figure, immediately under which stopper the (register) door of the ash-pit is situated.

The ash-pit of each of the fire-places of the stewpans is furnished with a register door. The passages into these ash-pits are expressed in the figure by dotted lines. The fuel (which is small pieces of wood about 5 inches in length) is introduced into the fire-place from above by removing the stewpan for a moment for that purpose.

The chimney C, by which the smoke goes off, is

situated in a corner of the room; and, when it is swept, the chimney-sweeper enters it by a door-way, which is situated in front, just above the level of the upper surface of the mass of brick-work, and which is closed by an iron door.

Each of the horizontal canals, by which the smoke is carried off from the fire-places of the two large boilers into the chimney, is furnished with a damper, which is faintly marked in the figure. Each of the horizontal canals, which carry off the smoke from the fire-places of the stewpans, is likewise furnished with a damper; but, to avoid confusion, they are not expressed in the engraving.

The bottoms of the ash-pit doors of the fire-places of the three stewpans are on a level with the upper surface of the step B; but the bottoms of the ash-pit doors of the fire-places of the two large boilers are on a level with the pavement of the kitchen.

The two large boilers (which are constructed of sheet copper, tinned) are 22 Rhinland inches in diameter above, $19\frac{1}{4}$ inches in diameter below, and 24 inches deep. They weigh each 62 lbs. avoirdupois, and contain 28 wine-gallons. The circular dishing-grates belonging to their fire-places are each 10 inches in diameter, measured externally; and the fire-place, properly so called, or the cavity in which the burning fuel is confined, is 10 inches in diameter below, 18 inches in diameter above, and $8\frac{1}{2}$ inches deep.

The largest stewpan is 12 inches in diameter, and 4 inches deep; and the two others are each 11 inches in diameter and 4 inches deep.

The fire-places belonging to the stewpans are cylindrical, 5 inches deep and 6 inches in diameter, and are furnished with circular dishing-grates.

Each of the large boilers is furnished with a circular wooden rim, 2 inches wide and 2 inches thick, which is accurately fitted to the brim of the boiler; and a circular wooden cover, consisting of three pieces of deal board attached to each other by two pairs of hinges, closes the boiler by being fitted accurately to the upper surface of its circular wooden rim.

One of the three pieces of board, which together form the flat circular cover of the boiler, is firmly fastened down to the wooden rim of the boiler, by means of two small hooks of iron; and from the middle of this part of the cover, so fastened down, a long tin tube, about 1¼ inches in diameter, rises up perpendicularly to the ceiling of the room, and carries off the steam from the boiler out of the kitchen.

As the cover of the boiler is composed of three flat pieces of board united by hinges, and as the cover, so formed, is merely laid down on the flat surface of the wooden rim which is connected with the brim of the boiler, it might very naturally be expected that some of the steam would be forced through between the joinings of the cover, or between the cover and the wooden rim; but this is what never happens. So far from it, steam seldom comes into the room even when the cover of the boiler is in part removed, by laying back the first division of it upon the second, — so strong is the draught of the steam-tube.

This phenomenon, which rather surprised me when I first observed it, was of considerable use to me; for it led me to discover the utility of dampers in the tubes or chimneys that are destined for carrying off the steam from boilers, and more especially from such boilers whose covers are not perfectly air-tight. If these steam-chimneys are of any considerable length, they cannot fail to occasion a strong draught through them, which will have a tendency to cause the cold air of the atmosphere to press in by every crevice between the brim of the boiler and its cover; which streams of cold air, being precipitated upon the surface of the boiling liquid, will be there warmed, and then passing off rapidly by the steam-chimney will occasion a very considerable loss of heat.

The rule for regulating the damper of the steam-chimney of a boiler, whose cover is not steam-tight, is this: close the damper just so much that closing it any more would cause some steam to be driven out between the joinings of the brim of the boiler and its cover. When this is done, it is evident that little or no cold air can enter the boiler by any small crevices in its cover that may remain open, consequently little or no heat will be carried off by the air of the atmosphere from the surface of the hot liquid.

I have been the more particular in explaining this matter, as I am persuaded that a great deal of heat is frequently lost in boiling and evaporating liquids, by causing or permitting the cold air of the atmosphere to come into contact with the surface of the hot liquid.

Some, I know, are of opinion that a stream of fresh air or a wind, which is made to pass over the surface of a liquid that is evaporated by boiling, tends rather to increase the evaporation than to diminish it; but it appears to me that there are strong reasons to conclude that this opinion is erroneous. A very simple experiment which I propose to make, and which others may perhaps be induced to make before I can find leisure to attend to it, will determine the fact.

The large boiler belonging to the fire-place, which is situated on the left hand in the mass of brick-work above described, is that which was used in the experiment mentioned on page 8.

It was once my intention to have published drawings and descriptions of every part and detail of the kitchen of the Military Academy at Munich, and also that of the House of Industry in that city. But as enough has already been said in this and in my sixth Essay to give clear and distinct ideas of the fundamental principles on which all the essential parts of the machinery in those kitchens were constructed; and as the peculiar arrangement of a kitchen must ever depend much on its size, and on the variety and kinds of food that are to be cooked in it, to avoid being tedious and tiresome to my readers, I have, after mature deliberation, concluded that it will be best to suppress these details.

Having now finished all the descriptions which I think it useful to publish of the various public and private kitchens that have been constructed under my direction in foreign countries, and having explained in the most ample manner in this Essay, and in my other writings on the management of fire, all the leading principles according to which, in my opinion, kitchens and fire-places of all kinds should be constructed, I shall in the next place proceed to show in what manner my plans may be so modified and accommodated to the opinions and practices in this country as to remove the objections that will probably be made to them, and facilitate their gradual introduction into general use.

I am well aware that it is by no means enough for those who propose improvements to the public to be in the right in regard to the intrinsic merit of their plans:

much must be done to prepare the way for, and to facilitate their introduction, or all their labours will be in vain.

CHAPTER III.

Of the Alterations and Improvements that may be made in the Kitchen Fire-places now in common Use in Great Britain. — All Improvement in Kitchen Fire-places impossible, as long as they continue to be incumbered with Smoke-jacks. — They occasion an enormous Waste of Fuel. — Common Jacks, that go with a Weight, are much better. — Ovens and Boilers that are connected with a Kitchen Range should be detached from it, and heated each by its own separate Fire. — The closed Fire-places for iron Ovens and Roasters can hardly be made too small. — Of the various Means that may be used for improving the large open Fire-places of Kitchens. — Of the Cottage Fire-places now in common Use, and of the Means of improving them. — Of the very great Use that small Ovens constructed of thin sheet Iron would be to Cottagers. — Of the great Importance of improving the Implements and Utensils used by the Poor in cooking their Food. — No Improvement in their Method of preparing their Food possible without it. — Description of an Oven suitable for a poor Family, with an Estimate of the Cost of it. — Of Nests of three or four small Ovens heated by one Fire. — Of the Utility of these Nests of Ovens in the Kitchens of private Families. — They may be fitted up at a very small Expense. — Occa-

sional Remarks respecting the Materials proper to be used in constructing the Sides and Backs of open Chimney Fire-places.

THE kitchen fire-place of a family in easy circumstances in this country consists almost universally of a long grate, called a kitchen range, for burning coals, placed in a wide and deep open chimney, with a very high mantel. The front and bottom bars of the grate are commonly made of hammered iron, and the back of the grate (which usually slopes backwards) of a plate of cast iron; and sometimes there is a vertical plate of iron, movable by means of a rack in the cavity of the grate, by means of which plate the capacity, or rather the length of that part of the grate that is occupied by the burning fuel, may occasionally be diminished. At one end of the grate there is commonly an iron oven, which is heated by the fire in the grate; and sometimes there is a boiler situated in a similar manner at the other end of it. To complete the machinery (which in every part and detail of it seems to have been calculated for the express purpose of devouring fuel), a smoke-jack is placed in the chimney!

I shall begin my observations on the smoke-jack.

No human invention that ever came to my knowledge appears to me to be so absurd as this. A wind-mill is certainly a very useful contrivance, but were it proposed to turn a wind-mill by an artificial current of air, how ridiculous would the scheme appear! What an enormous force would necessarily be wasted in giving velocity to a stream of air sufficient to cause the mill to work with effect! A smoke-jack is, however, neither more nor less than a wind-mill, carried round by an

artificial current of air; and to this we may add that
the current of air which goes up a chimney, in consequence of the combustion of fuel in an open chimney
fire-place, is produced in the most expensive and disadvantageous manner that can well be imagined. It
would not be difficult to prove that much less than *one
thousandth* part of the fuel that is necessary to be burned
in an open chimney fire-place, in order to cause a smoke-
jack to turn a loaded spit, would answer to make the
spit go round, were the force evolved in the combustion
of the fuel properly directed, — through the medium of
a steam-engine, for instance.

But it is not merely the waste of power or of mechanical force, that unavoidably attends the use of smoke-
jacks, that may be objected to them: they are very
inconvenient in many respects; they frequently render
it necessary to make a great fire in the kitchen, when
otherwise a great fire would not be wanted; they very
frequently cause chimneys to smoke, and always render
a stronger current of air up the chimney necessary than
would be so merely for the combustion of the fuel wanted
for the purposes of cooking; consequently they increase
the currents of cold air from the doors and windows to
the fire-place; and, lastly, they are troublesome, noisy,
expensive, frequently out of order, and never do the
work they are meant to perform with half so much
certainty and precision as it would be done by a common jack, moved by a weight or a spring.

There is, I know, an objection to common jacks that
is well founded, which is, that they require frequent
winding up; but for this there is an easy remedy. A
jack may without any difficulty (merely by using a
greater weight and a greater combination of pulleys)

be made to run almost any length of time: a whole day for instance, or even longer; and, if it should be necessary, the weight may be at a considerable distance from the kitchen. It may indifferently be raised up into the air, descend into a well, or may be made to descend along an inclined plane; and but little ingenuity will be required to contrive and dispose of the machinery in such a manner as to keep it out of the way, and, if it should be required, completely out of sight; and, with regard to the winding up of such a jack as I here recommend (that is, to go a whole day), it may easily be done by any servant of the house in less than five minutes.

Incomparably less labour will be required to wind up the weight of a common jack than to bring coals to feed the fire that is requisite to make a smoke-jack go.

I know that it is said in favour of smoke-jacks, that all the fire that is required to make them perform would be necessary in the kitchen for other purposes, and consequently that they occasion no additional expense of fuel; but that this statement is very far indeed from being accurate will be evident to any person who will take the trouble to examine the matter with care. That the sails of a smoke-jack will turn round with the application of a very small force, when the pivots on which its axle-tree rests are well constructed, and when its motion is not impeded by any load, is very true; but it requires a very different degree of force to move it when it is obliged to carry round one, or perhaps two or three, loaded spits. Even the heat given off to the air by the kitchen range in cooking, after the fire is gone out, will sometimes keep up the motion of the sails of the smoke-jack for many hours. But what a striking proof is this of the enormous waste of fuel in kitchens in this country!

Would to God that I could contrive to fix the public attention on this subject.

Nothing surely is so disgraceful to society and to individuals as unmeaning wastefulness.

But to return to the attack of my smoke-jack; which (although it be a *wind-mill*) is certainly not a *giant*, and cannot be personally formidable, however it may expose me to another species of danger.

There is one objection to smoke-jacks that must be quite conclusive wherever the improvements I have recommended, and shall recommend, in kitchen fireplaces, are to be introduced. Where smoke-jacks exist, these improvements cannot be introduced, it being quite impracticable to unite them.

On a supposition that I have gained my point, and that the smoke-jack is to be removed, I shall now proceed to propose several alterations and improvements that may be made in the kitchen range.

And, first, all ovens, boilers, steam-boilers, etc., which are connected with the back and ends of the range, and heated by the fire made in the grate, should be detached from it; and for each of the ovens, boilers, etc., a small, separate, closed fire-place must be constructed, situated directly under the oven or boiler, and furnished with a separate canal for carrying its smoke into the kitchen chimney, which separate canal may open into the chimney about a foot above the level of the mantel.

There is nothing so wasteful as the attempt to heat ovens and boilers by heat drawn off laterally from a fire in an open grate. The consumption of fuel is enormous, to say nothing of the expense of the machinery, and the inconvenience that must frequently arise from the heat being forcibly drawn away sidewise under an oven or boiler, when it is wanted elsewhere.

The separate closed fire-place under iron ovens and roasters must be made *very small*, otherwise the cook or his assistants will sometimes, in the hurry of business, make too large a fire; the consequences of which will be the spoiling of the food, and the burning and destroying of the oven or roaster.

Almost all the roasters that have been put up in England have been spoiled in consequence of their fire-places being made too large; and not one has ever received the slightest accident or injury, or failed to perform to entire satisfaction, that has been heated by a very small fire, and never overheated.

The fire-place for an oven or roaster of sheet iron, from 18 to 20 inches wide, and from 24 to 30 inches long, should never be more than 6 inches wide, 6 inches deep, and about 9, or at most 10, inches long; and this fire-place should seldom be half filled with coals. If the oven or roaster be set in such a manner that the flame or smoke from the fire must necessarily spread round it and embrace it on every side, there will be no want of heat for any of the common purposes of cookery, and its intensity may at all times be regulated by means of the damper in the chimney and the register in the ash-pit door.

It is not easy to imagine how much the business of cooking is facilitated by making the machinery so perfect that the quantity of heat may at any time be regulated with certainty merely by registers and dampers, and without adding to or diminishing the quantity of fuel in the fire-place. It is on these advantages, and the numerous other conveniences that will result from them, that my hopes are principally founded of gaining over the cooks, and engaging their cordial assistance in bringing forward into general use the improvements I recommend. I am well aware of their influence, and of the importance of their co-operation.

When all the ovens and fixed boilers are detached from the kitchen range, then, and not before, measures may be taken with some prospect of success for improving the kitchen fire-place, so as to economize fuel, and prevent the kitchen chimney from smoking, if it has that fault; and the measures proper to be adopted for obtaining those ends must depend principally on the size, or rather on the width, of the open fire that will be wanted in the kitchen. Where the family is small, and where great dinners are seldom or never given, and especially where closed roasters are introduced, a small fire-place, and consequently a narrow grate, will answer every purpose that can be wanted; and the fire-place of the kitchen may be fitted up nearly upon the principles laid down in my fourth Essay, on the construction of open chimney fire-places.

The kitchen of Mr. Summers, ironmonger, of New Bond Street (No. 98), has been fitted up in this manner, and has been found to answer perfectly well.

But if it be necessary to leave the grate of the kitchen range with its width undiminished, in order that a wide fire may occasionally be lighted in it, this can best be done in the manner that was lately adopted in altering and fitting up the kitchen in the house of the Countess of Morton in Park Street. The range being suffered to remain (or rather the front and bottom bars of the grate only, for the iron plate that formed the back of the range was taken away), the range, which is about 5 feet long, was divided into three unequal parts, which parts were built up with hard fire-bricks in such a manner as to form three distinct fire-places, the one contiguous to the other, and separated from each other by divisions so thin in front that when fires are burning in them all it appears like one fire, and has all the effect of one fire in roasting meat that is put before it. Each fire-place is, however, perfectly distinct from the others, and has its own distinct coverings (which are oblique), — back, throat, etc., — though the same front bars, which are of hammered iron, and made very strong, run through them all.

When a very small fire is wanted (merely for boiling a tea-kettle, for instance), it is kindled in the *first* or smallest fire-place; when a little larger fire is necessary, it is made in the *second* fire-place, which is at the opposite end of the range; when a still larger fire is required, it is made in the *third* fire-place, which occupies the middle of the range. If a large fire in the fourth degree is wanted, two neighbouring fires are kindled in the *first* and *third* fire-places; if in the fifth degree, the two contiguous fires are lighted in the second and third fire-places; and when the greatest fire that can be made is wanted, all the three fire-places are at the same time filled with burning fuel.

In cases where a single open chimney fire-place of a moderate size, that is to say, from 18 to 20 inches in width, might sometimes be too small, and a very wide fire, like that just described, would never be wanted, I would advise the construction of two separate but adjoining fire-places, the one about 12 inches, and the other about 18 or 20 inches in width. These would, I imagine, answer every purpose for which an open fire in the kitchen could be wanted by a large family, even though they should (contrary to all my recommendations) continue to roast their meat upon a spit.

That I am not unreasonable enough to expect that all my recommendations will immediately be attended to, is evident from the pains I take to improve machinery now in use, of which I do not approve, and which is perfectly different from that I am desirous to see introduced.

When my roasters shall become more generally known, and the management of them better understood, I have no doubt but that open chimney fire-places, and open fires of all descriptions, will be found to be much less necessary in kitchens than they now are.

I am even sanguine enough to expect that the time will come when open fires will disappear, even in our dwelling-rooms and most elegant apartments. Genial warmth can certainly be kept up, and perfect ventilation effected much better without them than with them; and though I am myself still child enough to be pleased with the brilliant appearance of burning fuel, yet I cannot help thinking that something else might be invented equally attractive to draw my attention and amuse my sight, that would be less injurious to my eyes, less expensive, and less connected with dirt, ashes, and other unwholesome and disagreeable objects.

It is very natural to suppose that those nations who inhabit countries where the winter is most severe must have made the greatest progress in contriving means for making their dwellings warm and comfortable in cold weather; and when, in milder climates, the growing scarcity of fuel has rendered the saving of that article an object of rational economy, it appears to me to be wise to search *there* for the means of doing it, where necessity has long since rendered the use and highest possible improvement of those means indispensable. And the truly liberal — that is to say, the enlightened, just, and generous — feel no difficulty in acknowledging the ingenuity and industry of their neighbours, and no humiliation in adopting their useful inventions and improvements.

Before I finish this publication I must say a few words on the construction of *cottage fire-places*. It is, I am sensible, a long time since I promised to publish an Essay on that subject, and still mean to do so; but a variety of weighty considerations has engaged me to postpone the putting of that Essay out of my hands. I conceived the subject to be of very great importance, and wished to have time to make myself fully acquainted with the present state of cottages, and of the different kinds of fuel used in them in different parts of these kingdoms. I had with pain observed the numerous mistakes that have been made in altering chimney fire-places on the principles recommended in my fourth Essay, and on that account I was very desirous of deferring the publication of my directions for constructing cottage fire-places, till I could inform the public where cottage fire-places, constructed on the principles recommended, might be seen.

I hope and trust that in the arrangement of the repository of the Royal Institution, now fitting up in this metropolis, an opportunity will be found for exhibiting cottage fire-places on the most perfect plans, as also of showing many other mechanical contrivances that may be of general utility.

Cottage chimneys, as they are now commonly constructed in most parts of Great Britain, have a very wide open fire-place, with a high mantel, and large chimney-corners, in which the children frequently sit on little stools, when in cold weather they hover round the fire. These chimney-corners are very comfortable; and, except the whole room could be made equally so, it would certainly be a pity to destroy them. But this, I am persuaded, may easily be done: in the mean time, much may be done to make cottages warm and comfortable, merely by a few simple alterations in their present fire-places.

As the principal fault of these fire-places is the enormous width of the throats of their chimneys, which frequently occasions their smoking, and always gives too free a passage for the warm air of the room to escape up the chimney, a smaller fire-place may be constructed in the midst of the larger one; and the little chimney of this small fire-place being carried up perpendicularly in the middle of the large fire-place, the large chimney-corners, without being destroyed, may be arched over and closed in above, so as to leave no passage in those parts for the escape of the warm air of the room into the chimney, and from thence into the atmosphere.

The back of the old chimney may serve for a back to the new fire-place, and the jambs of the new chimney need not project forward beyond the back more than 12 or 15 inches; so that the new chimney, and every part of it, may be completely included within the opening of the old fire-place. This is to be done in order to preserve the old chimney-corners; but in cases where the opening of the old fire-place is not sufficiently wide, high, and deep to permit of the leaving of chimney-corners sufficiently spacious to be useful, it will be best to sacrifice these corners, and to proceed in a different manner in constructing the new fire-place.

In this last case the back of the new fire-place should be brought forward, and the new work should be executed agreeably to the directions contained in my fourth Essay for the construction of open chimney fire-places. If void spaces should remain on the right and left of the new jambs, they will be found useful for various purposes.

It is of so much importance to facilitate the means of cooking to the poor, and to enable them to prepare food in different ways, that I think it extremely desirable that each cottager should have an iron pot or digester, so contrived as to be used occasionally over his open fire, or, what will be much more economical, in a small closed fire-place, which may be made with a few bricks on one side of his open fire-place.

But what would be of more use, if possible, to a poor family, even than a good boiler, would be a small oven of sheet iron, well put up in brick-work. Such an oven would not cost more than a few shillings, and if properly set would last for many years without needing any repairs. It would answer not only for baking household bread and cakes, but might likewise be used with great advantage in cooking rice puddings, potato pies, and many other kinds of nourishing food of the most exquisite taste, that might be prepared at a very trifling expense.

It is in vain to expect that the poor should adopt better methods of choosing and preparing their food, till they are furnished with better implements and utensils for cooking.

I put up an oven like that I now recommend last winter in my lodgings at Brompton, and have made a great number of experiments with it, from the results of which I am fully persuaded of its utility. I pulled it down on removing into the house I now occupy, but mean to put it up again as soon as my kitchen shall be ready to receive it. As I put up this oven merely as an experiment, in order to ascertain by actual trials how far it might be useful to poor families, the oven was made small, and it was set in the cheapest manner, merely with common bricks and mortar, without any iron or other costly material. The grate of the closed fire-place (which was 5 inches wide and about 8 inches long) was constructed of three common bricks placed edgewise, and a sliding brick was used for closing the door of the fire-place, and another for a register to the ash-pit door-way. The oven, which is of thin sheet iron, is 18¼ inches long, 12 inches wide, and 12 inches high, and it weighs just 10¼ lbs. exclusive of its front frame and front door, which together weigh 6¼ lbs.

For a small family the oven might be made of a smaller size, — 11 inches wide, for instance, 10 inches high, and 15 inches long; and it is not indispensably necessary that it should have either a front frame or a front door of iron. It might be set in the brick-work without a frame perfectly well; and a flat twelve-inch tile, or a flat piece of stone, or even a piece of wood, placed against its mouth, might be made to answer instead of an iron door.

The only danger of injury to these ovens from accident to which they are liable is that arising from carelessness in making too large a fire under them. They require but a very small fire indeed, and a large one is not only quite unnecessary, but detrimental on several accounts.

For greater security against accidents from too strong fires, I would advise the fire-place to be made extremely — I had almost said ridiculously — small, not more than from 4 to 5 inches wide, from 6 to 8 inches long, and about 5 inches deep; and I would place the bottom or grating of the fire-place 11 or 12 inches below the bottom of the oven. For still greater security, the bottom of the oven, immediately over the fire, might, if it should be found necessary, be defended by a thin plate of cast, hammered, or sheet iron, full of small holes (as large as peas), placed about half an inch from the bottom of the oven, and directly below it; but, if any common degree of attention be used in the management of the fire, this precaution will not, I am persuaded, be necessary.

In setting these ovens, care must be taken that room be left for the flame and smoke to come into contact with the oven, and surround it on every side; and it can hardly be necessary to add that a canal must be made by which the smoke can afterwards pass off into the chimney.

I once imagined that small ovens for poor cottagers might be made very cheap indeed, by making only the bottom of the oven of iron, and building up the rest with bricks; but, on making the experiment, it was not found to answer. I caused several ovens on this principle to be constructed in my kitchen, and made many attempts to correct their faults; but I found it impossible to heat them equally and sufficiently. I then altered my plan, by making both the bottom and the top of sheet iron. But this even did not answer. It might answer for a perpetual oven, like that which I caused to be made in the House of Industry at Dublin; but, if an oven of this kind is ever suffered to become cold, it will require a long time to heat it again, which is a circumstance that renders it very unfit for the use of a poor family. The ovens I have recommended, constructed entirely of thin sheet iron, have the advantage of being heated almost in an instant; and the heat which penetrates the walls of their closed fire-places, being gradually given off after all the fuel is burned out, keeps them hot for a long time. Care should, however, always be taken to keep these ovens well closed when they are used, and to leave only a very small hole, when necessary, for the escape of the generated steam or vapour.

For larger families the oven may be made larger in proportion; or, what will be still more convenient, a nest of two, three, or four small ovens, placed near to each other, may be so set in brick-work as to be heated by one and the same fire.

A nest of four small ovens, set in this manner, was fitted up in the kitchen of the Military Academy at Munich, and found very useful: they were rectangular, each being 10 inches wide, 10 inches high, and 16 inches long; and they were placed two abreast in two rows, one immediately above the other, the sides and bottoms of neighbouring ovens being at the distance of about 1¼ inch, that the flame and smoke which surrounded them on every side might have room to pass between them. The fire-place was situated immediately below the interval that separated the two lowermost ovens, at the distance of about 10 inches below the level of their bottoms; and by means of dampers the flame could be so turned and directed as to increase or diminish the heat in any one or more of the ovens at pleasure.

These four ovens were furnished with iron doors, movable on hinges, which, in order that they might not be in the way of each other, opened two to the right, and two to the left.

In a large kitchen, where a variety of different kinds of food is baked at the same time or on the same day, it is easy to perceive that a nest of small ovens must be very useful, much more so than one large oven equal in capacity to them all; for, besides the inconvenience in cooking a variety of different things in the same oven that arises from the promiscuous mixture of various exhalations and smells, the process going on in one dish must often be disturbed by opening the oven to put in or take out another, and the heat can never be so regulated as to suit them all.

But the cook of the Military Academy at Munich finds the nest of ovens useful not merely for baking: he uses them also for stewing and for boiling, with great success. A large quantity of cold liquid cannot, it is true, be heated and made to boil in a very short time in one of these ovens; but a saucepan or boiler, whose contents are already boiling-hot, being placed in one of them, a gentle boiling may be kept up for a great length of time, with the consumption of an exceedingly small quantity of fuel.

With regard to the expense or cost of such a nest of ovens, it could not, or at least ought not to, be considerable. If they were each 12 inches wide, 12 inches high, and 16 inches long, they would not weigh more than 15 lbs. each, their doors included; and this would make but 60 lbs. for the weight of the whole nest, supposing it to consist of four ovens. I do not know what price might be demanded by the artificers in this country, or by the trade, for work of this kind, but I should think they might well afford to sell these ovens,

properly made and ready for setting, at less than 6*d.*
the pound, avoirdupois weight. The sheet iron would
cost them in the market, at the first hand, not more than
about 3½*d.* per pound. The expense of setting the ovens
would not be considerable, especially as only one small
fire-place would be necessary.

In some future publication, or in a subsequent part
of this Essay, I shall give a design of one of these
nests of ovens, with an exact estimate of the expense of
it: in the mean time I will endeavour to get one of
them put up for the public inspection at the Royal
Institution.

I cannot close this chapter without once more calling
the attention of my reader to the necessity of furnishing the canal that carries away the smoke into the
chimney with a damper. If this is not done in setting
the ovens I have just been describing, it will be quite
impossible to manage the heat properly. For the fire-
place of a small oven for the family of a cottager, a
common brick may be made to answer very well as a
damper; and, indeed, a very good damper for any small
fire-place may be made with a brick or a tile or a
piece of stone.

If, in addition to the introduction of a good damper,
care be taken to cause the smoke to descend about
12 or 15 inches just after it has quitted the oven (or the
boiler), and before it is permitted to rise up and go off
into the chimney, this will greatly contribute to the
economy of fuel.

It is surely not necessary that I should again observe
how very essential it is in altering open chimney fire-
places — whether they belong to kitchens, to the dwelling-rooms of the opulent, or to cottages — to build up

their backs and sides, in that part especially which contains and is occupied by the burning fuel, with fire-bricks or with stone; and never in any case to kindle a fire against a plate of iron.

If all the metal in a register stove, except the front, and the front and bottom bars, were removed, and the back and sides built up properly with fire-bricks, or partly with fire-bricks and partly with fire-stone, it would make a most excellent fire-place.

This last observation is, I acknowledge, in some degree foreign to my present subject; but, as it is well meant, I hope it will be well received.

In a supplementary Essay now preparing for the press, in which will be published such additional remarks and observations to all my former Essays as may be necessary to their complete explanation and elucidation, I shall take occasion to enter fully into the subject of chimney fire-places, and shall endeavour to show, at some length, why it is improper and ill-judged to construct the sides and backs of their grates of iron, or of any other metallic substance.

In a second part which will be added to this (tenth) Essay, particular directions will be given for constructing boilers, steam dishes, ovens, roasters, and various other implements and utensils used in cookery; and a detailed plan will be laid before the public for improving the kitchen utensils of cottagers and other poor families.

I have been induced to reserve these various matters for a separate publication, in order to accommodate my writings as much as is possible to the convenience of the various classes of readers into whose hands they are likely to come. The plates, which were indispensably necessary to elucidate the descriptions contained in the preceding chapters (which have been admirably executed by that excellent artist Lowry), could not fail to enhance very considerably the price of this publication, and on that account I was desirous to detach and publish separately all such popular parts of the subjects I have undertaken to treat in this Essay as appeared to me to bid fair to be most read, and to be of most general utility.

Whether the reader agrees with me or not in respect to the validity of the reasons which have determined my judgment on this occasion, I hope and trust that he will do me the justice to believe that I have no wish so much at my heart as to render my labours of some real and lasting utility to mankind. How happy shall I be when I come to die, if I can *then* think that I have lived to some useful purpose!

APPENDIX TO PART I.

An Account of the Expense of fitting up a small Oven.

SINCE the foregoing sheets were printed off, I have caused a small oven of sheet iron to be made and set in brick-work, for the express purpose of ascertaining the cost of it. This oven, which is such as would be proper for the use of a small poor family, is 11 inches wide, 11 inches high, and 15¾ inches long; and it weighs 6 lbs. 2 oz. At its mouth or opening, the sheet iron is turned back in such a manner as to form a rim, half an inch wide, projecting outwards; which rim serves to strengthen the oven, and is likewise useful in fixing it in the brick-work.

The whole oven is constructed of two pieces of sheet iron, of unequal dimensions, the largest piece (which is about 16½ inches wide by 45 inches long) forming the top, bottom, and two sides; and the smallest (which is about 12 inches square) forming the end. These sheets of iron are united by seams without rivets. One seam only runs through the oven in the direction of its length, and that is situated in the middle of the upper part of it.

A good workman was employed just two hours in making this oven; but there is no doubt but the work might be done in a shorter time by a man accustomed to that kind of manufacture, especially if the proper means were used for facilitating and expediting the labour.

The sheet iron used in the construction of this oven, which was of the very best quality, cost 34*s.* per gross hundred of 112 lbs., which is at the rate of $3\frac{1}{4}d$. and $\frac{3}{4}$ of a farthing per lb. The quantity used, 6 lbs. 2 oz., must therefore have cost 1*s.* $10\frac{1}{2}d$. and $\frac{1}{12}$ part of a farthing.

If now we allow two ounces for wastage, this will bring the quantity necessary for constructing one of these ovens to $6\frac{1}{4}$ lbs., which quantity, at the rate above mentioned, would cost something less than 1*s.* 11*d.*; and if to this sum we add 1*s.* for the making, this will bring the prime cost of the oven to 2*s.* 11*d.*

Let us allow 20 per cent for the profit of the manufacturer, and still the price of the oven to buyers will be only 3*s.* 6*d.**

In order to ascertain the expense of setting one of these ovens in brick-work, I caused that above described to be put up in the middle of a wide chimney fire-place in my house in Brompton Row; and the work was executed with as much care and attention as was necessary, in order to render it strong and durable. In doing this 114 bricks were used, and something less than 3 hods of mortar; and the bricklayer performed the job in 3 hours and 10 minutes.

Three bricks set edgewise formed the grate or bottom of the fire-place; the middle brick being placed vertically, and those on each side of it inclining a little

---

* The oven I have here described was made by Mr. Summers, Ironmonger, of New Bond Street, who, before I acquainted him with the above computations, offered to furnish these ovens in any quantities at 4*s.* a piece. This, for the offer of a manufacturer, I thought not unreasonable.

inwards above, to give a more free passage to the falling ashes.

The entrance into the fire-place was closed with a sliding brick, and another brick served as a register to the ash-pit door-way; a third served as a damper to the canal that carried off the smoke into the chimney; and the oven itself was closed with a twelve-inch tile.

The expense of setting this oven was estimated as follows:—

	s.	d.
114 bricks, at 3s. per hundred	3	4
3 hods of mortar, at 4d.	1	0
1 twelve-inch tile, at 4d.	0	4
Bricklayer's labour	1	6
Total	6	2
If to this sum we add the amount of the Ironmonger's bill for the oven	3	6
The whole expense will turn out	9	8

The mass of brick-work in which this oven is set is just 2 feet wide, 19½ inches deep, measured from front to back, and 3 feet 3½ inches high. The chimney fire-place in which it is placed is 3 feet wide, 3 feet 3½ inches high, and 20 inches deep.

If the oven had been set in one corner of this fire-place, instead of occupying the middle of it, near one-quarter of the bricks that were used might have been saved; but if in building a new chimney a convenient place were chosen and prepared for it, an oven of this kind might be put up at a very small expense indeed, perhaps for 3s. or 3s. 6d., which would reduce the cost of the oven when set to about 7s. or 7s. 6d.

Though the bricklayer was above 3 hours putting up this oven, yet, as it was the first he ever set, there is no doubt but that he was considerably longer in doing the work on that account. He thinks he could put up another in two hours, and I am of the same opinion.

I think it would be advisable, in order to facilitate stowage and carriage of these small ovens, always to manufacture them in nests of four, one within the other, even when they are designed to be sold, and to be put up singly; for it can be of no great importance whether they be a quarter of an inch or half an inch wider or narrower; and it will often be a great convenience to be able to pack them one within the other, especially when they are to be sent to any considerable distance.

If care be taken in making them to preserve their forms and dimensions, and if the seams of the metal be properly beaten down, the difference in the sizes of two ovens that will fit one within the other need not be very considerable. But I forget that I am writing for the cleverest and most experienced workmen upon the face of the earth, to whom the utility of these contrivances is perfectly familiar, and who, without waiting for my suggestions, will not fail to put them all in practice.

Though there is nothing I am more anxious to avoid than tiring my reader with useless repetitions, yet I cannot help mentioning once more the great importance of causing the smoke that heats one of the ovens I have been describing to descend at least as low as the level of the bottom of the oven, after it has passed round and over it, before it is permitted to rise up freely and escape by the chimney into the atmosphere. In setting the oven, and forming the canal for carrying off the smoke from the oven into the chimney, this may easily be effected: and, if it be done, the oven will retain its heat for a great length of time even after the fire is gone out; but, if it be not done, the fire must constantly be kept up, or the oven will soon be cooled by the cold air that will not fail to force its way through the fire-place and up the chimney.

From the result of this experiment it appears that an oven of the kind recommended is very far from being an expensive article; and there is no doubt but that, with a little care in the management of the fire, an oven of this sort would last many years without wanting any repairs. It is hardly necessary for me to add that a nest of these small ovens, consisting of three or four, put up together, and heated by a single fire, would be very useful in the kitchen of a private gentleman, and indeed of every large family.

If nests of small ovens should come into use (which I cannot help thinking will be the case), it would be best, as well for convenience in carriage as for other reasons, to make those which belong to the same nest not precisely of the same dimensions, but varying in size just so much as shall be necessary in order that they may be packed one within the other.

PART II.

PREFACE.

I TOO often find myself in situations in which I feel it to be necessary to make apologies for delays and irregularities in the publication of my writings. This second part of my tenth Essay was announced in the beginning of the year 1800; and it ought certainly to have made its appearance long ago, but a variety of circumstances has conspired to retard its publication.

During several months, almost the whole of my time was taken up with the business of the Royal Institution; and those who are acquainted with the nature and objects of that noble establishment will, no doubt, think that I judged wisely in preferring its interests to every other concern. For my own part, I certainly consider it as being by far the most useful, and consequently the most important, undertaking in which I was ever engaged, and of course I feel deeply interested in its success. The distinguished patronage and liberal support it has already received afford good ground to hope that it will continue to prosper, and be a lasting monument of the liberality and enterprising spirit of an enlightened nation.

It is certainly a proud circumstance for this country that in times like the present, and under the accumulated pressure of a long and expensive war, individuals generously came forward and subscribed in a very short time no less a sum than *thirty thousand pounds sterling*, for the noble purpose of "diffusing the knowledge and facilitating the general introduction of new and useful inventions and improvements."

In the *repository* of this new establishment will be found specimens of all the mechanical improvements which I have ventured to recommend to the public in my Essays.

CHAPTER IV.

An Account of a new Contrivance for roasting Meat. — Circumstance which gave rise to this Invention. — Means used for introducing it into common Use. — List of Tradesmen who manufacture Roasters. — Number of them that have already been sold. — Description of the Roaster. — Explanation of its Action. — Reasons why Meat roasted in this Machine is better tasted and more wholesome than when roasted on a Spit. — It is not only better tasted, but also more in Quantity when cooked. — Directions for setting Roasters in Brick-work. — Directions for the Management of a Roaster. — Miscellaneous Observations respecting Roasters and Ovens.

THERE is no process of cookery more troublesome to the cook, or attended with a greater waste of fuel, than roasting meat before an open fire.

Having had occasion, several years ago, to fit up a large kitchen (that belonging to the Military Academy at Munich) in which it was necessary to make arrangements for roasting meat every day for near 200 persons, I was led to consider this subject with some attention; and I availed myself of the opportunity which then offered to make a number of interesting experiments, from the results of which I was enabled to construct a machine for roasting, which upon trial was found to answer so well that I thought it deserving of being made known to the public. Accordingly, during the visit I made to this country in the years 1795 and 1796, I caused two of these roasters to be constructed in London,—one at the house then occupied by the Board of Agriculture, and the other at the Foundling Hospital; and a third was put up, under my direction, in Dublin, at the house of the Dublin Society.

All these were found to answer very well, and they were often imitated; but I had the mortification to find, on my return to England in the year 1798, that some mistakes had been made in the construction, and many in the management of them. Their fire-places had almost universally been made three or four times as large as they ought to have been, as neither the cooks, nor the bricklayers who were employed in setting them, could be persuaded that it was possible that any thing could be sufficiently roasted with a fire which to them appeared to be *ridiculously small;* and the large quantities of fuel which were introduced into these capacious fire-places not only destroyed the machinery very soon, but, what was still more fatal to the reputation of the contrivance, rendered it impossible for the meat to be well roasted.

When meat, surrounded by air, is exposed to the action of very intense heat, its surface is soon scorched and dried; which preventing the heat from penetrating freely to the centre of the piece, the meat cannot possibly be equally roasted throughout.

These mistakes could not fail to discredit the invention, and retard its introduction into general use; but, being convinced by long experience of the utility of the contrivance, as well as by the unanimous opinion in its favour of all those who had given it a fair trial, I was resolved to persist in my endeavours to make it

known, and, if possible, to bring it into use in this
country. The roaster in the kitchen of the Military
Academy at Munich had been in daily use more than
eight years; and many others in imitation of it, which
had been put up in private families in Bavaria and
other parts of Germany, and in Switzerland, had been
found to answer perfectly well; and as that in the
kitchen of the Foundling Hospital in London had
likewise, during the experience of two years, been found
to perform to the entire satisfaction of those who have
the direction of that noble institution, I was justified in
concluding that, wherever the experiment had failed, it
must have been owing to mismanagement. And I was
the more anxious to get this contrivance brought into
general use, as I was perfectly convinced that meat
roasted by this new process is not merely as good, but
decidedly better; that is to say, more delicate, more
juicy, more savoury, and higher flavoured, than when
roasted in the common way,—on a spit, before an
open fire.

A real improvement in the art of cookery, which
unites the advantage of economy with wholesomeness,
and an increase of enjoyment in eating, appeared to me
to be very interesting; and I attended to the subject
with all that zeal and perseverance which a conviction
of its importance naturally inspired.

On my return to this country, in the autumn of the
year 1798, one of the first things I undertook in the
prosecution of my favourite pursuit was to engage an
ingenious tradesman, who lives in a part of the town
which is much frequented (Mr. Summers, ironmonger,
of New Bond Street), to put up a roaster in his own
kitchen; to instruct his cook in the management of it;

to make daily use of it; to show it in actual use to his customers, and others who might desire to see it; and also to allow other cooks to be present, and assist when meat was roasted in it, in order to their being convinced of its utility, and taught how to manage it. I likewise prevailed on him to engage an intelligent bricklayer in his service who would submit to be taught to set roasters properly, and who would follow without deviation the directions he should receive. All these arrangements were carried into execution in the beginning of the year 1799; and since that time Mr. Summers has sold and put up no less than 260 roasters, all of which have been found to answer perfectly well; and, although he employs a great many hands in the manufacture of this new article, he is not able to satisfy all the demands of his numerous customers.

Many of these roasters have been put up in the houses of persons of the highest rank and distinction; others in the kitchens of artificers and tradesmen; and others again in schools, taverns, and other houses of public resort; and in all these different situations the use of them has been found to be economical, and advantageous in all respects.

Several other tradesmen in London have also been engaged in the manufacture of roasters. Mr. Hopkins, of Greek Street, Soho, ironmonger to the king, made that which is at the Foundling Hospital, likewise that which was put up in the house formerly occupied by the Board of Agriculture; and he informs me that he has sold above 200 others, which have been put up in the kitchens of various hospitals and private families in the capital and in different parts of the country.

Messrs. Moffat & Co., of Great Queen Street, Lincoln's-Inn Fields, and Mr. Feetham, of Oxford Street, as also Mr. Gregory, Mr. Spotswood, Mr. Hanan, and Mr. Briadwood, in Edinburgh, have engaged in the manufacture of them. Other tradesmen, no doubt, with whose names I am not acquainted, have manufactured them; and as there is no difficulty whatever in their construction, and as all persons are at full liberty to manufacture and sell them, I hope soon to see these roasters become a common article of trade.

I have done all that was in my power to improve and to bring them forward into notice; and all my wishes respecting them will be accomplished if they should be found to be useful, and if the public is furnished with them at reasonable prices.

Several roasters, constructed by different workmen, may be seen, some of them set in brick-work, and others not, at the repository of the Royal Institution.

I have delayed thus long to publish a description of this contrivance, in order that its usefulness might previously be established by experience; and also that I might be able, with the description, to give notice to the public where the thing described might be seen. I was likewise desirous of being able at the same time to point out several places where the article might be had.

These objects having been fully accomplished, I shall now proceed by giving

An Account of the Roaster, and of the Principles on which it is constructed.

When I first set about to contrive this machine, meditating on the nature of the mechanical and chemical operations that take place in the culinary process in question, it appeared to me that there could not possibly be any thing more necessary to the roasting of meat than heat in certain degrees of intensity, accompanied by certain degrees of dryness; and I thought if matters could be so arranged, by means of simple mechanical contrivances, that the cook should be enabled not only to regulate the degrees of heat at pleasure, but also to combine any given degree of heat with any degree of moisture or of dryness required, this would unquestionably put it in his power to perform every process of roasting in the highest possible perfection.

The means I used for attaining these ends will appear by the following description of the machinery I caused to be constructed for that purpose.

The most essential part of this machinery, which I shall call the *body* of the roaster (see Fig. 14), is a

Fig. 14.

hollow cylinder of sheet iron (which, for a roaster of a moderate size, may be made about 18 inches in diameter and 24 inches long), closed at one end, and set in a horizontal position in a mass of brick-work, in such a manner that the flame of a small fire, which is made in a closed fire-place directly under it, may play all round it, and heat it equally and expeditiously. The open end of this cylinder, which should be even with the front of the brick-work in which it is set, is closed either with a double door of sheet iron, or with a single door of sheet iron covered on the outside with a panel of wood; and in the cylinder there is a horizontal shelf, made of a flat plate of sheet iron, which is supported on ledges riveted to the inside of the cylinder, on each side of it. This shelf is situated about three inches below the centre or level of the axis of the body of the roaster, and it serves as a support for a dripping-pan, in which, or rather over which, the meat to be roasted is placed.

This dripping-pan, which is made of sheet iron, is about 2 inches deep, 16 inches wide above, 15½ inches in width below, and 22 inches long; and it is placed on four short feet, or, what is better, on two long sliders, bent upwards at their two extremities, and fastened to the ends of the dripping-pan, forming, together with the dripping-pan, a kind of sledge; the bottom of the dripping-pan being raised by these means about an inch above the horizontal shelf on which it is supported.

In order that the dripping-pan on being pushed into or drawn out of the roaster may be made to preserve its direction, two straight grooves are made in the shelf on which it is supported, which, receiving the sliders of the dripping-pan, prevent it from slipping about from side to side, and striking against the sides of the roaster. The front ends of these grooves are seen in Fig. 14, as are also the front ends of the sliders of the dripping-pan, and one of its handles.

In the dripping-pan, a gridiron (seen in Fig. 14) is placed, the horizontal bars of which are on a level with the sides or brim of the dripping-pan, and on this gridiron the meat to be roasted is laid; care being taken that there be always a sufficient quantity of water in the dripping-pan to cover the whole of its bottom to the height of at least half or three quarters of an inch.

This water is essential to the success of the process of roasting: it is designed for receiving the drippings from the meat, and preventing their falling on the heated bottom of the dripping-pan, where they would be evaporated, and their oily parts burned or volatilized, filling the roaster with ill-scented vapours, which would spoil the meat by giving it a disagreeable taste and smell.

It was with a view more effectually to defend the bottom of the dripping-pan from the fire, and prevent as much as possible the evaporation of the water it contains, that the dripping-pan was raised on feet or sliders, instead of being merely set down on its bottom on the shelf which supports it in the roaster.

A late improvement has been made in the arrangement of the dripping-pan, by an ingenious workman at Norwich, Mr. Frost, who has been employed in putting up roasters in that part of the country; an invention which I think will, in many cases, if not in all, be found very useful. Having put a certain quantity of water into the principal dripping-pan, which is constructed of sheet iron, he places a second, shallower, made of tin, and standing on four short feet, into the first, and then places the gridiron which is to support the meat in this second dripping-pan. As the water in the first keeps the second cool, there is no necessity for putting water into this; and the drippings of the meat may, without danger, be suffered to fall into it, and to remain there unmixed with water. When Yorkshire puddings or potatoes are cooked under roasting meat, this arrangement will be found very convenient.

In constructing the dripping-pans, and fitting them to each other, care must be taken that the second do not touch the first, except by the ends of its feet; and especially that the bottom of the second (which may be made dishing) do not touch the bottom of the first. The lengths and widths of the two dripping-pans above, or at their brims, may be equal, and the brim of the second may stand about half an inch above the level of the brim of the first. The horizontal level of the upper surface of the gridiron should not be lower than the level of the brim of the second dripping-pan; and the meat should be so placed on the gridiron that the drippings from it cannot fail to fall into the dripping-pan, and never upon the hot bottom or sides of the roaster.

To carry off the steam which arises from the water in the dripping-pan, and that which escapes from the meat in roasting, there is a steam-tube belonging to the roaster, which is situated at the upper part of the roaster, commonly a little on one side and near the front of it, to which tube there is a damper, which is so contrived as to be easily regulated without opening the door of the roaster. This steam-tube is distinctly seen in Fig. 14; and the end of the handle by which its damper is moved may be seen in Fig. 15 (p. 261).

The heat of the roaster is regulated at pleasure, and to the greatest nicety, by means of the register in the ash-pit door of its fire-place (represented in Fig. 15) and by the damper in the canal, by which the smoke goes off into the chimney, which damper is not represented in any of the figures.

The *dryness* in the roaster is regulated by the damper of the steam-tube, and also by means of a very essential part of the apparatus — the *blowpipes* — which still remain to be described. They are distinctly represented in the Figs. 14, 15, and 16.

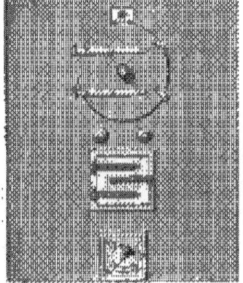

Fig. 15.

These blowpipes, which lie immediately under the roaster, are two tubes of iron, about 2¼ inches in diameter and 23 inches long, or about 1 inch shorter than the roaster; which tubes, by means of elbows at their farther ends, are firmly fixed to the bottom of the roaster, and communicate with the inside of it. The hither ends of these tubes come through the brick-work, and are seen in front of the roaster, being even with its face.

These blowpipes have stoppers, by which they are accurately closed; but when the meat is to be *browned* these stoppers are removed, or drawn out a little, and the damper in the steam-tube of the roaster being at the same time opened a strong current of hot air presses in through the tubes into the roaster, and through the roaster into and through the steam-tube, carrying and driving away all the moist air and vapour out of the roaster.

Fig. 16.

As these blowpipes are situated immediately below the roaster and just over the fire, and are surrounded on every side by the flame of the burning fuel (see Fig. 16), they are much exposed to the heat; and when the fire is made to burn briskly, which should always be done when the meat is to be browned, they will be heated red-hot, consequently the air which passes through them into the roaster will be much heated; and this *hot wind* which blows over the meat will suddenly heat and dry its surface in every part, and give it that appearance and taste which are peculiar to meat that is well roasted.

When these roasters were first proposed, and before their merit was established, many doubts were entertained respecting the taste of the food prepared in them.

As the meat was shut up in a confined space, which has much the appearance of an oven, it was natural enough to suspect that it would be rather *baked* than *roasted;* but all those who have tried the experiment have found that this is by no means the case. The meat is *roasted*, and not *baked;* and, however bold the assertion may appear, I will venture to affirm that meat of every kind, without any exception, roasted in a roaster, is *better tasted, higher flavoured, and much more juicy and delicate* than when roasted on a spit before an open fire.

I should not have dared to have published this opinion four years ago; but I can with safety do it now, for I can appeal for a confirmation of the fact to the results of a number of decisive experiments lately made in this metropolis, and by the most competent judges.

Among many others who, during the last year, have caused roasters to be put up in their kitchens, I could mention one person in particular, a nobleman, distinguished as much by his ingenuity and indefatigable zeal in promoting useful improvements as by his urbanity and his knowledge in the art of refined cookery, who had two roasters put in his house in town, and who informs me that he has frequently invited company to dine with him since his roasters have been in use, and that the dishes prepared in them have never failed to meet with marked approbation.

In enumerating the excellences of this new implement of cookery, there is one of indisputable importance, which ought not to be omitted. When meat is roasted in this machine, its quantity, determined by weight, is considerably greater than if it were roasted upon a spit before a fire. To ascertain this fact, two legs of mutton taken from the same carcass, and made perfectly equal in weight before they were cooked, were roasted on the same day, the one in a roaster, the other on a spit before the fire; and, to prevent all deception, the persons employed in roasting them were not informed of the principal design of the experiment. When these pieces of roasted meat came from the fire they were carefully weighed; when it appeared that the piece which had been roasted in the roaster was heavier than the other by a difference which was equal to six per cent, or six pounds in a hundred. But this even is not all; nor is it indeed the most important result of the experiment. These two legs of mutton were brought upon table at the same time, and a large and perfectly unprejudiced company was assembled to eat them. They were both declared to be very good; but a decided preference was unanimously given to that which had been roasted in the roaster, it was much more juicy, and was thought better tasted. They were both fairly eaten up, nothing remaining of either of them that was eatable. Their fragments, which had been carefully preserved, being now collected and placed in their separate dishes, it was *a comparison of these fragments* which afforded the most striking proof of the relative merit of these two methods of roasting meat, in respect to the economy of food. Of the leg of mutton which had been roasted in the roaster, hardly any thing visible remained except the bare bone; while a considerable heap was formed of scraps not eatable which remained of that roasted on a spit.

I believe I may venture to say that the result of this experiment is deserving of the most serious attention, especially in this country, where so much roasted meat is eaten, and where the economy of food is every day growing to be more and more an object of public concern.

I could mention several other experiments similar to that just described, which have been made, and with similar results; but it would be superfluous to bring many examples to ascertain a fact which is so well established by one.

There is one peculiarity more respecting meat roasted in a roaster, which I must mention; that is, the uncommon delicacy of the taste of the fat of the meat so roasted, especially when it has been done by a very slow fire. When good mutton is roasted in this manner, its fat is exquisitely sweet and well tasted, and when eaten with currant jelly can hardly be distinguished from the fat of the very best venison. The fat parts of other kinds of meat are also uncommonly delicate when prepared in this manner; and there is reason to think that they are much less unwholesome than when they are roasted before an open fire.

The heat which is generated by the rays which proceed from burning fuel is frequently most intense; and hence it is that the surface of a piece of meat that is roasted on a spit is often quite burned, and rendered not only hard and ill-tasted, but very unwholesome. The fat of venison is not thought to be unwholesome; but, in roasting venison, care is taken, by covering it, to prevent the rays from the fire from burning it. In the roasting machine, the bad effects of these direct rays are always prevented by the sides of the roaster, which intercepts them, and protects the surface of the meat from the excessive violence of their action; and even when, at the end of the process of roasting, the intensity of the heat in the roaster is so far increased as to brown the surface of the meat, yet this heat being communicated through the medium of a heated fluid (air) is much more moderate and uniform and certain in its effects, than direct rays which proceed from burning fuel, or from bodies heated to a state of incandescence.

Directions for setting Roasters.

There are two points to which attention must be paid by bricklayers in setting these roasters, otherwise they will not be found to answer. Their fire-places must be made extremely small; and provision must be made for cleaning out their flues from time to time when they become obstructed with soot.

When I first introduced these roasters into this country five years ago, I was not fully aware of the irresistible propensity to make too great fires on all occasions, which those people have who inhabit kitchens; but sad experience has since taught me that nothing short of rendering it absolutely impossible to destroy my roasters by fire will prevent their being so destroyed. The knowledge of this fact has put me on my guard, and I now take effectual measures for preventing this evil. I cause the fire-places of roasters to be made very small, and direct them to be situated at a considerable distance below the bottom of the roaster.

For a roaster which is 18 inches wide, and 24 inches long, the fire-place should not be more than 7 inches wide and 9 inches long; and the side walls of the fire-place should be quite vertical to the height of 6 or 7 inches. Small as this fire-place may appear to be, it will contain quite coals enough to heat the roaster, and many more than will be found necessary for keeping it hot when heated. The fact is that the quantity of fuel required to roast meat in this way is almost incredibly small. By experiments made with great care at the Foundling Hospital, it appeared to be only about one sixteenth part of the quantity which would be required to roast the same quantity of meat in the common way before an open fire. But it is not merely to save fuel that I recommend the fire-places to be made very small: it is to prevent the roasters from being wantonly destroyed, the meat spoiled, and a useful invention discredited.

With regard to the provision which ought to be made, in the setting of a roaster, for occasionally cleaning out its flues, this must be done by leaving proper openings (about 4 or 5 inches square, for instance) in the brick-work, to introduce a brush, like a bottle-brush, with a long handle; which openings may be closed with stoppers or fit pieces of brick or of stone, and the joinings made good with a little moist clay. To render these stoppers more conspicuous, they may each be furnished with a small iron ring or knob, which will likewise be useful as a handle in removing them and replacing them.

In Figs. 15 and 16, a simple contrivance may be seen represented, by means of which the soot which is apt to collect about the top of a roaster may be removed with very little trouble as often as it shall be found necessary, without injuring the brick-work or deranging any part of the machinery. By means of an oblong square frame, constructed of sheet iron, and fastened to the top of the roaster by rivets, a door-way is opened into the void space left for the flame and smoke between the outside of the roaster and the hollow arch or vault in which it is placed; and by introducing a brush with a flexible handle through this door-way, the soot adhering to the outside of the top of the roaster, and to the surface of the brick-work surrounding it, may be detached and made to fall back into the fire-place, from whence it may be removed with a shovel. The sides of the roaster may be cleaned by introducing a brush through the door-way of the fire-place.

The door-way at the top of the roaster may be closed either by a stopper made of sheet iron, or by a fit piece of stone or brick, furnished with a ring or knob to serve as a handle to it.

If cokes be burned under these roasters, instead of coal (which, as they will not be more expensive fuel, and as they burn longer, and give a more equal heat, I would strongly recommend), the flues will seldom if ever require to be cleaned out. I burn nothing but coke and a few pieces of wood in the closed fire-places of my own kitchen; and for my open chimney fires I use a mixture of coke and coals, which makes a very pleasant fire, and is, I believe, less expensive than coals. It appears to me that there is no subject which offers so promising a field for experimental investigation, and where useful improvements would be so likely to be made, as in the *combination and preparation of fuel*. But to return from this digression.

In constructing the fire-place of a roaster (and all other closed fire-places) care must be taken to place the iron bars on which the fuel burns at a considerable distance from the door of the fire-place; otherwise, this door being near the fire, its handle will become very hot, and it will burn the hand of a person that takes hold of it. I have more than once seen roasters and ovens condemned, disgraced, and totally neglected, merely from an accident of this kind. And yet how easy would it have been to have corrected this fault! If the door of the fire-place is found to become too hot, send for the bricklayer, and let him put the fire-place farther backward.

There should always be a passage or throat, of a certain length, between the mouth or door of a closed fire-place and the fire-place properly so called, or the cavity occupied by the burning fuel. Where fire-places are of large dimensions, it is very useful (as indeed it is customary) to keep this throat constantly filled and choked up with coal. This coal, which, as there is no supply of air in the passage, does not burn, serves to defend the fire-place door from the heat of the fire. It serves another useful purpose: it gets well warmed, and even heated very hot, before it is pushed forward into the fire-place, which disposes it to take fire instantaneously, and without cooling the fire-place and depressing the fire when it is introduced. If any part of it takes fire while it occupies the throat or passage of the fire-place, it is that part only which is in immediate contact with the burning fuel, and what is so burned is consumed under the most advantageous circumstances; for the thick vapour which rises from this coal, as it grows very hot, and which under other less favourable circumstances would not fail to go off in smoke, takes fire in passing over the burning fuel, and burns with a clear bright flame. I have had frequent opportunities of verifying this interesting fact; and I mention it now, in order, if possible, to fix the attention of those who have the management of large fires, to an object which perhaps is of greater importance than they are aware of.

When good reasons can be assigned for the advantages which result from any common practice, this not only tends to satisfy the mind, and make people careful, cheerful, and attentive in the prosecution of their business, but it has also a very salutary influence, by preventing those perpetual variations and idle attempts at improvement, *undirected by science*, which are the consequence of the inconstancy, curiosity, and restlessness of man.

Discoveries are always accidental; and the great use of science is by investigating the nature of the effects produced by any process or contrivance, and of the causes by which they are brought about, to explain the operation and determine the precise value of every new invention. This fixes as it were the *latitude* and *longitude* of each discovery, and enables us to place it in that part of the map of human knowledge which it ought to occupy. It likewise enables us to use it in taking *bearings* and *distances*, and in shaping our course when we go in search of new discoveries. But I am again straying very far from my humble subject.

In constructing closed fire-places for roasters, boilers, ovens, etc., for kitchens, I have found it to be a good general rule to make the distance between the fire-place door and the hither end of the bars of the grate just equal to the width of the fire-place, measured just above the bars. In fire-places of a moderate size, where double doors are used, it will suffice if the distance from the hinder side of the inner door to the hither end of the bars be made equal to the width of a brick, or $4\frac{1}{2}$ inches; but, if the door be not double, it is necessary that the length of the passage from the door into the place occupied by the burning fuel should be at least 6 or 7 inches.

In setting the iron frame of the door of a closed fire-place, care should be taken to mask the metal by setting the bricks before it in such a manner that no part of the frame *may be seen* (if I may use that expression) by the fire. This precaution should be used in constructing fire-places of all sizes, otherwise the frame of the fire-place door will be heated very hot by the rays from the burning fuel, especially when the fire-place is large, and its form will soon be destroyed by the frequent expansion and contraction of the metal. The consequences of this change of form will be the loosening of the frame in the brick-work, and the admission of air into the fire-place over the fire between the sides of the frame and the brick-work, and likewise between the frame and its door, which will no longer fit each other.

The expense of keeping large fire-places in repair is very considerable, as I have learned from some of the London brewers. More than nine tenths of that expense might easily be saved by constructing the machinery more scientifically, and using it with care.

Fig. 15, page 261, is a front view; and Fig. 16, page 262, represents a vertical section of a roaster, set in brick-work. The hollow spaces represented in Fig. 16 are expressed by strong vertical lines; namely, the ash-pit, A; the fire-place, B; the space between the outside of the roaster and the arch of brick-work which surrounds it, C; the broad canal at the farther end of the roaster, by which the smoke descends, D; and the place E, where it turns, in order to pass upwards into the chimney by the perpendicular canal, F. The brick-work is expressed by fainter lines drawn in the same direction.

The farther end of the roaster must be so fixed in the brick-work that no part of the smoke can find its way from the fire-place, B, directly into the canal, D, otherwise it will not pass up by the sides of the roaster to the top of it. At the top of the roaster, at its farther end, an opening must of course be left for the smoke to pass into the descending canal, D.

As I have already mentioned the necessity of causing the smoke which is used for heating an iron oven or a roaster *to descend* before it is permitted to pass off into the chimney, I shall insist no farther on that important point in this place. It may, however, be useful to observe that, if the place where a roaster is set is not deep enough to allow of the descending canal, D, and the canal, F, by which the smoke ascends and passes into the chimney, to be situated at the farther end of the roaster, both these canals may, without the smallest inconvenience, be placed on one side of the roaster; indeed, as houses are now built, it will commonly be most convenient to place them on one side, and not at the end of the roaster. When this is done, the smoke must be permitted to pass up behind the farther end of the roaster, as well as by the sides of it.

By taking away a large flat stone, or a twelve-inch tile, placed edgeways, a passage from A to E may be opened occasionally, in order to clean out the canals, D and F, and remove the soot. These passages may be cleaned out either from above or from below, by means of a brush with a long flexible handle.

The steam-tube (which is seen in this figure) must open into a separate canal (not expressed in the figure), which must be constructed for the sole purpose of carrying off the steam into the chimney or into the open air. If this steam-tube were to open into either of the cavities or canals, C, D, E, or F, in which the smoke from the fire which heats the roaster circulates, this smoke might, on some occasions, be driven back into the roaster, which could not fail to give a bad taste to the meat. The steam-tube must be laid on a descent, otherwise the water generated in it, in consequence of the condensation of the steam, might run back into the roaster.

Some care will be necessary in forming the vault which is to cover the roaster above. Its form should be regular, in order that it may be everywhere at the same distance from the roaster; and its concave surface should be as even and smooth as possible, in order that there may be the fewer cavities for the lodgement of soot. The distance between the outside of the roaster and the concave surface of this vault may be about 2 inches; and the same distance may be preserved below, between the brick-work and the sides of the roaster. In the Fig. 15 the outline of the fire-place and of the cavity in which the roaster is set is indicated by a dotted line.

Directions for the Management of a Roaster.

Care must be taken to keep the roaster very clean, and, above all, to prevent the meat from touching the sides of it, and the gravy from being spilt on its bottom. If by any means it becomes greasy in any part that is exposed to the action of the fire, as the metal becomes hot this grease will be evaporated, as has already been observed, and will fill the roaster with the most offensive vapour. When grease spots appear, the inside of the roaster must be washed, first with soap and water to take away the grease, and then with pure water to take away the soap, and it must then be wiped with a cloth till it be quite dry.

The fire must be moderate, and time must be allowed for the meat to be roasted *by the most gentle heat*. About one third more time should in general be employed in roasting meat in a roaster, than would be necessary to roast it in the usual way, on a spit before a fire.

The blowpipes should be kept constantly closed from the time the meat goes into the roaster till within 12 or 15 minutes of its being sufficiently done to be sent to the table; that is to say, till it is fit *to be browned*.

The meat is browned in the following manner: the fire is made to burn bright and clear for a few minutes, till the blowpipes begin to be red-hot (which may be seen by withdrawing their stoppers for a moment, and looking into them), when the damper of the steam-tube of the roaster being opened, and the stoppers of the blowpipes drawn out, a certain quantity of air is permitted to pass through the heated blowpipes into and through the roaster.

I say a certain quantity of air is allowed to pass through the blowpipes into the roaster. If the steam-tube and the blowpipes were set wide open, it is very possible that too much might be admitted, and that the inside of the roaster and its contents might be cooled by it, instead of being raised to a higher temperature. As the velocity with which the cold air of the atmosphere will rush into and through the blowpipes of a roaster will depend on a variety of circumstances, and may be very different even in roasters of the same size and construction, no general rules can be given in browning the meat for the regulation of the stoppers of the blow-pipes, and of the damper in the steam-tube: these must depend on what may be called *the trim of the roaster*, which will soon be discovered by the cook.

There is an infallible rule for the regulation of the damper of the steam-tube, *during the time the meat is roasting by a gentle heat*. It must then be kept just so much opened that the steam which arises from the meat, and from the evaporation of the water in the dripping-pan, may not be seen coming out of the roaster through the crevices of its door; for, if it be more opened, the cold air of the atmosphere will rush into the roaster through those crevices, and by partially cooling it will derange the process that is going on; and, if it be less opened, the room will be filled with steam.

In brightening the fire, preparatory to the browning of the meat, the register in the ash-pit door, and the damper in the canal by which the smoke passes off into the chimney, should both be opened; and it may be useful to stir up the fire with a poker, but this would be a very improper time for throwing a quantity of fresh coals into the fire-place, for that would cool the fireplace, and damp the fire for a considerable time. By far the best method of brightening the fire for this purpose would be to throw a small fagot into the fire, or a little bundle of dry wood of any kind, split into small pieces about six or seven inches in length. This would afford a clear bright flame, which would heat the blowpipes quickly, and without injuring them. Indeed, wood ought always to be used for heating roasters, in preference to coal, where it can be had; and the quantity of it required is so extremely small, that the difference in the expense would be very trifling, even here in London, where the price of fire-wood is so high. And if the durability of the machinery be taken into the account, which is but just, I am confident that, for heating roasters and ovens constructed of sheet iron, coals would turn out to be dearer fuel than wood.

I have already insisted so much on the necessity of keeping a quantity of water under meat that is roasting, in order to prevent the drippings from the meat from falling on any very hot metal, that I shall not now enlarge farther on the subject, except by saying once more that it is a circumstance to which it is indispensably necessary to pay attention.

When meat is roasted by a very moderate heat, it will seldom or never require being either turned or basted; but, when the heat in the roaster is more intense, it will be found useful both to turn it and to baste it three or four times during the process. The reason of this difference in the manner of proceeding will be evident to those who consider the matter with attention.

When roasters are constructed of large dimensions, several kinds of meat may be roasted in them at the same time. If care be taken to preserve their drippings separate, which may easily be done by placing under each a separate dish or dripping-pan, standing in water contained in a larger dripping-pan, there will be no mixture of tastes; and, what no doubt will appear still more extraordinary, a whole dinner, consisting of various dishes,—roasted, stewed, baked, and boiled, — may be prepared at the same time in the same roaster, without any mixture whatever of tastes. A respectable friend of mine who first made the experiment, and who has since repeated it several times, has assured me of this curious fact. It may, perhaps, in time turn out to be an important discovery. A simple and economical contrivance, by means of which all the different processes of cookery could be carried on at the same time and by one small fire, would, no doubt, be a valuable acquisition.

It is very certain that roasters will either bake or roast separately in the highest possible perfection; and it is not improbable that, with certain precautions in the management of them, they may be made to perform those two processes at the same time, in such a manner as to give general satisfaction. When roasters are designed for roasting and baking at the same time, they should be made sufficiently large to admit of a shelf above the meat, on which the things to be baked should be placed. I am told that above half the roasters lately put up in London are so constructed, and that they are frequently made to roast and bake at the same time. I shall take another opportunity of enlarging on the utility of this contrivance.

There is a precaution to be taken in opening the door of a roaster, when meat is roasting in it, which ought never to be neglected; that is, to open the steam-tube and both the blowpipes, for about a quarter of a minute, or while a person can count fifteen or twenty, before the door of the roaster be thrown open. This will drive away the steam and vapour out of the roaster, which otherwise would not fail to come into the room as often as the door of the roaster is opened.

As it will frequently happen that the meat will be done before it will be time to send it up to table, when this is the case, it may either be taken out of the roaster and put into a hot closet, which may very conveniently be situated immediately over the roaster, or it may remain in the roaster till it is wanted. If this last-mentioned method of keeping it warm be adopted, the following precautions will be necessary for cooling the roaster, otherwise the process of roasting will still go on, and the meat, instead of being merely kept warm, will be over done. The register in the ash-pit door should be closed; the fire-place door and the damper in the chimney should be set wide open; the fire should either be taken out of the fire-place or it should be covered with cold ashes; and, lastly, the damper in the steam-tube and both the blowpipes should be opened. By these means the heat will very soon be driven away up the chimney, and, as soon as it is so far moderated as to be no longer dangerous, the blow-pipes and the damper in the steam-tube may be nearly closed; and if there should be danger of the cooling being carried too far, the fire-place door may be shut. By these means the heat of the roaster and of the brick-work which surrounds it may be moderated and regulated at pleasure; and meat already roasted may be kept warm, for almost any length of time, without any danger of its being spoiled.

Miscellaneous Observations respecting Roasters and Ovens.

I shall, no doubt, be criticised by many for dwelling so long on a subject which to them will appear low, vulgar, and trifling; but I must not be deterred by fastidious criticisms from doing all I can do to succeed in what I have undertaken. Were I to treat my subject superficially, my writings would be of no use to anybody, and my labour would be lost; but, by investigating it thoroughly, I may perhaps engage others to pay that attention to it which, from its importance to society, it certainly deserves. If improvements in articles of elegant luxury, which not one person in ten thousand is rich enough to purchase, are considered as matters of public concern, how much more interesting to a benevolent mind must those improvements be which contribute to the comfort and convenience of every class of society, rich and poor.

But the subject now under consideration is very far from being uninteresting, even if we consider it merely as it is connected with science, without any immediate view to its utility; for in it are involved several of the most abstruse questions relative to the doctrine of heat.

Many have objected to the roaster, on the supposition that meat cooked in it must necessarily partake more of the nature of baked meat than of roasted meat. The general appearance of the machinery is certainly calculated to give rise to that idea, and when it is known that all kinds of baking may be performed in great perfection in the roaster, that circumstance no doubt tended very much to confirm the suspicion; but, when we examine the matter attentively, I think we shall find that this objection is not well founded.

When any thing is baked in an oven (on the common construction), the heat is gradually diminishing during the whole time the process is going on. In the roaster, the heat is regulated at pleasure, and can be suddenly increased towards the end of the process; by which means the distinguishing and most delicate operation, *the browning of the surface* of the meat, can be effected in a few minutes, which prevents the drying up of the meat and the loss of its best juices.

In an oven, the exhalations being confined, the meat seldom fails to acquire a peculiar and very disagreeable smell and taste, which, no doubt, is occasioned solely by those confined vapours. The steam-tube of a roaster being always set open, when in browning the meat the heat is sufficiently raised to evaporate the oily particles at its surface, the noxious vapours unavoidably generated in that process are immediately driven away out of the roaster by the current of hot and pure air from the blow-pipes. This leaves the meat perfectly free both from the taste and the smell peculiar to baked meat.

Some have objected to roasters, on an idea that, as the water which is placed under the meat is (in part at least) evaporated during the process, this must make the meat sodden, or give it the appearance and taste of meat boiled in steam; but this objection has no better foundation than that we have just examined. As steam is much lighter than air, that generated from the water in the dripping-pan will immediately rise up to the top of the roaster, and pass off by the steam-tube, and the meat will remain surrounded by air, and not by steam. But were the roaster to be constantly full of steam, to the perfect exclusion of all air, which however is impossible, this would have no tendency whatever to make the meat sodden. It is a curious fact that steam, so far from being a moist fluid, is perfectly dry, as long as it retains its elastic form; and that it is of so drying a nature that it cannot be contained in wooden vessels (however well seasoned they may be) without drying them and making them shrink till they crack and fall to pieces.

Steam is never moist. When it is condensed with cold, it becomes water, which is moisture itself; but the steam in a roaster, which surrounds meat that is roasting, cannot be condensed upon it; for the surface of the meat, being heated by the calorific rays from the top and sides of the roaster, is even hotter than the steam.

If steam were a moist fluid, it would be found very difficult to bake bread, or any thing else, in a common oven.

Meat which is *boiled* or *sodden* in steam is put cold into the containing vessel, and the hot steam which is admitted is instantly condensed on its surface, and the water resulting from this condensation of steam dilutes the juices of the meat and washes them away, leaving the meat tasteless and insipid at its surface; but when meat is put cold into a roaster, the water in the dripping-pan being cold likewise, long before it can acquire heat sufficient to make it boil, the surface of the meat will become too hot for steam to be condensed upon it; and, were it not to be browned at all, it could not possibly taste sodden.

It appears to me that these elucidations are sufficient to remove the two objections which are most commonly made to the roaster by those who are not well acquainted with its mechanism and manner of acting.

In my account of the blowpipes, I have said that the current of air which comes into the roaster through them, when they are opened to brown the meat, "drives away all the moist air and vapour out of the roaster." This I well know is not an accurate account of what really happens; but it may serve, perhaps better than a more scientific explanation, to give the generality of readers distinct ideas of the nature of the effects that are produced by them. The noxious vapour generated from the oily particles that are evaporated by the strong heat are most certainly driven away precisely in the manner described; and we have just seen how very essential it is that these vapours should not be permitted to remain in the roaster. And whether the surface of the meat be in fact dried by the immediate contact of a current of hot and dry air, or whether this effect is produced in consequence of an increase of calorific rays from the top and sides of the roaster occasioned by the additional heat communicated to the internal surface of the roaster by this hot wind, the utility of the blowpipes is equally evident in both cases.

CHAPTER V.

More particular Descriptions of the several Parts of the Roaster, designed for the Information of Workmen. — Of the Body of the Roaster. — Of the Advantages which result from its peculiar Form. — Of the best Method of proceeding in covering the iron Doors of Roasters and Ovens, with Panels of Wood, for confining the Heat. — Method of constructing double Doors of sheet Iron and of cast Iron. — Of the Blowpipes. — Of the Steam-tube. — Of the Dripping-pan. — Precautions to be used for preventing the too rapid Evaporation of the Water in the Dripping-pan. — Of large Roasters that may be used for roasting and baking at the same Time. — Precautions which become necessary when Roasters are made very large. — Of various Alterations that may be made in the Forms of Roasters, and of the Advantages and Disadvantages of each of them. — Account of some Attempts to simplify the Construction of Roasters. — Of a Roasting-oven. — Of the Difference between a Roasting-oven and a Roaster.

ALTHOUGH it will be easy for persons acquainted with the mechanic arts, and accustomed to examine drawings and descriptions of machines, to form a perfect idea of the invention in question from what has already been said, yet something more will be necessary for the instruction of artificers who may be employed in executing the work, and more especially for such as may from these descriptions undertake to construct roasters without ever having seen one. By going into these details, I shall no doubt find opportunities for introducing occasional remarks on the uses and management of the various parts of the machinery, which will tend not a little to illustrate the foregoing descriptions, and enable the reader to form a more precise and satisfactory opinion respecting the merit of the contrivance.

Of the Body of the Roaster.

Although I have directed the body of the roaster to be made cylindrical, it may, without any considerable inconvenience, be constructed of other forms. The reasons why I preferred the cylindrical form to all others were because I was told by workmen that it was the form of easiest construction; and because I knew it to be the form best adapted for strength and durability.

There is another reason, which I did not dare to communicate to the workmen (iron-plate workers) whom I was obliged to employ, in order to introduce this contrivance into common use in this country; when roasters are of this form, it will be easy to make them of cast iron, which will render the article not only cheaper to the purchaser, but also much more durable, and better on many accounts.

As there is a certain proportion of sulphur in the coal commonly used in this country, I was always perfectly aware of the consequences of burning it under roasters constructed of sheet iron. I knew that the sulphurous vapour from such fuel would be much more injurious to the roaster, and especially to its blowpipes (which are much exposed) than the clear flame of a wood fire; but I trusted to the remedy, which I knew might easily be provided for this defect. I thought that cast iron, which is much less liable to be injured by a coal fire than wrought iron, would soon be substituted in lieu of it, first for the blowpipes, and then for the body of the roaster. In this expectation I have not been disappointed, for the blowpipes of roasters are now commonly made of cast iron by the London workmen; and, where sea-coal is used as fuel, they never should be made of any other material.

The first roasters I caused to be made had all flat bottoms, and their sides were vertical, and their tops were arched over in the form of a trunk; but several inconveniences were found to result from this shape. Their bottoms were too much exposed to the heat, and this excessive heat in that part heated the bottom of the dripping-pan too much, and caused the water in it to be soon evaporated; it likewise caused them to warp, and sometimes prevented their doors from closing them with that precision which is necessary.

If the hot air in a roaster be permitted to escape by the crevices of its door, or, what is still worse and more likely to happen, if cold air be permitted to enter the roaster by those openings, it is quite impossible that the process of roasting can go on well.

As cold air will always tend to press into the body of the roaster by every passage that is left open, whenever, the roaster being hot, the damper of its steam-tube is open, — this shows how necessary it is, in roasting meat, not to leave that damper open at any time when it ought to be kept closed.

As iron doors for confining heat are very liable to be warped by the expansion of the metal, they should never be made to shut into grooves, but they should be made to close tight by causing the flat surface of the inside of the door to lie against and touch in all parts the front edge of the door frame, which front edge must of course be made to be perfectly level, and as smooth as possible.

When the body of the roaster is made cylindrical, it will be easier to make the front of it, against which its door closes, level, than if it were of any other form; and when the door is circular, by making it a little dishing, it will not be liable to be warped, especially when it is made double.

If the front end of the cylinder of sheet iron which forms the body of the roaster be turned outwards over a very stout iron wire (about one third of an inch in diameter, for instance), this will strengthen the roaster very much, and will render it easier to make the end of the roaster level to receive the flat surface of its door: it can most easily be made level by placing the cylinder in a vertical or upright position, with its open end downwards, on a flat anvil, and hammering the wire above mentioned till its front edge, which reposes on the anvil, is quite level.

In order that the door of the roaster may close well, its hinges should be made to project outwards two or three inches beyond the sides of the roaster; and it should be fastened not by a common latch, but by two turn-buckles, situated just opposite to the two hinges. The distance at which the two hinges (and consequently the two turn-buckles) should be placed from each other should be equal to half the diameter of the roaster.

The hooks for the hinges, and also the support for the turn-buckles, should be situated at the projecting ends of strong iron straps, fastened at one of their ends to the outside of the roaster, by means of riveting-nails. The manner in which these turn-buckles are constructed, and the manner in which they are fastened to the roaster, may be seen by examining Fig. 17, where they are represented on a large scale.

The first roasters that were made were furnished with two separate doors, the one placed about four inches within the body of the roaster, the other even with its front. As the inside door had no hinges, but, like a common oven door, was taken quite away when the roaster was opened, there was some trouble in the management of it; and it was found that the cooks, to avoid that trouble, frequently threw it away, and used the roaster without it. This contrivance of the cooks to save trouble came very near to discredit the roasters altogether, and to put a final stop to their introduction in this country. The circumstance upon which the principal merit of the roaster depends, and on which the excellence of the food cooked in it depends entirely, is the *equality of the heat*. When the heat is equal on every side, it may be more moderate than when it is unequal; and the more moderate and equal the heat is by which meat can be properly roasted, the better tasted

Fig. 17.

and more wholesome will it be. Now it is quite impossible to keep up an equal heat in a roaster which is closed only by a single door of sheet iron; for so much heat will pass off through such a thin metallic door, and be carried away by the cold air of the atmosphere which is lying against the outside of it, that the degrees of heat in different parts of the roaster must necessarily be very different; and the consequence of this inequality will be either that the meat will not be sufficiently done in some parts, or that the heat must be so much increased as to prevent its being well done in any part.

In order to induce persons to be careful in the management of machinery of any kind which is new to them, it is necessary to point out the bad consequences which will result from such neglects and inattentions as they are most liable to fall into in the use of it; for, however particular instructions may be, strict attention to them cannot be expected from those who are not aware of the bad effects that may result from what may appear to them very trifling deviations or neglects.

Those who make roasters must take the greatest care to construct them in such a manner that they may be accurately closed, and that the heat may not be able to make its way through their doors; and those who use them must be careful to manage them properly.

There are two ways in which the door of a roaster may be constructed, so as to confine the heat perfectly well, without giving any additional trouble to the cook in the management of it. It may be made of a single sheet of iron, and covered on the outside with a panel of wood; or it may be constructed of two sheets of iron, placed parallel to each other at the distance of about an inch, and so fastened together that the air between them may be confined.

When a door of single sheet iron is made to confine the heat by means of an outside covering of wood, care must be taken to make such outside wooden covering in the form of a panel, otherwise it will not answer. If a board be used instead of a framed panel, it will most certainly warp with the heat, and will either detach itself from the iron door to which it is fastened, or will cause the door to bend and prevent its closing the roaster with sufficient accuracy. I have seen several attempts made to use boards instead of panels, in covering the outsides of the iron doors of roasters and iron ovens; but they were all unsuccessful. It is quite impossible that they ever should answer, as will be evident to those who will take the trouble to consider the matter with attention.

As doors of sheet iron, covered with wood on the outside, when they are properly constructed, are admirably calculated for confining heat, I think it worth while to give a detailed account of the precautions that are necessary in the construction of them.

Of the best Method of covering the iron Doors of Roasters and Ovens, etc., with wooden Panels, for confining the Heat.

The object principally to be attended to in this business is to contrive matters so that the shrinking and swelling of the wood by alternate heat and moisture shall have no tendency either to detach the wood from the iron door, or to change its form, or to cause openings in the wood by which the air confined between the wood and the iron can make its escape.

The manner in which this may, in all cases, be done, will be evident from an examination of the Fig. 18, which represents a front view of the door of a cylindrical roaster, 18 inches in diameter, covered with a square wooden panel.

It will be observed that this panel consists of a square frame tenanted, and fastened together at each of its four corners with a single pin; and filled up in the middle with a square board or panel, which is confined in its place, by being made to enter into deep grooves or channels, made to receive it, in the insides of the pieces which form the frame. The circular iron door to which this panel is fixed cannot be seen in the figure, being covered and concealed from view by the

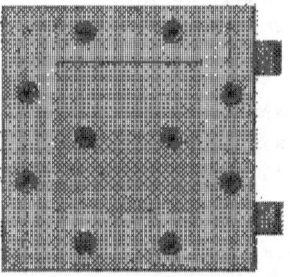

Fig. 18.

wood, but its size and position are marked out by a dotted circle; and the heads of ten rivets are seen, by which the wooden panel is fastened to the iron door. These rivets are made to hold the wood fast to the iron by means of small circular plates of sheet iron, which are distinctly represented in the figure.*

If the positions of the pins by which the wooden frame is fastened together, and of the rivets which fasten the panel to the iron door, are considered, it will be evident that all bad effects of the shrinking of the wood by the heat are prevented by the proposed

* Instead of these rivets, short wood screws may be used for fastening the wooden panel to the iron door; but care must be taken to place these screws in the same places which are pointed out for the rivets. The heads of the wood screws must of course be on the inside of the iron door.

construction. The four pieces of wood which constitute the frame of the panel (which may be of common deal, and about four inches wide and one inch thick), being fastened with one pin only at each of their joinings at the corners, and these pins being situated in the centre of those joinings, if upon the frame, in the middle of each of the four pieces which compose it, a square be drawn in such a manner that the corners of this square may coincide with the centres of the four pins which hold the frame together, as neither heat nor dryness makes any considerable alteration in the length of the fibres of wood, it is evident that the shrinking of the four pieces which compose this frame cannot alter the dimensions of this square, or in any way change its position. If, therefore, care be taken in fastening the panel to the iron door to place the riveting-nails *in the lines which form the four sides of this square*, the shrinking of the wood will occasion no strain on the iron door, nor have any tendency whatever to change its form; and with regard to the centre piece of the panel, if it be fastened to the iron door by two rivets, situated *in the direction of the fibres of the wood*, in a line dividing this piece into two equal parts, its shrinking will be attended with no kind of inconvenience. Care should, however, be taken to make this panel enter so deeply into the grooves in its frame that, when it has shrunk as much as possible, its width shall not be so much reduced as to cause it to come quite out of the grooves. This piece may be made about one third of an inch thick, and the grooves which receive it may be made of the same width, and about three quarters of an inch deep.

When wooden covers of this kind are made for iron

doors of large dimensions, they should be divided into a number of compartments, otherwise the centre pieces, or the panels properly so called, being very large, the shrinking of the wood with heat will be apt to make them quit the grooves of their frames, which would open a passage for the cold air to approach the surface of the iron door.

In fastening the wooden panel to its iron door, it will be best that the wood should not come into immediate contact with the iron. Two or three sheets of cartridge paper, placed one upon the other, may be interposed between them; and, to prevent the possibility of this paper taking fire, it may previously be rendered incombustible by soaking it in a strong solution of alum, mixed with a little Armenian bole or common clay. This paper will not only assist very much in confining the heat, but will also effectually prevent the wood from being set on fire by heat communicated through the iron door of the roaster. It is, indeed, highly improbable that the roaster should ever be so intensely heated as to produce this effect; but, as the strangest accidents sometimes do happen, it is always wise to be prepared for the worst that can happen.

As the centre piece of wood, or panel properly so called, which fills up the wooden frame, is only one third of an inch in thickness, while the frame is one inch in thickness, it is evident that, if the face of the frame be made to apply everywhere to the flat surface of the iron door, the centre piece will not touch it. This circumstance will be rather advantageous than otherwise, in confining the heat; but still it will require some attention in fastening the wood to the iron. Each of the two rivets which pass through this centre piece must also be made to pass through a small block of wood, about an inch square for instance, and one third of an inch thick, which will give these rivets a proper bearing, without any strain on the iron door which can tend to alter its form.

When the wood and the iron are firmly riveted together, the superfluous paper may be taken away with a knife.

The hinges of the door, which in the Fig. 18 are seen projecting outwards on the right hand, are to be riveted to the outside surface of the circular iron door; and, in order that they may not prevent the panel from applying properly to the door, they are to be let into the wood. The turn-buckles, by which the door is fastened, must be made to press against the outside or front of the wooden frame.

No inconvenience of any importance will arise from leaving the wooden panel square, while the door itself is circular; but, if it should be thought better, the corners of the panels may be taken off, or the wooden panel may be made circular. This should not, however, be done till after the panel has been fixed to the door. After this has been done, as the rivets will be sufficient to hold the sides of the frame in their places, the cutting off of the corners of the frame will produce no bad consequences.

I have been the more particular in my account of the manner of covering iron doors with wooden panels, for the purpose of confining heat, as this contrivance may be used with great advantage, not only for roasters and ovens, but also for a variety of other purposes; for the covers of large boilers, for instance, for the doors of hot closets, steam closets, etc.

Of double Doors for Roasters, constructed of two circular Pieces of sheet Iron seamed together.

No difficulty will be found in the construction of these doors; and though they may not, perhaps, confine the heat quite so perfectly as the doors we have just described, they answer very well; and, when the outside of the door is japanned, they have a very handsome and cleanly appearance.

There are two ways of constructing them, either of which may be adopted: the circular sheet of iron which forms the inside of the door may be flat and the outside sheet dishing, or the outside sheet may be flat and the inside sheet dishing; but, whichever of these methods is adopted, the hinges must be attached to the outside of the door, and care must be taken to make that part of the inside of the door quite flat which lies against the end of the roaster, and closes it. The distance of the inside sheet of iron and the outside sheet is not very essential: it should not, however, be less than one inch in the centre of the door; and these two sheets should not touch each other anywhere, except it be at their circumference, where they are fastened together. In the centre of the outside sheet there should be fixed a knob of iron or of brass, to serve as a handle for opening and shutting the door.

Double doors of this kind might easily be constructed of two circular pieces of cast iron, fastened together by rivets; or of one piece of cast iron, cast dishing, and a flat piece of sheet iron turned over it. When the latter construction is adopted, the cast iron must form the inside of the door, and its convex side must project into the roaster. It should be quite flat near its circumference, in order that it may close the roaster with accuracy; and it should be at least three quarters of an inch larger in diameter than the roaster, in order that no part of the circular plate of sheet iron, which should be fastened to it by being turned over its edge, may get between it and the end of the roaster.

Of the Blowpipes.

There are various ways in which the blowpipes may be fastened to the roaster. The common method, when they are made of sheet iron, is to fasten them with rivets; but as blowpipes of sheet iron are liable to be burned out in a few years, if much used, it is better to procure them of cast iron from an iron founder, in which case they should be cast with flanges, and should be keyed on the inside of the roaster; and their joinings with the bottom of the roaster must be made tight with some good cement that will stand fire, and is proper for that use.

The effect of the blowpipes will be considerably increased if a certain quantity of iron wire, in loose coils, or of iron turnings, be put into them. These being heated by the fire, the air which passes through the tubes, coming into contact with them, will be more heated than it would be if the tubes were empty; but care must be taken that the quantities of these substances used be not so great as to choke up the tube and obstruct too much the passage of the air.

The stoppers of the blowpipes must be made to close them well, otherwise air will find its way through the blowpipes into the roaster at times when it ought not to be admitted. One of these stoppers, represented on a large scale, is seen drawn a little way out of its blowpipe, in the Fig. 17, page 287; and in that figure part of the iron strap is seen which supports the front ends of the two blowpipes, and confines them in their places. This strap will not appear when the roaster is set, for it will then be entirely covered and concealed by the brick-work.

Where blowpipes are made of sheet iron, they should be so constructed and so fastened to the roaster that they may at any time be removed and replaced without taking the roaster out of the brick-work. This is necessary, in order that they may be taken away to be repaired or replaced with new ones, when by long use they become burned out and unfit for service. If they be made with flanges, and keyed on the inside, and if they be supported in front on an iron strap of the form represented in Fig. 14, page 257, they may at any time be removed with little trouble, by unkeying them and removing a few bricks. When the bricks in front, which it will be necessary to take away, are removed, this will open a passage into the fire-place sufficiently large to come at the wall at the farther end of the fire-place, which must come away in order to disengage the farther ends of the blowpipes, which are fixed in it. This wall must be carefully built up again, after the new blowpipes have been introduced and fastened to the roaster.

Of the Steam-tube.

This is an essential part of the machinery of a roaster, and must never be omitted. It should be situated somewhere in the upper part of the roaster, but it is not necessary that it should be placed exactly at the top of it. It might perhaps be thought that a hole in the upper part of the door would serve the purpose of a steam-tube; but this contrivance would not be found to answer. A steam-tube, properly constructed, will have what is called *a draught* through it, which on some occasions will be found to be very useful; but a hole in the door unconnected with a tube could have no draught. It is absolutely necessary that there should be a damper in the steam-tube. The simplest damper is a circular plate of iron, a very little less in diameter than the tube, which, being placed in it, is movable about an axis, which is perpendicular to the axis of the tube. This circular plate being turned about, and placed in different positions in the tube by means of its axis, which, being prolonged, comes forward through the brick-work, the passage of the steam through the tube is more or less obstructed by it. This prolonged axis, which may be called the projecting handle of this damper, is represented in the Figs. 14, 15, and 17. This appears to me to be one of the simplest kind of dampers I am acquainted with; and it has this in particular to recommend it. that it may be regulated without opening any passage into the steam-tube, or into the roaster, by which the air could force its way.

Of the Dripping-pan.

As the principal dripping-pan of a roaster is destined for holding water, and as it is of much importance that it should not leak, it should be hammered out of one piece of sheet iron, in the same manner as a frying-pan is formed; or, if the metal be turned up at the corners, it should be lapped over, but not cut, and all riveting-nails should be avoided, except such as can be placed very near the edge of the pan, and above the common level of the water that is put into it. To avoid the necessity of placing any riveting-nail at the bottom of the pan or near it, in fastening the sliders on which the pan runs, these sliders should be made to pass upwards by the ends of the pan, in order to their being fastened to it near its brim.

The dripping-pan should not be made quite so long as the roaster, for room must be left between the farther end of it and the farther end of the roaster for the hot air from the blowpipes to pass up into the upper part of the roaster. In order to stop the dripping-pan in its proper place when it is pushed into the roaster, the farther end of the shelf on which it slides may be turned upwards, and the brim of the dripping-pan made to strike against this projecting part of the shelf. The opening between this projecting part of the shelf and the farther end of the roaster should be about 1 inch or $1\frac{1}{4}$ inches wide, and it may be just as long as the dripping-pan is wide at the brim. This part of the shelf which projects upwards should be $\frac{1}{4}$ an inch higher than the brim of the dripping-pan, in order to prevent the current of hot air from the blowpipes from striking against the end of the dripping-pan, and heating it too much. The shelf may be stopped in its proper place by means of two horizontal projecting slips of iron about 1 inch or $1\frac{1}{4}$ inches long each at its farther end, which, striking against the end of the roaster, will prevent the shelf from being pushed too far into it. The dripping-pan should have two falling handles, one at each end of it, which handles should have stops to hold them fast when they are raised into a horizontal position. As these handles will necessarily project a little beyond the ends of the pan, even when they are not raised up, the handle at the farther end of the pan will prevent the brim of the pan from actually touching the projecting end of the shelf; which circumstance will be advantageous, as it will serve to defend the end of the pan, and prevent its being so much heated as otherwise it would be by the hot air from below.

I find, on inquiry from several persons who have lately made the experiment, that it is by far the best method to use two dripping-pans, one within the other, with water between them. As the upper pan is very thin, being made of tin * (tinned sheet iron), it is kept as cool as is necessary by the water; and, the surface of the water being covered and protected, it does not evaporate so fast as when it is left exposed to the hot air in the roaster.

Of the Precautions that may be used to prevent the Dripping-pan from being too much heated.

This is a very important matter, and too much attention cannot be paid to it by those who construct roasters. From what has been said, it is evident that, if in roasting meat the water in the dripping-pan ever happens to be all evaporated, the drippings from the meat which fall on it cannot fail to fill the roaster with noxious fumes. It is certainly not surprising that those who, in roasting in a roaster, neglected to put water into the dripping-pan should not much like the flavour of their roasted meat.

There is a method of defending the dripping-pan from heat, which many have put in practice with success;

---

* Some persons have used a shallow earthen dish, instead of this second dripping-pan; but earthen-ware does not answer so well for this use as tin, as it is more liable to be heated too much by the radiant heat from above.

but, although it effectually answers the purpose, yet it is attended with a serious inconvenience, which, as it is not very obvious, ought to be mentioned. When the bottoms of roasters were made flat, their dripping-pans were much more liable to be too much heated than they are when, the body of the roaster being made cylindrical, the dripping-pan is placed on a shelf in the manner I have here recommended. And several persons, finding the water in the dripping-pans of their roasters to boil away very fast, covered the (flat) bottoms of their roasters with sand, or with a paving of thin tiles or bricks. This produced the desired effect; but this contrivance occasions the bottom of a roaster to be very soon burned out and destroyed. The heat from the fire communicated to the under side of the bottom of the roaster, not being able to make its way upwards into the body of the roaster through the stratum of sand or bricks (which substances are non-conductors of heat), it is accumulated in the bottom of the roaster, and becomes there so intense as to destroy the iron in a short time.

The best method that can be adopted for preventing the dripping-pan from being too much heated is to defend the bottom of the roaster from the direct action of the fire by interposing a screen of some kind or other between it and the burning fuel. This screen may be a plate of cast iron, about one third of an inch thick, with a number of small holes through it, supported upon iron bars at the distance of about an inch below the bottom of the roaster; or it may be formed of a row of thin flat tiles laid upon the blowpipes, and supported by them.

Roasters which are made of a cylindrical form will hardly stand in need of any thing to screen them from the fire, especially if their fire-places are situated at a proper distance below them, and if the size of the fire is kept within due bounds. But, after all, if the person to whom the management of a roaster is committed is determined to destroy it, no precautions can prevent it; and hence it appears how very necessary it is to secure the good-will of the cooks. They ought certainly to wish well to the success of these inventions; for the introduction of them cannot fail to diminish their labour, and increase their comforts very much.

Of large Roasters, that will serve to roast and bake at the same Time.

It has been found by experience that any roaster may be made to roast and bake at the same time, in great perfection, when the proper precautions are taken; but this can best be done when the roaster is of a large size, from 20 inches to 24 inches in diameter, for instance; for in this case there will be room above the meat for a shelf on which the things to be baked can be placed. And even when there is no roasting going on below it, any thing to be baked should be placed on this shelf, in order to its being nearer to the top of the roaster, where the process of baking goes on better than anywhere else. In baking bread, pies, cakes, etc., it seems to be necessary that the heat should descend in rays from the top of the oven; and as the intensity of the effects produced by the calorific rays which proceed from a heated body is much greater near the hot body than at a greater distance from it (being most probably as the squares of the distances inversely), it is evident why the process of baking should go on best in a low oven, or when the thing to be baked is placed near the top of the oven, or of the roaster, when it is baked in a roaster.

The shelf in the upper part of a roaster for baking may be made of a single piece of sheet iron, but it will be much better to make it double; that is to say, of two pieces of sheet iron, placed at a small distance from each other, and turned inwards, and fastened together at their edges, in the manner which will presently be more particularly described. This shelf, whether it be made single or double, should be placed upon ledges, riveted to the sides of the roasters; and, to prevent the hot air from the blowpipes from passing up between the farther end of this shelf and the farther end of the roaster, the shelf should be pushed quite back against the end of the roaster. It should be made shorter than the roaster by about two inches, in order that there may be sufficient room, between the hither end of the shelf and the inside of the door of the roaster, for the vapour that ought to be driven out of the roaster to pass upwards to the opening of the steam-tube. This shelf should not be fastened in its place, for it may sometimes, when very large pieces of meat are roasted, be found necessary to remove it.

As it seems probable that radiant heat from the top and sides of the roaster acts an important part, even in the process of roasting, if a roaster of very large dimensions were to be constructed, I think it would be advisable not to make its transverse section circular, but elliptical, the longest axis of the ellipse being in a horizontal position. This form would bring the top of the roaster to be nearer to the meat than it would be if its form were cylindrical, its capacity remaining the same. How far a horizontal shelf of sheet iron, placed immediately over the meat, and very near it, would answer as a remedy for the defect of a roaster, the top of which, on account of its great size, should be found to be too far from the surface of the meat, I cannot pretend to determine, as I never have made the experiment; but I think it well deserving of a trial. If the farther end of this shelf were made to touch the farther end of the roaster, so as to prevent the current of air from the blowpipes from getting up between them, it is very certain that this hot air would be forced to impinge against the shelf, and run along the under side of it, to the hither end of the roaster. The only question remaining, and which can only be determined by experiment, is whether this hot air would heat the shelf sufficiently, or to that temperature which is necessary in order that the iron may throw off those calorific rays which are wanted.

If this shelf were covered above with a pavement of tiles, or if it were constructed of two sheets of iron placed parallel to each other, at the distance of about one inch, turned in or made dishing at their edges, and seamed together at their ends and sides in such a manner as to confine the air shut up between them, either of these contrivances, by obstructing the heat in its passage through the shelf, would promote its accumulation at its under surface, which would not only increase the intensity of the radiant heat where it is wanted, but, by diminishing the quantity of heat which passes through the shelf, would be very useful when any thing is placed on it in order to be baked.

Whenever a shelf is made in a roaster, whether it be situated above the dripping-pan or below it, I think it would always be found advantageous to construct it in the manner here described, viz., of two sheets of iron, with confined air between them; or perhaps it may be still better to fill this cavity with finely pulverized charcoal. The additional expense of constructing the shelves of roasters in this manner would be but trifling; and the passage of the heat through them, which it is always desirable to prevent as much as possible, will, by this simple contrivance, be greatly obstructed. If the lower shelf be so constructed, it will no doubt be found very useful in preventing the too quick evaporation of the water in the dripping-pan.

Of various Alterations that have been made in the Forms of Roasters, and of the Advantages and Disadvantages of each of them.

The blowpipes of all the roasters that were constructed, till very lately, were made to pass round to

Fig. 19.

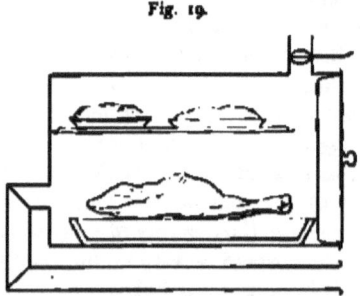

the farther end of the roaster; and, after forming two right angles each, they entered the roaster, in a horizontal direction, just above the level of the brim

Fire-places and Kitchen Utensils.

of the dripping-pan, in the manner represented in the Fig. 19.

The Fig. 20 shows the manner in which the blow-pipes have been constructed of late.

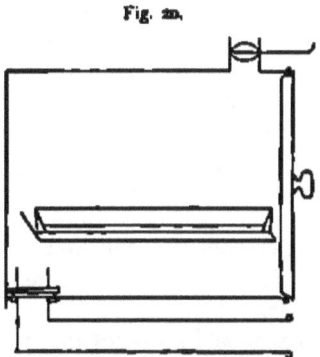

Fig. 20.

The advantages of the former construction were a great length of tube, and consequently a greater effect on that account; and a good direction to the current of hot air. The disadvantages were the difficulty of removing the tubes to repair them, without unsettling the roaster; and the difficulty of procuring blowpipes of this form of cast iron; and, lastly, the great depth of space that was required for setting the roaster.

The advantages of the blowpipe, represented in Fig. 20, have already been noticed. The disadvantage from want of length is compensated by a small increase of diameter. When this blowpipe is fastened to the roaster, its flange is covered with a cement; and the vertical end of the pipe being introduced into the roaster through the circular hole in the bottom of it, which is made to receive it, a flat iron ring, covered with cement on its under side, is then slipped over the end of the tube within the roaster, and a key of iron, in the form of a wedge, being passed through both sides of the tube in holes prepared to receive it, by driving this wedge-like key with a hammer, the ring is forced downwards, and at the same time the flange of the blowpipe is forced upwards against the bottom of the roaster, by which means the blowpipe is firmly fixed in its place, and the cement makes the joinings airtight. By removing this key, the pipe may at any time be removed without deranging the roaster.

The Fig. 19 represents the section of a flat-bottomed roaster. In this there is a shelf on which two pies are seen baking, and a piece of meat is represented lying on the gridiron.

In the Figs. 14 and 15, pages 257, 261, the front or hither end of the roaster is represented as being turned over a stout iron wire. The first roasters that were constructed were all made in a different manner. The hither end of the roaster was riveted to a broad flat frame, constructed of stout plate iron; and to this frame, or flat front, which projected before the brickwork, the hinges and turn-buckles of the door were fastened. An idea of this manner of constructing the front of a roaster may be formed from the Fig. 21, page 310, although this figure does not represent the front of a roaster, but that of an oven, which will be described presently.

There is no objection to this method of constructing roasters but the expense of it.

Of some Attempts to simplify the Construction of the Roaster.

Finding that much more heat was always communicated to the under sides of roasters, especially as they were first constructed (with flat bottoms), than was there wanted, meditating on the means I could employ to defend the bottom of the dripping-pan from this excessive heat, without at the same time exposing the bottom of the roaster to the danger of being soon destroyed, in consequence of the accumulation of it on its passage upwards being prevented, it occurred to me that if the bottom of the roaster were covered with a shallow iron pan turned upside down, with a row of holes from side to side at the farther end of it, and if a certain quantity of fresh air could occasionally be admitted under this inverted pan, this cold air, on coming into contact with the bottom of the roaster, would take off the heat, and, becoming specifically lighter on being heated, would pass upwards through the holes at the farther end of this pan into the roaster, serving at the same time three useful purposes; namely, to defend the dripping-pan; to cool the bottom of the roaster; and to assist in heating the inside of the roaster above, where heat is most wanted. This invention was put in practice, and was found to answer very well all the purposes for which it was contrived. It was likewise found that with proper management the current of heated air from below the inverted pan might be so regulated as to roast meat very well without making any use of the blowpipes; and consequently that roasters might be constructed without blowpipes.

As the substitution of the contrivance above described, in lieu of the blowpipes, would simplify the construction of the roaster very much, and enable tradesmen to afford the article at a much lower price, I took a great deal of pains to find out whether a roaster on this simple construction could be made to perform as well as those which are made with blowpipes. I caused one of them to be put up in my own house, and tried it frequently; and I engaged several of my friends to try them; and they were found to answer so well that I ventured at length to recommend it to manufacturers to make them for sale. As they were called roasters, and as they cost little more than half what those with blowpipes were sold for, many persons preferred them on account of their cheapness; and more than two hundred of them have already been put up in different parts of the country, and I am informed that they have answered to the entire satisfaction of those who have tried them.

Although they are undoubtedly inferior in some respects to roasters which are furnished with blowpipes, meat may, with a little care and attention, be roasted in them in very high perfection; and, as nothing can possibly answer better than they do for all kinds of baking, they will, I am persuaded, find their way in due time into common use.

Roasters on this simple construction (without blowpipes), which I shall call *Roasting Ovens*, were at first made with flat bottoms, but of late they have been made cylindrical; and, as I think the cylindrical form much the best in many respects, I shall give a description of one of them.

Fig. 21 represents a front view of a cylindrical

roasting oven with its door shut. The front end of the large cylinder, which constitutes the body of this oven, instead of being turned over a stout wire, is turned outwards, and riveted to a flat piece of thick sheet iron, which in this figure is distinguished by vertical lines, and which I shall call *the front* of the oven.

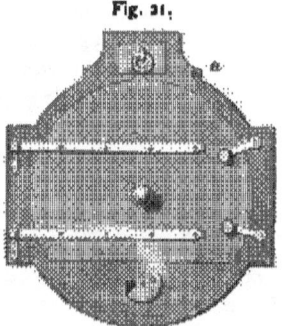

Fig. 21.

The door of the oven is distinguished by horizontal lines. The general form of the front of the oven is circular; but it has two projections on opposite sides of it, to one of which the hinges of the door, and to the other the turn-buckles for fastening it when it is closed, are fastened. It has another projection above, which serves as a frame to the doorway, through which a brush is occasionally introduced for the purpose of cleaning the flues. On one side of this projection there is a small hole, which is distinguished by the letter *a*, through which the handle or projecting axis of the circular register of the vent-tube (which is not seen) passes.

In the body of the oven, at the distance of half its

semi-diameter below its centre or axis, there is a horizontal shelf, which is fixed in its place, not by resting on ledges, or by being riveted to the sides of the oven, but by its hither end being turned down, and firmly riveted to the vertical plate of iron, which I have called the front of the oven. This shelf, which should be made double to prevent the heat from passing through it from below, must not reach quite to the farther end of the oven; there must be an opening left, about one inch in width, between the end of it and the farther end of the oven, through which opening the air heated below the shelf will make its way upwards into the upper part of the oven.

From what has been said, it will be evident that the hollow space below the shelf we have just been describing, which I shall call the *air-chamber*, is intended to serve in lieu of the blowpipes of a roaster; and this office it will perform tolerably well, provided means are used for admitting cold air into it, from without, occasionally. This is done by means of a register, which is situated at the lower part of the vertical front of the roaster, a little below the bottom of the door. This register is distinctly represented in the Fig. 21.

Fig. 22, which represents a vertical section of the oven through its axis, shows the (double) door of the roaster shut, and the two dripping-pans, one within the other, standing on the shelf we have just been describing, and a piece of meat above them, which is supposed to be laying on a gridiron placed in the second dripping-pan. The register of the air-chamber below the shelf, which supplies the place of the blowpipes, is represented as being open; and a part of the steam-tube is shown, through which the steam and vapour are driven out of the oven, by the blast of hot air from the air-chamber.

The cylinder which constitutes the body of the oven is two feet long, and is supposed to be of cast iron. It is cast with a flange, which projects outwards about one inch at the opening of the cylinder, by means of which flange it is attached, by rivets, to the front of the oven, which, as I have already observed, must be made of strong sheet iron, which may be near one eighth of an inch in thickness.

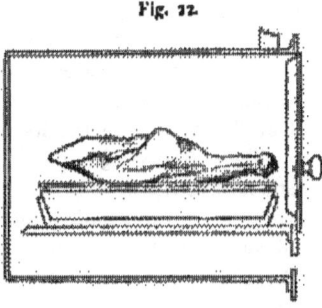

Fig. 22.

As the shelf is not attached to the sides of the oven, but to its front, the body of the oven need not be perforated, except in one place, namely, where the steam goes off; and as the bottom or farther end of the cylinder, and the flange at its hither end, and the cylinder itself, are all cast at the same time, and as the form of the oven is such as will deliver well from the mould, it appears to me that the article might be afforded at a low price, especially in this country, where the art of casting in iron is carried to so high a pitch of perfection.

The shelf might easily be made of cast iron, as might also the dripping-pans and the double door of the oven; and I should not be surprised if English workmen should succeed in making even the front of the oven and the register of the air-chamber, and every other part of the machinery, of that cheap and most useful metal.

If the shelf be made of cast iron, to save the trouble of riveting in making it double, it may be covered by an inverted shallow pan of cast iron; and in the bottom of this pan, which will be uppermost when it is inverted, there may be cast two shallow grooves, both in the direction of the length of the pan, and consequently parallel to each other, in which grooves (which may be situated about an inch from the sides of the inverted pan) two parallel projections at a proper distance from each other, cast at the bottom of the lower dripping-pan, may pass. These projections, passing freely in the grooves which receive them, will serve to keep the dripping-pan steady in its proper direction when it is pushed into or drawn out of the oven.

To increase the effect of the air-chamber when this oven is used for roasting meat, a certain quantity of iron wire in loose coils, or of iron turnings, may be put into the air-chamber.

The door of the oven, which is very distinctly represented in the Fig. 21, should be about 19 inches in diameter, if the oven is 18 inches in diameter within, or in the clear. In this figure the internal edge or corner of the hither end of the body of the oven is indicated by a dotted circle, and the position of the shelf is pointed out by a horizontal dotted line.

In fastening the vertical plate, which forms the front of the oven, to the projecting flange at the hither end of the cylindrical body of the oven, care must be taken to beat down the heads of the riveting nails in front, otherwise they will prevent the door of the oven from closing it with that nicety which is requisite.

In setting this roasting-oven, the whole of the thickness of the vertical front of it should be made to project forward before the brick-work. The fire-place doors, ash-pit, register-door, damper in the chimney, etc., should be similar in all respects to those used for roasters; and the flues should likewise be constructed in the same manner.

I have been the more particular in my description of this roasting-oven, because I think it bids fair to become a most useful implement of cookery. As an oven, it certainly has one advantage over all ovens constructed on the common principles, which must give it a decided superiority. By means of the air-chamber and the steam-tube it may be kept clear of all ill-scented and noxious fumes without the admission of cold air.

Of the Difference between a Roasting-oven and a Roaster.

From the account of the roasting-oven that has just been given it might be imagined that it possesses all the properties of the roaster, and in the same degree; but this is not the case. The essential difference between them is this: the blowpipes of the roaster being surrounded by the flame on all sides, they are heated above as well as below, and the air in passing through them is much more exposed to the heat than it is in passing through the air-chamber of the roasting-oven. The particles of air which happen to come into contact with the bottom of the oven will of course be heated;

but if, in consequence of their acquired lightness on being heated, they rise upwards to the top of the air-chamber, they will there come in contact with the bottom of the shelf, which, instead of communicating more heat to them, will deprive them of a part of that which they bring with them from below. But circumstances are very different in the blowpipes of a roaster: in them the particles of air acquire continually additional heat from every part of the surface with which they come into contact in their passage through the tube.

From this view of the subject, we see how very essential it is that the shelf of a roasting-oven should be so composed or constructed that heat may not readily find its way through it; and we see likewise how necessary it is to manage the registers of blowpipes and of air-chambers with proper care.

CHAPTER VI.

Of the Usefulness of small iron Ovens, and of the best Methods of constructing them and managing them. — Reasons why they have not succeeded in many Cases where they have been tried. — Ovens may be used for other Processes of Cookery besides Baking. — Curious Results of some Attempts to boil Meat in an Oven. — Explanation of these Appearances. — Conjectures respecting the Origin of some national Customs.

IN the first part of this tenth Essay I recommended small iron ovens for cottagers, and nests of small ovens for the kitchens of large families; and I have had occasion to know since that several persons have adopted them. I have likewise been made acquainted with the results of many of the trials that have been made of them, and with the complaints that have been brought against them. As I am more than ever of opinion that iron ovens will always be found useful when they are properly constructed and properly managed, I shall in this place add a few observations to what I have already published concerning them.

And, in the first place, I must observe that a small iron oven stands in need of a good door; that is to say, of a door well contrived for confining heat; and the smaller the oven is, so much the more necessary is it that the door should be good.

The door must not only fit against the mouth of the oven with accuracy, but it must be composed of materials through which heat does not easily make its way.

An oven door constructed of a single sheet of plate iron will not answer, however accurately it may be made to fit the oven; for the heat will find its way through it, and it will be carried off by the cold air of the atmosphere which comes into contact with the outside of it. The bottom of the oven may be made hot by the fire under it; but the top and sides of it cannot be properly heated while there is a continual and great loss of heat through its door. But an oven, to perform well, must be very equally heated in every part of it.

If the flame and smoke of the fire be made to surround an oven on every side, and if the fire be properly managed, there can be no difficulty in heating an iron oven equally, and of keeping it at an equal temperature, provided the loss of heat by and through the door be prevented.

If the door be constructed of sheet iron, it must either be made double, or it must be covered on the outside with a panel of wood. By a *double door* I do not here mean *two doors*, but one door constructed of two sheets or plates of iron placed parallel to and at a certain distance from each other; and so constructed that the air which is between the two plates may be shut up and confined. The two plates or sheets of iron, of which the double door of an oven is made, must not touch each other, except at their edges (where they must join in order to their being fastened together); for, were they to lie one flat upon the other, the heat would pass too rapidly through them, notwithstanding there being two of them; but it is not necessary that they should be farther asunder than an inch or an inch and a half. One of the plates may be quite flat, and the other a little convex. The end of the oven must be made quite flat or level, so as to be perfectly closed by a flat surface placed against it. The door is that flat surface; and the greatest care must be taken that it apply with accuracy, or touch the end of the oven in every part when it is pressed against it; for if any opening be left, especially if it be near the top of the oven, the hot air in the oven will not fail to make its escape out of it.

It never should be attempted to make the door of an oven or of a closed fire-place fit, by causing it to *shut into a rabbet*. That is a very bad method; for, besides the difficulty of executing the work with any kind of accuracy, the expansion of the metal with heat is very apt to derange the machinery, when the door is so constructed.

From what has been said of the necessity of causing the door of an oven to fit with accuracy, it is evident that care must be used to place its hinges properly; and I have found, by experience, that such a door is closed more accurately by two turn-buckles, placed at a proper distance from each other, than by a single latch. I beg pardon for repeating what has already been said elsewhere.

Of the Management of the Fire in heating an iron Oven.

If a certain degree of attention is always necessary in the management of fire, there is certainly nothing on which we can bestow our care that repays us so amply; and, with regard to the trouble of managing a fire in a closed fire-place, it is really too inconsiderable to deserve being mentioned.

Whenever a fire is made under an iron oven, in a closed fire-place, constructed on good principles, there is always *a very strong draught* or pressure of air into the fire-place; and this circumstance, which is unavoidable, renders it necessary to keep the fire-place door constantly closed, and to leave but a small opening for the passage of the air through the ash-pit register. The fire-place, too, should be made very small, and particularly the bottom of it, or the grate on which the fuel burns.

If any of these precautions are neglected, the consequences will be, — the rapid consumption of the fuel, the sudden heating and burning of the bottom of the oven, and the sudden cooling of the oven as soon as the fire-place ceases to be filled with burning fuel.

It is a fact which ought never to be forgotten, "that of the air that forces its way into a closed fire-place, that part only which comes into actual contact with the burning fuel, and is decomposed by it in the process of combustion, contributes any thing to the heat generated; and that all the rest of the air that finds its way into and *through* a fire-place is a thief that steals heat, and flies away with it up the chimney."

The draught occasioned by a fire in a closed fire-place being into the chimney and not into the fire, cold air is as much disposed to rush in over the fire as through it; and it violently forces its way into the hot fire-place by every aperture, even after all the fuel is consumed, carrying the heat away with it up the chimney and into the atmosphere. It even makes its way between the bars of the grate whenever they are not quite covered with burning fuel; hence it appears how necessary it is to make the grate of a closed fire-place small, and to give to that part of the fire-place which is destined for holding the fuel the form of an inverted truncated cone or pyramid, or else to make it very deep in proportion to its length and width.

But the prevention of the air from finding its way through the fire-place without coming into contact with the burning fuel is not the only advantage that is derived from constructing closed fire-places in the manner here recommended: it serves also to increase the intensity of the heat in that part of the fire-place which contains the fuel, which tends very powerfully to render the combustion of the fuel complete, and consequently to augment the quantity of heat generated in that process.

To prevent the bottom of the oven (or boiler) from being too much affected by this intense heat, nothing more is necessary than to make the fire-place sufficiently small, and to place it at a sufficient distance below the bottom of the oven. It will be indispensably necessary, however, with such a (small) fire-place, situated far below the bottom of an oven, to keep the fire-place door well closed, otherwise so much cold air will rush in over the fire that it will be quite impossible to make the oven hot.

I have found by recent experiments that a fire-place in the form of an oblong square or prism, 6 inches wide, 9 inches long, and 6 inches deep, is sufficient to heat an iron oven 18 inches wide, 24 inches long, and from 12 to 15 inches in height; and that the grate of this fire-place should be placed about 12 inches below the bottom of the oven. More effectually to prevent the fire from operating with too much violence upon any one part of the bottom of the oven, the brick-work may be so sloped outwards and upwards on every side from the top of the burning fuel to the extreme parts of the sides and ends of the bottom of the oven, that the whole of the bottom of the oven may be exposed to the direct rays from the fire.

In some cases I have suffered the flame to pass freely up both sides of the oven to the top of it, and then caused it to descend by the end of the oven to the level of its bottom, or rather below it, and from thence to pass off by a horizontal canal into the chimney; and in other cases I have caused it to pass backwards and forwards in horizontal canals by the sides of the oven, before I permitted it to go off into the chimney. Either of these methods will do very well, provided the smoke be made to descend after it has left the top of the oven, till it reaches below the level of the bottom of it, before it is permitted to pass off into the chimney; and provided the canal by which the smoke passes off be furnished with a damper.

In setting an oven, provision should be made, by leaving holes to be stopped up with stoppers, for occasionally cleaning out all the canals in which the smoke is made to circulate; and, in order that these canals may not too often be choked up with soot, they should never be made less than two inches wide, even where they are very deep or broad; and, where they are not more than four or five inches deep, they should be from three to four inches wide, otherwise they will be very often choked up with soot.

To clean out the flues of an oven, roaster, or large fixed boiler, a strong cylindrical brush may be used, which may have a flexible handle made of three or more iron wires, about $\frac{1}{8}$ or $\frac{1}{16}$ of an inch in diameter, twisted together.

Holes closed with fit stoppers must of course be left in the brick-work for occasionally cleaning out these flues.

If the iron door of an oven be made double, the outside of it may with safety be japanned black or white, which will prevent its rusting, and add much to the cleanliness and neatness of the appearance of the kitchen.

These details may by some be thought unimportant and tiresome, but those who know how much depends on minute details in the introduction of new mechanical improvements will be disposed to excuse the prolixity of these descriptions. I wish I could make my writings palatable to the generality of readers, but that, I fear, is quite impossible. My subjects are too common and too humble to excite their curiosity, and will not bear the high seasoning to which modern palates are accustomed.

A great disadvantage under which I labour is that, of those who *might* profit most from my writings, many *will not read*, and others *cannot*.

But to return to my subject. To save expense, small ovens for poor families may be closed with flat stones or with tiles; and the fire-place door for such an oven, and its ash-pit register, may be made of common bricks placed edgewise, and made to slide against those openings.

There is a circumstance respecting the iron ovens I am describing, which is both curious and important. The fire-place for an oven of the smallest size should be nearly as capacious as one which is destined for heating a much larger oven; and I have found, by repeated experiments, that a nest of four small ovens, set together, and heated by the same fire, will require but very little more fuel to heat them than would be necessary to heat one of them, were it set alone. An attentive consideration of the manner in which the heat is applied — of the smallness of the quantity, in all cases, that is applied to the heating of the contents of the oven, and the much greater quantity that is expended in heating the fire-place and the flues — will enable us to account for this curious fact in a manner that is perfectly philosophical and satisfactory.

A cottage oven 11 inches wide, 10 inches high, and 16 inches long, will require a fire-place 5 inches wide, 5 inches high, and 7 inches long; and for four of these ovens, set together in a nest, the fire-place need not be more than 6 inches wide, 6 inches high, and 8 inches long.

I have in my house at Brompton two iron ovens, each 18 inches wide, 14 inches high, and 24 inches long, set one over the other, and heated by the same fire; and their fire-place is only 6 inches wide, 6 inches high, and 9 inches long.

If the fire-place of an iron oven be properly constructed, and if the fire be properly managed, it is almost incredible how small a quantity of fuel will answer for heating the oven, and for keeping it hot. But if the fire-place door be allowed to stand open, and a torrent of cold air be permitted to rush into the fire-place and through the flues, it will be found quite impossible to heat the oven properly, whatever may be the quantity of fuel consumed under it; and neither the baking of bread nor of pies, nor any other process of cookery, can be performed in it in a suitable manner.

A very moderate share indeed of ingenuity is required in the proper management of a fire in a closed fire-place, and very little attention. And as it requires no bodily exertion, but saves labour and expense and anxiety; and as moreover it is an interesting and amusing occupation, attended by no disgusting circumstance, and productive of none but pleasing, agreeable, and useful consequences, we may, I think, venture to hope that those prejudices which prevent the introduction of these improvements will in time be removed.

It is not obstinacy, it is that *apathy* which follows a total corruption of taste and morals, that is an *incurable* evil; for that, alas! there is no remedy but calamity and extermination.

Ovens may be used in boiling and stewing, and also in warming Rooms.

There are so many different ways in which the heat necessary in preparing food may be applied, that it would not be surprising if one should sometimes be embarrassed in the choice of them; and I am not without apprehension that I may embarrass my readers by describing and recommending so many of them. The fact is, they all have their different kinds of merit, and in the choice of them regard must always be had to the existing circumstances.

Desirous of contriving a fire-place on as simple a construction as possible, that should serve at the same time for heating a room and for the performance of all the common processes of cookery for a small family, and which moreover should not be expensive nor require much attendance, I caused four small iron ovens to be set in the opening of a common chimney fire-place. These ovens, which were constructed of sheet iron, and were furnished with doors of the same sheet iron, each covered with a panel of wood to confine the heat, were 16 inches long, 11 inches wide, and 10 inches high each; and they were set in brick-work in such a manner that the fronts of the doors of the ovens being even with the side of the room, the original opening of the chimney fire-place, which was large, was completely filled up. These ovens were all heated by one small fire, the closed fire-place being situated about 12 inches below the level of the bottoms of the two lowermost ovens, and perpendicularly under the division between them, and the passage into the fire-place was closed by a fit stopper.

From this description, it will not be difficult for any person who has perused the preceding chapters of this Essay to form a perfect idea of this arrangement; and it is equally easy to perceive that, had not the open chimney fire-place in which these four ovens were set been very large, I should have been under the necessity of enlarging it, or at least of raising its mantel, in order to have been able to introduce these ovens, and set them at proper distances from each other.

I shall now proceed to give an account of the experiments that were made with this fire-place.

My first attempt was to warm the room by means of it. A small fire being made in its closed fire-place, its oven doors were all set wide open, and the room, though by no means small, soon became very warm. This warming apparatus was now, to all intents and purposes, a German stove. By shutting two of the oven doors, the heat of the room was sensibly diminished; and by leaving only one of them open it was found that a moderate degree of warmth might be kept up even in cold weather.

As no person in this country would be satisfied with any fire-place, if in its arrangement provision were not made for boiling a tea-kettle, I caused a very broad shallow tea-kettle, with a bottom perfectly flat, to be constructed of common tin, and, filling it with cold water, placed it in one of the two lower ovens, and shut the oven door. Although the fire under the ovens was but small, it burned very bright, and the water in the tea-kettle was soon made to boil.

I was not surprised that the water boiled in a short time, for it was what I expected; but on removing the tea-kettle I observed an appearance which did surprise me, and which indicated a degree of heat in the oven which I had no idea of finding there. The handle of the tea-kettle resembled very much in form the handle of a common tea-kettle, but, like the rest of the kettle, was constructed of tin, or, to speak more properly, of tinned sheet iron.

On removing the kettle from the oven I found that the tin on its handle had been melted, and had fallen down in drops, which rested on the body of the kettle below, where they had congealed, having been cooled by the water in the kettle.

This discovery convinced me that I should not fail of obtaining in these ovens any degree of heat that could possibly be wanted in any culinary process whatever: it showed me likewise that degrees of temperature much higher than that of boiling water may exist in a closed oven in which water is boiling; and it seemed to indicate that all the different culinary processes of boiling, stewing, roasting, and baking might be carried on at the same time in one and the same oven. Subsequent experiments have since confirmed all these indications, and have put the facts beyond all doubt. These facts are certainly curious, and the knowledge of them may lead to useful improvements; for they may enable us to simplify very much the implements used in cookery.

Having found that I could boil water in my small ovens, my next attempt was to boil meat in them. I put about three pounds of beef, in one compact lump, into an earthen pot, and filling the pot to within about two inches of its brim with cold water, I set it in one of the lower ovens, shutting the door of the oven, and keeping up a small steady fire in the fire-place. In about two hours and three quarters the meat was found to be sufficiently boiled; and all those who partook of it (and they were not fewer than nine or ten persons) agreed in thinking it perfectly good and uncommonly savoury. On my guard against the illusions which frequently are produced by novelty, I should have had doubts respecting the reality of those superior qualities ascribed to this boiled beef, had not an uncommon appearance in the water in which it had been boiled attracted my attention. This water, after the meat had been boiled in it, appeared to be nearly as transparent and as colourless as when it was brought from the pump. It immediately occurred to me that this effect could be owing to nothing else but to the state of perfect quiet in which the water must necessarily have been during the greater part of the time it remained in the oven; and, to determine whether this was really the case or not, I made the following decisive experiment.

Having provided two equal pieces of beef from the same carcass, I put them into two stewpans of nearly the same form and dimensions; one of them, which had a cover, being constructed of earthen-ware, while the other, which had no cover, was made of copper.

Into these stewpans I now put equal quantities of water,—with this difference, however, that while the water put into the copper stewpan was cold, that put into the other was boiling hot. A small fire being now made in the fire-place, these two stewpans, with their contents, were introduced into the two lower ovens. The earthen stewpan was set down upon a ten-inch tile, which had previously been placed in the oven to serve as a support for it, in order to prevent the bottom of the stewpan from coming into immediate contact with the bottom of the oven, and the door of that oven was shut; but the copper stewpan was set down immediately on the bottom of its oven, and the door of that oven was left open 'during the whole time the experiment lasted.

At the end of three hours the stewpans were taken out of the ovens, and their contents were examined.

The appearances were just what I expected to find them. The meat in each of the stewpans was sufficiently boiled, but there was certainly a very striking difference in the appearance of the liquor remaining in the two utensils; and, if I was not much mistaken, there was a sensible difference in the taste of the two pieces of meat, that boiled in the earthen stew-pan being the most juicy and most savoury. The water remaining in this vessel — and little of it had evaporated — was still very transparent and colourless, and nearly tasteless, while the liquor in the copper stewpan was found to be a rich meat broth.

The result of this experiment recalled very forcibly to my recollection a dispute I had had several years before, in Germany, with the cook of a friend of mine, who at my recommendation had altered his kitchen fire-place; in which dispute I now saw I was in the wrong, and, seeing it, felt a desire more easy to be conceived than to be described to make an apology to an innocent person whom I had unjustly suspected of wilful misrepresentation. This woman (for it was a female cook), on being repeatedly reprimanded for sending to table a kind of soup of inferior quality, which, before the kitchen was altered, she had always been famous for making in the highest perfection, persisted in declaring that she could not make the same good rich soup in the new-fashioned boilers (fitted up in closed fire-places, and heated by small fires) as she used to make in the old boilers, set down upon the hearth before a great roaring wood fire.

The woman was perfectly in the right. To make a rich meat soup, the juices must be washed out of the meat, and intimately mixed with the water; and this washing out in boiling must be greatly facilitated and expedited by the continual and rapid motion into which the contents of a boiler are necessarily thrown when heat is applied to one side of it only, especially when that heat is sufficiently intense to keep the liquid continually boiling with vehemence. I ought, no doubt, to have foreseen this; but how difficult is it to foresee any thing! It is much easier to explain than to predict.

If it be admitted that fluids in receiving and giving off heat are necessarily thrown into internal motions in consequence of the changes of specific gravity in the particles of the fluid, occasioned by the alteration of their temperatures, we shall be able to account, in a manner perfectly satisfactory, not only for the appearances observed in the experiments above mentioned, and for the superior richness of the soup made by the Bavarian cook in her boiler, but also for several other curious facts.

When the copper stewpan, containing cold water and a piece of meat, was put into an iron oven, heated by a fire situated below it, as the bottom of the oven on which the stewpan was placed was very hot, the heat, passing rapidly through the flat bottom of this metallic utensil, communicated heat to the lower stratum of the water, which, becoming specifically lighter on being thus heated, was crowded out of its place, and forced upwards by the superincumbent colder and consequently heavier liquid. This necessarily occasioned a motion in every part of the fluid, and this motion must have been rapid in proportion as the communication of heat was rapid; and it is evident that it could never cease, unless all the water in the stewpan could have acquired and preserved an equal and a permanent temperature, which, under the existing circumstances, was impossible; for, as the door of the oven was left open, the upper surface of the water was continually cooled by giving off heat to the cold atmosphere, which, rushing into the oven, came into contact with it; and, as soon as the water was made boiling hot, an internal motion of another kind was produced in it, in consequence of the formation and escape of the steam, which last motion was likewise rapid and violent in proportion to the rapidity of the communication of heat. Hence we see that the water in the copper stewpan must have been in a state of continual agitation from the time it went into the oven till it came out of it; and the state in which this liquid was found at the end of the experiment was precisely that which might have been expected, on a supposition that these motions would take place. Let us now see what, agreeably to our assumed principles, ought to have taken place in the other stewpan.

In this case, its contents having been nearly boiling hot when the stewpan was put into the oven, and the door of the oven having been kept closed, and the stewpan covered with its earthen cover, and the stewpan being moreover earthen-ware, which substance is a very bad conductor of heat, and being placed not immediately on the bottom of the oven, but on a thick tile, every circumstance was highly favourable not only for keeping up the equal heat of the water, but also for preventing it from receiving additional heat so rapidly as to agitate it by boiling. There is therefore every reason to think that the water remained at rest, or nearly so, during the whole time it was in the oven; and the transparency of this fluid at the end of the experiment indicated that little or none of the juices of the meat had been mixed with it.

When the Bavarian cook made soup in her own way, the materials (the meat and water) were put into a tall cylindrical boiler, and this boiler was set down upon the hearth against a wood fire, in such a manner that the heat was applied to *one side only* of the boiler, while the other sides of it were exposed to the cold air of the atmosphere; consequently the communication of the heat to the water produced in it a rapid circulatory motion, and, when the water boiled, this motion became still more violent. And this process being carried on for a considerable length of time, the juices of the meat were so completely washed out of it that what remained of it were merely tasteless fibres; but when the ingredients for this meat-soup, taken in the same proportions, were cooked during the same length of time in a boiler set in a closed fire-place and heated by a small equal fire,—this moderate heat being applied to the boiler on every side at the same time, while the loss of heat at the surface of the liquid was effectually prevented by the double cover of the boiler,—the internal motions in the water, occasioned by its receiving heat, were not only very gentle, but they were so divided into a vast number of separate ascending and descending small currents, that the mechanical effects of their impulse on the meat could hardly be sensible; and as the fire was so regulated that the boiling was never allowed to be at all vehement (the liquid being merely kept gently simmering) after the contents of the boiler were once brought to the temperature of boiling, the currents occasioned by the heating ceased of course, and the liquid remained nearly in a state of rest during the remainder of the time that the process of cooking was continued. The soup was found to be of a very inferior quality, but on the other hand the meat was uncommonly juicy and savoury.

These minute investigations may perhaps be tiresome to some readers; but those who feel the importance of the subject, and perceive the infinite advantages to the human species that might be derived from a more intimate knowledge of the science of preparing food, will be disposed to engage with cheerfulness in these truly interesting and entertaining researches; and such readers, and such only, will perceive that it has not been without design that, in chapters devoted to the explanation of subjects the most humble, I have frequently introduced abstruse philosophical researches and the results of profound meditation.

I am not unacquainted with the manners of the age. I have lived much in the world, and have studied mankind attentively, and am fully aware of all the difficulties I have to encounter in the pursuit of the great object to which I have devoted myself. I am even sensible, fully sensible, of the dangers to which I expose myself. In this selfish and suspicious age, it is hardly possible that justice should be done to the purity of my motives; and in the present state of society, when so few who have leisure can bring themselves to take the trouble to read any thing except it be for mere amusement, I can hardly expect to engage attention. I may write, but what will writing avail if nobody will read. My bookseller, indeed, will not be ruined as long as it shall continue to be fashionable to have fine libraries. But my object will not be attained unless my writings are read, and the importance of the subjects of my investigations are felt.

Persons who have been satiated with indulgences and luxuries of every kind are sometimes tempted by the novelty of an untried pursuit. My best endeavours shall not be wanting to give to the objects I recommend not only all the alluring charms of novelty, but also the power of procuring a pleasure as new, perhaps, as it is pure and lasting.

How might I exult could I but succeed so far as to make it fashionable for the rich to take the trouble to choose for themselves those enjoyments which their money can command, instead of being the dupes of those tyrants who, in the garb of submissive fawning slaves, not only plunder them in the most disgraceful manner, but render them at the same time perfectly ridiculous, and fit for that destruction which is always near at hand when good taste has been driven quite off the stage.

When I see in the capital of a great country, in the midst of summer, a coachman sitting on a coach-box dressed in a thick heavy greatcoat with sixteen capes, I am not suprised to find the coach door surrounded by group of naked beggars.

We should tremble at such appearances, did not the shortness of life and the extreme levity of the human character render us insensible to dangers while at any distance, however great and impending and inevitable they may be.

But to return from this digression.

It is frequently useful, and is always amusing, to trace the differences in the customs and usages of different countries to their causes. The French have for ages been remarkable for their fondness for soups, and for their skill in preparing them. Now as national habits of this kind must necessarily originate at a very early period of society, and must depend on peculiar local circumstances, may not the prevalence of the custom of eating soup in France be ascribed to the open chimney fire-places and wood fires which have ever been common in that country?

It is certain that in the infancy of society, before the arts had made any considerable progress, families cooked their victuals by the same fire which warmed them. Kitchens then were not known; and the utensils used in cooking were extremely simple, an earthen pot perhaps set down before the fire. We have just seen that, with such an apparatus, soups of the very best qualities would naturally be produced; and it is not surprising that a whole nation should acquire a fondness for a species of food not only excellent in its kind, but cheap, nutritious, and wholesome, and easily prepared.

Had coals been the fuel used in France, it is not likely that soups would have been so generally adopted in that country; for a common coal fire is not favourable for making good soups, although with a little management the very best soups may be made, and every other process of cooking be performed, *in the highest perfection* with any kind of fuel.

When the *science* of cookery is once well understood, or an intimate knowledge is acquired of the precise nature of those chemical and mechanical changes which are produced in the various culinary processes, we may then, and not till then, take measures with certainty for improving the *art* of preparing food. Experience, unassisted by science, may lead, and frequently does lead, to useful improvements; but the progress of such improvement is not only slow, but vacillating, uncertain, and very unsatisfactory. On that account, no doubt, it is that men of science have in all ages been respected as valuable members of society.

PART III.

CHAPTER VII.

Of the Construction of Boilers, Stewpans, etc. — Choice of the Material for constructing Kitchen Utensils. — Objections to Copper. — Iron much less unwholesome. — Of the Attempts that have been made in different Countries to cover the Surface of iron Boilers with an Enamel. — Of Earthen-ware glazed with Salt. — Stewpans and Saucepans of that Substance recommended. — Kitchen Utensils of Earthen-ware may be covered and protected by an Armor of sheet Copper. — Wedgewood's Ware unglazed would answer very well for Kitchen Utensils. — Directions for constructing Stewpans and Saucepans of Copper in such a Manner as to make them more durable, and more easy to be kept clean. — These Utensils are frequently corroded and destroyed by the Operation of what has been called the Galvanic Influence. — Of the Construction of Covers for Kitchen Boilers, Stewpans, etc.

THE choice of the material to be used in constructing kitchen boilers, stewpans, etc., is a matter of so much importance that I cannot pass it over in silence; though I am very sensible that all I can offer on the subject will not be sufficient to remove entirely the various difficulties I shall be obliged to point out.

The objects principally to be had in view in the choice of materials to be used in the construction of kitchen utensils are wholesomeness, cheapness, and durability. The material most commonly used for constructing kitchen boilers and saucepans is *copper;* but the poisonous qualities of that metal, and the facility with which it is corroded and dissolved by the acids which abound in those substances that are used as food, has long been known and lamented. And numerous attempts have been made to prevent its deleterious effects, by covering its surface with tin and with other metallic substances, and with various kinds of varnish and enamel; but none of these contrivances have completely answered the purpose for which they were designed.

The method which has been found to be most effectual is to keep the copper utensils well tinned, or to tin them afresh as often as the copper begins to appear, and this is what is now commonly practised; but still it were to be wished that some good substitute might be found for that unwholesome metal.

Iron has often been proposed; and though it is more liable to be corroded even than copper, yet as the rust (oxide) of iron is not poisonous, though it changes the colour of some kinds of food that are cooked in it, and in some cases communicates an astringent taste to them, it is not thought to make food unwholesome.

There is, however, one precaution by means of which the disagreeable effects produced by this metal on food that is prepared in utensils constructed of it may be very much diminished, and indeed in most cases almost entirely prevented, especially when the utensil is made of *cast iron.* If, instead of scouring the inside of iron boilers and stewpans with sand, and keeping them bright, which notable housewives are apt to do, in order that their kitchen furniture may appear neat and clean, they be simply washed and rinsed out with warm water, and wiped with a soft dishcloth or towel, the surface of the metal will soon become covered with a thin crust or coating of a dark brown colour resembling enamel; which covering, if it be suffered to remain and to consolidate, will at last become so hard as to take a very good polish, and will serve very efficaciously to defend the surface of the metal from farther corrosion, and consequently to prevent the food from acquiring that taste and colour which iron is apt to impart to it.

The process by which this covering is gradually formed is similar to that by which some gunsmiths brown the barrels of fowling-pieces, and could no doubt be greatly expedited by the same means which they employ for that purpose. The object had in view is likewise the same in both cases, namely, by causing a hard and impenetrable covering of rust to be formed on the surface of the iron to defend it from a contact with those substances which are capable of dissolving or corroding it; or, in other words, to prevent the farther progress of the rust.

For iron utensils designed merely for *frying* or cooking in fat there is an easy and a very effectual precaution that may be taken for preventing rust. It is to avoid putting hot water into them, and above all to avoid boiling, or even heating, water in them. They may occasionally be washed out with warm water; but as often as this is done great care must be taken to wipe them perfectly dry with a dry cloth before they are put away.

The effects produced by this management may be explained in a satisfactory manner. As fatty or oily substances cannot communicate oxygen to iron (with which that metal must unite in order that rust may be formed), and as they prevent the approach of other substances which could furnish it (air, water, acids, etc.) as long as the surface of the iron is completely covered by them, it is evident that no rust can be formed. But boiling-hot water, and more especially water heated and actually made to boil in such a vessel, could not fail to dislodge the fat from the surface of the metal, and leave it naked and exposed to every thing that is capable of corroding it.

Kitchen utensils made of iron may be tinned on the inside to preserve them from rust; and this is frequently done. But even tin, though it be much less liable to be dissolved by those substances which are used in cookery than iron or copper, yet it is sometimes sensibly corroded by them, and consequently is taken into the stomach with our food.

What its effects may be on the human body, when taken in very small quantities, I cannot pretend to determine. In large doses it is well known to be a fatal poison.

That the tin with which the insides of kitchen boilers and stewpans are covered is actually corroded in many of the processes of cookery is rendered highly probable by the very short time that such a coating lasts, when the utensil is in daily use; but I had, not long since, a still more striking proof of that fact. Learning by accident, from my cook, that a dish of which I am very fond (*stewed pears*), which I frequently eat with bread and milk for my supper), required three hours' boiling, it occurred to me that, as this process was performed in a copper stewpan tinned, and as it lasted so long a time, the tin might perhaps be attacked, and some part of it dissolved by the acid of the pears, or by that of the sugar which was mixed with them. In order that I might be able to enjoy my favourite dish free from all apprehensions of being poisoned, I ordered it to be always prepared in future in a stewpan of porcelain; but, several of these vessels having been destroyed in a short time by the fire in this process, I found myself obliged to abandon this scheme on account of these frequent accidents; and I now had recourse to my roaster.

The pears, being previously cut in quarters, and freed from their skins, seeds, and cores, were put, with a sufficient quantity of water and sugar, into a shallow glass basin fitted with a glass cover, and this basin, being placed upon a brick, was put into the roaster; and, a small fire being made under it, the water in the basin was soon brought to boil, and in less than three hours the pears were found to be sufficiently done.

When they were served up, I observed that their colour was different from what it had always been before; and, inquiring into the cause of it, I was let into a secret which explained the matter completely. The cook informed me that it was absolutely impossible to give *a beautiful red colour* to stewed pears without some metal, and that their colour would not have been so fine as it was when they were cooked in porcelain, had not the precaution been taken *to boil a pewter spoon with them*. The reader can easily imagine how much I was surprised at receiving this unexpected information.

This ingenious contrivance is similar to one sometimes used in this country, — that of boiling *half-pence* with greens to give them a fine colour.

Several years ago a variety of attempts was made in Sweden to improve cooking utensils made of iron, by covering them on the inside with a kind of enamel, to protect them from rust; and since that time a considerable manufacture of cast iron boilers and stewpans, covered within with white enamel, was established by Count Heinitz, on his estate in Silesia; but this scheme has not succeeded entirely, owing to the difficulty of finding an enamel capable of uniting with iron, the expansion of which with heat shall be so nearly equal to the expansion of iron as not to be liable to crack and fly off upon being suddenly exposed to heat and to cold; and even were it possible to compose an enamel that would withstand the effects of the heat and the cold, and the blows to which it would be exposed in the business of the kitchen, there would still remain a very important point to be ascertained, which is whether the matter of which the enamel is composed *is not itself of a poisonous nature*, and whether there is not reason to apprehend that it might communicate its deleterious qualities to the food.

Lead is an essential ingredient in most, if not all, enamels, and as its effects are known to be extremely pernicious to health, under all its various forms, when taken internally, it would be highly necessary to ascertain, by the most rigid experimental investigation, whether the enamel of kitchen utensils contains any lead or other noxious metals or unwholesome substance; and, if this be the case, whether such poisonous substance be liable to be corroded and dissolved, or mixed in any other manner with the food.

It is possible that a poisonous substance may be so fixed, on being mixed and united with other substances, as to render it perfectly insoluble, and consequently perfectly inert and harmless; but still the fact ought to be well ascertained before it is admitted.

A large proportion of the calx of lead enters into the composition of flint glass, yet it is not probable that flint glass ever communicates any thing poisonous to food or drink that is kept in it. But, on the other hand, there is reason to conclude that the glazing of common pottery, which is likewise composed in part of calx of lead, is not equally safe, when earthen vessels covered with it are used as implements of cookery. In some countries the use of such vessels in the processes of boiling and stewing is forbidden by the laws, under severe penalties; and in this country it is not customary to use earthen vessels, so glazed, for preserving pickles, and other substances designed for the use of the table which contain strong acids.

The best glazing for earthen vessels that are to be used in preparing or preserving food is most undoubtedly made with common salt, as this glazing (which appears to be merely the beginning of a vitrification of the earth at the surface of the vessel) is not only very hard and durable, but it is also perfectly insoluble in all the acids and other substances in common use in kitchens, and contains nothing poisonous or unwholesome.

A large proportion of lead enters into the composition of pewter; but it has lately been proved, by many ingenious experiments made to ascertain the fact, that the lead, united to tin and the other metallic substances that are used in composing pewter, is incomparably less liable to be dissolved by acids, and consequently much less unwholesome than when it is pure or unmixed with other metals. This fact is very important, as it tends to remove all apprehension respecting the unwholesomeness of a very useful compound metal, which, from its cheapness, as well as on account of its durability, renders it peculiarly well adapted for many domestic uses. It would not, however, be advisable to boil or stew any kind of food, especially such as contain acids, in pewter vessels; nor should acid substances ever be suffered to remain long in them.

The best, or at least the most wholesome, material for stewpans and saucepans is, undoubtedly, earthen-ware glazed with salt.* Several manufactories of this kind of pottery have lately been established in this country, and one in particular in the King's Road, at Chelsea, which belonged to the late Mrs. Hempel, which is, I believe, now carried on by her sons. The principal reason why this article has not long since found its way into common use is, no doubt, the brittleness of earthen-ware, and its being so liable to crack on being suddenly exposed to heat or to cold; for, excepting this imperfection, it has every thing to recommend it. It is perfectly wholesome (when glazed with salt), and is kept clean with little trouble; and things cooked in

---

* Nothing is more pernicious than the glazing of common coarse earthenware. There is no objection to *unglazed* earthen-ware but its being apt to imbibe moisture, which renders it difficult to be kept clean. I have lately seen some kitchen utensils of very fine, compact, unglazed earthen-ware, bought at Mr. Wedgewood's manufactory, which I thought very good. They were made thin, and seemed to stand the fire very well; and, as their surface was very smooth, they were easily kept clean. I wish that the intelligent gentlemen who direct that noble manufactory would turn their attention to the improvement of an article so nearly connected with the health, comfort, and peace of mind of a great portion of society. Stewpans of this material, suspended in a cylindrical armor of sheet iron, would be admirably calculated for the register stoves I shall recommend. Some of these stoves may be seen in the great kitchen of the Royal Institution.

it are much less liable to be burned to the sides of the vessel, and spoiled, than when the utensil is formed of a metallic substance.

There is a very great difference in earthen-ware in respect to its power of withstanding the heat without injury, on being suddenly exposed to the action of a fire, some kinds of it being much less liable to crack and fly, when so exposed, than others; and, in order to take measures with certainty for diminishing this imperfection, we have only to consider the causes from which it proceeds. Now it is quite certain that the cracking of an earthen vessel, on its being put over a fire, is owing to *two* circumstances,—the brittleness of the substance, and the difficulty or slowness with which heat passes through it; for it is evident that neither of these circumstances alone, or acting singly, would be capable of producing the effect.

As heat expands all solid bodies, if one side of a vessel, composed of a brittle substance, be suddenly heated and expanded, it must crack, or rather it must cause the other surface to crack, unless the heat can make its way through the solid substance of the vessel, and heat and expand that other surface so expeditiously as to prevent that accident. Now, as heat passes through a vessel which is thin sooner than through one (composed of the same material) which is thicker, it is evident that the thinner an earthen vessel for cooking is made, the less liable will it be to receive injury on being exposed to sudden heat or cold.

I mention sudden cold as being dangerous, and it is easy to see why it must be equally so with sudden heat. If a brittle vessel be (by slow degrees) made very hot, if the heat be equally distributed throughout the whole

of its substance, this heat, however intense it may be,
will have no tendency whatever to cause the vessel to
crack; for, the expansion being equal at the two opposite surfaces, the tension at those surfaces will be equal
also. But, if cold water be suddenly poured into a
vessel so heated, its internal surface will be suddenly
cooled and as suddenly contracted; and as the external surface cannot contract, being forcibly kept in
a state of expansion by the heat, the inside surface
must necessarily crack, in consequence of its contraction, and this fracture will make its way immediately
through the whole solid substance of the vessel from
the inside to the outside surface.

Sudden heat applied to one side or surface of a
brittle vessel causes the *opposite* side of it to crack;
but sudden cold *causes the side to crack to which the
cold is applied.*

By forming distinct ideas of what happens in these
two cases, every thing relative to the subject under
consideration will be rendered perfectly clear and intelligible.

The *form* of a vessel has a considerable effect in
rendering it more or less liable to be cracked and
destroyed by sudden heat or cold. All flat surfaces,
sharp corners, and inequalities of thickness, should, as
much as possible, be avoided. The globular form is
the best of all, and next to it are those forms which
approach nearest to it; and the thinner the utensil is
made, consistent with the requisite strength to resist
occasional blows, the better it will be in all respects.

The best composition for earthen-ware for culinary
purposes is, I am told, pounded Hessian crucibles, or
any kind of broken earthen-ware of that kind, reduced

to powder, and mixed with a very small proportion of Stourbridge clay.

The method of glazing this ware with salt is by throwing decrepitated common salt into the top of the kiln, with an iron ladle, through six or eight holes made for that purpose in different parts of the top of the kiln. These holes, which need not be more than four inches in diameter each, may be kept covered with common bricks laid over them.

The salt should not be thrown in till the ware is sufficiently burned and till it has acquired the most intense heat that can be given it; and the holes should be immediately closed as soon as the salt is thrown in. If as much as a large handful of salt be thrown into each hole, that will be sufficient, unless the kiln be very large.

The salt is immediately reduced to vapour by the intense heat, and this vapour expands itself and fills every part of the kiln, and disposes the ware to vitrify at its surface.

I have made several attempts to protect stewpans and saucepans of earthen-ware from danger from sudden heat, and from accidental blows, by covering them on the outside with sheet copper and with sheet iron; and in these attempts I have succeeded tolerably well. Several stewpans covered in this manner may be seen in the kitchen and in the repository of the Royal Institution. As the subject is of infinite importance to the health and comfort of mankind, I wish that some ingenious and enterprising tradesman would turn his attention to it.

As cooking utensils of tinned iron are incomparably less dangerous to health than those which are made of copper, I have taken considerable pains to get serviceable stewpans and saucepans made of that material. The great difficulty was to unite durability with cheapness and cleanliness. How far I have succeeded in this attempt will be seen hereafter.

As it is probable the copper stewpans and saucepans will continue to be used, at least for a considerable time to come, notwithstanding the objections which have so often been made to that poisonous metal, I shall proceed to an investigation of the best forms for those utensils.

Before I proceed to a consideration of the improvements that may be made in the forms of kitchen utensils, I must bespeak the patience of the reader. It is quite impossible to make the subject interesting to those who read merely for amusement, and such would do well to pass over the remainder of this chapter without giving it a perusal; but I dare not treat any part of a subject lightly which I have promised to investigate. Besides this, I really think the details, in which I am now about to engage, of no inconsiderable degree of importance; and many other persons will, no doubt, be of the same opinion respecting them. The smallest real improvement of any utensil in general and daily use must be productive of advantages that are incalculable. It is probable that more than a million of kitchen boilers and stewpans are in use every day in the United Kingdom of Great Britain and Ireland; and the providing and keeping kitchen furniture in repair is a heavy article of expense in housekeeping. I am certain that this expense may be considerably lessened; and, in doing this, that kitchen utensils may be made much more convenient, neat, and elegant than they now are.

As it is indispensably necessary, in recommending new mechanical improvements, not only to point out what alterations ought to be made, but also to show distinctly *how the work to be done can be executed in the easiest and best manner,* the fear of being by some thought prolix and tiresome must not deter me from being very particular and minute in my descriptions and instructions.

In justice it ought always to be remembered that my object in writing is professedly to be useful, and that I lay no claim to the applause of those delicate and severe judges of literary composition, who read more with a view to being pleased by fine writing than to acquire information. If those who are quick of apprehension are sometimes tempted to find fault with me for being too particular, they must remember that it is not given to all to be quick of apprehension, and that it is amiable to have patience and to be indulgent. But to proceed.

As the fire employed in heating stewpans, saucepans, etc., may be applied in a variety of different ways, and as the form of the utensil ought in all cases to be adapted to the form of the fire-place and to the mode of applying the heat, it is necessary, in laying down rules for the construction of stewpans and kitchen boilers, to take into consideration the construction of the fire-places in which they are to be used. But kitchen fire-places, constructed on the best principles, are susceptible of a variety of different forms.

In the spacious dwellings of the rich, where large rooms are set apart for the sole purpose of cooking, a number of separate fire-places, in large masses of brick-work constructed on the principles adopted in the kitchen of Baron de Lerchenfeld, at Munich, will be found most convenient (see page 203*); but for persons of moderate fortunes, to whom the economy of house-room is an object of importance, a less expensive arrangement may be chosen.

It is very easy (as will be shown hereafter) so to arrange the implements necessary in cooking for a moderate family, as to leave the kitchen not merely a habitable, but also a perfectly comfortable and even an elegant room. All those who have seen the kitchen in my house, at Brompton (which was fitted up principally with a view to exemplify that important fact), will not doubt the truth of this assertion.

In treating the subject I have proposed to investigate in this chapter, I shall first consider what forms will be best for saucepans and stewpans that are designed to be used in fixed fire-places, and shall then show how those should be constructed which are designed to be heated in a different manner.

Of the Construction of Saucepans and Stewpans for fixed Fire-places.

The reasons have already been given why stewpans and saucepans ought always to be circular. They are indeed always made in that form; but still, as they are commonly constructed, they have a fault which renders

---

* For all such fire-places, at least for all such as are destined for heating stewpans and saucepans, I am quite sure that wood is the cheapest fuel that can be used, even here in London, where it bears so high a price. It is certainly the most cleanly and most convenient, and makes the most manageable fire. I found by an experiment, made on purpose to ascertain the fact, that any given quantity of wood, burned in a closed fire-place, gives very near three times as much heat as it would give if it were first reduced to charcoal, and then burned in the same fire-place. But the great advantage of using wood as fuel in the small fire-places of stewpans and saucepans is the facility with which it may be kindled, and the facility and quickness with which the fire may be put out (by shutting the dampers) when it is no longer wanted.

them but ill adapted for the closed fire-places I have recommended. Their handles being fastened to them on their outsides (by rivets), the regularity of their form is destroyed, and they cannot be made to fit well to the circular openings in their fire-places, which they ought to occupy and to fill.

There are two ways in which this imperfection may be remedied: the first, which is the least expensive, but which is also at the same time the least perfect, is to rivet the handle to the *inside* of the saucepan. This leaves the *outside* of the saucepan circular or cylindrical, that is to say, if care is taken to beat down the heads of the riveting nails, and to make them flat and even with the outside surface of the vessel; but the regularity of the form of the inside of the saucepan will in this case be spoiled by that part of the handle that enters the saucepan, which circumstance will not only render it more difficult to keep the saucepan clean, but will also make it impossible to close it well with a circular cover. The cover may indeed be so contrived as to fit the opening of the saucepan by making a notch in one

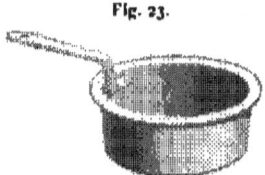

Fig. 23.

side of it to receive that part of the handle which is in the way; and in this manner I have sometimes caused kitchen utensils already on hand to be altered and made to serve very well for closed fire-places. The Figs. 23

and 24 will give a perfect idea of the manner in which these alterations were executed.

Fig. 24.

But, when new saucepans and stewpans are constructed, I would strongly recommend the following more simple and more advantageous contrivance.

A circular rim of iron should be provided for each saucepan with a handle belonging to it, of the form here represented; and, by forming the saucepan to this

Fig. 25.

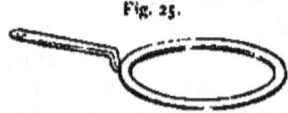

rim, its form at its brim will be circular *within* and *without*; and consequently the saucepan will exactly fit the circular opening of its fire-place, and will at the same time be exactly fitted by its *circular cover*. No attention will in that case be necessary, in putting on the cover, to place it in any particular manner or situation; and the saucepan, not being pierced with holes for rivets, will, on that account, be less liable to leak, and will also be more durable and more easily kept clean.*

* One reason is obvious why stewpans without rivets should be more durable than those which have their handles riveted to them; but there is another reason more occult, which requires the knowledge of a late discovery in chemistry to understand. When iron and copper, in contact with each other, are placed in a situation in which they are exposed to be frequently wetted, they act on each other very powerfully, and one of the metals will soon be destroyed by rust.

Fire-places and Kitchen Utensils. 351

The circular iron rim above recommended should be broad and flat, from $\frac{1}{8}$ to $\frac{3}{16}$ of an inch in thickness, and from $\frac{1}{2}$ an inch to $\frac{3}{4}$ of an inch in width. Its handle, which must be welded fast to it, and must project from one side of it, may be from 1$\frac{1}{4}$ inch to 1$\frac{1}{2}$ in width, from 6 to 8 or 10 inches long, and of the same thickness as the circular rim where it joins it.

The under side of this flat iron rim should be made perfectly flat, in order that the saucepan, by being suspended by it in its fire-place, may so completely close the circular opening of the fire-place as to prevent the smoke from coming into the room; and also to prevent (what would be much more likely to happen) the cold air of the room from descending into the fire-place, and mixing there with the flame and smoke, and afterwards going off thus heated through the chimney into the atmosphere.

The copper saucepan or stewpan is to be fastened

When ships first began to be covered with copper, this fact was not known, and great inconvenience was found to arise from the rapid decay of the iron bolts in the vessels so covered. As there appeared to be no remedy for this evil, it was found necessary to substitute copper bolts for iron bolts in constructing ships intended to be coppered. These effects are now known to depend on what (from the name of its discoverer) has been called the *Galvanic influence*.

It appears to me to be highly probable that stewpans and saucepans, constructed in the manner above described, would last more than twice as long as those made in the usual manner. Frequent attempts have been made to line copper boilers and saucepans with tinned iron (commonly called sheet iron) in order to guard against the poisonous qualities of the copper; but none of these have succeeded so well as was expected, the tin being found to be destroyed by rust with uncommon rapidity. This, no doubt, was owing to the influence of the same cause by which the iron bolts of coppered ships were so suddenly destroyed.

If handles must be riveted to the sides of copper saucepans or boilers, such handles should be made of copper and not of iron; and the nails by which they are fastened should likewise be copper. They would cost something more at first, but the utensils would last so much longer that they would turn out to be much the cheapest in the end.

to its iron rim by being turned over its outward edge;
and in order that the copper, thus turned over the outward edge of the iron rim, may hold fast without projecting below the level of the lower flat surface of the ring (which would be attended with inconvenience), the lower part of the outward edge of the ring must be chamfered away in the manner represented in the following figure (26), which shows a vertical section of the ring, of the full size, with the copper turned over it.

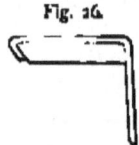

Fig. 26.

The upper inside edge of this iron ring may be rounded off, as it is represented to be in the above figure. In this figure the section of the ring is distinguished by diagonal lines, and that of the copper (which is turned over it) by two parallel crooked lines.

When stewpans and saucepans are constructed on the principles here recommended (with flat circular iron rings), an advantage will be attained, which in many cases will be found to be of no small importance: they will be well adapted for being used in small portable fire-places heated by charcoal, or in portable stoves heated (or rather kept hot) by heaters. Descriptions of these portable fire-places and heater-stoves will be given in the sequel of this work.

As the upper part of the circular opening of the fire-place (Fig. 27), on the top of which the lower part of the circular rim of the saucepan reposes, is nearly on a level with the top of the solid mass of the brick-work,

Fire-places and Kitchen Utensils. 353

it is necessary that the handle of the saucepan should be bended upwards, so as to be above the level of the brim of the saucepan; otherwise, when the saucepan is in its place, there would not be room between the handle and the surface of the brick-work for the fingers to pass in taking hold of the handle to remove the saucepan. This is evident from a bare inspection of the following figure (27), which represents the section of a saucepan constructed on the plan here proposed, fitted into its fire-place.

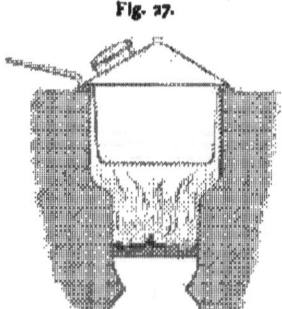

Fig. 27.

There should be a round hole, about a ¼ of an inch in diameter, near the end of the handle, by which the saucepan may occasionally be hung up on a nail or peg when it is not in use. The cover belonging to the saucepan may be hung up on the same nail or peg, by means of the projection of its rim.

These will be thought trifling matters; but it must not be forgotten that convenience and the economy of time are often the result of attention to the arrangement of things apparently of little importance.

In constructing the cover of a saucepan, care must be taken to avoid a fault, into which it is easy to fall, and which, as I have found by experience, will be attended with disagreeable consequences. The circular plate of tin, or of thin sheet copper tinned, which forms the bottom of the cover, should be of the same diameter *precisely* as the outside of the brim of the saucepan.

I once thought it would be better to make the bottom of the cover rather *larger* than the top of the brim of the saucepan, as it is represented in the following section:—

Fig. 28.

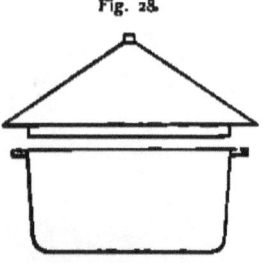

I imagined that it would prevent any thing that happened by accident to be spilled on the cover from finding its way into the saucepan and spoiling the victuals, and this indeed it would do most effectually; but it often occasioned another accident not less disagreeable in its effects. It drew the smoke into the saucepan, which happened to escape by the sides of the circular opening of the fire-place.

When the cover is precisely of the same diameter as the brim of the saucepan, there is little danger of any thing entering the saucepan in this manner, as will be evident from an inspection of the following figure:—

Fire-places and Kitchen Utensils. 355

Fig. 29.

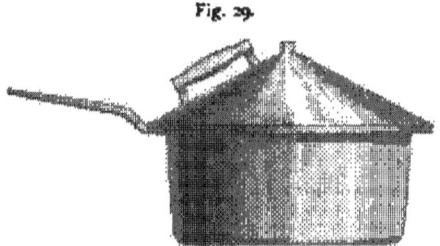

The bottom of the cover may either be made quite flat, as in this section:—

Fig. 30.

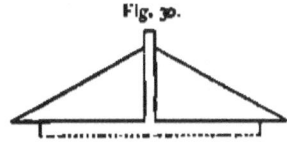

Or it may be made concave, and of a conical form, thus:—

Fig. 31.

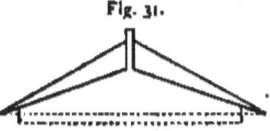

Or concave, and of a spherical figure, as is represented in the following figure:—

Fig. 32.

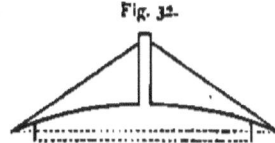

The only utility derived from making the bottom of the cover hollow instead of flat is that a little more room is left for the boiling up or swelling of the contents of the saucepan. Cooks will be best able to judge how far this is an object of importance.

In each of the three last figures a section of the tube which carries off the steam is shown, as also a section of the rim of the cover that enters the saucepan. This rim, which may be from ¼ of an inch to 1 inch in breadth, should be made to fit the opening of the saucepan with some degree of nicety; but it should not be fitted so closely as to require any effort in removing it, or so as to render it necessary to use both hands in doing it, — one to hold the saucepan fast in its place, and the other to take off its cover.

The steam-tube of the cover, which may be ½ an inch or ¼ of an inch in diameter, and should project about ½ an inch above the top of the cover, must pass through both the top and the bottom of the cover, and must be well fitted and soldered in both, in order that the air between the top of the cover and its bottom may be confined and completely cut off from all communication with the steam, and also with the external air. This steam-tube should have a fit stopple, which may be made of wood, and which, to prevent its being lost, should be attached to the top of the cover by a small wire chain about 2 or 3 inches long.

In respect to the handles of these covers, the choice of the form to be adopted may be left to the workman who is employed to make the cover; for, excepting in certain cases, which will be particularly noticed hereafter, it is a point of little importance.

It is right that I should observe here that though the covers I have here described are such as I have generally recommended, yet others of different forms may be constructed on the same principles, that very possibly may answer quite as well as these, and cost less. The steam-tube, for instance, for small saucepans, may with safety be omitted, and the steam be left to make its way between the rim of the cover and the saucepan; and, should it be thought an improvement, the upper part of the cover, instead of being a cone, may be a segment of a sphere.

The following figure is the section of the cover of a saucepan now in general use in this country. It is

Fig. 33.

made of a circular piece of sheet copper, and its handle, which is of iron, is fastened to it by rivets; and it is tinned on the under side. Its form is such that it fits without a rim into the saucepan to which it belongs.

This cover might be greatly improved, and perhaps rendered as well adapted for confining heat as any metal cover whatever, merely by covering it above with a thin circular plate of tinned iron or of copper, either quite flat or convex, like that represented by this figure:—

Fig. 34.

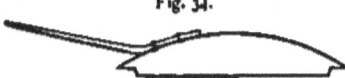

It can hardly be necessary for me to observe that this thin circular plate must be well soldered to the cover all round its circumference, in order to confine the air that is intercepted between the upper surface of the cover and the lower surface of this plate.

For the mere purpose of confining the heat in a stewpan or small boiler — were superior neatness and cleanliness not objects of particular attention — one of the very best covers that could be used would be a common saucepan cover, defended above from the cold air of the atmosphere by a circular cover of wood firmly fixed to it by means of a screw or a rivet.

The following figures represent covers so defended; and were the circular piece of wood to prevent its

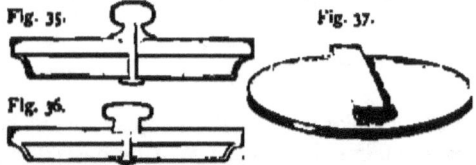

warping to be composed of two or three very thin boards, glued fast to each other and nailed or riveted together to unite them more strongly, I am inclined to think that this would be one of the best covers for common use, especially for large stewpans, that could be made. Its handle might be made of wood, and of either of the forms represented in these figures, or of any other simple form.

The covers for large stewpans should always be furnished with steam-tubes, in order that the steam, when it becomes too strong to be confined, may escape without deranging or lifting up the cover.

A cover made entirely of wood might answer very well for confining heat, especially if care were taken to construct it in such a manner as to prevent its being liable to be warped by the heat and by the moisture to which it is continually exposed; but the wooden covers of boilers, saucepans, and stewpans, require much attention to keep them clean, unless they be lined with tin or with sheet copper.

Having now finished my observations on the covers of small boilers and saucepans, *in their most simple state,* when they are designed merely for confining heat, it remains to consider of the means that may be put in practice to render them useful in *directing* the heat that escapes in the steam, which is formed when liquids are boiled in the various processes of cookery, and *employing this heat to useful purposes.*

As the quantity of heat that exists in steam is very considerable (as has been elsewhere observed), the recovery of this heat is frequently an object deserving of attention; but, before we proceed in this inquiry, it will be necessary to say something respecting the method of *cooking in steam.* This subject will be treated in the following chapter.

CHAPTER VIII.

Of cooking in Steam. — Objections to the Steam-kitchens now in Use.—Principles on which a steam Apparatus for cooking should be constructed. — Descriptions of fixed Boilers for cooking with Steam.—A particular Description of a STEAM-RIM *for Boilers by Means of which their Covers may be made steam-tight. — Description of a* STEAM-DISH *to be used occasionally for cooking with Steam over a Kitchen Boiler. — Account* of what has been called a FAMILY BOILER: many of them have already been sold, and have been found very useful. — *Hints to Cooks concerning the Means that may be used for improving some popular Dishes.*

As the art of cooking with steam is well known, and has long been successfully practised in this country, it would be a waste of time to attempt to prove what is universally acknowledged; namely, that almost every kind of food usually prepared for the table in boiling water may be as well cooked, and in many cases better, by means of boiling-hot steam. I shall therefore confine my present inquiries to the investigation of the best methods of confining and directing steam, and employing it usefully with the most simple and least expensive apparatus.

Steam-kitchens, as they are called, consist of very expensive machinery, and I have been informed, by several persons who have used them, that they do not produce any considerable saving of fuel. Bare inspection is, indeed, sufficient to show that they cannot be economical in that respect; for the surface of the tin steam-vessel filled with hot steam that is exposed quite naked to the cold air of the atmosphere is so great, that it must necessarily occasion a very considerable loss of heat.

A primary object in contriving a steam apparatus for cooking should be to prevent the loss of heat *through the sides of the containing vessels;* and this is to be done, first, by exposing as small a surface as possible to the atmosphere; and, secondly, by covering up that surface with the warmest covering that can conveniently be used, to defend it from the cold air.

The steam-vessel in the kitchen of the Foundling Hospital is a large wooden box lined with tin, capable of containing a large quantity of potatoes; and the steam comes through a small tin tube from an oblong quadrangular iron boiler which is used daily for boiling meat, etc., for the Hospital. As this boiler is furnished with what I have called a *steam-rim* (which will presently be described), when the (wooden) cover of the boiler is down, all the steam that is generated in the boiler is forced to pass through the steam-box, and the potatoes, greens, etc., that are in the box are cooked without any additional expense of fuel.

The steam-box has a steam-rim and also a wooden cover which, when it is down, closes the box and makes it perfectly steam-tight.

When steam is generated faster than it can be condensed in the steam-box, that which is redundant passes off by a waste-tube, which conducts it into a neighbouring chimney.

The apparatus for cooking with steam in the kitchen of the House of Correction, at Munich, is still more simple. Here two equal quadrangular boilers are set, one at the end of the other, at the same level, in the same mass of brick-work; and the flame and smoke from the same fire pass under them both (see Plate X., Fig. 7, and Plate XI., Fig. 9). Both boilers being enclosed in brick-work and being covered with wooden covers, it is evident that no part of the apparatus is exposed to the cold air. I say *no part* of it; for the covers of the boilers being of wood, which is one of the worst conductors of heat, very little heat can make its way through them; and to prevent even this loss, inconsiderable as it is, these wooden covers may, if it should be thought necessary, be defended from the cold air by warm rugs thrown over them.

The smoke which passes under the second boiler not only prevents the approach of the cold air to the under surface of its bottom, but, acting on the small quantity of water that is contained in it, actually assists in the generation of steam. It even happens sometimes (namely, when there is but a small quantity of water in the second boiler, and the first is nearly filled with cold water) that the water in the second boiler actually boils and fills the boiler with steam, before the water in the first boiler is heated boiling-hot.

This appears to me to be one of the most economical methods that can be used for cooking, and that it is well adapted for hospitals and also for large private families. If it should be necessary to make provision for cooking a great number of different dishes in steam at the same time, either the steam-boiler may be made sufficiently large to receive them, or, instead of it, two or more steam-boilers of a moderate size may be put up; and, if the different kinds of food that are cooked at the same time in the same steam-boiler be placed each in a separate dish and covered over with some proper vessel in the form of a bell (a common earthen pot, for instance, turned upside down), the exhalations from the different kinds of food will be prevented from so mixing together as to give an improper taste or flavour to any of the victuals.

These covers to the different dishes will likewise be useful on another account. When the cover of the steam-boiler is opened for the purpose of examining or of introducing or removing any dish, the process of cooking going on in the other dishes will not be interrupted, for their bell-like covers, remaining filled with steam, will prevent the cold air from coming into contact with the victuals. It is true that the cover or lid of the steam-boiler must not be kept open too long, otherwise the steam confined under the covers of the dishes will be condensed, and the cold air will find its way under them.

In order that these boilers may be perfectly steam-tight when their lids are down, they must all be furnished with *steam-rims;* and there must be a tube of communication between them for the passage of the steam, and another tube to carry off the redundant steam from the boiler which is situated farthest from the fire.

If it should be necessary, the principal boiler may, without any difficulty or inconvenience, be divided into two compartments, so as to render it possible to prepare two different kinds of soup, or to boil two different things separately at the same time. Suppose, for instance, that the apparatus is designed for the kitchen of a large family, and that the principal boiler is 12 inches wide, 24 inches long, and 12 inches deep. This may be so divided by a vertical partition as to form two compartments: the one, that immediately over the fire, for instance, 12 inches by 10; and the other, 12 inches by 14. In this case I should make the second, or *steam-boiler*, 24 inches square by 12 inches deep, and should cause the smoke to circulate in three flues parallel to each other. The first (in the hither end of which the fire-place should be situated) should be immediately under the first boiler, and the second and third should be under the second boiler.

364   *On the Construction of Kitchen*

The following figure shows the manner in which these boilers should be set:—

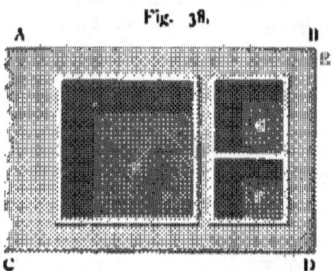

Fig. 38.

A, B, is the side of the room; A, C, D, E, the mass of brick-work in which the boilers are set; F and G are the two compartments of the first boiler, which is shown with its steam-rim; H is the larger boiler, which is also represented with its steam-rim.

The covers of these boilers (which do not appear in the figure) should be so attached to the boilers by hinges as to be laid back when the boilers are opened, and rested against the side of the room; and these covers should be lined with tin or with thin sheet copper tinned.

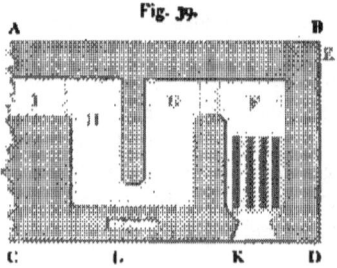

Fig. 39.

The foregoing figure represents a horizontal section of the brick-work in which these boilers are to be set, taken at the level of the tops of the flues.

A, B, is the side of the room; and A, C, D, E, the mass of brick-work which is placed against it; F, G, and H are the three parallel flues; and I is the canal that carries off the smoke from the second boiler to the chimney; K is the opening into the fire-place by which the fuel is introduced; and L is a passage, closed up with a tile or with loose bricks, which is occasionally opened to clean the flues, G and H. The damper in the canal, I, may be placed near the left-hand side of the second boiler. The situations of the boilers are indicated by dotted lines.

As it is not necessary that I should repeat in this place the directions which have already been so amply explained concerning the proper method of proceeding in setting boilers, I shall not enlarge farther on that subject, but shall proceed to give an account of a very essential part, not yet described, of the apparatus necessary for cooking with steam in the simple way I have here recommended: the part I mean is the *steam-rim* of the boiler.

Description of a Steam-rim for a Boiler, by Means of which its Cover may easily be made steam-tight.

To give a more complete idea of this contrivance, I have, in the following figure, represented a vertical section of a small part of one side of a boiler and its steam-rim with its (wooden) cover in its place, both of one half size.

A, B, is a section of part of the flat wooden cover; the crooked line, C, D, is a section of the steam-rim, and part of the side of a boiler; E is a section of a descending rim of wood belonging to and making an essential part of the cover, which rim, when the cover is down, enters the steam-rim of the boiler, and reposes on the bottom of it. In the figure it is represented in this situation: the wooden rim of the cover is fastened

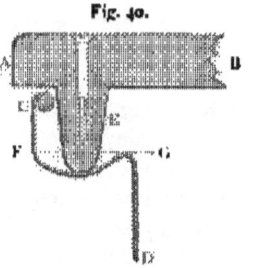

Fig. 40.

to the flat part of it by means of wood-screws, one of which is represented in the figure.*

Now it is evident, from an inspection of the figure, that a small quantity of water will lodge in the steam-rim, and will stand at the level of the dotted line, F, G; and, as the rim of the cover will enter this water when the cover is shut down, all communication between the steam in the boiler and the external air must necessarily be cut off, and of course the steam will be completely confined.

It is true that, if in consequence of the increase of its temperature above the heat of water boiling in the open air the elasticity of the steam should become sufficient to overcome the pressure of the atmosphere,

---

* The cover itself is supposed to be framed and panelled in the manner described in the 6th chapter of this Essay, and it should be lined with tin or with thin sheet copper tinned, in order to prevent the wood from being cracked and destroyed by the steam.

it will force the water in the steam-rim to ascend toward C, and, getting under the rim, E, of the cover of the boiler, it will make its escape, but no bad consequences will result from this loss; on the contrary, the steam-rim will in this case serve instead of a *safety-valve*. And, although this contrivance may not be adequate to the confining of *strong* steam, it certainly answers perfectly well for confining that kind of steam which is most proper to be used for cooking. It will likewise be found useful in many cases for covering boilers, where the principal object in view is to prevent the contact of the cold air with the contents of the boiler. It will be useful for the boilers of bleachers, as also for laundry boilers, for brewers' boilers, and for all boilers destined for the evaporation of liquids under a boiling heat.

It appears to me that this contrivance might, with a little alteration, be used with great advantage for covering the boilers used by distillers. By making the steam-rim deeper, the cover of the boiler would be tight, under a considerable pressure; and by making the boiler broad and shallow, with several separate fire-places under it (the flat bottom of the boiler being supported on the tops of the flues of these fire-places), a variety of important advantages would be gained, and these would not be compensated by any disadvantages that I can foresee. The boiler might be constructed of very thin sheet copper, which would not only render it less expensive, but would also make it more durable.

When steam-rims were first introduced, they were made of the form represented in the following figure, which represents a vertical section of part of one side of a boiler with a steam-rim, covered with a conical double cover made of tin:—

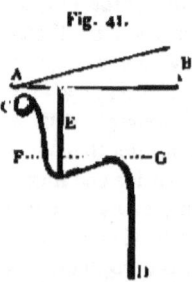

Fig. 41.

In this and the following figures, A, B, represents a section of part of one side of the (double) cover of the boiler; C, D, the steam-rim and part of one side of the boiler; E, the descending rim of the cover; and F, G, the level of the water in the steam-rim,—all of one half size.

This construction was found to be attended with an inconvenience, which, indeed, might easily have been foreseen. When the steam, on being confined, became strong enough to force its way under the descending rim, E, of the cover of the boiler, the water in the steam-rim was frequently blown out of it with considerable violence and dispersed about the room. To prevent these disagreeable accidents, the form of the upper part of the steam-rim was altered. To make a proper finish to the boiler, the edge of its brim (which forms the top of its steam-rim) had been turned *outwards* over a strong wire. It was now turned *inwards* over the wire; and the outside or rising part of the steam-rim, instead of being made *sloping outwards*, was now made *vertical*.

A complete idea of these different alterations, and of

the effects necessarily produced by them, may be formed by comparing the foregoing figure (No. 41) with the following:—

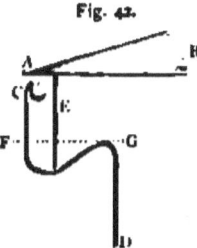

Fig. 42.

It is evident that in this case, as there is sufficient room between the outside of the descending rim of the cover and the vertical side of the steam-rim to contain all the water that can be forced upwards between them by the steam, there is little danger of any part of this water being blown out of the steam-rim by the steam when it makes its escape under the rim of the cover.

Of the Manner in which Kitchen Boilers and Stewpans may be constructed so as to be rendered useful in cooking with Steam.

If a common kitchen boiler be furnished with a steam-rim, and the descending rim of its cover be made to shut down into it, the steam in the boiler will be effectually confined, and may in various ways be usefully employed in cooking. One of the simplest methods of doing this is to set what I shall call a *steam-dish* upon the boiler. The bottom of this steam-dish being furnished with a descending rim or projection, fitting into the steam-rim of the boiler, the steam-dish may be made to serve as a cover to the boiler; and, if a number of small holes be made in the bottom of this dish near its circumference, the steam will pass up into it from below; and, if it be properly closed above, any victuals placed in it will be cooked in steam.

If this dish be furnished with a steam-rim of the same form and size with that of the boiler, the cover of the boiler will then serve for covering the steam-dish, whenever that dish is in use.

The following figure, which represents a vertical section of the apparatus, will show this contrivance in a clear and distinct manner:—

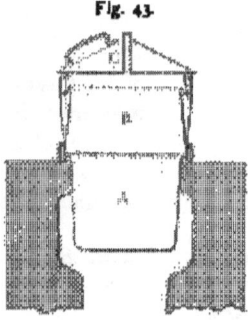

Fig. 43.

A is the boiler, which is seen set in brick-work; B is the steam-dish; and C is the cover of the boiler, which is here made to serve as a cover for the steam-dish.

The sides of the steam-dish (which is made of tin) are double, for the purpose of confining the heat more effectually.

If it be required to cook several kinds of food at the same time, a steam-dish may be used that is divided into several compartments; or two or more steam-dishes may be placed one above another over the same boiler, that which is uppermost being covered with the cover of the boiler.

A very complete apparatus of this kind may be seen in the kitchen of Mr. Summers, of New Bond Street, ironmonger, who makes and sells these articles, and who has sold no less than 225 sets of these family boilers, as they are called, since he first began to manufacture them; and Mr. Feetham, of Oxford Street, has sold 110 sets of them. A cooking apparatus of this kind may likewise be seen at the Royal Institution; and at Heriot's Hospital, at Edinburgh; and in the houses of many private families in England and Scotland. There are several tradesmen who now manufacture them; and all persons desirous of making and selling them are at full liberty to do so.

When different kinds of food, placed one above the other, are cooked in steam, the drippings of those above might, in some cases, be apt to spoil those below if means were not used to prevent it. This inconvenience may be avoided in the apparatus I am describing by introducing the food into the steam-dishes, placed in deep plates or in shallow basins, sufficiently capacious, however, to contain as much water as will be generated in consequence of the condensation of the steam on the surface of the food in heating it boiling-hot. I say "in heating it boiling-hot;" for, after it is once heated to that temperature, no more steam will be condensed upon it, however long the process of cooking may be continued.*

---

* It is not difficult to determine with great precision what the size or contents of the dish must be, in order that it may contain all the water that can possibly be produced by the condensation of the steam, in heating the victuals

This is a curious circumstance, and the knowledge of the fact may be turned to a good account. If, for instance, it were required to make the strongest extract of the pure juices of any kind of meat, unmixed with water, this may be done by heating the meat nearly boiling-hot, either in boiling water or in steam, and then putting it, placed in a shallow dish, into a steam-dish, or into any closed vessel filled with hot steam, and leaving it in this situation two or three hours, or for a longer time. Whatever liquid is found collected in the dish at the end of the process must necessarily be the purest juices of the meat. In this manner the richest gravies may no doubt be prepared.

that are cooked in it to the temperature of boiling water. Suppose, for instance, that a piece of beef weighing six pounds is to be cooked in the steam-dish, and that this meat, when it is put into the dish, is at the temperature of $55°$ of Fahrenheit's thermometer, which is the mean annual temperature of the atmosphere at London. Now as this piece of meat is to be made boiling-hot, its temperature must be raised 157 degrees, namely, from $55°$ to $212°$. But we have seen that any given quantity, by weight, of beef, requires less heat to heat it any given number of degrees, than an equal weight of water, in the proportion of 74 to 100 (see the introduction to this Essay, page 183); consequently these 6 lbs. of beef will be heated 157 degrees, or from $55°$ to the boiling point, with a quantity of heat which would be required to heat 4 lbs. 7 oz. of water 157 degrees.

Now if we suppose, with Mr. Watt, that the steam which produces, in its condensation, 1 lb. of water gives off as much heat as would raise the temperature of 5½ lbs. of water 180 degrees, namely, from the point of freezing to that of boiling water, the same quantity of heat must be sufficient to raise the temperature of 6 lbs. 5 oz. of water 157 degrees, or from $55°$ to $212°$.

And if 6 lbs. 5 oz. of water require 1 lb. of condensed steam to heat it 157 degrees, 4 lbs. 7 oz. of water, or 6 lbs. of beef, will require only 11⅜ oz. of condensed steam to raise its temperature the same number of degrees, for it is 6 lbs. 5 oz. is to 1 lb. as 4 lbs. 7 oz. to 11⅜ oz.

Consequently, if 6 lbs. of beef at the temperature of $55°$ were placed in a steam apparatus, in a shallow dish capable of containing 11¼ oz., or a little less than *three quarters of a pint*, this dish would contain all the water that could possibly result from the condensation of steam on the surface of the meat, in heating it boiling-hot.

This computation may be of some use in determining the dimensions of the vessels proper to be used for holding the victuals that are cooked in the steam-dishes above described.

Thick steaks or cutlets of beef, boiled in this manner, and made perfectly tender throughout, and then broiled on a gridiron, and served up in their own gravy, with or without additions, would, I imagine, be an excellent dish, and very wholesome. But it must be left to cooks and to professed judges of good eating to determine whether these hints (which are thrown out with all becoming humility and deference) are deserving of attention. For, although I have written a whole chapter on the pleasure of eating, I must acknowledge, what all my acquaintances will certify, that few persons are less attached to the pleasures of the table than myself. If, in treating the subject, I sometimes appear to do it *con amore*, this warmth of expression ought, in justice, to be ascribed solely to the sense I entertain of its infinite importance to the health, happiness, and innocent enjoyments of mankind.

CHAPTER IX.

Description of a UNIVERSAL KITCHEN BOILER, *for the Use of a small Family, to answer all the Purposes of Cookery; and also for boiling Water for Washing, etc.* — *Description of a* PORTABLE FIRE-PLACE *for a universal Kitchen Boiler.* — *Account of a Contrivance for warming a Room by Means of this Fireplace and Boiler.* — *Of* STEAM STOVES *for warming Rooms.* — *They are probably the best Contrivance for that Purpose that can be made Use of, — they warm the Air without spoiling it, they economize Fuel, and may be made very ornamental.*

Description of a UNIVERSAL KITCHEN BOILER *for the Use of small Families, to answer all the Purposes of Cookery ; and also for boiling Water for Washing, etc.*

THE following figure represents a vertical section of this boiler, and also of its fire-place and cover.

This boiler is supposed to be made of cast iron, and its section is represented by a double line. The lower

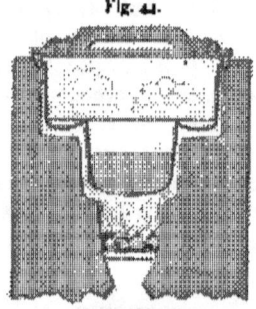

Fig. 44.

part of it, which is represented as being filled about half full with water, is 12 inches in diameter above, about 11 inches in diameter below, and 9¼ inches deep. The upper part of it, which is furnished with a steam-rim, is 24 inches in diameter above — where its steam-rim begins — and 23 inches in diameter below — where it joins the flat part which unites it to the lower part of the boiler.

The lower part of this boiler (which might, without any impropriety, be called the *lower boiler*) is destined for containing the soup or the water that is made to boil, while the upper and broader part is used for boiling with steam. The brim of the lower boiler projects upward, about an inch above the level of the flat bottom of the upper boiler. This projection prevents the water resulting from the condensation of steam against the sides of the upper boiler from descending into the lower boiler. The upper boiler is 8½ inches deep, from the top of the inside of its steam-rim to the flat part of its bottom. The whole depth of both boilers is 18 inches, from the top of the steam-rim to the lower boiler.

A circular piece of tin, about 22 inches in diameter, with many holes through it to give a free passage to the steam, being laid down in a horizontal position upon the top or projecting brim of the lower boiler, upon this circular plate the shallow dishes are placed, which contain the victuals that are to be cooked in steam. Two such dishes are faintly represented in the foregoing figure by dotted lines.

The cover of this universal boiler is a shallow circular dish, 26 inches in diameter at its brim, and about 1¼ inches deep, turned upside down, and covered above with a circular covering of wood to confine the heat. The handle to this cover is a strong cleat of wood, fastened to the circular wooden cover by means of four wood screws. This handle is distinctly represented in the figure.

The circular wooden cover for confining the heat must be constructed in panels, and must be fastened to the shallow metallic dish by means of rivets or wood screws. In doing this, all the precautions must be taken that are pointed out in the fifth chapter of this Essay, page 289; otherwise the wood and the metal will be separated from each other, in consequence of the shrinking of the wood on its being exposed to heat.

The inverted shallow dish, which, properly speaking,

constitutes the cover of this boiler, may be made either of tin or of sheet iron or of sheet copper; or it may be made of cast iron. Whatever the material is of which it is constructed, care must be taken to make it of such dimensions precisely that its brim may enter the steam-rim, and occupy the lower or deepest part of it, otherwise the steam will not be properly confined in the boiler.

The following figure represents a vertical section, *of one half size*, of the steam-rim of one of these boilers (of cast iron), together with a section of a part of an inverted shallow cast iron pan, which serves as a cover to the boiler, and also of the circular covering of wood which is attached to the pan, and defends it from the cold air of the atmosphere.

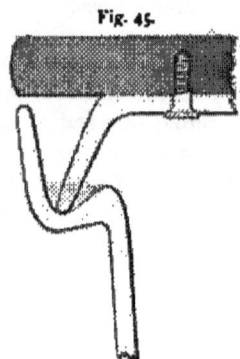

Fig. 45.

In this figure the steam-rim is represented as being full of water, and one of the screws is seen which fasten the circular wooden cover to the inverted shallow pan which confines the steam in the boiler.

On examining the two preceding figures, it will be

found that both the boiler and its cover are of forms that will readily deliver from their moulds; and that circumstance will enable iron-founders to sell these articles at low prices.

The mass of brick-work in which this boiler is set may be a cube of 3 feet; or, by sinking the ash-pit in the ground, its height may be reduced to 2½ feet.

In order that the flame may be made to separate and spread equally on all sides under the lower boiler, the smoke should be made to pass off in two small canals situated on opposite sides of the boiler. The openings of these canals may be a little below the level of the bottom of what has been called the upper boiler; and the smoke, being made first to descend nearly to the level of the bottom of the lower boiler, may then pass off horizontally towards the chimney. The situation of the two horizontal canals (on opposite sides of the boiler) by which the smoke goes off is indicated (in Fig. 44) by dotted lines.

So much has already been said in the foregoing chapters relative to the construction of closed fire-places for kitchen boilers, that it would be quite superfluous to give any particular directions respecting the construction of the fire-place for this boiler. The manner in which the boiler is set in brick-work, and the means that are used for causing the smoke to surround it on every side, are distinctly shown in the figure.

In order more effectually to confine the heat, the boiler should be entirely enclosed in the brick-work on every side, in such a manner that the brim of its steam-rim should not project above it more than half an inch. To preserve the brick-work from being wetted, the top of it may be covered with sheet lead, which may be made to turn over the top of the brim of the steam-rim of the boiler.

There may either be a steam-tube in the cover of the boiler, or the steam may be permitted to force its way under the descending rim of the inverted shallow pan which constitutes the cover. If there be a steam-tube, it should be half an inch in diameter and about one inch in length; and it should be made very smooth on the inside, in order that another tube of tin or of tinned copper, about 10 inches in length, may pass freely in it. The use of this movable tube is to cause the air to be expelled from the upper boiler, while it is used for cooking with steam. This will be done if, while the water below is boiling, the long tube be thrust down into the boiler through the steam-tube till its lower end comes to the level of the brim of the lower boiler. For, as steam is considerably lighter than common air, it will of course rise up and occupy the upper part of the upper boiler, and the air below it being compressed will escape through the tube we have just described; and, although that tube should remain open, the upper boiler will nevertheless remain filled with steam, to the total exclusion of atmospheric air. The inside of the steam-tube and the outside of the movable tube should be made to fit each other with accuracy, in order that no steam may escape between them. The necessity of this precaution is too evident to require any elucidation.

It will be best to place the steam-tube within about an inch of the side of the cover, in which case it will be easy, by turning the cover about, to place it in such a position that the movable tube may descend into the upper boiler without being stopped by meeting with any of the dishes that are placed in it.

It is hardly necessary that I should observe here that boilers on the principles above described may be constructed of sheet iron or sheet copper as well as of cast iron, and that they may be made of any dimensions. That which is represented in the foregoing figure (No. 44) is of a moderate size, and would, I should imagine, be suitable for the family of a labourer consisting of eight or ten persons. The lower part of the boiler would hold about 3⅛ gallons; but the whole boiler, filled up to within an inch of the level of the inside of the steam-rim, would hold 14¼ gallons. When so filled up, I should suppose the boiler to be sufficiently capacious to heat water for washing or for any other purpose that could be wanted by an industrious family consisting of the number of persons above-mentioned.

Description of a PORTABLE FIRE-PLACE *for a* UNIVERSAL KITCHEN BOILER.

The following figure represents a vertical section of the fire-place with its boiler in its place:—

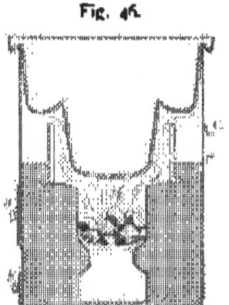

Fig. 46.

This figure is drawn to a scale of 20 inches to the inch.

The boiler is supposed to be of cast iron, and the section of it is represented by a double line. To render its form more conspicuous, its cover is omitted.

The portable fire-place is a cylinder of sheet iron, 24¼ inches in diameter, and 34¼ in height, open above and closed below. The sections of this cylinder and of its bottom are marked by strong black lines.

The fire-place, properly so called, is the centre or axis of this cylinder. It is built of fire-bricks and Stourbridge clay, and the fire burns on a circular cast iron dishing-grate, 8 inches in diameter.

The opening (at *a*) by which the fuel is introduced is marked by dotted lines, as is also another opening below it (at *b*) which leads to the ash-pit. These openings are closed by doors of sheet iron, which are attached by hinges to the outside of the cylinder, and fastened by means of turn-buckles.

The door of the ash-pit is furnished with a register for regulating the admission of air.

The smoke is carried off by a horizontal tube, a part of which is seen at C.

There is a particular and very simple contrivance for causing the smoke to come into contact with the sides of the lower boiler and with the flat bottom of the upper boiler, and then to *descend* before it is permitted to pass off. This is a cylinder of cast iron or of earthenware, which is 16 inches in diameter within or in the clear, and 8 inches high, with a thin flange about an inch wide at its lower extremity. This flange serves as a foot for keeping it steady in its vertical position, and also for fastening it in its place by laying the ends of a circular row of short pieces of brick upon it. The lower end of this cylinder being set down at the level of the bottom of the lower boiler, upon the top of the hollow cylindrical mass of brick-work which constitutes the fire-place, the smoke is obliged to pass up between the inside of this cylinder and the outside of the lower boiler and to strike against the flat bottom of the upper boiler. It then passes horizontally over the top of this cylinder, and, turning downwards into the space which is left for it between the outside of this short cylinder and the great cylinder of sheet iron in which the boiler is suspended, it passes off by the small horizontal tube which carries it to the chimney.

This short cylinder is so distinctly represented in the figure that letters of reference are quite unnecessary.

A piece of brick or of fire-stone, about 2½ inches thick, is supposed to be attached to the inside of the fire-place door, to prevent its being too much heated by the fire; and this is represented in the figure by dotted lines. The knobs in the fire-place door and in the door of the ash-pit are designed to be used as a handle in opening them.

This portable fire-place may have two strong handles for transporting it from place to place; and, as the boiler may be removed and carried separately, the fire-place will not be too heavy to be carried very conveniently by two men.

Without stopping to expatiate on the usefulness of this new implement of cookery, I shall proceed to show how its utility may be made still more extensive. With a trifling additional expense it may be changed into one of the very best stoves for warming a room in cold weather that can be contrived. I say one of the *very best*, for it will warm the air of the room without its being possible for it ever to heat it so much as to make it unwholesome; and it will do it with the least trouble and at the expense of the least possible quantity of fuel.

Description of a Contrivance for warming a Room by Means of a portable universal Kitchen Boiler.

The following figure represents an elevation, or front view, of the machinery that may be used for this purpose: —

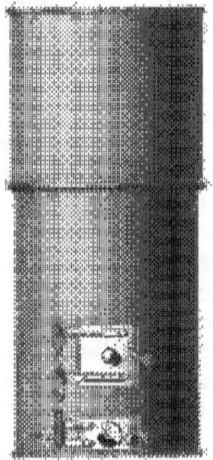

Fig. 47.

This machinery is very simple. It consists of the portable boiler and fire-place represented in the preceding figure (No. 46), with an inverted cylindrical vessel, constructed of tin or of very thin sheet copper, placed over the boiler. This cylindrical vessel, which I shall call a steam-stove, must be just equal in diameter to the steam-rim of the boiler at the lowest or deepest part of that rim; and it may be made higher or lower, according to the size of the room that is to be heated by it. That represented in the foregoing figure is 26 inches in diameter and 24 inches high, which gives 17 square feet of surface for heating the room.

This *steam-stove* may be made of common sheet iron; but in that case it should be japanned within and without, to prevent its rusting. In japanning it, it might be painted or gilded, and rendered very ornamental. The portable fire-place might likewise be japanned and ornamented; but in that case it would be necessary to line that part of it with clay or cement with which the smoke comes into contact, otherwise the heat in that part might injure the japan.

There must be a small tube about $\frac{1}{4}$ of an inch in diameter in one side of the steam-stove, just above the top of the steam-rim of the boiler. This tube should be about 2 inches in length, and it should project inwards, horizontally, into the cavity of the steam-stove. Into this tube one end of another longer tube should be introduced, which is designed to carry off the redundant steam into the chimney.

The reason why this tube should be placed near the bottom of the steam-stove will be evident to those who recollect that steam is lighter than air. Were it placed at the top of it, no steam would remain in the stove, and the object of the contrivance would be defeated.

This small steam-tube at the lower part of the stove may, with safety, be kept quite open; for, unless the water in the boiler be made to boil with vehemence, little or no steam will issue out of it; for the greater part, if not the whole of it, will be condensed against the top and sides of the steam-stove.

As the water which results from this condensation of steam will all return into the boiler, it will seldom be necessary to replenish the boiler with water.

When cooking is going on in the boiler in cold weather, the steam-stove will supply the place of a cover for the boiler; but, when the weather is warm, the cover of the boiler may be used instead of it, and the air of the room will be very little heated.

Steam-stoves on these principles would be found very useful in heating halls and passages, and I think they might be used with advantage for heating elegant apartments. They are susceptible of a variety of beautiful forms, and are not liable to any objections that I am aware of. A most elegant steam-stove might be made in the form of a Doric temple, of eight or ten columns, standing on a pedestal. The fire-place might be situated in the pedestal, and the columns and dome of the temple might be of brass or bronze, and made hollow to admit the steam. In the centre of the temple a small statue might be placed as an ornamental decoration; or an Argand's lamp might be placed there to light the room. In case a lamp should be placed in the centre of the temple, there should be a circular opening left in the top of the dome for the passage of the smoke of the lamp.

The fire under the boiler may be lighted and fed without the room or within it; or the steam may be brought from a distance in a leaden pipe or copper tube. If the boiler that supplies the steam is situated in the pedestal of the temple, and if the fire is lighted from within the room, the fire-place and ash-pit doors may be masked by tablets and inscriptions.

But I need not enlarge on the means that may be

Fire-places and Kitchen Utensils.

used for rendering a useful mechanical contrivance ornamental and expensive; for many persons will be ready to lend their assistance in that undertaking.

Those who wish to see one of these universal kitchen boilers will find one set in brick-work in the kitchen of the Royal Institution. It is constructed of copper, and tinned on the inside; and it is considerably larger than that I have here described. The method used for confining the steam in this boiler is different from that here recommended, and there is a contrivance for heating the contents of the boiler occasionally by means of steam, which is brought from another boiler; but this contrivance has no particular connection with the invention in question, and is introduced here merely to show how steam may be employed for making liquids boil.

In order that these universal kitchen boilers, with steam-stoves, may the more easily find their way into common use in this country, some method should be contrived for making tea in them. Now I think this might be done by putting the tea with cold water into a shallow tin tea-pot, or rather kettle, and placing it in the upper boiler, directly over the lower boiler. I once made an experiment of this kind; and, if I was not much mistaken, the tea that was so made was uncommonly good and high-flavoured. It certainly appeared to be considerably stronger than it would have been, if, with the same quantities of tea and of water, it had been made in the common way.

Boiling water poured upon a vegetable substance does not always extract from it all that might be extracted by putting the substance to cold water and heating them together. This fact is well known; and it renders it probable that the method here proposed of making tea would be advantageous. If this should be the case, no implement could be better contrived for that purpose than our universal kitchen boiler.

CHAPTER X.

Description of a new-invented REGISTER-STOVE *or* FURNACE *for heating Kitchen Boilers, Stewpans, etc.* — *Of the Construction of Boilers and Stewpans peculiarly adapted to those Stoves.* — *Particular Method of constructing Stewpans and Saucepans of Tin, by which they may be rendered very durable.* — *Description of a small* PORTABLE FIRE-PLACE *for Stewpans and Saucepans.* — *Of cast-iron* HEATERS *for heating Kitchen Utensils.*

HAVING learned, by frequenting kitchens while the various processes of cookery were going on in them, how very desirable it would be that the cook might be enabled to regulate and occasionally to moderate the fires by which stewpans and saucepans are heated, I set about contriving a fire-place for that purpose, which on trial was found to answer very well. The first fire-place of this kind that was constructed was put up in my own kitchen, at Munich, where it was in daily use for more than twelve months; and soon after I returned to this country (in the year 1798) one of them was put up in the kitchen of Mr. Summers, ironmonger, No. 98 New Bond Street, where it has been exhibited to the view of those who frequent his shop. Since that time a great number of them have been put up in the kitchens of private families, and, as I am informed, are much liked. As their usefulness appears to me to have been sufficiently ascertained by experience to authorize me to recommend them to the public, I shall now lay before the reader the most exact and particular description of them that I can give; premising, however, that it will be difficult to give so clear an account of this contrivance as to enable a person to form a perfect idea of it without having seen it.

I shall perhaps be most likely to succeed in this attempt, if I begin by exhibiting a view of the thing to be described.

Fig. 48.

This plate represents a view of a register-stove fireplace for two stewpans, actually existing in Heriot's Hospital, at Edinburgh. It is placed in a mass of brick-work, 2 feet 6 inches high, 4 feet 6 inches long, and 2 feet wide from front to back, situated in a corner of the room on the right-hand side of the fire-place. In the middle of the front of this mass of brick-work are seen the front of the fire-place door (which is double), and the ash-pit register-door; and near the end of it, on the left, in the upper front corner, may be discovered the stone stopper, which closes a canal, which is occasionally opened for cleaning out the soot from the flues in the interior parts of the mass of brick-work. A like stopper, and which serves for a like purpose, may be seen at the end of the mass of brick-work, near the right-hand corner above. Each of these stoppers is furnished with an iron ring, fastened by a staple, which serves as a handle in removing and replacing it.

On the top of this mass of brick-work there is laid a horizontal plate of cast iron, 18 inches wide, 3 feet long, and about ⅜ of an inch in thickness; and on the right and left of this iron plate, and level with its upper surface, there are placed two flat stones, each 9 inches wide and 18 inches long, being just as long as the iron plate is wide.

At the back of this iron plate runs a flue, 4 inches wide and 5 inches deep, which is covered above, at the level of the upper surface of the iron plate, with a flat stone, 6 inches wide.

One of the most essential parts of this contrivance is the iron plate, with its circular register, both which are represented by the following figure; but only one half of the plate is represented, being shown broken off in the middle.

In this figure the circular movable register (which is distinguished from the oblong plate to which it belongs

Fire-places and Kitchen Utensils. 389

by marking the latter by fine horizontal lines) is shown in its place; and the projecting piece of metal is also seen which serves as a handle to turn it about on its centre. This circular register has a shallow circular groove near its circumference, about ¼ an inch deep and

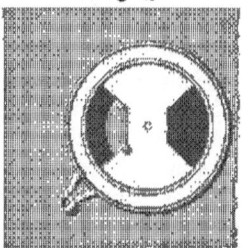

Fig. 49.

1¼ inches wide; and between the inside of this groove and the centre of the register there are two holes or openings on opposite sides of the centre which answer to two other openings of like form and dimensions, which are in each half of the oblong plate to which the registers belong. By one of these openings (that next the middle of the oblong plate) flame rises from a fire situated below, and spreads under the bottom of a boiler which is suspended over the circular register; and by the other it descends, and, again entering the mass of brick-work, it goes off by a horizontal canal which communicates with the chimney.

The boiler or stewpan is suspended over the circular register-plate, and the heat is confined about it by means of a hollow cylinder of sheet iron or of earthenware (about one inch longer or higher than the boiler is deep), and open at both ends, the lower end of which, entering the shallow groove of the register, reposes on it, while its upper end is closed by the boiler which, resting on it by its brim, is suspended in it, and consequently is surrounded by the flame.

This cylinder must be made quite flat or even at its two ends by grinding it on a flat stone, and the boiler must be made to fit it accurately, not however by fitting too nicely into its opening (which method would not be advisable), but by making the under part of the iron ring which forms the projecting brim of the boiler perfectly flat, and causing the boiler to be suspended by that ring on the flat end of the cylinder.

To prevent the escape of the flame under the bottom of the cylinder or between its lower end and the circular register-plate on which it stands, a small quantity of sand or (what will be still better) of fine filings of iron or brass may be put into the groove in which the cylinder is placed; and the same means may be used for making the joinings tight between the circular registers and the flat plate to which they belong.

The following figure, which shows a vertical section of this register-stove with its fire-place and its two boilers, or rather stewpans, will give a clear idea of the arrangement of the machinery.

These stewpans, which are $10\frac{1}{2}$ inches in diameter above and 6 inches deep each, are constructed according to the directions given in the seventh chapter of this Essay. They are of copper, tinned, and are turned over flat iron rings at their brims. Their handles are not seen in this figure. Their covers, which are of tin and made double, are on a peculiar construction. They are so contrived that a small saucepan for melting butter or warming gravy may be placed upon them and heated by the steam from their stewpans.

From a careful inspection of the three foregoing figures, and a comparison of them with the short description that has been given of the various parts of this machinery, it will, I fancy, be possible to form so distinct an idea of this contrivance as to enable any person conversant in matters of this kind to imitate

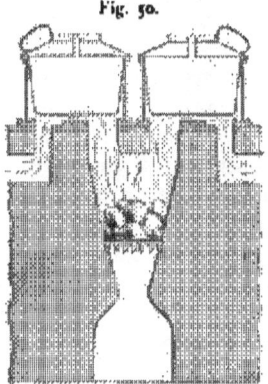

Fig. 50.

the invention, even without ever having seen the work executed. The principles at least on which this contrivance is founded will be perfectly evident; and, when they are understood, ingenious men will find little difficulty in the application of them to practice. It is indeed highly probable that simpler and better means of applying them will be found than those I have adopted, when the use of the contrivance shall become more general. I am indeed aware of several alterations of the machinery which I think would be improvements; but, as I have not tried them, I dare not recommend them as I recommend things which I know from experience to be useful.

I shall now proceed to give an account of several precautions in the construction and use of these register-stoves for boilers, which have been found to be necessary and useful.

The circular registers are so constructed that, by turning them round, they may be so placed as either to close entirely the holes in the flat plate on which they lie, or to leave them open more or less. Now, as there is no passage by which the smoke can go off from the fire-place into the chimney but through these holes, care must be taken never to attempt to kindle the fire when both these registers are closed, and never to open one of them without having first placed a hollow cylinder on it and a fit saucepan or boiler in the cylinder, to close it above. It can hardly be necessary that I should add that care must always be taken to put water or some other liquid into the boiler to prevent its being burned and spoiled by the heat.

The state of the register, in regard to its being more or less open, cannot be seen when the boiler is in its place, as the openings of the register are concealed by it and by the cylinder in which it is suspended. But, although the state of the register under these circumstances is not seen, it is nevertheless known; and the heat which depends on the dimensions of the opening left for the passage of the flame may at any time be regulated with the utmost certainty. By means of a projecting pin or short stub, represented in the Fig. 49, belonging to the lower (fixed) plate, and which is cast with it, the movable circular register is stopped in two different positions, in one of which the openings for the flame are as wide as possible, and in the other they are quite closed. When the handle by which the circular plate is turned round is pulled as far forward as possible towards the front of the brick-work, the register is wide open. In this situation it is represented in the Fig. 49. When it is pushed as far backwards as possible, the register is closed; and its situation at any intermediate station of the handle between these two limits of its motion will at any time show the exact state of the register.

That the handles of the register plates may not interfere with each other, they are placed on the sides of their plates which are farthest from the fire; consequently they are as far from each other as possible. The form of these handles is such that they never become very hot, although they are of iron and of a piece with their plates, being cast together. The cold air of the atmosphere passing freely upward through a conical hole (left in casting) in the centre of the knob of the handle, the heat is carried off by this current of air almost as fast as it arrives from the circular plate.

There is a circumstance to which it is absolutely necessary to pay attention in setting the large flat iron plate in the brick-work, otherwise the machinery will be liable to be soon deranged by the effects of the expansion of the metal by heat. The bottom or under side of this plate must be everywhere completely covered and defended from the action of the flame by bricks or tiles. This is very easy to be done; but at the same time, as it requires some care and attention, it is what workmen are very apt to neglect if they are not well looked after. As this plate is very large, if great care be not taken to prevent its being exposed to the flame, it will soon be warped and thrown out of its place. If, instead of casting this plate in one piece, it be formed of two pieces, each 18 inches square, the bad effects produced by the expansion of the metal by heat will be greatly lessened, and this precaution has been taken in most of the register-stoves on these principles that have been put up in London; but by an experiment lately made at Heriot's Hospital, at Edinburgh, I have been convinced that the large plates may be depended on if they are properly set.

I have described the cylinder in which the stewpan or boiler is suspended as being a separate thing. It is right, however, that I should inform the reader that, in almost all cases where register fire-places of this kind have hitherto been put up, this cylinder has been firmly and inseparably united to the stewpan, so much so as to make a part of it, the handle even being attached to this cylinder instead of being joined immediately to the stewpan. The following figure, which represents a vertical section of one of these stewpans and its cylinder, will show how they have hitherto generally been constructed:—

Fig. 51.

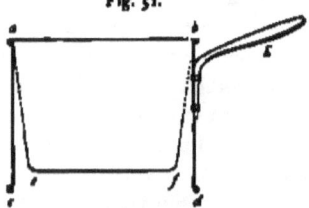

$a, b, c, d,$ represents a vertical section of the cylinder, which is $11\frac{1}{2}$ inches in diameter and 8 inches high. Into this cylinder, which is open at both ends, the boiler or stewpan, *a, e, f, d* (which is distinguished by dotted lines), is made to pass with so much difficulty as to require a considerable force to bring it into its place, and not to be in danger of being separated from it by any accidental blow. The handle, *g*, is riveted to the cylinder previously to its being united to its stewpan.

It having been found that this cylinder was liable to become very hot, and even to be destroyed by the heat in a short time if care was not taken to keep the fire low; and it having likewise been found that the heat that made its way upwards, between the outside of the stewpan and the inside of the cylinder, frequently heated the upper part of the stewpan so intensely hot as to cause the victuals cooked in it to be burned to the sides of the stewpan, especially when the stewpan was almost empty, — with a view to remedy both these evils, and at the same time to construct stewpans and saucepans of large dimensions of common sheet tin (tinned iron) which should be more durable, and superior in many respects to those of that material now in common use, some alterations were made in this utensil, which will be easily understood by the help of the following figure: —

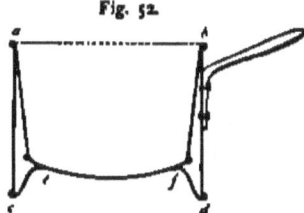

Fig. 52.

In order to prevent the flame from passing upwards between the saucepan and its cylinder, and occupying the vacant space, *c, a, e,* this space was enclosed by means of a circular piece of sheet copper, *c, e, f, d,* with a large circular opening in its centre, of the diameter *e, f.* This copper, being a little larger in diameter than the cylinder, was firmly attached to it all round by being turned over the same wire, which strengthened and made a finish to the bottom of the cylinder; while the inside edge, *e, f,* of this circular perforated sheet of copper, being raised upwards with the hammer about an inch, as it is represented in the figure, the saucepan is made of such a form that, on being brought into its place, its bottom is forced down upon the upper edge of this copper, by which means the empty space between the saucepan and its cylinder is closed up below by the copper, and the flame prevented from entering it. Sheet iron might have been used instead of sheet copper for closing up this space; but copper was preferred to it on account of its not being so liable as iron to be destroyed by the action of the flame.

This contrivance was found to answer so well for preventing the cylinder from being destroyed by heat, that, when it was made of tinned sheet iron (commonly, but improperly, called tin), the tin by which the surface of the iron was covered was not melted by it; and so completely did it prevent the sides of the saucepan from becoming too hot, that a quantity of fluid of any kind, so small as barely to cover the bottom of the vessel, might be boiled in it without the smallest danger of its being burned to its sides.

Having found that the sides of the saucepan were so effectually defended by this contrivance from intense heat, it occurred to me that a saucepan of common tin might perhaps be so constructed as, with this precaution for the preservation of its sides, it might be made to last a great while, which would not only save a considerable expense for kitchen utensils,— tin being much cheaper than copper,— but would also remove the apprehension of being poisoned by any thing injurious to health communicated to the food by the vessel in which it is prepared, which those cannot help feeling who eat victuals cooked in copper utensils, and who know the deleterious qualities of that metal.

Concluding that if I could contrive to prevent the seams or joinings of the tin in a saucepan or boiler from ever coming into contact with the flame of the fire, it could not fail to contribute greatly to the durability of the utensil, I caused the saucepan represented in the foregoing figure to be made of that material. The bottom of this saucepan, *e, f,* was made dishing (instead of being flat, as the bottoms of tin saucepans are commonly made); and, being joined to the body of the saucepan by a strong double seam, the vacuities of the seam, both within and without, were well filled up with solder.

Now as care was taken in adjusting the conical band of copper, *c, e, f, d,* to the bottom of the saucepan, to make its circular opening above, at *e, f,* something less in diameter than the bottom of the saucepan at its extreme breadth, or where it joins the sides or body of the utensil, and also to cause the upper edge of this copper actually to touch the bottom of the saucepan, and even to press against it in every part of its circumference, it is evident that the seam by which the body of the saucepan and its dishing bottom were united was completely covered by the copper, and defended from the immediate action of the fire. It is likewise evident that the side-seams in the body of the saucepan were likewise protected most effectually from all the destructive effects of intense heat; and, if care were taken to cover the outside of the body of the saucepan with a good thick coating of japan to prevent its being injured by rust, there is little doubt but that saucepans so constructed would last a long time indeed.

The cylinder in which the saucepan is suspended might likewise be japanned, both within and without, which would not only preserve it from rust, but would also give it a very neat appearance. All these improvements have been made, and a variety of saucepans constructed on the principles here recommended may be seen in the Repository of the Royal Institution.

Of the Means that may be employed for using indifferently Saucepans and Boilers of different Sizes, with the same Register-Stove Fire-place.

Although the diameter below of the cylinder or cone (for it may be either the one or the other) in which the saucepan or boiler is suspended is limited by the diameter of the groove of the circular register-plate in which it stands over the fire, yet the sizes of the cooking utensils used with them may be greatly varied. They may, without the smallest inconvenience, be made either broader or narrower above at their brims than the bottom of the cylinder or cone in which they are suspended; and, with any given breadth above, their depths (and consequently their capacities) may be varied almost at pleasure. When, however, the diameter of one of these boilers, at its brim, is greater than the diameter of the groove of the register-plate of the fire-place, it must be suspended in an inverted hollow cone, and its body must necessarily be made conical.

The following figure shows how a boiler 15 inches in diameter, with a steam-rim (with which the steam-dishes of a 15-inch family boiler may occasionally be used), may be adapted to a register-stove fire-place of the usual dimensions:—

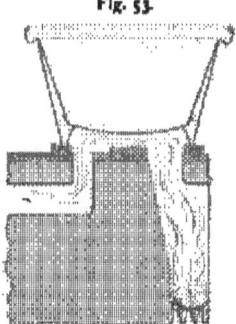

Fig. 53.

This boiler requires no handle, as its steam-rim may be used instead of a handle in moving it from place to place.

The following figure shows how very small sauce-pans are to be fitted up, in order to their being used with these register-stove fire-places:—

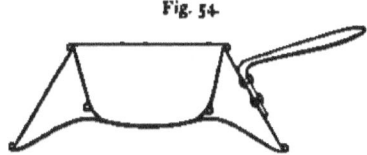

Fig. 54.

This saucepan is only 6 inches in diameter at its brim, and 3 inches deep. The hollow cone in which it is suspended is about 6 inches in diameter above, 10½ inches in diameter below, and 4 inches in height.

In kitchens of a moderate size it will seldom be convenient to devote more space for stoves for stewpans and saucepans than would be necessary for erecting one register stewing-stove fire-place, which, if the fire-place has only two registers, will heat only two stewpans or boilers at the same time; but in cooking for a large family it will frequently be necessary to have culinary processes going on at the same time in several stewpans and saucepans. It remains therefore to show how this may be done with the apparatus and utensils just described; and it is certain that this object is so important that any arrangement of culinary apparatus would be essentially deficient and imperfect, which did not afford the means of attaining it completely, and without any kind of difficulty. There are two ways in which it may be done with the utensils above described. A stewpan or saucepan having been placed upon one of the register-plates of the stove till its contents are boiling-hot, it may be removed and placed over a very small fire made with charcoal in a small portable furnace resembling a common chafing-dish; or it may be set down upon a circular iron heater, made red-hot, and placed in a bed of dry ashes in a shallow earthen pan. By either of these methods a boiling heat may be *kept up* for a long time in the stewpan; and any common process of boiling or stewing carried on in a very neat and cleanly manner. It must however be remembered that it is only with stewpans and boilers constructed on the principles here recommended, and constantly kept well covered with double covers to prevent the loss of the heat, that the processes of boiling and stewing can be carried on with very small portable furnaces and with heaters; but with these utensils, which are so well calculated to confine the heat, it is almost incredible how small a supply of heat will be sufficient, when the contents of the vessel have previously been made boiling-hot, to keep up that temperature, and carry on any of the common processes of cookery.

In the following figure (Fig. 55) A represents a vertical section of a stewpan, 11 inches wide at its brim and

Fig. 55.

6 inches deep, suspended in its cylinder and placed upon a *portable furnace*, B, which is 7 inches in diameter at its opening above, 11 inches in diameter below, and 9 inches high. A small saucepan, C, for melting butter, is placed on the cover of the stewpan, and is heated by the steam from the stewpan.

This small saucepan is suspended in a cylinder, which serves for confining the steam about it which rises from the stewing-stove.

The cover of this small saucepan is double, and, instead of a handle, it is furnished with a kind of a knob (*d*) formed of a hollow inverted cone of tin, which occasionally serves as a foot for supporting the cover when it is taken off from the saucepan and laid down in an inverted position. This contrivance is designed to prevent the inside of the cover from being exposed to dirt when it is occasionally taken off and laid down. The saucepan is furnished with a handle of the common form (*e*), which is represented in the figure. The handle (*f*) of the stewpan is also shown, and that (*g*) of the portable fire-place.

The following figure is a perspective view of the portable furnace without the stewpan:—

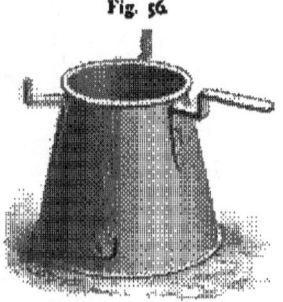

Fig. 56.

In this figure the three horizontal projecting arms are distinctly seen, which serve to support the stewpan. One of these arms, which is longer than the rest, serves as a handle to the furnace.

This little furnace, which is constructed principally of sheet iron, is made double, that part of it which contains the burning charcoal being cylindrical, or nearly so, and being suspended in the axis of a hollow cone, which forms the body of the furnace, and serves as a covering for confining the heat.

The following figure, which represents a vertical section of this furnace through its axis, will give a clear idea of the manner in which it is constructed:—

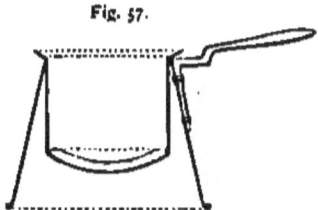

Fig. 57.

The air is introduced into the fire-place first through a circular hole (represented in the Fig. 56), about 1½ inches in diameter, situated in the side of the hollow cone near its bottom; and from thence it passes up through a small dishing-grate of cast iron which lies at the bottom of the hollow cylinder which contains the burning fuel. At the upper end of this cylinder there is a narrow rim about half an inch wide, turned outwards, by which the cylinder is suspended in its place; and a similar rim being turned inwards below serves as a support for the dishing-grate.

When this fire-place is used, it will be proper to place it on a flat stone or on a tile; or, what will be still better, to set it in a thin earthen dish.

The same earthen dishes which would be proper for

holding these portable fire-places would also answer perfectly well for holding the cast-iron heaters that may occasionally be used for finishing the processes of cooking that have been begun in stewpans and saucepans heated over the fire of a register-stove, or otherwise made boiling-hot.

The following figure, which represents a vertical section of a stewpan placed over a heater of the kind here recommended, will give a perfect idea of this arrangement:—

Fig. 58.

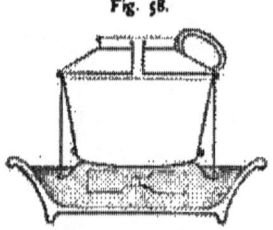

The heater is here represented as lying in a bed of ashes, and there is likewise a thin layer of ashes seen between the top of the heater and the bottom of the stewpan. By the quantity of ashes suffered to remain on the upper surface of the heater, the heat communicated to the stewpan is to be moderated and regulated.

The heater is perforated in its centre by a hole of a peculiar form, which serves for introducing an iron hook, which is used in taking it from the fire and placing it in the earthen dish.

The form of the hook, and the shape of the aperture through which it passes in the heater, may be seen in the following figure.

The circular excavation in the heater, on each side of it, surrounding the hole (which is in the form of the key-hole of a lock) by which the hook is introduced, serves to give room for the hook (or key, as it might be called) to be turned round when the heater is laid

Fig. 59.

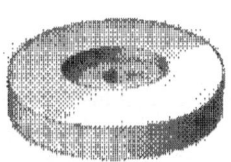

upon or against a flat surface. As this excavation, as well as the hole through which the key passes, may be cast with the heater, this arrangement will cause no additional expense.

CHAPTER XI.

Of the Use of PORTABLE FURNACES *for culinary Purposes.* — *Description of a portable Kitchen Furnace, for Boilers, etc., on the common Construction.* — *Description of a small portable Furnace of cast Iron for heating Tea-kettles, Stewpans, etc.* — *Description of another of sheet Iron, designed for the same Uses.* — *Description of a portable Kitchen Furnace of Earthen-ware.* — *An Account of a very simple Apparatus for cooking used in China.*

IN China and in several other countries, all, or nearly all, the fire-places used in cooking are portable, and real advantages might certainly be derived in many cases from the use of portable kitchen fire-places in this country. Convinced of the utility of this method of cooking, I have taken considerable pains to investigate the subject experimentally, and to ascertain the best forms for the furnaces and utensils necessary in the practice of it.

Portable furnaces for cooking are of two distinct kinds: the one has a fire-place door for introducing the fuel, the other has none; and either of these may or may not be furnished with a tube for carrying off the smoke into the air or into a neighbouring chimney.

When a portable kitchen furnace is constructed without a fire-place door, as often as fuel is to be introduced it will be necessary to remove the boiler, in order to perform that operation. When the boiler is small, that may easily be done; and when the furnace stands out of doors, or on the hearth within the draught of a chimney, or when the fuel used produces little or no smoke, it may be done without any considerable inconvenience. But, if the boiler be large, it cannot be removed without difficulty; and when the furnace is placed within doors, and the fuel used produces smoke or other noxious vapours, the removing of the boiler, though it were but for a moment, would be attended with very disagreeable consequences.

Small portable furnaces without fire-place doors may be used within doors, provided they be heated with charcoal; but it will in that case always be advisable to furnish them with small tubes of sheet iron for carrying off the unwholesome vapour of the charcoal into the chimney. Without such tubes to carry off the smoke, they would not, it is true, be more disagreeable or more detrimental to health than the stoves now generally used for burning charcoal in kitchens; but I should be sorry to recommend an invention to which there appear to me to be so great objections.

I have caused a considerable number of portable kitchen furnaces, of both the kinds above-mentioned, to be constructed; and I shall now give descriptions of such of them as seem to answer best the purposes for which they were designed. They may all be seen at the Repository of the Royal Institution.

A very simple and useful portable kitchen furnace, with its stewpan in its place, is represented by the following figure:—

Fig. 60.

This furnace is made of common sheet iron, and it may be afforded at a very low price. It is composed of a hollow cylinder, and two hollow truncated cones of different sizes. The large cone, which is erect, is closed at its base or lower end. The smaller is inverted, and is open at both ends. This smaller cone is suspended in the larger, by means of a rim about half an inch wide, which projects outwards from its upper (larger) end. A rim of equal width, projecting inwards at its lower extremity, supports a circular grate, on which the fuel burns. The cylinder, which is about two inches less in diameter than the larger cone at its base, and which rests upon the surface of that cone, serves to support the boiler or saucepan. This cylinder is firmly fixed to the cone on which it rests by means of rivets, two of which are represented in the figure. The upper end of this open cylinder is strengthened, and its circular form preserved, by means of a strong iron wire, over which the sheet iron is turned. There is a short horizontal tube (A) on one side of the cylinder, which is destined for receiving a longer tube which carries off the smoke. The air necessary for the combustion of the fuel is admitted through a circular hole (B), about 1¼ inches in diameter, in the side of the larger cone near its bottom, and below the joining of the cone with the cylinder which rests on it. This hole for the admission of air should be furnished with a register, by means of which the fire may be regulated. The handle of the stewpan is omitted in this plate, as is also that of the fire-place. This figure is drawn to a scale of 8 inches to the inch.

The following figure (which is drawn to a scale of 12 inches to the inch) is a perspective view of one of these portable furnaces without its stewpan.

A part of the handle of this furnace is seen on the left hand; and the short tube is seen on the right hand, that receives another tube (a part of which only is shown) by which the smoke passes off.

The stewpan represented in the Fig. 60 is supposed to be made of copper, and to be constructed on the principles recommended in the seventh chapter of this (tenth) Essay. These portable furnaces are peculiarly adapted to kitchen utensils constructed on those principles, and also to boilers and stewpans with steam-rims, which are not made double; but for double or

Fig. 61.

armed boilers, stewpans, etc., the furnace must be made in a different manner. The simplest form for portable furnaces adapted to armed boilers is that represented by the Figs. 55, 56, and 57; but I shall now give an account of a furnace of this sort constructed on different and better principles.

The following figure represents a vertical section of a small portable kitchen furnace of *cast iron*.

On examining this figure, it will be found that care has been taken, in contriving this furnace, to divide it in such a manner into parts, and to give to those parts such forms as to render the whole of easy construction. It consists of three principal parts; namely, of the fire-place, A, which is a hollow cylinder, or rather an inverted hollow truncated cone, 7 inches in diameter above measured internally, 4 inches long or high, ending below with a hemispherical hollow bottom, 6 inches in diameter, perforated with many holes for the admission of air.

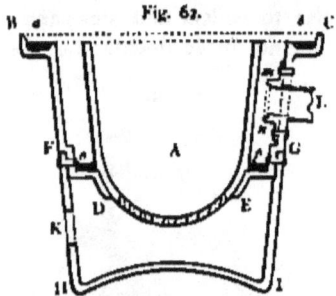

Fig. 62.

This fire-place is suspended in the axis of the furnace by means of the projecting hollow ring, D, E, belonging to the upper and principal piece, B, C, D, E, of the furnace. At the upper part of this piece there is a circular cavity, *a*, *b*, about 1 inch wide and a quarter of an inch deep, which is destined to receive the lower extremity of the hollow cylinder in which the boiler is suspended. At L is a circular hole, 1¼ inches in diameter, which receives the end of the tube by which the smoke is carried to the chimney. A part of this tube, which is of sheet iron, is represented in the figure. To give it a more firm support in its place, there is a short tube, *m*, *n*, of cast iron, which projects inwards into the furnace about ⅝ of an inch. This short tube is cast with a flange, and it is fastened to the inside of the piece which constitutes the upper part of the body of the furnace by means of three or four rivets. Two of these rivets are distinctly represented in the figure.

The lower part of the body of the furnace consists of the piece, F, G, H, I, and it is fastened to the upper part by means of rivets, two of which are seen at F and at G. In one side of this lower part there is a circular hole at K, about 1¼ inches in diameter, which serves for the admission of air, and which is furnished with a register-stopper. The bottom of this furnace, instead of being made flat, is spherical, projecting upwards; which form was chosen in order to prevent as much as possible the heat from the fire from being communicated downward. This furnace will require no handle, as its projecting brim will serve instead of one.

It will be observed that all the pieces of which this furnace is composed are of such forms that the moulds for casting them will readily deliver from the sand; and that circumstance will contribute greatly to the lowness of the price at which this most useful article of kitchen furniture may be afforded.

The perforated cast iron bowl, A, which constitutes the fire-place, is not confined in its place, and its form and its position are such that its expansion with heat can do no injury to the outside of the furnace.

When the two pieces which form the body of the furnace are fastened together, their joinings may be made tight with cement.

A little fine sand should be put into the hollow rim, $a, b,$ of the furnace, in order that it may be perfectly closed above by the lower end of the hollow cylinder of its boiler; and a little sand or ashes may be thrown upon the bottom of the circular cavity, $o, p,$ into which the smoke descends before it goes off by the tube, L, into the chimney. This last precaution will prevent the air from making its way upwards from the ash-pit directly into the cavity, $o, p,$ occupied by the smoke, without passing through the fire-place.

The register-stopper to the opening, K, into the ash-pit, may be constructed on the same principle as that of the blowpipe of a roaster. One of these stoppers is represented on a large scale in the Fig. 17, at the end of the second part of this (tenth) Essay; or, what will be still more simple and quite as good, the admission of the air may be regulated by a register like that represented in the preceding Fig. No. 61.

This portable kitchen furnace will answer a variety of useful purposes; and, if I am not much mistaken, it will come into very general use. It is cheap and durable, and not liable to be broken by accidents or put out of order; and it is equally well adapted for every kind of fuel. No particular care or attention is required in the management of it, and it is well calculated for confining heat, and directing it.

As the fire-place belonging to this furnace is nearly insulated, and as it contains but a small quantity of matter to be heated, a fire is easily and expeditiously kindled in it; and the fuel burns in it under the most favourable circumstance.

It will be found extremely useful for boiling a tea-kettle, especially in summer, when a fire in the grate is not wanted for other purposes; and, when the tea-kettle is constructed on the principles that will presently be described, a very small quantity indeed of fuel will suffice.

But the most important use to which these portable furnaces can be applied is most undoubtedly for cooking for poor families. I have hinted at the probable utility of a contrivance of this kind in some of my former publications; but since that time I have had opportunities of examining the subject more attentively, and of ascertaining the fact by the test of actual experiment.

As the subject strikes me as being of no small degree of importance, I shall make no apology for enlarging on it, and giving the *most particular account* of several kinds of *portable kitchen furnaces*.

That just described (of cast iron) is, it is true, as perfect in all respects as I have been able to make it, and will probably be found to be quite as economical and as useful as any that I shall describe; but cast iron is not everywhere to be found, and, even where foundries are established for casting it, moulds must be provided, and these are expensive, and not easy to be had. As it is probable that some persons may be desirous of being provided with portable furnaces of this kind, who may not have it in their power to procure them of cast iron, I shall now show how they may be constructed (by any common workman) of sheet iron, and also how they may be made of earthen-ware.

Of small portable Kitchen Furnaces constructed of sheet Iron.

The following figure represents a vertical section of one of these furnaces, drawn to a scale of 6 inches to the inch.

The construction of this furnace will be easily understood from this figure. The circular hollow horizontal rim, *a, b*, which I shall call the *sand-rim*, is $8\frac{4}{10}$ inches in diameter within, and $12\frac{4}{5}$ inches in diameter without. Its width at its bottom, which is flat, is just 1 inch. Its sides are sloping and of different heights: that which is towards the centre of the furnace is 1 of an inch high, but the side which is outwards is ⅜ an inch in height.

The sand-rim is confined and supported in its place by being fastened, by means of rivets or otherwise, to an inverted hollow truncated cone, *c, d, e, f,* which forms the upper part of the body of the furnace. This inverted cone, which is turned over a strong circular iron wire at its upper edge, *c, d,* is 12⅛ inches in diam-

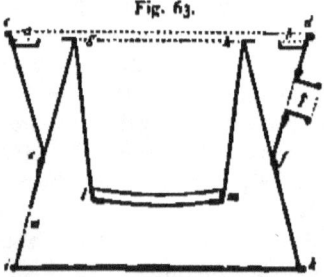

Fig. 63.

eter above measured within the wire, and 5⅕ inches in height measured from *c* to *e* or from *d* to *f,* and is 9⅕ inches in diameter from *e* to *f,* where it is fastened to the erect hollow truncated cone, *g, h, i, k.*

This last-mentioned erect cone, which is closed below by a circular plate of sheet iron, forms the lower part of the body of the furnace. It is 7 inches in diameter above, 12 inches in diameter below, and its perpendicular height is just 9 inches. Its sloping side, *g, i,* measures about 9⅒ inches.

The *fire-place* of this little portable furnace is an inverted hollow truncated cone, *g, h, l, m,* which is 7 inches in diameter above, at *g, h,* and 5¼ inches in diameter below, at *l, m;* and its length is 6½ inches, measured from *g* to *m*. This conical fire-place has a flat rim above, which is ½ an inch wide, and turned outwards; and another below of equal width which is turned inwards. The first serves to suspend it in its place, the second serves to support its circular grate on which the fuel burns.

The air is admitted into the fire-place through a hole, *n*, about 1½ inches in diameter, in the side of the furnace. This aperture must be furnished with a register similar to that shown in the Fig. 61.

The provision for carrying off the smoke is similar in all respects to that used in the portable furnace above described, constructed of cast iron; and it will easily be understood, from a bare inspection of the Fig. 63, without any farther explanation.

Having shown how this portable kitchen furnace may be constructed of cast iron, and also how it may be made of sheet iron, I shall now show how it may be made partly of cast iron and partly of sheet iron. A fire-place of cast iron, like that represented in the Fig. 62, may be used in a furnace of sheet iron; but, when this is done, the fire-place must be cast with a projecting rim above, in order that it may be suspended in its place. The sand-rim may likewise be of cast iron, and it may be fastened to the inverted hollow cone, *c*, *d*, *e*, *f*, by rivets.

The short tube, *p*, which serves to support the tube which carries off the smoke, may also be made of cast iron, and it may be fastened to the outside of the furnace by three rivets. As it may be made of such a form that its mould will deliver from the sand, it will cost less when made of cast iron than when made of sheet iron; and it will have another advantage,—its form on the inside will be more regular, and it will be better adapted on that account for receiving the end of the tube, which it is designed to receive. Its length need not exceed 1 inch or $1\frac{1}{4}$ inches, and its internal diameter may be about $1\frac{1}{4}$ inches at its projecting extremity, and something less at its other end, where it joins the side of the furnace.

Of small portable Kitchen Furnaces constructed of Earthen-ware.

The following figure represents a furnace of this kind (of earthen-ware) destined for heating boilers of the same kind and of the same dimension as those proper to be used with the two (iron) furnaces last described:—

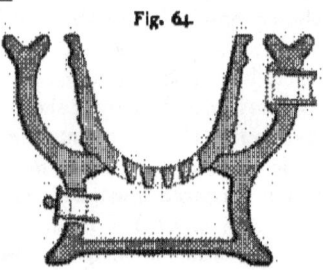
Fig. 64.

This figure represents a vertical section of the furnace, drawn to a scale of 6 inches to the inch; and it gives an idea so clear and satisfactory of the form of this furnace that a detailed description of it would be superfluous.

The fire-place is distinct from the body of the furnace, and its form and position are such that it cannot crack and injure the body of the furnace by its expansion with heat. It resembles very much the cast iron fire-place just described, and the same principles regulated the contrivance of both of them. It should be bound round with iron wire, in order to hold it together, in case it should crack with the heat of the fire. Two places for the wire, one near its brim and the other lower down, are shown in the figure.

The aperture by which the air enters the ash-pit is closed by a register-stopper, represented in the figure, or a conical stopper of earthen-ware may be used for that purpose.

If such earths are used in constructing these small portable furnaces as are known to stand fire well, there is no doubt but these furnaces may, with proper usage, be made to last a great while; and, for confining heat, they are certainly preferable to all others.

The portable kitchen furnaces in China are all constructed of earthen-ware; and no people ever carried those inventions which are most generally useful in common life to higher perfection than the Chinese. They, and they only, of all the nations of whom we have any authentic accounts, seem to have had a just idea of the infinite importance of those improvements which are calculated to promote the comforts of the lowest classes of society.

What immortal glory might any European nation obtain by following this wise example!

The emperor of China, the greatest monarch in the world, who rules over one full *third part* of the inhabitants of this globe, condescends *to hold the plough* himself one day in every year. This he does, no doubt, to show to those whose example never can fail to influence the great bulk of mankind how important that art is by means of which food is provided.

Let those reflect seriously on this illustrious example of provident and benevolent attention to the wants of mankind who are disposed to consider the domestic arrangements of the labouring classes as a subject too low and vulgar for their notice.

If attention to the art by which food is provided be not beneath the dignity of a great monarch, that art by which food is prepared for use, and by which it may be greatly *economized*, cannot possibly be unworthy of the attention of those who take pleasure in promoting the happiness of mankind.

As the implements used in China for cooking are uncommonly simple, it may perhaps be amusing to the reader to be made acquainted with them. They consist of the two articles represented below:—

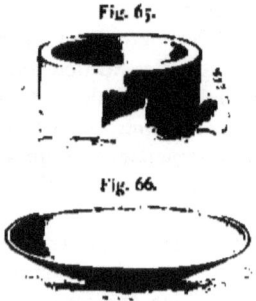

Fig. 65.

Fig. 66.

This Fig. 65, which is made of earthen-ware, is the fire-place, which is set down on the ground. The shallow pan, represented by the Fig. 66, is of cast iron, and serves for every process of Chinese cookery. It is cast very thin, and, if by any accident a hole is made in it, their itinerant tinkers mend it by filling up the hole, which they do with so much dexterity that scarcely a mark is left behind.

When the dinner consists of several dishes, they are all cooked in this pan, one after the other; and those which are done first are kept warm till they are sent to table.

I leave it to the ingenuity of Europeans to appreciate these specimens of Chinese industry.

But to return from this digression to our portable kitchen furnaces. Although these furnaces are peculiarly adapted for heating boilers and stewpans that are *armed*, yet boilers on the common construction, or such as are not suspended in cylinders, may easily be used with them. When this is to be done, a detached hollow cylinder or cone must be used in the manner described in the preceding chapter, and represented in the Fig. 50. This cylinder or cone (which may be constructed either of sheet iron, of cast iron, or of earthen-ware) must be about an inch higher than the boiler is deep, with which it is to be used; and just so wide above as to admit the boiler to be suspended in it by its circular rim. Its diameter below must be such as to fit the sand-rim, in which it must stand when it is used.

CHAPTER XII.

Of the Construction of Tea-kettles *proper to be used with Register-Stoves and portable Kitchen Furnaces.* — *These Utensils may be constructed of Tin, and ornamented by Japanning and Gilding.* — *When they are properly constructed and managed, they may be heated over a small portable Furnace in a very short Time, and with a surprisingly small Quantity of Fuel.—Descriptions of four of these Tea-kettles of different Forms and Sizes.— Description of several very SIMPLE and CHEAP STEWPANS for portable Furnaces.—Description of a STEWPAN of EARTHEN-WARE on an improved Construction.— This will probably turn out to be a most useful Utensil for cooking with portable Furnaces.*

AS tea-kettles are so much used in this country, and as they occasion so great a consumption of fuel (a large fire being frequently made in a grate or kitchen range, morning and evening, for the sole purpose of heating a few pints of water to make tea), the saving of this unnecessary trouble and expense is an object deserving of attention. And in doing this it will be possible to improve very essentially the forms of tea-kettles in several respects, and at the same time to render their external appearance more neat and cleanly. If the forms I shall recommend should not happen to please at first sight, it should be remembered that utility, cleanliness, and wholesomeness are objects of more importance in cases like that in question than mere elegance of form; and, after all, I am not sure whether the forms I shall propose are not in reality quite as elegant as those with which they will be compared. They will, no doubt, at first sight appear uncouth to many persons, but the eye will soon become accustomed to them; and their superior cheapness, cleanliness, and usefulness will in the end procure them that preference which they deserve. They may, no doubt, be constructed of the most elegant forms, on the principles I shall recommend; but I shall confine my descriptions to such forms as are most simple, and of the easiest and least expensive construction, leaving it to those to beautify the article whose business and interest it is to set off their goods to the best advantage.

The following figure represents a tea-kettle of the simplest form, suited to a register kitchen stove, or to a portable furnace such as has just been described:—

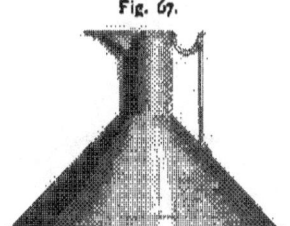

Fig. 67.

This tea-kettle is constructed of tin, and it may be japanned on the outside to prevent its rusting, and to give it an elegant and cleanly appearance. Its bottom, which is 11 inches in diameter, is not flat, but it is raised up about half an inch in the manner pointed out by a dotted line. The body of this tea-kettle is of a conical form, ending above in a cylinder, 3 inches in length and 2 inches in diameter. The spout, which resembles that of a coffee-pot, is situated at the top of this cylinder; and it has a flat cover, fastened by a hinge, which prevents dust or soot from falling into it when it stands on the hearth. When this tea-kettle is put over the fire, it should not be filled higher than to the top of the cone, or lower end of the cylinder, otherwise it will be liable to boil over. The kettle so filled will contain 4 pints of water; and, if it be heated over one of the small portable furnaces described in the foregoing chapter, it may be made to boil in about 10 minutes, with 6¼ oz. of dry wood, which, at the price at which wood is commonly sold in London, would cost ⅛ of a farthing.*

The tea-kettle represented by the following figure is rather more complicated, but still its form is more simple, and more advantageous in several respects than those which are in common use, and it is well adapted for the fire-places we have recommended. It is drawn to a scale of 6 inches to the inch.

Fig. 68.

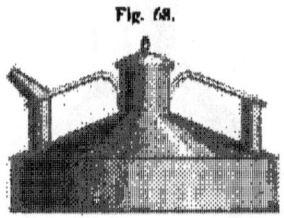

This kettle has two handles, each of which is supported on the outside, or near the circumference of the kettle, by a small vertical tube, ⅜ of an inch in diameter and 1¾ inches in height. That on the left hand is open, and forms a part of the spout; but that on the right hand is closed at both ends. The bottom of this kettle, also the bottoms of those represented in the two following figures, like that of the last (Fig. 67), is not flat, but is raised up about half an inch above the level of the lower part of the cylindrical sides of the kettle.

* One pint of water only being put into this tea-kettle, over a very small wood fire, made in the portable furnace represented in the foregoing Fig. 63 (see page 414), it was heated and made to boil *in two minutes and a half.*

This kettle holds about 3 quarts of water, which can be made to boil with the combustion of 9¼ oz. of wood.

The following kettle holds about 1 gallon, and may be made to boil with ¼ lb. of wood, which would cost just ¼ of a farthing: —

Fig. 69.

The following kettle is not essentially different from those two last described, except in the form of its handle. It holds about 3 quarts.

Fig. 70.

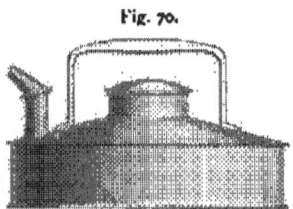

The cylindrical opening of this kettle above, where the water is introduced, is considerably wider than those in the two foregoing figures. It was made wider because it was necessary to make it lower, in order to make room for the hand without raising the handle too high. When this part of a tea-kettle is made very narrow, it must be made high to afford room for the expansion of the water with heat, and prevent the kettle from boiling over. These kettles should never be filled higher than to the level of the lower part of this cylindrical space, otherwise there will be danger of their boiling over.*

It will be observed that the cover of this tea-kettle projects a little beyond the cylindrical opening to which it belongs. This projection serves instead of a handle in removing and replacing the cover. The cover of a tea-kettle is usually furnished with a knob for that purpose; but these knobs are in the way when the kettle is lifted up by its handle, unless the handle be made much higher than otherwise would be sufficient.

It has, no doubt, already been remarked by the reader that all the tea-kettles here recommended are of forms that are perfectly easy to be executed in tin. There are several reasons which have induced me to give a decided preference to that material for constructing culinary utensils. It is not only wholesome, — which copper is not, — but it is also very cheap, and easy to be procured in all places, and it is easily worked. It is moreover light and strong, and not liable to be injured by accidents; and if measures be taken to prevent the effects of rust it is very durable.

The four tea-kettles represented in the four last figures are all particularly designed to be used with the portable furnaces described in the last chapter; and for that purpose they are well calculated, although they are not suspended in cylinders. They may likewise be used with the register kitchen stoves described

---

* I find, by experiments made since the above was written, that tea-kettles of this kind should never be filled above two thirds full, otherwise they will be very apt to boil over.

in the tenth chapter of this Essay. As their bottoms are raised up, and as their diameters are such that their conical or vertical sides enter into and fit the sand-rims of those furnaces and stoves, the heat is effectually confined under them; and their outsides, not being exposed either to flame or to smoke, may be japanned, and they may easily be kept so clean as to be fit to be placed upon a table, over a lamp, or upon a heater placed in a shallow dish of china or earthen-ware. They are even capable of being elegantly ornamented by gilding or painting, or both.

They are likewise well calculated for being heated by a lamp; and if an Argand's lamp be used for that purpose they may be made to boil in a short time and at a small expense. Placed on a handsome tripod on a table, with an elegant Argand's lamp under it, one of these kettles, handsomely ornamented by japanning and gilding, would make no mean appearance, and would cost much less than the commonest tea-urn that could be bought.

But it is not solely for making tea that these kettles will be found useful: they will answer perfectly well for boiling water for many other purposes; and, if portable kitchen furnaces should come into use, boiling-hot water will often be wanted for filling saucepans and stewpans; and no utensil can be better contrived for heating and boiling water over a portable kitchen furnace than these kettles.

In constructing them, care should be taken to fill all their seams well with solder, which, by covering the naked edges of the iron, will contribute more than any thing to the prevention of rust and the durability of the article; and they should likewise be well japanned on the outside in every part except the bottom, which should not be japanned.

The reason why I have not made these tin-tea-kettles double is this: Tea-kettles are commonly used merely for *making water boil*, which, with the kettles here recommended, can be done *in a very short time*, consequently much heat cannot possibly be lost during that process in consequence of the top and sides of the kettle being exposed naked to the cold air of the atmosphere. Were these utensils designed for *keeping water boiling-hot* a great length of time, the case would be very different; and then it might be well worth while to make them double, in order more effectually to confine the heat in them.

The *saving of time* in making them boil by making them double would be very trifling indeed, for till the water has become very hot there is but little loss of heat through the sides and top of the kettle; the communication of heat being rapid in proportion as the temperature of the hot body is high compared with that of the colder body into which the heat passes.

If a tea-kettle filled with water at the temperature of the atmosphere at the time, on being put over a fire, be brought to boil in 10 minutes, it will, during that time, have lost only half as much heat as it will lose in the next 10 minutes, if it be kept boiling-hot during that time.

All these kettles are of such forms as will render it very easy to cover them, should it be thought advisable to make them double; and by covering them with plated or gilt copper they may be made very elegant at a small expense.

Of the Construction of cheap Boilers and Stewpans to be used with small portable Kitchen Furnaces.

The best boilers and stewpans that can be used with these furnaces are undoubtedly those which were described in the tenth chapter of this Essay; but utensils on a simpler construction may be made to answer very well, and may perhaps be preferred by many on account of their cheapness.

The following figure represents a vertical section of a stewpan on a much more simple construction than any of those already described:—

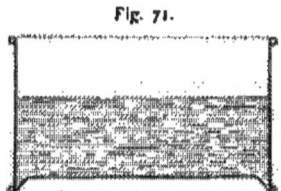

Fig. 71.

This stewpan (which is drawn to a scale of 6 inches to the inch) being of a proper diameter below to fit the sand-rim of the portable furnace, and its bottom being raised up about half an inch in order to allow its vertical sides to descend into that sand-rim, it is plain that it may be used with the furnace in the same manner as the tea-kettles just described are used with it. It may likewise be used with the register-stoves described in the tenth chapter of this Essay.

In order that this stewpan may the more easily be kept clean, the joinings of its bottom and sides should be well filled up on the inside with solder.

The following figure represents another and smaller

stewpan, constructed on the same principles with that just described and designed for the same use:—

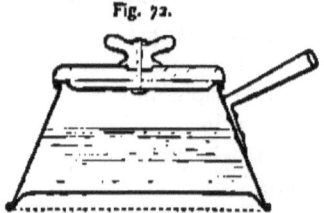

Fig. 72.

The diameter of this stewpan below is the same as that of the last. This is necessary, in order that it may fit the sand-rim of the same register-stove or portable furnace; but its diameter above is much less, and it is also less deep, consequently its capacity is much smaller. The cover of this stewpan is of wood lined with tin. It is in all respects like that represented by the Fig. 35 (see Chapter VII. of this Essay, page 358). Both these stewpans are supposed to be constructed of tin, but they might be made of tinned copper. The handle of the stewpan represented by the Fig. 71 is omitted.

The following figure represents a vertical section of a double or armed stewpan on a very simple construction:—

Fig. 73.

The stewpan (which is drawn to a scale of 6 inches to the inch) is supposed to be made of tin, and it is supposed to be turned over a wire at its brim. The cylinder by which it is surrounded is of sheet iron, and the stewpan and the cylinder are fastened together by the former being driven into the latter with some degree of force, and sticking in it above where they come into close contact. The lower edge of the cylinder being turned inwards forms a narrow rim on which the lower end of the stewpan rests.

Of the Construction of Stewpans of EARTHEN-WARE *and* PORCELAIN, *to be used with Register-Stoves and portable Kitchen Furnaces.*

The following figure shows how, by means of a hoop or cylinder of sheet iron, a stewpan or saucepan of earthen-ware or of porcelain of a suitable form and size may be fitted to be used with a register kitchen stove or portable furnace: —

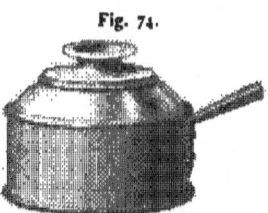

Fig. 74.

This figure is drawn to a scale of 9 inches to the inch. The form of the lower part of the stewpan is pointed out by a dotted line. The top and the bottom of the cylinder of sheet iron are both turned over circular iron wires. The handle of this stewpan is of iron, and it is fixed to the cylinder by rivets. The stewpan is firmly fastened to its metallic hoop or cylinder, first, by making this cylinder of a proper size to fit it; and, secondly, by wedging it both above and below with very thin wedges made of narrow pieces of sheet iron, and by filling up the vacuities above and below with good cement.

The cover of this stewpan, which is of earthen-ware (or porcelain), is made of a peculiar form. It has a kind of foot instead of a handle, which serves for supporting it when it is taken off from the stewpan and laid down in an inverted position. By means of this simple contrivance it is rendered less liable to be dirtied on the inside and of communicating dirt to the victuals.

If an earthen stewpan of the form represented in this figure be made of good materials, — that is to say, of a proper mixture of the different earths well worked, — and if its bottom be made thin and of equal thickness in every part of it that is exposed to the fire, there is little doubt, I think, of its standing the heat of a register-stove or of a small portable kitchen furnace; and, if this should be the case, I should certainly never think of recommending any other kitchen utensils in preference to these.

It appears to me to be very probable that unglazed Wedgewood's ware would be as good a material as could be found for these stewpans. The intelligent gentleman who directs Mr. Wedgewood's manufactory caused several of them to be made after drawings which I gave him, and those I found, upon trial, to answer very well.

If it should be found that kitchen utensils, constructed and fitted up, or mounted, on the principles here pointed out, should answer as well as there is reason to expect, as nothing would be easier than to make earthen boilers with *steam-rims* and to form *steam-dishes* of earthen-ware to fit them, every utensil for cooking, by *boiling* and *stewing*, might be constructed of that most cleanly, most elegant, and most wholesome material,—*earthen-ware*.

I hesitated a long time before I resolved to publish this last observation; for, however anxious I am to promote useful improvements, and especially such as tend to the preservation of health and the increase of rational enjoyments, it always gives me pain when I recollect how impossible it is to introduce any thing new, however useful it may be to society at large, without occasioning a temporary loss or inconvenience to some certain individuals, whose interest it is to preserve the state of things *actually existing*.

It certainly requires some courage, and perhaps no small share of enthusiasm, to stand forth the voluntary champion of the public good; but this is a melancholy reflection, on which I never suffer my mind to dwell. There is no saying what the consequences might be, were we always to sit down before we engage in a laudable undertaking and meditate profoundly upon all the dangers and difficulties that are inseparably connected with it. The most ardent zeal might perhaps be damped and the warmest benevolence discouraged.

But the enterprising seldom regard dangers, and are never dismayed by them; and they consider difficulties but to see how they are to be overcome. To them *activity* alone is life, and their glorious reward the consciousness of having done well. Their sleep is sweet when the labours of the day are over; and they await with placid composure that rest which is to put a final end to all their labours and to all their sufferings.

CHAPTER XIII.

Of cheap Kitchen Utensils for the Use of the Poor.— The Condition of the lower Classes of Society cannot be improved without the friendly Assistance of the Rich.— They must be TAUGHT *Economy, and they cannot be instructed by Books, for they have not Leisure to read.— Advice intended for their Good must be addressed to their benevolent and more wealthy Neighbours.— An Account of the Kitchen Utensils of the poor itinerant Families that trade between Bavaria and the Tyrol.— These Utensils were adopted by the Bavarian Soldiers.— An Account of some Attempts that were made to improve them.— Description of a very simple closed Fire-place constructed with seven loose Bricks.— How this Fire-place may be improved by using three Bricks more, and a few Pebbles.— Description of a very useful* PORTABLE KITCHEN BOILER *of cast Iron, suitable for a small Family. — An Account of a very simple Method of* COOKING WITH STEAM, *on the Cover of this Boiler.— Description of a* STEAM-DISH *of Earthen-ware or of cast Iron, to be used with this Boiler.— Description of a Boiler still more simple in its Construction, proper to be used with a small portable Kitchen Furnace.— The cooking Apparatus here recommended for the Use of the Poor may, with a small Addition, be rendered serviceable for warming their Dwellings in cold Weather.*

AMONGST the great variety of enjoyments which riches put within the reach of persons of fortune and education, there is none more delightful than that which results from doing good to those from whom no return can be expected; or none but gratitude, respect, and attachment. What exquisite pleasure then must it afford to collect the scattered rays of useful science, and direct them *united* to objects of general utility! to throw them in a broad beam on the cold and dreary habitations of the poor, spreading cheerfulness and comfort all around!

Is it not possible to draw off the attention of the rich from trifling and unprofitable amusements, and engage them in pursuits in which their own happiness and reputation and the public prosperity are so intimately connected? What a wonderful change in the state of society might, in a short time, be affected by their *united efforts!*

It is hardly possible for the condition of the lower classes of society to be essentially improved without that kind and friendly assistance which none can afford them but the rich and the benevolent. They must be *taught*, and who is there in whom they have confidence that will take the trouble to instruct them? They cannot learn from books, for they have not time to read; and, if they had, how few of them would be able from a written description to comprehend what they ought to know! If I write for their instruction, it is to the rich that I must address myself; and, if I am not able to engage *them* to assist me, all my labours will be in vain. But to proceed.

In contriving kitchen utensils for cottagers, two objects must frequently be had in view,— viz., the cooking of victuals and the warming of the habitation; and as these objects require very different mechanical arrangements, some address will be necessary in combining them.

Another point to which the utmost attention must be paid is to avoid all complicated and expensive machinery. Instruments for general use should be as simple as possible; and such as are destined for the use of those who must earn their daily bread by their labour should be cheap, durable, and not liable to accidents, or to be often in want of repairs.

As food is more indispensably necessary than a warm room, and as the most common process of cookery is boiling, I shall first show how that process may be performed in the most economical manner possible, and shall then point out the means that may be used for rendering the kitchen fire useful in warming the room in which cookery is carried on.

One of the cheapest utensils for cooking for a family that ever was contrived is, I verily believe, that used by the itinerant poor families that trade between Bavaria and the Tyrol, bringing raisins, lemons, etc., from the south side of the mountains (which they transport in light carts drawn by themselves) and carrying back earthen-ware.

As these poor people have no fixed abode, and never stop at an inn or other public-house, but, like the gypsies in this country, sleep in empty barns and under the hedges by the road-side, they carry with them in their cart all that they possess; and among the rest the whole of their kitchen furniture, which consists of *one single article*,—a deep frying pan of hammered iron, with a short iron handle.

In this they bake their cakes, boil their brown soup, make their hasty pudding, stew their greens, fry their meat, and in short perform every process of their cookery; and, when their victuals are done, their boiler serves them for a dish, which, being placed on the ground, the family sit round it, each individual capable of feeding himself being provided with a wooden spoon.

This is precisely the same kind of kitchen utensil as that used by the Bavarian wood-cutters when they go into the mountains to fell wood; and it is likewise used by many poor families in the Tyrol and in Bavaria.

These broad stewpans, with the addition of a tripod of hammered iron, were adopted many years ago in Bavaria, for the use of the soldiers in barracks; and they still continue to be used by them. Some successful attempts to improve them have, however, lately been made, and it was the experiments which led to those improvements that first induced me to turn my attention to this useful article of kitchen furniture.

Before I proceed any farther in my account of these shallow pans, and of the improvements of which they have been found to be capable, it may perhaps be proper to give an account of the manner in which they are constructed, and of the price at which they are sold.

All those which are used in Bavaria come from the Tyrol or from Styria, where there are considerable manufactories of them; and they are sold at Munich by wholesale at 22 kreutzers (about 7½d. sterling) the pound, Bavarian weight, which is at the rate of 6d. sterling per lb. avoirdupois weight.

One of these pans of large dimensions, — namely, 18 inches in diameter above or at its brim, 15 inches in diameter below, and 4 inches deep, — bought at an ironmonger's shop at Munich, cost me three shillings sterling.

In manufacturing these pans, five of them, one placed within the other, are brought under the hammer at the same time; and, in being hammered out and brought to their proper form and thickness, they are frequently heated red-hot. When they come from the hammer, they are carried to the lathe and are turned on the inside, and made clean and bright, and their edges are turned and made even. They are then packed up one within the other, or in nests (as these parcels are called), and are sold by weight.

The following figure represents one of these pans in its most simple state, placed on three stones, over a fire made with small sticks of wood on the ground in the open air: —

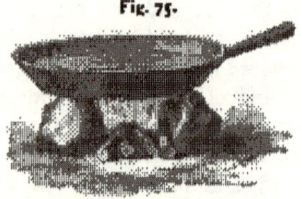

Fig. 75.

The pan used by the Bavarian soldiers — which, as I just observed, is placed on a tripod or trivet of iron — is about 20 inches in diameter above, 16 inches in diameter below, and 4½ inches deep.

As a great part of the heat generated in the combustion of the fuel that is burned under this pan escaped by its sides, to prevent in some measure this loss, I enclosed the pan in a circular hoop or cylinder of sheet iron. The diameter of this hoop was just equal to the diameter of the pan above or at its brim, and its height or width was 6 inches, and the upper part of it was fastened by rivets to the upper part or brim of the pan. This alteration, and a double cover fitted to the pan which prevented the heat from being carried off by the cold air of the atmosphere from the broad surface of the hot liquid in the pan, produced a saving of considerably more than half the fuel, even when this fuel — which was dry pine wood — was burned on the hearth or on the ground in the open air, and no means were used for confining the heat on either side. But the saving was still greater when the fire was made in a closed fire-place.

For a pan of this kind of 14 or 15 inches in diameter at its brim, a very good temporary fire-place may be constructed in a moment, and almost without either trouble or expense, merely with seven common bricks. Six of them, laid down upon the hearth in pairs one upon the other in the manner represented in the following figure,

Fig. 76.

form the fire-place; and the seventh, placed edgewise, serves as a sliding door to close this fire-place in front more or less, as shall be found best.

This little fire-place, which is better calculated for wood or for turf than for coals, is represented filled with fire-wood ready to be kindled, and a dotted circular line shows where the bottom of the circular hoop of sheet iron (in which the pan is suspended) should be set down upon the top of the three bricks which are uppermost.

If, in constructing this fire-place, its walls be made higher by using nine bricks instead of six (laid down flat upon one another by threes), and if a few loose pebbles or stones of any kind, about as large as hens' eggs, be put into it under the fuel, these additions will improve it considerably. The fuel being laid upon these pebbles instead of lying on the hearth or on the ground, the air necessary for its combustion will the more readily get under it, which will cause the fire to burn brighter and more heat to be generated.

These small stones will likewise serve other useful purposes. They will grow very hot, and when they are so they will increase the violence of the combustion and the intensity of the heat; and, even after the fuel is all consumed, they will still be of use by giving off gradually to the pan the heat which they will have imbibed.

Savages, who have few implements of cookery, make great use of heated stones in preparing their food; and civilized nations would do wisely to avail themselves oftener than they do of *their* ingenious contrivances.

I have already mentioned that a considerable saving of fuel was made in consequence of furnishing the broad and shallow boilers of the Bavarian soldiers with double covers; but for boilers of this kind, that are destined for poor families, I would recommend wooden or earthen dishes, turned upside down, instead of these double covers; which dishes may also be used for serving up the victuals after it is cooked. By this contrivance an article necessary in housekeeping will be made to serve two purposes; and, besides this advantage, as a deep bowl or platter turned upside down over the shallow boiler will leave a considerable space above the level of the boiler, which, as steam is lighter than air, will always be filled with hot steam when the water in the shallow pan is boiling, notwithstanding that the joinings of this inverted dish with the rim of the pan will not be steam-tight, a piece of meat much larger than could be covered by the water in this shallow pan might be cooked in it, or potatoes or greens, placed above the surface of the water in the pan, might be cooked in steam.

The following figure, which represents a vertical section of one of these shallow iron boilers, 14 inches in diameter above, surrounded by a cylindrical hoop of sheet iron for confining the heat, and covered by an inverted earthen dish, will give a clear idea of the proposed arrangement:—

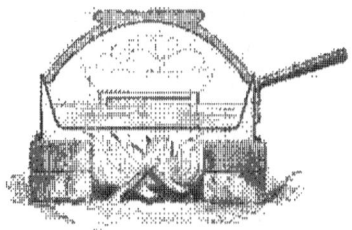

Fig. 77.

The fire-place represented in this figure is that shown in the preceding figure (Fig. 76), and is constructed of six loose bricks. The brick which occasionally serves to close the opening into the fire-place in front is not shown.

A shallow dish is represented (by dotted lines) standing on a small tripod above the surface of the water in the boiler and filled with potatoes, which are supposed to be boiled in steam.

The earthen dish which covers the boiler is represented with a small projection like the foot which is frequently given to earthen dishes. This projection serves instead of a handle when the dish is placed upon, or removed from, the boiler.

This I believe to be the cheapest contrivance that can be used for cooking victuals for a poor family, especially when the durability of the utensil is taken into the account, and also the small quantity of fuel that is required to heat it. The following contrivance will, however, be found more convenient and not much more expensive.

Description of a very useful portable Kitchen Boiler of cast Iron, suitable for a small Family.

The form of this boiler is such that it may easily be cast, and consequently it may be afforded at a low price; and it is equally well calculated to be used with one of the small temporary fire-places just described, constructed with six or with nine loose bricks, or to be heated over one of the small portable kitchen furnaces, of which an account has been given in Chapter XI. It may be made of any dimensions, but the size I would recommend for a small poor family is that indicated by the following figure, which is drawn to a scale of 6 inches to the inch.

This boiler is 10¼ inches in diameter above on the inside of the steam-rim, 9¼ inches in diameter below, and 8¼ deep, measured from the top of the inside of

Fig. 78.

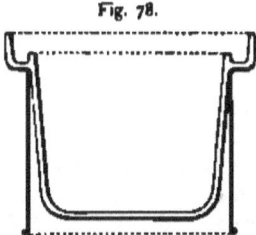

the steam-rim; consequently it will hold about 3 gallons. Its greatest diameter at its brim is 13¼ inches, and total height to the top of its steam-rim is 9¾ inches.

The hollow cylinder of sheet iron in which this boiler is suspended, and which confines the heat by defending its sides from the cold air of the atmosphere, is 8¼ inches high and just 11 inches in diameter.

When this boiler is used for preparing only one dish of victuals, or for cooking several things that may, without inconvenience, be all boiled together in the same water, it may be covered with the cover represented in the following figure : —

Fig. 79.

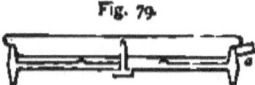

This cover is composed of one piece of cast iron, covered above with a flat circular piece of wood which serves for confining the heat. The wood is fastened to the iron by means of a strong wood screw, with a flat square head, which passes through a hole in the centre of the piece of cast iron.

The handle of this cover must project on one side, and must be fastened to the metal and not to the wood. A piece of it is seen (at *a*) in the figure. It may either be cast with the cover, or it may be of wrought iron and fastened to it by rivets.

The figure, which is a vertical section of the cover, shows the form of it distinctly, and it will be perceived that the piece of cast iron is of a shape which renders it easy to be moulded and cast. The two small projections on the right and left of the hole in the centre of the cover are sections of a circular projection, about $\frac{1}{16}$ of an inch in height, which, as will be seen presently, is designed to serve a particular purpose. In the circumference of this horizontal projecting ring there are three equi-distant projecting blunt points, each about $\frac{1}{16}$ of an inch high above the level of the upper flat surface of the cover, or about $\frac{1}{16}$ of an inch higher than the ring from the upper part of which they project. These three points serve for supporting a shallow dish in which vegetables or any other kind of victuals is put in order to its being cooked in steam.

Of the Manner of using this simple Apparatus for cooking with Steam.

This may easily be done in the following manner. The flat circular piece of wood belonging to the cover of this boiler being removed and the (cast iron) cover being put down upon the boiler, a shallow dish about 2 inches less in diameter than the cover at its brim or upper projecting rim, containing the victuals to be cooked in steam, is to be set down upon the cover, just in the centre of it; and an inverted earthen pot, or any other vessel of a form and size proper for that use, being put over it, the steam from the boiler passing up through the hole in the centre of the cover will find its way under the shallow dish, and passing upwards by the sides of this dish will enter the inverted earthen pot, and, expelling the air, will take its place, and the victuals in the dish will be surrounded on every side by hot steam.

Instead of an earthen pot, an inverted glass bell may be used for covering the victuals in the shallow dish, which will not only render the experiment more striking and more amusing, but will also in some respects be more convenient; for, as the process that is going on may be seen distinctly through the glass, a judgment may, in many cases, be formed, from the *appearance* of the victuals when they are sufficiently done, without removing this vessel by which the steam is confined.

I would not, however, recommend glass vessels for common use, as they would be too expensive for poor families and too liable to be broken. For *them*, a pot of the commonest earthen-ware, or a small wooden tub, would be much more proper. But, for those who can afford the expense and who find amusement in experiments of this kind, the glass bell will be preferable to an opaque vessel.

The manner in which this simple apparatus for cooking with steam is to be arranged will be so easily understood from what has been said, that a figure can hardly be necessary to form a clear and satisfactory idea of it. I shall therefore now proceed to a description of another method of cooking with steam with these small portable kitchen boilers.

The following figure, which is drawn to a scale of 8 inches to the inch, represents a vertical section of a steam-dish of earthen-ware, proper to be used with the boiler represented by the Fig. 78 :—

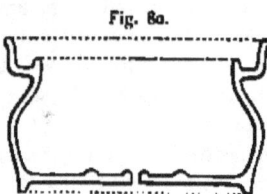

Fig. 80.

The following figure represents a vertical section of an earthen bowl, which, being inverted, may be used occasionally as a cover for the steam-dish represented above, or as a cover for the boiler :—

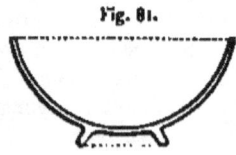

Fig. 81.

When this dish is not in use as a cover for the steam-dish or the boiler, it may be made use of for other purposes. It may, for instance, serve for bringing the soup or any other kind of food upon the table, or for containing any thing that is to be put away. In short, it may be employed for any purpose for which any other earthen bowl of the same form and dimensions would be useful.

In like manner the steam-dish may be made use of for many other purposes besides cooking with steam.

This steam-dish, and the bowl which serves as a cover to it, may both be made of cast iron; but, when this is done, they should be tinned on the inside and japanned on the outside, to give them a neat and cleanly appearance, and prevent their rusting. They may likewise be made of pewter; or, by changing their forms a little, they may be made of tin. The choice of the material to be employed in constructing them must, in each case, be determined by circumstances.

The inverted bowl which covers the steam-dish may be used likewise for covering the boiler when the steam-dish is not in use. Or the cover of the boiler, which is represented by the Fig. 79, may be made use of instead of the inverted bowl for covering the steam-dish, and the bowl may be omitted altogether. One principal reason why I proposed this bowl was to show how by a little contrivance, an article useful in housekeeping might, without any inconvenience or impropriety, be made to serve different purposes.

It is the interest of so many persons to *increase* as much as possible the number of articles used in housekeeping, and to render them as expensive as possible, that I could not help feeling a strong desire to counteract this tendency in some measure, at least in as far as it affects the comforts and enjoyments of the poor.

The natural and the fair object of the exertions of the industrious part of mankind being the acquirement of wealth, *their* ingenuity is employed and exhausted in supplying the wants and gratifying the taste of the rich and luxurious.

It is not *their* interest to encourage the practice of economy, except it be *privately*, in their own families.

Though I sometimes speak with indignation of some of those ridiculous forms under which unmeaning and ostentatious dissipation too often insults common decency, and mortally offends every principle of good taste and elegant refinement, I am very, very far from wishing to diminish the expenses of the rich.

I well know that the free circulation of the blood is not more essentially necessary to the health of a strong athletic man than the free and *rapid* circulation of money is necessary to the prosperity of a great manufacturing and commercial country, whose power at home and abroad is necessarily maintained at a great expense.

Those who would take the trouble to meditate profoundly on the influence which taxes and luxury necessarily have, and ever must have, in promoting that circulation, would, I am confident, become more reconciled to the present state of things, and less alarmed at the progressive increase of public and private expense.

It is apathy and a general *corruption of taste* (which is inseparably connected with avarice and *a corruption of morals*), and not the progress of elegant refinement, that is a symptom of national decline.

But to return to my subject. The boiler above recommended (see Fig. 78) is peculiarly well adapted for being used with the small portable furnaces described in the *eleventh* chapter of this Essay; and, as these furnaces will not be expensive, I would strongly recommend them for the use of poor families, to be used with the utensils I have just been describing.

A cast-iron portable furnace, with one of these boilers and one of the cheap tea-kettles described in the last chapter, which might all be purchased for a small sum, would be a most valuable acquisition to a poor family. It would not only save them a great deal in fuel and in time employed in watching and keeping up the fire in cooking their victuals, but it would also have a powerful tendency to facilitate and expedite the introduction of essential improvements in their cookery, which is an object of much greater importance than is generally imagined.

The boiler in question (represented in the Fig. 78) is made double, or rather it is suspended in a hollow cylinder of sheet iron. This hollow cylinder is certainly useful, as it serves to confine the heat about the boiler; but as it renders the implement more expensive, and may wear out or be destroyed by rust after a certain time, I shall now show how a boiler, proper to be used with one of the portable furnaces before recommended, may be so constructed as to answer without a hollow cylinder.

The following figure represents a vertical section of such a boiler of cast iron drawn to a scale of 8 inches to the inch: —

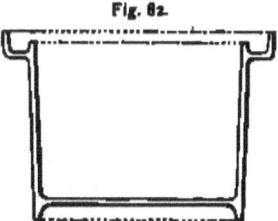

Fig. 82.

The essential difference between this boiler and that last described consists in a rim of about ⅜ of an inch in depth, which descends below its bottom, and forms a kind of foot, on which it stands. This foot being made of such diameter as to fit the sand-rim of the furnace, into which it enters when the boiler is placed over the furnace, the flame and smoke of the fire are confined under the bottom of the boiler quite as effectually as if the boiler were suspended in a cylinder.

It can hardly be necessary that I should observe here — what would probably occur to the reader without my mentioning it — that stewpans and saucepans for register-stoves, and for portable furnaces of all kinds with steam-rims, might be constructed on this simple principle.

It is on this principle that the tea-kettles are constructed that were recommended in the last chapter.

I shall finish this chapter by a few observations respecting the means that may be used for combining the method of cooking here recommended for poor families, with the warming of their habitations in cold weather. This can most readily be done by using an inverted, tall, hollow, cylindrical vessel of tin, thin sheet iron, or sheet copper, as a cover to the boiler (or to the steam-dish, when that is used).

This will change the whole apparatus into a steam-stove, which, as I have elsewhere shown, is one of the best kinds of stoves that can be used for warming a room.

Whenever this is done, care must be taken to stop up the chimney fire-place with a chimney-board, otherwise all the air warmed by the stove, and rendered lighter than the external air, will find its way up the chimney, and escape out of the room. A small opening must, however, be left for the tube which carries off the smoke from the portable furnace into the chimney.

But, whenever it is intended that a portable kitchen furnace should be used occasionally for warming a room by means of steam, it will be very advisable to construct the furnace with an opening on one side of it, for the purpose of introducing the fuel without removing the boiler.

But even should no use whatever be made of this cooking apparatus in warming the room, the use of it will nevertheless be found to be very economical. The quantity of fuel consumed in preparing food will be greatly diminished; and, as a fire may at any time be lighted in one of these portable furnaces almost in an instant, there will be no longer any necessity nor any excuse for constantly keeping up a fire on the hearth in warm weather, which is but too often done in this country, even in places where fuel is neither cheap nor plenty. And even in winter, when a fire in the grate is necessary to render the room warm and comfortable, it will still be good economy to light a small separate fire in a portable furnace, or other closed fire-place, for the purpose of cooking; for nothing is so ill-judged as most of those attempts that are so frequently made by ignorant projectors *to force the same fire to perform different services at the same time.*

The *heat* generated in the combustion of fuel is a *given quantity;* and the more *directly* it is applied to the object on which it is employed, so much the better, for the less of it will escape or be lost on the way, and what is taken away on one side for a particular purpose can produce no effect whatever on the other, where it is not.

CHAPTER XIV.

Miscellaneous Observations respecting culinary Utensils of various Kinds, etc.—Of cheap Boilers of Tin and of cast Iron, suitable to be used with portable Furnaces. — Of earthen Boilers and Stewpans proper for the same Use. — Of LARGE PORTABLE KITCHEN FURNACES, *with Fire-place Doors.— Description of a very cheap* SQUARE BOILER *of sheet Iron, suitable for a* PUBLIC KITCHEN. *— Of* PORTABLE BOILERS *and Fire-places that would be very useful for preparing Food for the Poor in Times of Scarcity.— Of the* ECONOMY OF HOUSE-ROOM *in the Arrangement of a Kitchen for a large Family.— A short Account of the* COTTAGE GRATE *and of a small* GRIDIRON GRATE *for open Chimney Fire-places. — A Description of a* DOUBLE DOOR *for closed Fire-places.*

ALTHOUGH my Essays are professedly *experimental*, and I seldom or never presume to trouble the public with mere speculations, or to recommend any mechanical contrivance till I have been convinced of its utility *by actual experiment*, yet my inquiries have been so numerous and so varied that I am frequently apprehensive of embarrassing my reader, and perhaps tiring and disgusting him by too great a variety of detail. To avoid that evil (which would be fatal to all my hopes) I shall, in this chapter, pass as rapidly as possible over a great number of different objects, many of which will, no doubt, be considered as curious and important. And to relieve the attention of the reader, and also to make it easy for him to pass over what he may have no curiosity to examine, I shall divide my subject as much as possible, and shall treat each distinct branch of it under a separate head of inquiry.

I shall likewise make a liberal use of figures, for by means of them it is often possible to convey more satisfactory information at a single glance than could be obtained by reading many sentences. Whenever I sit down to write, I feel my mind deeply impressed with a sense of the respect which I owe, as an individual, to the public, to whom I presume to address myself; and often consider how blamable it would be in me, especially when I am endeavouring to recommend economy, to trifle with the time of thousands.

Too much pains cannot be taken by those who write books to render their ideas clear, and their language concise and easy to be understood.

Hours spent by an author in saving *minutes* or even *seconds* to his readers is time well employed. But I must hasten to get forward.

Of the Construction of cheap Boilers and Stewpans of Tin or cast Iron, proper to be used with small portable Furnaces.

These utensils, when they are made of tin, may be constructed on the same principles as the tea-kettles described in the last chapter; that is to say, their bottoms being raised up about half an inch above the level of the lower part of their conical or cylindrical sides, and being moreover made of a proper diameter to fit the sand-rim of the furnace, they may be used without being made double. When they are of cast iron, they may be made of the same form below as the boiler represented by the Fig. 82, and particularly described in the last chapter.

Of earthen Boilers and Stewpans proper to be used with portable Furnaces.

Although the earthen stewpan represented by the Fig. 74 (see chapter XII.) is of a good form, yet those represented by the two following figures have likewise their peculiar merit. They are of forms which render them well adapted for being suspended in hollow cylinders of sheet iron, and for their being defended by those cylinders from being broken by accidental falls and blows. From a bare view of them the reader will

Fig. 83.   Fig. 84.

be able to appreciate their relative merit, and also to discover the particular objects had in view in the contrivance of them. The second (Fig. 84) has a steam-rim, and consequently may be used for cooking with steam by means of a steam-dish.

It would no doubt be very possible to construct earthen boilers and stewpans of such forms as to render them capable of being used with portable furnaces without being suspended in hollow cylinders. An earthen stewpan or saucepan, of the form represented by the following figure, would probably answer for that purpose:—

Fire-places and Kitchen Utensils. 453

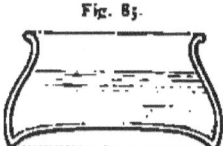
Fig. 85.

Of large portable Kitchen Furnaces with Fire-place Doors.

The following figure represents a vertical section (drawn to a scale of 12 inches to the inch) of a portable furnace of this kind, constructed of sheet iron: —

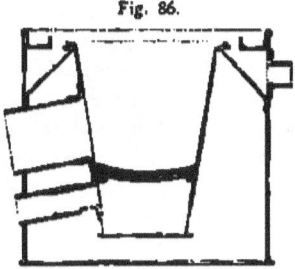
Fig. 86.

Furnaces of this kind might, I am confident, be made very useful in many cases. Wood, coals, charcoal, or turf, might indifferently be used with them; and no contrivance is better calculated for promoting both the economy of fuel and that of house-room.

Portable furnaces on this principle might easily be made of cast iron, which would be both cheap and durable; or they might be constructed partly of cast iron and partly of sheet iron, in the manner recommended in the eleventh chapter, in respect to portable furnaces without fire-place doors.

The door belonging to this fire-place is not represented in the foregoing figure. It may be a hollow cylindrical stopper made of sheet iron.

Description of a very cheap square Boiler of sheet Iron, suitable for a public Kitchen.

As some of the most wholesome and nourishing as well as most palatable kinds of food that can be prepared are rich and savoury soups and broths, and as many of these can be afforded at a very low price, especially when they are made in large quantities, there is no doubt but the use of them will become more general, and that they will in time constitute an essential, if not the principal, part of the victuals furnished to the poor, in every country, from public kitchens; and also to those who are lodged in hospitals or confined in prisons. And as the rich flavour and nutritious quality — or, in other words, the *goodness* of any soup — depend very much on *the manner of cooking it*, — that is to say, on its being boiled or rather *simmered* for a long time over a very slow fire, — the form of the boiler and the form of the fire-place are both objects of great importance.

The simplicity and cheapness of the machinery, and the facility of procuring it in all places and getting it fitted up, are also objects to which much attention ought to be paid. Refined improvements, which require great accuracy in the execution and much care in the management of them, must not be attempted.

The boiler I would propose for the use of public kitchens is similar in all respects to that which has been adopted at Hamburg, after a model sent from Munich; for, although there is nothing about this boiler that indicates the display of much ingenuity in its contrivance, yet it has been found to answer very well as often as it has been tried; and its great simplicity renders it peculiarly well adapted for the use for which it is recommended.

A perfect idea of this boiler may be formed from the following figure, where it is represented without the wooden curb to which it is fixed when it is set in brickwork:—

Fig. 87.

This boiler is 24 inches wide, 36 inches long, and 15 inches deep; consequently, when it is filled to within 3 inches of its brim, or when the liquor in it stands at the depth of 12 inches, it contains 10,364 cubic inches, which make above 36½ beer-gallons.

It should be constructed of sheet iron tinned on the inside; and, when it is not in use, care should be taken to wipe it out very dry with a dry cloth to prevent its being injured by rust; and, as often as it is put away for any considerable time, it should be smeared over with fresh butter or any other kind of animal fat unmixed with salt.

The sheet iron will be sufficiently thick and strong if the boiler when finished weigh 40 pounds; and, as the best sheet iron costs no more than about 3½d. per lb., the manufacturer ought not to charge more than 6d. per lb. for the boiler when finished, which, if it weigh 40 lbs., will amount to 20s.

To strengthen the boiler at the brim, it must be fastened to a curb of wood, which may be a frame of board 1¼ or 1½ inch thick, 5 inches wide, and just large enough to allow the boiler to pass into it and be suspended by its projecting brim. This brim, which may be made about an inch wide, must be fastened down upon the wooden curb with tinned nails or with small wood screws.

This curb will be 3 feet 10 inches long and 2 feet 10 inches wide; and, as the stuff used is 5 inches wide, it will measure very nearly 2¾ feet, superficial measure, which, at 6*d*. the foot (which would be a fair price in London for the work when done), would amount to 1*s*. 4½*d*.

The boiler must be furnished with a cover, which may be made of wood, and should consist of three distinct pieces framed and panelled, and united by two pair of hinges as they are represented in the following figure:—

Fig. 88.

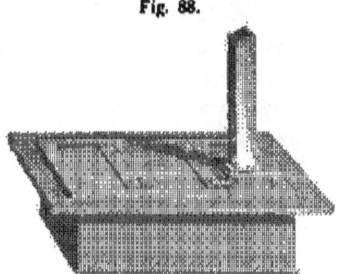

This cover will measure about 7 superficial feet, and, at 7*d*. the foot, will cost 4*s*. 1*d*. The hinges may cost about 4*d*. the pair, consequently the cover will cost, all together, about 4*s*. 9*d*.

This figure represents the boiler fixed in its wooden curb and with its cover in its place.

The first division of the cover (which is 12 inches wide) is laid back on the second (which is 14 inches wide) whenever it is necessary to open the boiler to put anything into it or to take anything out of it, or merely to stir about its contents. When the boiler is to be washed out and cleaned, the opening into it is made larger by throwing back the first and second divisions of its cover, folded one upon the other, and leaning them against the steam-tube which stands upon the third division of the cover, which division is firmly fixed down upon the curb of the boiler by means of wood screws.

The steam-tube (which should be of sufficient length to carry the steam from the boiler out of the room into the open air or into a neighbouring chimney) may be made of four slips of $\frac{3}{4}$ inch thick deal boards fastened together (by being grooved into each other and nailed together) in such a manner as to form a hollow square trunk, measuring about 1$\frac{1}{2}$ inches wide in the clear.

In setting this boiler in brick-work, the flame and smoke from the fire should be made to act on its bottom only, but its sides and ends should be bricked up, in order more effectually to confine the heat. The mass of brick-work should be just 3 feet 8 inches long and 2 feet 8 inches wide, in order that the curb of the boiler may cover it above and project beyond it horizontally on every side about $\frac{1}{2}$ an inch. The bars of the fire-place on which the fuel burns should be situated 12 or 14 inches below the bottom of the boiler, in order that the boiler may not be injured when the fire happens by accident or by mismanagement to be made too intense.

It is not necessary that I should mention here any of the precautions which are to be observed in setting boilers of this kind in brick-work; for that subject has already been so amply treated in various parts of these Essays that to add any thing to what has already been said upon it could be little better than an unnecessary and tiresome repetition.

This boiler would be sufficiently large for cooking for about 300 persons. If it were necessary to feed a much greater number from the same kitchen, I would rather recommend the fitting up of two or more boilers of this size than constructing one large boiler to supply the place of a greater number of others of a moderate size; for I have found by much experience that very large boilers are far from being either economical or convenient.

Large boilers of sheet iron, and especially such as are not kept in constant use, are always *very expensive*, on account of their being so liable to be destroyed by rust.

Of portable Boilers and Fire-places that would be very useful for preparing Food for the Poor in Times of Scarcity.

There is always much trouble and inconvenience, and frequently much danger, in collecting together great numbers of idle people; and these assemblies are never so likely to produce mischievous effects as in times of public calamity, when it is peculiarly difficult to preserve order and subordination among the lower and most needy classes of society.

I have often trembled at seeing the immense crowds of poor people, without occupation, who were sometimes

Fire-places and Kitchen Utensils.

collected together at the doors of the great public kitchens in London during the scarcity of the year 1800.

Two or three hundred people may, without any considerable inconvenience, be supplied with food from the same kitchen; but when public kitchens are not connected with asylums or houses or schools of industry where the poor assemble to work during the day, and when there is no other object in view but merely to enable the poor to purchase good and wholesome food at the lowest prices possible, without any interference at all with their domestic employments or concerns, it appears to me that it would always be best to select from amongst the poor a certain number of honest and intelligent persons, and encourage them to prepare and sell to their poor neighbours, under proper regulation and inspection, such kinds of food and at such prices as should be prescribed by those who have the charge of providing for the relief of the poor.

A plan of this sort might be executed at any time on the pressure of the moment, without the smallest delay, and almost without either trouble or expense, if each parish or community were to provide and keep ready in store a certain number of portable kitchen furnaces, with boilers belonging to them, to be lent out occasionally to those who should be willing to undertake to cook and sell victuals to the poor on the terms that should be proposed.

If these boilers were made to hold from 8 to 10 gallons, they would serve for preparing food for 60 or 70 persons; and, as they would require very little fuel, and so little attendance that a woman who should undertake the management of one of them might perform that service with great ease by devoting to it each day the labour of half an hour, and giving to it occasionally a few moments of attention, which would hardly interrupt her in her common domestic employments, this method of preparing food would be very economical, — perhaps more so than any other, — and, with proper inspection, it would be little liable to abuse.

How very useful would these portable boilers and furnaces be for providing a warm and cheap dinner for children who frequent schools of industry!

No furnace could, in my opinion, be better contrived for this use than that represented in the Fig. 86; and the boiler might be made either of sheet iron tinned, or of copper tinned, or of cast iron. It cannot be necessary that I should give any particular directions respecting its form, and its dimensions may easily be computed from its capacity, when that is determined on.

A portable cooking apparatus of this kind, which is designed as a model for imitation, may be seen in the repository of the Royal Institution.

Of the Economy of House-room in the Arrangement of a Kitchen for a large Family.

There is nothing which marks the progress of civil society more strongly than the use that is made of house-room; and nothing would tend more to prevent the too rapid progress of destructive luxury among the industrious classes than a taste for neatness and true elegance in all the inferior details of domestic arrangement. The pleasing occupation which those objects of rational pursuit afford to the mind fills up leisure time in a manner that is both useful and satisfactory and prevents *ennui* and all its fatal consequences.

The poor cook their victuals in the rooms in which they dwell; but those who can afford the expense — and many indeed who cannot — set apart a room for the purpose of cooking, and call it a kitchen. I am far from desiring to alter this order of things, for I think it perfectly proper. What I wish is, that each class of society may be made as comfortable as possible, and that all their domestic arrangements may be *neat* and *elegant*, and at the same time *economical*.

I always fancy that teaching industrious people economy, and giving them a taste for the improvement of all those useful contrivances and rational enjoyments that are within their reach, is something like showing them how, without either toil or trouble, and with a good conscience, they may obtain all those advantages which riches command, together with many other very sweet enjoyments which money cannot buy. And whose heart is so cold as not to glow with ardent zeal at a prospect so well calculated to awaken all the most generous feelings of humanity?

But to return from this digression. There are various methods that may be used for economizing house-room in making the necessary arrangements for cooking. If the family be small, the use of portable furnaces and boilers will be found to be very advantageous.

For a large family I would recommend what I shall call a *concealed kitchen*. There are two very complete kitchens of this kind, which have been fitted up under my direction at the Royal Institution: the one, which is small, is in the housekeeper's room; the other is in the great kitchen. These were both made as models for imitation, and may be examined by any person who wishes to see them.

There are also two kitchens of this kind in my house at Brompton in two adjoining rooms, which have been fitted up principally with a view to showing that all the different processes of cookery *may* be carried on in a room which, on entering it, nobody would suspect to be a kitchen. The following figure is the ground plan of one of them:—

Fig. 89.

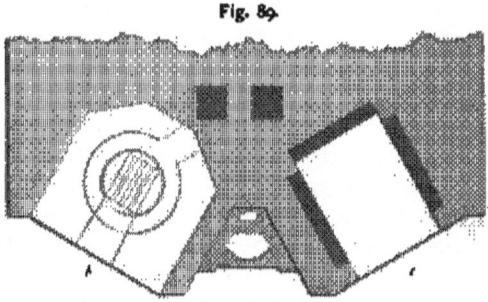

a is the opening of the fire-place, which is brought forward into the room about 14½ inches. This was done, in order to give more room for the family boiler, which is situated at *b*, and the roaster, which is placed on the other side of the open chimney fire-place at *c*.

The two broad spaces on the two sides of the roaster, by which the smoke from the fire below it rises up round it, and another at the farther end of it, by which the smoke descends, are distinguished by dark shades, as are also the two square canals by which the smoke from the roaster and that from the boiler rise up into the chimney.

The top of the grate is seen which belongs to the open chimney fire-place: it is represented by horizontal lines. It is what I have called a *cottage grate*, and

Fire-places and Kitchen Utensils. 463

what is sold in the shops under that name. The retail price of this grate, with its fender and trivet, is *ten shillings and sixpence*. The Carron Company entered into an engagement with me to furnish them by wholesale to the trade, delivered in London, at *seven shillings and sixpence*. A front view of this grate may be seen in the next figure. As this figure (Fig. 89) is designed merely for showing *where* the different parts of the apparatus are to be placed, and not *how* they are to be fitted up, none of the details of the setting of the roaster or boiler were in this place attempted to be expressed with accuracy. Information respecting those particulars must be collected from other parts of the work.

The grate represented in this figure is calculated for boiling a pot or a tea-kettle, and for heating flat-irons for ironing. Its bottom is so contrived as to be easily taken away and replaced. By removing it at night, or whenever a fire is no longer wanted, the coals in the grate fall down on the hearth, and the fire immediately goes out. This contrivance not only saves much fuel, which otherwise would be consumed to waste, but it is also very convenient on another account. As all the coals and ashes fall out of the grate when its bottom is removed, on replacing it again the grate is empty and ready for a new fire to be kindled in it.

The top of this grate, which is a flat piece of cast iron, has one large hole in it for allowing the smoke to pass upwards, and another behind it, which is much smaller, through which it is forced to *descend* into what has been called a *diving-flue*, whenever the boiler belonging to this fire-place is used,—which boiler is suspended in a hollow cylinder of sheet iron, about

11½ inches in diameter, resembling in all respects the boilers used with the register-stoves described in the tenth chapter of this Essay.

I intend, as soon as it shall be in my power, to publish a particular detailed account of this grate, and also of several others for open chimney fire-places, which at my recommendation have lately been introduced in this country. In the mean time, I avail myself of this opportunity of pointing out one fault which has been committed by almost all those who have undertaken to set *cottage grates* in brick-work. They have made what has been called the *diving-flue* much too deep. It is more than probable that the name given to this flue has contributed not a little to lead them into this error. When properly constructed, it hardly deserves the name of *a flue*, for it ought not to be above *two inches deep*, measured from the under surface of the flat plate of cast iron which forms the top of the grate. There are two important advantages that result from making this opening in the brick-work for the passage of the smoke *very shallow:* the one is, that in this case it may easily be cleaned out when coals happen to fall into it by accident when it is left uncovered; and the other is, that the back wall of the fire-place, against which the fuel burns, may in that case be made thick and strong, and not so liable to be destroyed by the end of the poker in stirring the fire as it is when there is a hollow flue just behind it.

Both these are important objects, and for want of due attention being paid to them cottage grates have, to my knowledge, often been disgraced and rejected. When they are properly set and properly managed, they are very useful fire-places where coal or turf is burned; and it never was designed that they should be used with wood.

When kitchens are fitted up on the plan here recommended in places where wood is used as fuel, the open chimney fire-place, which is situated between the roaster and the boiler, may be constructed *of the form* represented in the foregoing figure, but without any fixed grate; and the wood may be burned on andirons or on a small movable *gridiron grate* placed on the hearth.

These *gridiron grates* are very simple in their construction, cheap and durable; and they make an excellent fire, either with coals or turf, or with wood, if it be sawed or cut into short billets. Five of these grates may be seen at the house of the Royal Institution: one in the great lecture-room, one in the apparatus-room, one in the manager's room, one in the clerks' room, and one in the dining-room. They have hitherto been made of two sizes only; namely, of 16 inches and of 18 inches in width in front. The width of the back part of the grate is always made just equal to half its width in front, and the two sloping sides or ends of the grate are each just equal in width to the back. The form and dimensions of the grate determine the form and dimensions of the open chimney fire-place in which it is used; for the back of the fire-place must always be made just equal in width to the back of the grate, and the sloping of the covings must be the same as the sloping of the ends of the grate.

From what has been said of the proportions of the front, back, and sides of these grates, it is evident that the covings and backs of their fire-places must make an angle with each other just equal to 120 degrees. This angle I have been induced to prefer to one of

135 degrees, which I formerly recommended for open chimney fire-places. The reasons for this preference will be fully explained in another place. To give them here would take up too much time, and would moreover be foreign to my present subject.

For the information of the public, and to prevent, in as far as it is in my power, exorbitant demands being made for these useful articles, I would just observe that the smallest or 16-inch *gridiron grate*, together with all the apparatus belonging to it, ought to cost, *by retail*, no more than *seven shillings*. This apparatus consists of a cast-iron fender, a trivet for supporting a boiler or a tea-kettle over the fire, and a small plate of cast iron (to be fastened into the back of the chimney), by means of which, and a small bolt or nail, the grate is fastened in its place on the hearth.

The second-sized or 18-inch *gridiron grate*, with all its apparatus (consisting of the three articles mentioned above), ought to be sold, by retail, for *seven shillings and sixpence*.

The *wholesale price* of these articles, at the Carron Company's warehouse, in London (Thames Street, near Blackfriars' Bridge), to the trade, and to gentlemen who buy them by the dozen, to distribute them to the poor, is: —

For the gridiron-grate No. 1, with
the articles belonging to it . . . *four shillings*.
For that No. 2, with the articles
belonging to it . . . . . . *four shillings and sixpence*.

These are the wholesale and retail prices which I fixed with the agent of the Carron Company, at their works in Scotland, in the autumn of the year 1800, when I made a journey there for the purpose of establishing these regulations; and when I made a present to the Company of all my patterns, which I had got made in London, and which had been rendered as perfect as possible by previous experiments, — namely, by getting castings taken from them by the best London founders, and altering them occasionally, till they were acknowledged to be quite complete.

If it had been possible for me to have done more to prevent impositions, I should have done it with pleasure; and I should have felt, at the same time, that I had done no more than what it was my duty to do.

But to return from this long digression. I shall now hasten to finish my account of the means which have been used in one of the rooms in my house (that destined for the large kitchen) for concealing the roaster and the family boiler.

The following figure is an elevation of that part of the side of the room where these implements are concealed:—

Fig. 90.

The open chimney fire-place and the front of the grate are distinctly shown in the middle of this figure, in the lower part of it. The panelled door, immediately above the mantel of the chimney fire-place, which reaches nearly to the ceiling of the room, serves to shut up a small closet with narrow shelves, which has no connection with culinary affairs, but is used for putting away candlesticks, and any other small articles used in housekeeping, which are occasionally laid by when not in actual use. The two other panelled doors by the side of it serve, — the one (that on the right hand) for concealing the roaster, and the other for concealing the family boiler.

The two (shorter) panelled doors, on the right and left of the open chimney fire-place, and on the same level with it, serve for concealing the fire-place doors and ash-pit doors of the closed fire-places of the roaster and of the boiler.

The steam from the boiler (after passing through the steam-dishes, when they are used) is carried off by a tin tube into a small canal, which conveys it into the chimney in such a manner that no part of it comes into the room. The steam from the roaster is carried off in like manner by its steam-tube.

If a void space, about 2 or 3 inches in depth, be left between the outside of the door of the roaster and the inside of the panelled door which shuts it up and conceals it, and if this panelled door be lined on the inside with thin sheet iron, the process of roasting may be carried on with perfect safety with this door shut. And if similar precautions be used to defend the other panelled doors from the heat, they may also be kept shut while the processes of boiling and roasting are actually going on.

By these means it would be *possible* to prepare a dinner for a large company in a room where there should be no appearance of any cooking going on. But I lay no stress on this particular advantage resulting from this arrangement of the culinary apparatus. The real advantage gained by it is this: that the kitchen is left an *habitable*, and even an *elegant room*, when the business of cooking is over.

The kitchen in Heriot's Hospital at Edinburgh, which was fitted up in the autumn of the year 1800, is arranged in this manner, — with this difference, however, that all the panelled doors are omitted. The boiler is shut up by a door of sheet iron, japanned; and the door of the roaster and the two fire-place doors and two ash-pit register doors are exposed to view.

As the brick-work is whitewashed and kept clean, and as the doors are all either japanned black or kept very clean, the whole has a neat appearance.

The roaster and principal boiler in the great kitchen of the house of the Royal Institution are put up nearly in the same manner as those in Heriot's Hospital, excepting that in the former there is a hot closet, which is situated immediately above the roaster, whereas there is none belonging to the latter.

In one of the kitchens in my house there is, in the place of the roaster, a roasting-oven, with a common iron oven of the same dimensions placed directly over it, and heated by the same fire.

The door of my roaster and that of my roasting-oven are made single, of thin sheet iron, and they are covered on the outside with panels of wood, for confining the heat. Instead of doors to their closed fire-places, I use square stoppers, made of fire-stone or hard fire-brick, fastened to flat pieces of sheet iron, to which knobs of wood are fixed, which serve instead of handles.

These stoppers answer for confining the heat quite as well, and perhaps even better, than double doors, and they cost much less. They are fitted into square frames of cast iron (nearly similar to that represented in the Fig. 91), which are firmly fixed in the brick-work by means of projecting flanges, which are cast with them. The front edge of this frame or doorway is ground and made perfectly level; and the plate of sheet iron, which forms a part of the stopper, being made quite flat, shuts against the front edge of this doorway, and closes the entrance into the fire-place with the greatest accuracy.

The entrance into the ash-pit is likewise closed by a stopper, which is so contrived as to serve occasionally as a register for regulating the quantity of air admitted into the fire-place.

As this *register-stopper* for the ash-pit of a small closed fire-place is very simple in its construction, and as I have found it to answer very well the purpose for which it was contrived, I shall present the reader with the following sketch of it, which will, I trust, be sufficient to enable a workman of common inge-

Fig. 91.

nuity to construct, without difficulty, the thing which is represented.

The box with a flange at each of its ends forms the

door-way into the ash-pit. It is of cast iron, and its opening in front is 7¼ inches wide and 3¾ inches high. It is concealed in the brick-work in such a manner that its front edge only is seen, projecting about ⅛ of an inch before the brick-work.

When the register-stopper belonging to this door-way (which is shown in this figure) is pushed quite home, its flat plate comes into contact with the front edge of the door-way, and closes the passage into the ash-pit so completely that no air can enter. By withdrawing this stopper more or less, more or less air is admitted. The narrow, thin, elastic bands of iron, the ends of which are fastened by rivets to the flat plate of the stopper, serve to confine the stopper in any situation in which it is placed, which service they are enabled to perform (in consequence of their elasticity and of their peculiar shape) by pressing against the sides of the door-way.

The only objection that I am acquainted with to this kind of register for the door-way of the ash-pit of a small closed fire-place is that it is not quite so easy to see the precise state of the register as it is when the air is admitted through a hole in the front of the ash-pit door in the usual manner; but this objection is of no great importance, especially as means may easily be devised to remedy that trifling defect.

The door-way frames to all the closed fire-places in my own kitchen are in all respects like that represented in the foregoing figure (Fig. 91), with this difference only, that they are 5 inches high instead of being 3¾ inches in height. An account has already been given of the manner in which their stoppers were constructed.

It is right that the reader should be informed that although I have made use of stoppers to close the passage into each of the closed fire-places in my own kitchen, yet very few persons have adopted this simple and cheap contrivance. The reason why it has not come into more general use might easily be explained; but I fancy it will be best that I should say nothing now on that subject. Instead of recommending what nobody would find much advantage in furnishing at a fair price, it will be more wise and prudent to give a short description of a more complicated, more elegant, and more expensive contrivance, which has already found its way into the shops of several of the most respectable ironmongers in London. As this contrivance has often been used, and has always been found to answer perfectly well, I can venture to recommend it to all those to whom an additional expense of a few shillings or a guinea or two in fitting up a kitchen is not considered as an object of importance.

A short Description of a DOUBLE DOOR for a closed Fire-place.

The following figure (which is drawn to a scale of 6 inches to the inch) represents a horizontal section of one of these double doors, and also of a part of the brick-work in which it is set.

A is the inside door, and B is the outside door. These doors are so connected by means of a crooked rod of iron f, and the two joints g and h, that when the outside door is opened or shut the inside door is necessarily opened or shut at the same time. The inside door, which is of cast iron and near $\frac{1}{2}$ an inch in thickness, is movable on two pivots, one of which is represented at *e*. The outside door is movable on two hinges, one of which is shown at *d*.

c is the latch by which the outside door is fastened. This is of such a form that it may be used as a latch, and may serve at the same time as a handle for opening and shutting the door.

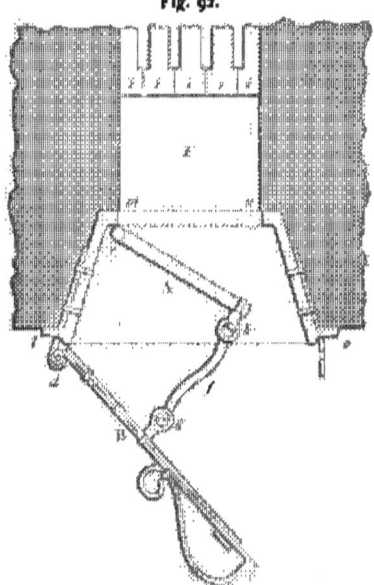

Fig. 92.

The door-way, which is of cast iron, is in the shape of a hollow truncated quadrangular pyramid, with a flange in front, about an inch wide, which flange, when seen in front, seems to form a kind of frame to the outside door; the flange, which is about ⅛ of an inch in thickness, projecting before the vertical front of the brick-work.

l, m, n, o, represents a horizontal section of this cast iron door-way. The brick-work in which it is set is distinguished by diagonal lines.

k is the passage leading to the fire-place: it is 6 inches wide in the clear from *m* to *n*, 5 inches high, and 6 inches long, measured from the inside of the inside door, when it is shut, to the hither ends of the openings between the iron bars of the fire-place, through which openings the air comes up from the ash-pit into the fire-place. The hither ends of these bars (five in number) are represented in the figure. They are each distinguished by the letter *i*. The opening of the inside door-way is 6 inches wide and 5 inches high in the clear; and the door itself is 6¼ inches wide and 5¼ inches high.

The outside door-way is 10 inches wide and 9 inches high in the clear; and the door, which is about $\frac{1}{16}$ of an inch in thickness, is 10¼ inches wide and 9¼ high. The extreme width of the door-frame to the outward edge of the flange is 12¼ inches, and its extreme height is 11¼ inches.

The two straps of iron to which the hooks of the hinges of the outside door are fastened pass through two holes in the flange, provided for them in casting the door-way, and are riveted to the sloping side of the door-way on the left-hand side of it.

These holes are each ⅜ of an inch in length from top to bottom, and about ¼ of an inch in width. There is another similar hole in the flange on the opposite side of the door-way, through which a strap of iron passes, the end of which projecting forward before the level of the front edge of the door-way serves as a catch or hook, into which the latch of the door falls when the door is closed.

These three holes in the side flanges of the doorway are distinctly represented in the following figure, which is an elevation or front view of this door-way, without its doors:—

Fig. 93.

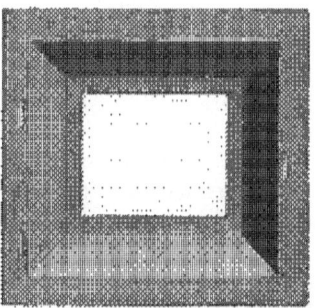

It appears by this figure, but still more distinctly by the last (Fig. 92), that the flange or front of this door-way is not quite flat. It is raised at its inward edge, which projects forward about ¼ of an inch. This projecting rim, which is cast as thin as possible, is ground upon a flat sand-stone and made quite level, in order that the outside door, which is flat, by shutting against the front of this projecting edge may close the opening into the fire-place with the greatest possible accuracy.

It will likewise be remarked, on examining this figure (Fig. 93) with attention, that the opening which is closed by the inside door is not precisely in the middle of the vertical flat surface against which that door shuts, being situated a little above the middle of it. This particular arrangement has been found to be of considerable use, as it serves to prevent small pieces of coal from getting between the inside door and that flat surface when the door is shut.

These double doors (of a size larger than that represented by the two preceding figures) have lately been introduced in a considerable number of hothouses in the neighbourhood of London; and I have been told, by several persons who have tried them, that they have been found very useful indeed. I was lately assured by a very respectable gardener, who has adopted them in all his hothouses, that since he has used them and the register ash-pit doors which belong to them and are always sold with them, and since he has altered the construction of his fire-places, his consumption of coals has been little more than half as much as it used formerly to be.

In setting these double doors in brick-work, great care should always be taken to make the entrance into the fire-place of some considerable length, or to keep the hither ends of the iron bars on which the fuel burns at some distance from the inside door; otherwise, if the burning fuel be near that door, it will heat it and its frame red-hot, which will soon destroy their form and prevent the door from closing the entrance of the fire-place with accuracy.

I have found it to be a good general rule to place the hither ends of the bars, which form the grate of the fire-place, as far beyond the inside door as that door-way is wide in the clear. And it will be found to be an excellent precaution to defend the door from the heat, if that part of the passage into the fire-place which lies beyond the inside door be kept constantly rammed quite full of small coals; or, what would be still better, of coal-dust mixed up with a certain proportion of moist clay.

I have already, in a former part of this Essay, mentioned how necessary it is, in setting double doors in brick-work, to take care to mask the farther end of the door-way in such a manner (by means of bricks interposed before it, or between it and the fire) that the rays from the burning fuel may never fall on it. The manner in which this is to be done is clearly represented in the Fig. 92.

All these precautions for preventing these double doors from being injured by excessive heat will be the more necessary in proportion as the fire-places are larger to which they belong.

There is one essential part of this apparatus which, for want of room, was omitted in the two last figures,— that is, the straps of wrought iron, by means of which the door-way is firmly fixed in the brick-work; but this omission can be of no consequence, as every common artificer will know, without any particular directions, how that part of the work should be executed. These straps must of course be fastened to the cast-iron doorway by means of rivets.

CHAPTER XV.

Apology for the great Length of this Essay. — Regret of the Author that he has not been able to publish Plans and Descriptions of the various culinary Inventions that have lately been put up in the Kitchen belonging to the House of the Royal Institution and

478   On the Construction of Kitchen

in the Kitchen of Heriot's Hospital at Edinburgh.— A short Account of a BOILER, on a new Construction, lately put up at the House of the Royal Institution, for the purpose of GENERATING STEAM for warming the Great Lecture-Room. — This Boiler would probably be found very useful for STEAM-ENGINES. — An Account of a Contrivance for preventing metallic STEAM-TUBES from being injured by the alternate Expansion and Contraction of the Metal by Heat and Cold. — An Account of a simple Contrivance which serves as a Substitute for SAFETY-VALVES.

I CANNOT finish this Essay without apologizing for the great length of it. I had no idea when I began it that it would ever have grown to such a voluminous size; but I am not conscious of having inserted any thing that could well have been omitted.

I was very desirous of laying before the public complete plans and descriptions of the various culinary inventions that have lately been put up in the great kitchen of the house of the Royal Institution in Albemarle Street, and also of those erected in Heriot's Hospital at Edinburgh, in the autumn of the year 1800; but my stay in this country will be too short for me to undertake so considerable a work at this time. I am happy, however, that these new contrivances, some of which have already been proved to be very useful, are situated in places of public resort where persons desirous of examining them may at all times obtain free admission.

There are also several other new and useful contrivances at the house of the Royal Institution, which I should have had great pleasure in laying before the public, had it been in my power, as I am persuaded that correct accounts of them would have been very acceptable to men of science, and to all those who take pleasure in promoting new and useful mechanical improvements.

I should, in particular, have been very glad to have given plans and descriptions of all the various parts of the steam-apparatus that has been put up for the purpose of warming the great lecture-room. The boilers for generating the steam are, if I am not much mistaken, well worthy of the attention of those who make use of steam-engines; and as the subject is of infinite importance in this great manufacturing country, where the numerous advantages which result from the use of machinery are known and every day more and more felt by individuals and by the public, I cannot resist the strong inclination which I feel, to attempt in a few words to give a general idea of this contrivance. Those who wish to know more of the matter may get all the information respecting it which they can want by applying at the house of the Royal Institution.

A short Account of the BOILERS *lately put up at the House of the Royal Institution for* GENERATING STEAM *for warming the Great Lecture-Room.*

Over an oblong closed fire-place, furnished with double doors, ash-pit register door, etc., are placed two cylinders of copper, laid down horizontally by the side of each other over the fire, each cylinder being 15 inches in diameter and 48 inches long. Immediately over these two cylinders, and resting on them, are placed two other cylinders of copper of the same length and diameter; and over these last, and resting on them, are placed two other like cylinders, making six cylinders in the whole, all made of the same material and being of the same dimensions.

The fire-place being situated under the hither ends of the two lower cylinders, the flame runs along under them to their farther ends, where it passes upwards and comes forward between the upper sides of the two lower cylinders, and the lower sides of the two cylinders immediately above them. Being arrived at the front wall of the brick-work, it there rises up again, and then passes along horizontally between the two middle cylinders and the two upper cylinders, till it comes to the back wall; and, passing up by the farther ends of the upper cylinders, it comes forwards horizontally, for the last time, in an arch or vault of brick-work which covers the two upper cylinders. Being arrived once more at the front wall of the brick-work, it there enters a canal (furnished with a good damper) by which it goes off into a neighbouring chimney.

These cylinders are confined in their places by being placed in pairs, over each other, between two parallel vertical walls, which are built just so far asunder as to admit two cylinders, placed horizontally by the sides of each other; and the flame is prevented from finding its way upwards between the two cylinders which lie by the sides of each other, or between the outsides of those cylinders and the sides of the vertical walls with which they are in contact, by filling up the joining between them with good clay, mixed with small pieces of firebricks.

The farther ends of all the cylinders are closed up, and all the tubes which are necessary for the admission of water and for the passage of the steam are fixed to a circular plate of metal, which closes (by means of flanges and screws) the front ends of the cylinders.

In consequence of this particular arrangement it will be perfectly easy to make all the cylinders of *cast iron*, even when these boilers are destined for steam-engines of the largest dimensions. The number of sets of cylindrical boilers, which in each case it will be necessary to put up, must be determined by the size of the cylinders and by the quantity of steam that will be wanted. Six cylindrical boilers put up in a separate mass of brick-work, in the manner above described, I call *one set*.

It will always be found to be very advantageous to have at least three or four sets of cylindrical boilers to each steam-engine, instead of having one set of larger cylinders; and this not only on account of the wear and tear of small fire-places being incomparably less expensive than in those which are large, but also on account of the economy of fuel which will be derived from that arrangement, and the great convenience that will be found to result from the use of small boilers, which may at any time be heated and made to boil in a very few minutes; and from the advantage of being able at all times to regulate the number of sets of boilers in use to the load on the engine.

It is quite impossible to make a small fire in a large fire-place without a great loss of heat; but, by having a number of small separate fire-places, an engine may be made to work with a light load with almost as small a proportion of fuel as when it is made to perform its full work. But to return to our cylindrical boilers.

The two lower cylinders, and those two which lie immediately over them, being destined for the generation of steam, are kept constantly about half full of water, which water they receive, already hot, from the two upper cylinders, in which last the water should never boil.

These upper cylinders communicate, by an open pipe, with a reservoir of water, which is situated several feet above them; consequently, as fast as they furnish water to the four cylinders which lie below them, that water so furnished is immediately replaced by water which comes from the reservoir above.

As the pipe which brings this water from the reservoir enters the cylinders some considerable distance below their centres, and as the pipes which convey the water from them to the cylinders below are fixed in their centres, as cold water is heavier than warm water, it is evident that the water which enters them cold from the reservoir will take its place at the lower parts of these cylinders, while only the lighter hot water will be furnished to the cylindrical boilers below.

The method of regulating the admission of water into the boilers below, where the steam is generated, is so well known that it would be superfluous to give a particular account of it.

In the set of boilers that has been put up at the house of the Royal Institution, the open ends of all the cylinders are on one side; that is to say, they all come through the front wall of the brick-work. This arrangement was rendered necessary in that particular case by local circumstances: it would, however, have been better if only the lower and upper pairs of cylinders had come through the front wall, and the open ends of the middle pair had passed through the back wall; for in that case it would have been easier to provide a passage for the flame round the ends of the middle cylinders.

One evident advantage that will be derived from constructing steam-engine boilers on the principles here recommended is their superior strength to resist the efforts of the steam, which will render it possible to use very thin sheet copper or sheet iron in constructing them, when they are made of those materials. Another advantage will be the great facility of removing and repairing any of the cylinders which may happen to leak, or which may be found to be damaged or worn out. When several sets of cylinders are put up for the same engine (which I would always recommend, even for engines of the smallest size), any of these occasional repairs may be made without stopping the engine.

If these cylindrical steam boilers should be found to be useful for steam-engines, they cannot fail to be equally so for generating steam for heating dyers' coppers by means of steam, for bleaching by means of steam, and, in general, for every purpose where steam is wanted in large quantities.

They must, I think, be peculiarly well adapted for dyers; for, as water less hot than boiling water is frequently wanted by them in the course of their business, the upper cylinders will at all times afford a plentiful supply of warm water, which may, without the smallest inconvenience, be drawn off whenever it is wanted.

To prevent in the most effectual manner the loss of heat which is occasioned by the passage of steam through the safety-valve, that steam which so escapes out of the boiler may be carried off in a tube provided for that purpose, and conducted into the upper cylinders or into the reservoir which feeds them. In doing this, care must be taken to cause the steam to descend perpendicularly, from the height of eight or ten feet, before it enters the water where it is intended that it should be condensed; and the end of the tube through which the steam descends and enters the water should be plunged to a certain depth below the surface of the water.

I shall finish this chapter and conclude this Essay by giving a short description of two very simple contrivances, which have been put in practice at the house of the Royal Institution, and which have been found to be very useful. The one is a contrivance for preventing most effectually the bad effects of the alternate expansion and contraction by heat and cold of the metallic tubes which are used in conveying steam to a considerable distance; and the other is a substitute for safety-valves in an apparatus for heating rooms by means of steam.

Of the Means that may be used for preventing metallic Steam-tubes, of considerable Length, from being injured by the alternate Expansion and Contraction of the Metal by the different Degrees of Heat and Cold to which those Tubes are occasionally exposed.

We will suppose the tube in question to be of copper, and eight inches in diameter (which is the size of that used for warming the great lecture-room at the Royal Institution). Let this tube be made in lengths of ten feet; and instead of joining the ends of these tubes together immediately, to form one long tube, let a very short tube or cylinder, of only one or two inches in length and 24 inches in diameter, closed at each end with a flat circular plate of sheet copper, like the head of a drum, be interposed between their joinings. These two circular sheets of copper, which form two ends of this very short cylinder, must be perforated in their centres with holes 8 inches in diameter, to give a passage to the steam; and the ends of the tubes must be firmly fastened to them by means of flanges and rivets.

The following figure, which represents an outline of a portion of a steam-tube constructed in this manner, will give a clear idea of this contrivance:—

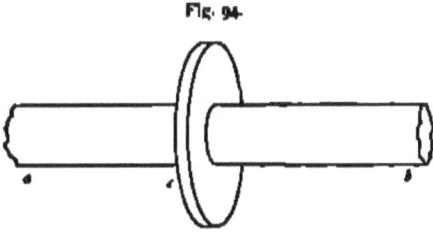

Fig. 94.

a, b, are portions of two of the tubes which are united together by means of the short flat cylinder *c*.

Now if we suppose one of these tubes (10 feet long) to be immovably fixed *in the middle of its length* to a beam of wood or to a solid wall, the increase or diminution of the length of each half of it — arising from its being occasionally heated to the temperature of boiling water by steam, or cooled to the mean temperature of the air of the atmosphere, — being free will cause its two ends to push inwards or to draw outwards the two flat ends of the two neighbouring short cylinders to which they are attached; and, as these short cylinders are 24 inches in diameter, while the tube is only 8 inches in diameter, the elasticity of the large circular thin plates of metal will allow it to be pressed inwards or drawn outwards without injury, much more than will be necessary in order to give room for the expansions and contractions of the tubes.

Hence it appears that, by this simple contrivance, steam may be conveyed to any distance, however great, in closed metallic tubes, without any danger of injury to the tubes from the expansions and contractions of the metal.

A short Description of a Contrivance which serves instead of Safety-valves for a Steam Apparatus, which is used for heating the Great Lecture-Room at the House of the Royal Institution.

The following figure, which represents a vertical section of this contrivance, will give a clear idea of it, and of the manner in which it acts: —

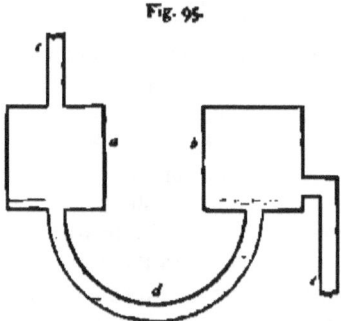

Fig. 95.

a and *b* are two cylinders of copper, 6 inches in diameter and 6 inches in length, placed in an erect position. The cylinder *a* is closed both above and below; the cylinder *b* is closed below, but is open above.

The semi-circular tube *d*, which is represented filled with water, serves to connect the two cylinders together.

By the tube *c*, the water, which results from the condensation of the steam in the steam-tubes which warm the room, returns to the reservoir which feeds the boiler. This water, after falling into the cylinder *a*, passes through the semi-circular tube *d* into the cylinder *b*, and then goes off from that cylinder, and is conveyed, still warm, to the reservoir, by the tube *e*.

This simple apparatus serves as a safety-valve in the following manner: When the steam in the steam-tubes is redundant, it descends through the tube *c*, and forcing the water out of the semi-circular tube *d* into the cylinder *b*, it follows it through that tube, and escapes into the open air through the open end of that cylinder. When the strength of the steam is sufficiently diminished, a small quantity of water, still remaining in the lower part of the cylinder *b*, returns back into the tube *d*, and cuts off the communication between the external air and the inside of the steam-tubes.

When, in consequence of the fire under the boiler being extinguished or being much diminished, a vacuum begins to be formed in the steam-tubes, the external air, pressing against the surface of the small quantity of water remaining in the lower part of the cylinder *b*, forces it through the semi-circular tube *d* into the cylinder *a*, and following it into that cylinder opens for itself a passage into the steam-tubes, and prevents their being crushed by the pressure of the atmosphere, on the condensation of the steam.

When the fire is gone out, and the whole apparatus

becomes cold, the steam-tubes will be entirely filled with air.

When, on lighting the fire again, fresh steam is generated, as this steam enters the large steam-tubes in the *highest* or *most elevated* part of them, and as steam is specifically lighter than atmospheric air, the steam remains above the air which still occupies the steam-tubes, and accumulating there presses this air downwards, and by degrees forces it out of the apparatus through the same passage by which it entered; the water in the semi-circular tube supplying the place of a valve, or rather of two valves, in these different operations.

[This paper is printed from the English edition of Rumford's Essays, Vol. III., pp. 1-384.]

SUPPLEMENTARY OBSERVATIONS

RELATING TO

THE MANAGEMENT

OF

FIRES IN CLOSED FIRE-PLACES.

OF THE MANAGEMENT OF FIRES IN CLOSED FIRE-PLACES.

Necessity of keeping the Doors of closed Fire-places well closed, and of regulating the Air that is admitted into them. — Account of some Experiments which showed in a striking Manner the very great Importance of those Precautions. — A Method is proposed for preventing the Passage of cold Air into the large Fire-places of Brewhouse Boilers, Distillers' Coppers, Steam-Engine Boilers, etc., while they are feeding with Coals. — Bad Consequences which result from overloading closed Fire-places with Fuel. — Computations which show in a striking Manner the vast Advantages that will be derived from the Use of proper Care and Attention in the Management of Fire, and in the Direction and Economy of the Heat which results from the Combustion of Fuel.

THOUGH I have already mentioned, more than once, the necessity of preventing the entrance of air into a closed fire-place by any other passage than by the register of the ash-pit door, and have strongly recommended the keeping of the door of the fire-place constantly closed; yet, as I have since found that those precautions are even of more importance than I had imagined, I conceived that it might be useful to mention the subject again, and give an account of the series of experiments from the results of which I have acquired new light in respect to it.

In fitting up a large shallow circular kitchen boiler (one of those I put up in the kitchen of the house formerly occupied by the Board of Agriculture), I made an experiment which, though it appeared to me at the time to have succeeded perfectly, led me into an error that afterwards caused me a great deal of embarrassment. I constructed the fire-place of the boiler of a peculiar form for the express purpose of *burning the smoke;* imagining that if I could succeed in that attempt I should not only get more heat from any given quantity of coals, but also that the narrow horizontal canal that carried off the smoke from the fire-place to the chimney would be much less liable to be choked up by soot or dust. The fire-place was made rather longer than usual; and near the farther end of it there was a thin piece of fire-stone, placed edgewise, which run quite across it from side to side, a space being left about 2¼ inches wide between the lower edge of this stone and the bars of the grate, while the bottom of the boiler reposed on its upper edge.

From this description it is evident that the flame of the burning fuel, after rising up and striking against that part of the bottom of the boiler which was situated over the hither part of the fire-place, must necessarily pass under the lower edge of the stone just mentioned, in order to get into the canal leading to the chimney; and I fancied that, by taking care to keep that *narrow passage* constantly occupied by red-hot coals, the smoke being forced to pass through between them would necessarily take fire and burn. This actually happened; and, when I left a small opening in the door of the fire-place to give admittance to a little fresh air to facilitate and excite the combustion, the flame became so exceedingly vivid and clear that I promised myself great advantages from this new arrangement.

Being soon after engaged in putting up a large square boiler in the kitchen of the Foundling Hospital, I there introduced the same contrivance; but how great was my surprise on finding that, notwithstanding the extreme vivacity of the fire, the contents of the boiler could not be brought to boil in less time than five hours! The fire-place, it is true, was small, and the brick-work was new and wet; but I found that the quantity of coals consumed was such that, had there been no essential fault in the construction of the fire-place, nor in the management of the fire, the contents of the boiler ought, notwithstanding these unfavourable circumstances, to have boiled in less than one third part of the time that had been found necessary to bring it into a state of ebullition.

Having wasted two or three days in attempting to remedy the defects of this fire-place, without changing entirely the principles of its construction; concealing my disappointment from those who it was necessary should have confidence in my skill, by representing to them all that had been done as being a mere experiment, I pulled down the work to the foundation, and caused it to be rebuilt on principles which I knew could not fail to succeed, and which did succeed to the utmost of my expectations.

Though I ruminated often on this disappointment, I did not find out the real cause of my ill success for some months. This discovery was, however, at length made, and in such a manner as to leave no room for doubt.

Having, as an experiment, constructed in the kitchen of the Military Academy at Munich an apparatus for the performance of all the different processes of cookery, and to serve occasionally for warming a room with one and the same fire, thinking that the principles of the invention might be employed with advantage in the construction of cottage fire-places, on my return to this country I made the experiment at my lodgings in Brompton Row, Knightsbridge; and, desirous of accommodating the contrivance to what I think may be called a prejudice of Englishmen, I contrived the machinery in such a manner as to render the fire *visible*.

A small low grate was fixed in the middle of a large open kitchen fire-place, and on each side of it were fixed in brick-work two Dutch ovens, one above the other, the bottom of the lower oven on each side being nearly on a level with the top of the grate; and, as each of the ovens was surrounded by flues, I had hopes that by causing the flame and smoke of the open fire to incline downwards and enter a horizontal canal, situated just behind the fire, and there to separate to the right and left and circulate under the iron bottoms of the ovens, they would by that means be sufficiently heated to bake or to boil; and, even if the two upper ovens should not be found to be sufficiently heated to perform those processes of cookery, I thought, by leaving their doors open, they might at least be very useful, occasionally for warming the room, acting in the manner of a German stove. But the experiment was far from succeeding as I expected.

The current of flame and smoke which arose from the open fire was, without difficulty, made to bend its course downwards into the canal destined to receive it, and to circulate in the flues of the ovens; but, to my astonishment, I found that the ovens, instead of being heated, were barely warmed. An accident, however, very fortunately for me, discovered to me the real cause of the ill success of the experiment. Throwing a piece of paper on the top of the coals that were burning in the grate, in order to see if *the whole* of the large flame which I knew the paper must produce would be drawn downwards into the horizontal opening of the canal, situated behind the back of the grate, I was surprised to find that this flame was not only drawn into this opening, but that it appeared to be violently *driven downwards* to the very bottom of the canal.

In short, every appearance indicated that there was a very strong vertical *wind* that was continually blowing *directly downwards* into the opening of the canal; and it immediately occurred to me that, as this wind consisted of a stream of cold air, this air must necessarily cool the ovens almost as fast as the flame heated them; and I was no longer surprised at the ill success of my experiment.

On considering the subject with attention, I saw how impossible it must be for the current of hot vapour, flame, and smoke that rises from burning fuel, to be made to pass off *horizontally*, or to deflect considerably from its direct ascension *in contact with the cold air of the atmosphere*, without drawing after it a great deal of that cold air; and I now saw plainly why so much time and fuel were required to heat the boiler in the kitchen of the Foundling Hospital, in the experiments that were made with its first fire-place.

The cold air which entered the fire-place at its door,

and passing *over* the surface of the burning fuel entered the flues of the boiler with the flame, cooled the bottom of the boiler almost as fast as the flame heated it.

The waste of heat that is occasioned *precisely in this manner* in the fire-places of steam-engines, brewers' coppers, distillers' coppers, etc., must be very great indeed. To be convinced of this fact, nothing more is necessary than to see how very imperfectly the entrance into one of these fire-places is closed by its single door, ill fitted to its frame; what a length of time the door is left *wide open* while the fire is stirring or fresh coals are putting into the fire-place; and what an impetuous torrent of cold air rushes into the fire-place on those occasions.

As the cold air that comes into the fire-place in this manner, and passes *over* the burning coals, has very little to do in promoting the combustion of the fuel, and must necessarily be heated very hot in passing through the fire-place and through the whole length of the flues of the boiler, it is easy to see what an immense quantity of heat this air must steal and carry off into the atmosphere in its escape up the chimney.

To remedy this evil, the doors of all closed fire-places should be double, and they should be fitted to their frames with the greatest nicety, which may easily be done by making them shut against the front edge of their frames, instead of being fitted *into them* or into grooves made to receive them; and, when the fire is burning, these doors should be opened as seldom as possible and for as short a time as possible. I have already mentioned the necessity of these precautions in my sixth Essay, but they are of so much importance that they can hardly be too often recommended, nor can too much pains be taken to show why they are so necessary.

In all cases where a fire-place is very large, and where, in consequence of the large quantity of coals consumed in it, the fire-place door is necessarily kept open a great deal, I would earnestly recommend the adoption of a contrivance which I think could not fail to turn out a complete remedy for the evil we have been describing; viz., the entrance of a torrent of cold air into the fire-place through its door-way.

The contrivance is this: to construct the floor or pavement of the area before the fire-place door in such a manner as to cut off all direct communication, without the fire-place in front of it, between the ash-pit and the fire-place door-way; and, when this is done, to build a porch, well closed above and on every side, immediately before the fire-place door, and in such a manner that the fire-place door may open into it.

This porch must have a door belonging to it, situated on the side opposite to the fire-place door, which door (that belonging to the porch) must open outwards, and must fit its door-frame with considerable nicety. There must also be a glass window either in this door or over it, or on one side of it, or in one of the side walls of the porch; and there must be sufficient room in the porch to allow of a certain provision of coals being lodged there and kept ready for use.

When fresh coals are to be thrown into the fire-place (as also when the door of the fire-place is to be opened for the purpose of stirring the fire, or for any other purpose), the person who is charged with the care of the fire enters the porch, and then, carefully shutting the door of the porch after him, he opens the fire-place door.

As no air can get into the porch from without, its door being closed, none can pass through it into the fire-place, and the fire-place door may be left open without the smallest inconvenience; and the person who tends the fire may take up as much time as he pleases in stirring it or feeding it with fresh fuel, for little or no derangement of the fire or loss of heat will result from these operations. The fire will continue to burn nearly in the same manner as it did before the fire-place door was opened; and those immense clouds of dense smoke which, to the annoyance of the whole neighbourhood, are now thrown out of the chimneys of all great breweries, distilleries, steam-engines, etc., as often as they are fed with fresh coals, will no longer make their appearance.

When these operations are finished, and the fire-place door is again closed, the door of the porch may be opened, and the provision of coals kept in the porch for immediate use may be again completed.

If the flame from the fire-place should be found to have any tendency to come into the porch, this may be easily checked by leaving a very small hole in the door of the porch for the admission of a small quantity of air, just enough to prevent this accident. This small hole might be furnished with a register.

But it is not merely through the opening by which the fuel is introduced that cold air furtively finds its way into closed fire-places. It frequently enters in much too large quantities by the ash-pit door-way, and, rushing up between the bars of the grate and mixing with the flame, serves to diminish instead of increasing the heat applied to the bottom of the boiler; and this never fails to happen when a *small fire is made in a large fire-place*, or when a part of the grate happens not to be covered with burning fuel, especially when there is no register to the ash-pit door.

It should be remembered that whenever more air enters a closed fire-place than is actually *decomposed* by the burning fuel, all that superabundant air not only is of no service whatever, but being itself heated at the expense of the fire, and going off hot by the chimney, occasions the loss of a quantity of heat that might have been usefully employed.

Ash-pit doors should always be furnished with registers of whatever size the fire-place may be, for they are always indispensably necessary to the good management of a fire; and, where small fires are occasionally made in large closed fire-places, the ascent of air through that part of the grate that is not covered with burning fuel should be prevented by sliding an iron plate under the bars of the grate, or by some other contrivance equally effectual.

If the closed fire-places of boilers, great and small, were properly constructed, and if due care were taken to introduce in a proper manner and to regulate the quantity of the air that is necessary to the perfect combustion of the fuel, their grates might be made considerably narrower than they now are, and the bottoms of their boilers might be placed at a greater height above them, from which arrangement several advantages would be derived; but as long as so little care is taken to keep the door of the fire-place well closed, and to prevent too much air from coming up through the grate by the openings between its bars, the bottom of the boiler must be placed very near the surface of the burning coals, otherwise so much more cold air than is wanted will find its way into the fire-place and mix with the flame that the bottom of the boiler cannot fail to be sensibly cooled by it.

When a boiler is properly set, if a fire of a moderate size that burns well does not heat it in a reasonable time, the fault must necessarily lie in the bad management of the doors and registers of the fire-place; for, as the heat required to heat the boiler is *a certain quantity*, which cannot vary, if the boiler is not found to be heated as fast as it ought to be by the quantity of fuel consumed, a part of the heat generated must necessarily go to heat something else; and there is nothing at hand that can take it, except it be the cold air of the atmosphere, which, whenever it is permitted to enter a fire-place in an improper manner or in too large quantities, never fails to rob it of a great deal of heat, which it takes with it up the chimney, as has already been observed.

If the door by which the fuel is introduced into the closed fire-place of a kitchen boiler is not kept constantly closed, it is quite impossible that a well-constructed fire-place can answer. With such neglectful management, *a bad fire-place* is certainly *preferable* to a good one; for, when an enormous quantity of fuel is consumed under a boiler, some part of it must necessarily find its way into it, even if, instead of being set in brick-work, it were suspended over the fire in the open air; but, when a fire-place is made no larger than is necessary in order to heat the boiler in a proper time when the door of the fire-place is kept closed, it is not surprising that the boiler should be much slower in acquiring heat when a stream of cold air is permitted to strike against its bottom and blow all the flame and hot smoke out of its flues into the chimney.

It would be just as unreasonable to object to the fire-places I have recommended, on account of the *trouble of keeping them closed*, as it would be to object to a scheme for warming a dwelling-house merely because it required that the street door should not be left open. The cases are exactly similar; and, if insisting on the attention of servants in the one case is not unreasonable, it cannot be so in the other.

There was a time, no doubt (when the doors of rooms first came in fashion), that the trouble they occasioned to servants was considered as a hardship and severity in exacting attention to the proper management of them as a grievance; but all improvements are progressive, and we may hope that a time will come when it will be considered as careless and slovenly to leave open the door of a closed fire-place. In the mean time, it is my duty to declare, in the *most serious and public manner*, that those who have not influence enough with their servants to secure due attention being paid to this important point, would do wisely not to attempt to introduce the improvements in closed fire-places which I have recommended. And it is not sufficient merely to be attentive to the shutting of the fire-place door. Care must be taken also to manage properly the register of the ash-pit door; otherwise, if it be left too much opened, a great deal too much cold air will find its way into the fire-place between the bars of the grate.

When a closed fire-place is properly constructed, it is hardly to be believed how small a passage is sufficient to admit as much air as is necessary or useful to maintain the combustion of the fuel.

A fault which is often committed in the management
of the closed fire-places I have recommended is the
overloading them with fuel. This mistake has several
bad consequences, and among them there is one which
would not naturally be expected. It prolongs the kindling of the fire, and very frequently so much so as to
prolong the heating of the boiler, notwithstanding the
fierceness of the fire when the fuel is all inflamed.

Great care should at all times be taken not to overcharge a fire-place with fuel, but more especially when
the fire is first kindled and the fire-place and every
thing about it is cold. It should be remembered that
a great deal of heat is necessary to warm the fuel itself,
and bring it to that degree of heat which it must have
in order to its being capable of taking fire; and, as long
as there remains any cold fuel in the fire-place to be
heated, very little heat will reach the bottom of the
boiler.

All the money that is expended in the purchase of
wood to kindle coal fires is money well laid out; and
it is by no means good economy to be sparing of wood
in kindling such fires. In many cases it would, I am
convinced, be cheaper to burn wood than coals, even
in London, especially in the closed fire-places of small
kitchen boilers and stewpans, where a fire is wanted but
for a short time. This proposal to burn wood instead
of coals or charcoal has already been made more than
once; and the more I have considered the subject, the
more I am convinced that the former would turn out
to be the cheapest fuel.

A great deal of fuel is consumed in this country for
boiling water to make tea. I was curious to know how
low it would be possible to reduce that expense, and

ascertained that point by the following experiments and computations.

I supposed a small family, consisting of two persons, to drink tea twice every day (morning and evening) during one whole year, and that 2 pints of water, at the temperature of 55° (the mean annual temperature of the atmosphere in Great Britain), was heated and made to boil every time tea was made.

I found on inquiry that the most costly fire-wood that is sold in London,—dry beech in billets,—at the highest price it is ever sold at, cost one farthing per lb., avoirdupois weight; that is, at the rate of *twopence* per billet, weighing at an average 8 lbs. By wholesale, these billets are sold in London at *one penny halfpenny* each.

I had some of these billets sawed into lengths of about 5 inches, and then split into small pieces (about the size of the end of one's little finger), and bound up with a pack-thread into little small bundles weighing about 4 or 5 ounces each. In the middle of each bundle there were a few smaller splinters and a very small piece of paper, that the bundle might easily be set on fire with a candle or with a common match.

On using the small portable furnace represented in the Fig. 63, and described in Chapter XI. of the tenth Essay, page 414, and the small tin tea-kettles represented in the Fig. 68, in that Essay, I found by an experiment, which was repeated several times, that I could boil 2 pints of water with a bundle of wood weighing 4 ounces.

Hence it appears that the daily consumption of wood in boiling water for tea for two persons would be 8 ounces, or half a pound weight; consequently, for one year, or 365 days, 182¼ lbs. would be required, and that quantity, at 1 farthing the pound, would cost 182¼ farthings = 45⅝ pence, or *three shillings* and *ninepence half-penny* and *half a farthing*.

Were it possible to heat so small a quantity of water with the consumption of the same proportion of firewood as was found to be sufficient for heating water in some of the experiments, of which an account is given in the sixth Essay, the annual expense for fire-wood, for boiling water for making tea for two persons twice a day, would amount to no more than 57 lbs. weight, which, at the London price of this wood, one farthing in the pound, would cost 57 farthings, or *one shilling and twopence farthing*.

It is by computations of this sort, founded on the results of unexceptionable experiments, that we are enabled to appreciate the vast saving to individuals and to the public that would result from proper attention being paid to the management of fire and to the economy of heat.

[This paper is printed from the English edition of Rumford's Essays, Vol. III., pp. 455–471.]

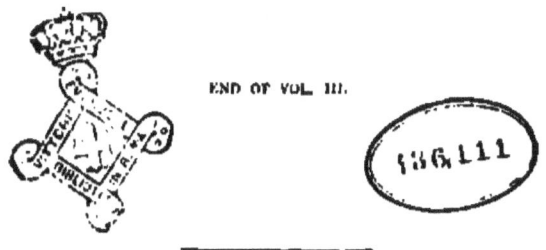

END OF VOL. III.

Cambridge: Press of John Wilson & Son.

www.ingramcontent.com/pod-product-compliance
Lightning Source LLC
Chambersburg PA
CBHW031947290426
44108CB00011B/710